Governance and Citizenship in Asia

Aims and Scope

This series explores how citizenship is shaped by social, political, cultural and historical contexts and how it may be moulded to serve the nation state in the age of globalization. In these publications we see how governance relates to all aspects of civic life, including politics, public policy, administration, civil society and the economy, as well as the core values of society.

Titles cover themes including public trust and trust building, the role of civil society, citizens' rights and obligations, citizenship identities including those related to gender, class and ethnicities. Authors explore how young people are shaped by democratic and traditional value systems and the importance of citizenship challenges in the Asia Pacific region.

Research collaborations in this interdisciplinary series probe questions such as: What are the links between 'good governance' and new forms of citizenship? What is the role of citizenship education as a tool in state formation and the development of active citizenship cultures? How do we explain the distinctive features of governance and citizenship in Asian societies?

Through these publications we see that citizenship is an integral part of 'good governance' and that such governance ultimately enriches citizenship. Scholarly investigation and academic dialogue in this series describe the interdependence and mutuality of governance and citizenship.

More information about this series at http://www.springer.com/series/11911

Hooi Lai Wan

Organisational Justice and Citizenship Behaviour in Malaysia

Springer

Hooi Lai Wan
The University of Nottingham
Nottingham University Business School
Semenyih, Selangor Darul Ehsan, Malaysia

ISSN 2365-6255 ISSN 2365-6263 (electronic)
Governance and Citizenship in Asia
ISBN 978-981-10-0028-7 ISBN 978-981-10-0030-0 (eBook)
DOI 10.1007/978-981-10-0030-0

Library of Congress Control Number: 2015958097

Springer Singapore Heidelberg New York Dordrecht London

Printed on acid-free paper

Springer Science+Business Media Singapore Pte Ltd. is part of Springer Science+Business Media (www.springer.com)

Preface

Globalisation and the advancement of technology have triggered much interest among organisational researchers to study the discretionary behaviour of employees at the workplace. As baby boomers retire, the core workforce in most organisations is dominated by Generation X and Generation Y, who generally are less likely to remain in an organisation for their entire working life. Being more techno-savvy, these human capitals have access to information that provides career advancement opportunities which increase the incidence of leaving. Therefore, research on organisational citizenship behaviour in the new millennium has attracted much attention as discretionary and extra-role behaviours of organisational citizens are instrumental for employee retention, job performance and the sustainability of organisations. Various predictors of organisational citizenship behaviour have been examined, and among the most robust attitudinal predictors of organisational citizenship behaviour are employees' perceptions of organisational justice, job satisfaction and leader–member exchange. As perceptions of organisational justice have been associated with job performance and organisational citizenship behaviour, and organisational citizenship behaviour with job satisfaction and leader–member exchange, facilitating organisational justice becomes crucial.

Perceptions of organisational justice are widely recognised as an influential factor in employee attitudes at the workplace. Employees who perceive unfairness are likely to limit their commitment to citizenship, whereas employees who perceive equity will contribute to the system through continued citizenship. Generally, employees are more likely to exhibit organisational citizenship behaviour if they perceive that their organisations treated them fairly. But, do employee perceptions of organisational justice have similar relationships with organisational citizenship behaviour in a high power distance and collectivist orientation culture like Malaysia? In the Malaysian context, there is limited study on organisational justice and organisational citizenship behaviour, specifically with job satisfaction and leader–member exchange as mediators. Furthermore, the limited literature available shows that the findings of prior studies are rather ambiguous. Specifically, the significance of each justice component on each dimension of organisational citizenship behaviour, job satisfaction and leader–member exchange in the manufacturing sector in

Malaysia is still inconclusive. Nonetheless, despite being a high power distance country, where open expression of dissatisfaction is much constrained, interest in research on organisational justice in Malaysia has increased. Considering the spiralling effects of negative work attitudes and the job switching habits of the current Malaysian workforce, the question of how employee perceptions of organisational justice are related to job satisfaction, leader–member exchange and organisational citizenship behaviour remains to be addressed. That question is the focus of this book. The growing competitiveness of the manufacturing sector especially in terms of career mobility of managerial staff makes organisational citizenship behaviour an important facet that is worth considering.

This book provides a comprehensive exploration of the current developments in organisational behaviour and human capital management in the new millennium in an academically rigorous manner. A review of related literature and an in-depth study among managerial staff in the manufacturing sector in Malaysia offer a profound insight of the subject domain. The study presents an integrated analysis of the organisational justice–organisational citizenship behaviour relationship in the manufacturing environment in Malaysia by embracing job satisfaction and leader–member exchange as mediators to unveil a holistic perspective of the associations between these constructs. The study has expounded on the importance of job satisfaction and the quality of leader–member exchange in the organisational justice–organisational citizenship behaviour relationship, and, therefore, the correlation between these constructs must not be overlooked. The relevant content of the study has been incorporated in the text of the chapters. Concisely, the findings indicate that personal factors are imperative for advancing organisational citizenship behaviour among managerial staff in the manufacturing sector in Malaysia.

The primary sources of information are discussions with practising managers and questionnaire survey. Practitioners provide real-life examples of the challenges that arise at the workplace. Data collected through questionnaire survey reflects employee perceptions of organisational justice, organisational citizenship behaviour, job satisfaction and leader–member exchange in Malaysia's manufacturing sector. Analysing data drawn from a sample of 267 managerial employees in a range of manufacturing entities using well-established scales, the study examines the effect of distributive justice, procedural justice, informational justice and interpersonal justice on five dimensions of organisational citizenship behaviour, namely, altruism, courtesy, conscientiousness, sportsmanship and civic virtue. As employee perceptions of organisational justice are likely to affect job satisfaction and leader–member exchange, this study includes these variables as mediators to enrich the understanding of the justice–citizenship relationship. Full use has been made of other comparable studies, which provided secondary data for this book. The reference list provides readers appropriate sources of additional information as well as creates a desire for further research. The reader is, thus, facilitated to continue with the research if sufficiently interested to do so.

The strongest significance of this study is probably providing indicators that influence organisational citizenship behaviours. Understanding the direct and indirect factors that affect organisational citizenship behaviours helps organisations to increase focus on those factors that encourage organisational citizenship behaviours. The inclusion of all four types of organisational justice in the study enlightens organisations on the relative importance of each and its effects on the employees. A corollary of this is that organisations in the manufacturing sector are able to see the effects of each type of organisational justice on each dimension of organisational citizenship behaviour. This facilitates organisations to decide which aspect of justice to work on to improve citizenship behaviours among their employees. It engenders organisations to promote a culture of fairness and shapes employees' perception of a quality relationship between organisational justice and organisational citizenship behaviour. As the study looks at job satisfaction and leader–member exchange as well, it offers an insight of whether these two factors are primary antecedents of organisational citizenship behaviour. If these two variables are indeed strongly related to organisational citizenship behaviour, then measures may be taken to improve job satisfaction and leader–member exchange. The study also gives an indication of the importance of organisational justice on job satisfaction and leader–member exchange. Furthermore, by comparison, one would be able to see which type of organisational justice would have a greater impact on organisational citizenship behaviour, job satisfaction and leader–member exchange.

In essence, this book is intended to be of value not only to academicians and practitioners but also students writing their dissertations. The book is a product of careful planning and constant reviews of the currents of change. Updates, additions and revisions are made at every level of writing. Grammar, syntax and vocabulary are continually revised to make the language more meaningful to the broadest possible range of people in the English reading audience. Writing that is directed towards one level of educational attainment and away from another, to one gender rather than to both, to some socioeconomic, ethnic or language groups rather than all, is eliminated whenever it is found. Much effort has been taken to be consistent without pedantry and to guide the reader, without being misleading. The author feels confident that this book offers a relevant and interesting look at organisational behaviour and human capital management and is optimistic that those who read this book will agree.

Semenyih, Malaysia Hooi Lai Wan

Contents

List of Figures

List of Tables

Chapter 1
Introduction to Organisational Justice and Organisational Citizenship Behaviour

Abstract This chapter introduces the research topic and outlines the areas of research. It presents a simplified overview of the study on the effect of organisational justice on organisational citizenship behaviour. The objectives, research framework and methodology for the research are clearly stated and laid the groundwork for this study. It also highlights the implications of a sustainable Malaysian workforce. The significance of the study justifies the importance of conducting the study. The scope of the study is to help the audience follow through the research process and provides a profound understand of the development of the research study. The chapter concludes with defining the key terms to develop an understanding of the concepts and terminology used in the study.

Introduction

In an era of dynamic change due to rapid technological advancement and globalisation, business has become increasingly competitive, tortuous and mutually dependent. Literally, the world has become a global village. Businesses are competing on a global arena, and organisations can no longer afford to be complacent. Organisations need to move with the paradigm shift; otherwise, aggressive players that are continuously redefining the rules of the game will eclipse them. In the midst of these, the human capital practitioner as the principal driver of change initiatives has to play a strategic role in the organisation. As a change agent and strategic partner of the organisation, the human capital practitioner needs to implement and develop effective human capital practices and policies that can achieve high performance workplace culture that is beneficial to the organisation. External and internal influences that will affect the organisation have to be identified and strategies formulated to overcome or nullify them.

In today's turbulent global economy, the emphasis is on 'people' as a source of competitive advantage. The growing recognition of human capital as the primary source of competitiveness in the first decade of the twenty-first century makes it necessary for human capital practitioners to continue monitoring changes and trends in the nature of work and the employment relationship. As organisational citizenship behaviour makes an organisation more effective over time and across people (Organ 1988a), this study intends to explore further the interactive effects of

L.W. Hooi, *Organisational Justice and Citizenship Behaviour in Malaysia*, Governance and Citizenship in Asia, DOI 10.1007/978-981-10-0030-0_1

organisational justice, job satisfaction, leader–member exchange and organisational citizenship behaviour in the manufacturing sector in Malaysia – making a contribution to the sustainability of the nation's effort to achieve Vision 2020. The manufacturing sector plays a prominent role in the Malaysian economy, and it is imperative that organisations groom employees, specifically the millennials, to be the leaders of tomorrow. The presence of organisational citizenship behaviour among employees is likely to enhance succession management and improve the quality of industry captains. However, due to the perilous nature of the work environment in the manufacturing sector, instilling organisational citizenship behaviour is probably more challenging comparatively.

Additionally, perceptions of organisational injustice may further dampen the spirit of organisational citizenship behaviour. Glaring organisational injustice is likely to result in much discontentment among employees. This leads to lower job satisfaction, which is further aggravated by poor quality leader–member exchange relationship. Such discontentment then cascades into lackadaisical attitude and translates into undesirable work attitudes among those affected. Employee intention to leave will probably increase. Based on the theory of reasoned action, behavioural intentions are much dependent on attitudes and subjective norms. Considering the spiralling effects of negative work attitudes and peer influence, maintaining organisational justice may be imperative for the well-being of the organisations. The growing competitiveness of the manufacturing sector makes organisational citizenship behaviour an important facet that is worth considering. It is, therefore, vital that organisations formulate human capital practices that promote impartial treatment of employees and train supervisors in the fair enactment of these practices.

This chapter begins with a deliberation of organisational justice and organisational citizenship behaviour, followed by a discussion on the sustainability of the Malaysian workplace. It then examines the objectives of the study and the importance of studying the manufacturing industry in Malaysia, before delineating the methodology and significance of the study. The chapter concludes with the organisation of chapters and definition of key terms used throughout the book.

Organisational Justice and Organisational Citizenship Behaviour

Perceptions of justice, equity or fairness in the workplace are widely recognised as an influential factor in employee attitudes at the workplace (Adams 1965; Cropanzano and Greenberg 1997; Fields et al. 2000; Leventhal 1976; Ramamoorthy and Flood 2004). Employees would probably hold positive attitudes about their work, their work outcomes and their supervisors if they perceived that they are treated fairly (Moorman 1991). Organisational justice concerns three distinct, but related, components of justice, namely, distributive, procedural and interactional justice. Distributive justice is established in literature on equity theory (Adams 1965) and refers to the fairness of decision outcomes. Studies have shown that employee performance may increase or decrease in relation to perceptions of inequitable outcomes (Adams 1965; Greenberg 1988, 1989). Procedural justice concerns perceived justice of the decision-making procedures used to determine the distribution of the outcome and is grounded in dispute resolution models (Kim and Mauborgne 1997; Leventhal 1976; Thibaut and Walker 1975). Distributive justice and procedural justice have been consistently related to employee work-related attitudes and behaviours such as job satisfaction, prosocial behaviours, tenure intent, team attachment, job performance and absenteeism (Colquitt et al. 2001; Greenberg 1990; Lee et al. 2000; Phillips 2002). Interactional justice relates to the perceived quality and equity of the interactions between recipient and the decision-maker (Ramamoorthy and Flood 2004).

DeConinck (2010) asserts that in order to increase interactional justice, it is imperative for the supervisor to explain the procedure as well as to take questions from the employee regarding the process. The supervisor has to ascertain that employees perceive the procedures as impartial. Concisely, perceived procedural justice augments interactional justice. Thus, the interactive effects of the three dimensions of organisational justice could not be ignored. Furthermore, meta-analysis has confirmed the three types of justice to be strongly related, but distinct from each other (Alexander and Ruderman 1987; Cohen-Charash and Spector 2001; Colquitt et al. 2001; Folger and Konovsky 1989; Konovsky et al. 1987).

Organ (1988a) identifies five dimensions of organisational citizenship behaviour that contribute to effectiveness: altruism, courtesy, conscientiousness, sportsmanship and civic virtue. Altruism is associated with how an employee helps others on the job. Courtesy represents helpful behaviours that involve checking with colleagues about actions that could affect their responsibilities. Conscientiousness is the dutiful respect of organisational rules, procedures and regulations beyond what is required by the organisation (Eskew 1993; Koopmann 2002; Tansky 1993). Sportsmanship relates to negative behaviours employees refrain from doing (Tansky 1993), and, finally, civic virtue concerns how employees respond appropriately and responsibly to how the organisation governs.

Employees who perceive unfairness are likely to limit their commitment to citizenship, whereas employees who perceive equity will contribute to the system through continued citizenship (Moorman 1991). A variety of studies have found a robust relationship between perceptions of procedural justice and organisational citizenship behaviour. Procedural justice accounts for a linear relationship with altruism (Farh et al. 1990) and altruism, courtesy, sportsmanship and conscientiousness (Moorman 1991). Their results were further substantiated by the findings of Niehoff and Moorman (1993). Additionally, Moorman (1991) emphasised that interactional justice was the sole dimension of fairness to relate significantly to organisational citizenship behaviour. Moreover, Robinson and Morrison (1995) assert that employees are likely to engage in civic behaviour if fairness is perceived. In essence, employees are more likely to exhibit organisational citizenship behaviours if they perceive that their supervisors personally treated them fairly.

In an organisational environment, employees use economic exchange and social exchange to view their relationship with the organisation (Blau 1964). Economic exchange is based on the fairness of contractual demands and predetermined obligations (e.g. pay), while social exchange goes beyond contractual obligations (e.g. trust). As far as organisational justice is concerned, employees are more likely to view their relationship with the organisation as one of social exchange. However, people will shift to more economic exchange view if their perception of justice is low. When employees feel that they are treated unfairly, they restore equity by containing extra-role behaviour. In contrast, they reciprocate with discretionary behaviours when they are treated fairly (Organ 1997). Nonetheless, employees are more likely to be in a reciprocal social exchange relationship with the organisation as organisational citizenship behaviour is reflected more in social exchange (Organ and Konovsky 1989). Thus, social exchange is more important than economic exchange to the use of organisational citizenship behaviour (Organ 1988b, 1990; Organ and Konovsky 1989).

In addition to studies in the organisational environment, the concepts of organisational citizenship behaviour and organisational justice have also been discussed in the field of education, albeit rather limited (DiPaola and Hoy 2005; Hoy and Tarter 2004). Oplatka (2006) asserts that there are only ten research papers on organisational citizenship behaviour in schools worldwide. DiPaola and Hoy (2005) conceive that organisational citizenship behaviour does exist in public schools. Nonetheless, studies concerning the adaptation of organisational citizenship behaviour (Bogler and Somech 2005; Christ et al. 2003; DiPaola and Hoy 2005; DiPaola and Tschannen-Moran 2001; Somech and Drach-Zahavy 2000) and organisational justice (Hoy and Tarter 2004) to schools are relatively new. Yilmaz and Tasdan (2009) study the relationship between organisational citizenship behaviour and organisational justice in terms of gender, field of study and seniority. The study shows that teachers have positive perceptions regarding organisational citizenship behaviour and organisational justice. Organisational citizenship behaviour perceptions did not vary according to gender, field of study and seniority, but organisational justice perceptions varied according to seniority, but not gender and field of study. A moderate positive relationship can be observed between the teachers' organisational citizenship behaviour and organisational justice perceptions. Other studies found that school teachers have moderately positive perceptions of organisational citizenship behaviour (Tschannen-Moran 2001; Yilmaz and Tasdan 2009). These studies suggest that a positive organisational justice perception may increase a positive citizenship perception. Similar findings are present in university settings (Erturk 2007; Skarlicki and Latham 1995). The study on organisational justice and organisational citizenship behaviour could be further extended to cover other sectors.

Sustainability of the Malaysian Workplace

The Malaysian economy is projected to grow stronger in 2015, primarily because of resilient domestic demand and improved external demand following the global recovery. During the first half of 2014, Malaysia benefited from the faster pace of recovery in advanced economies, particularly the USA and UK, and selected euro area economies as well as moderate growth in emerging economies. This in tandem with the upswing in global electronic demand which led to better performance of Malaysian exports. Therefore, the manufacturing sector should leverage this to stimulate not only market share in the short-term but also improve the long-term capacity of the business. Manufacturing organisations should be well prepared to immediately seize the opportunities as the global economy recovers. Moreover, the government's commitment to the ongoing programmes and projects under the Tenth Malaysia Plan (10MP), the Economic Transformation Programme (ETP) and Government Transformation Programme (GTP) has resulted in significant economic benefits as well as improved sustainability in the long run. In addition, accommodative monetary and fiscal policies will continue to support growth, and, therefore, the manufacturing sector should be ready with a pool of competent manpower to capitalise on this. In this study, it is argued that organisational citizenship behaviour would be a probable answer to a resilient workforce.

In this regard, the solidarity and engagement of the workers is of paramount importance. To sustain growth momentum and to encourage value creation, organisations have to, among others, ensure greater transparency and perceived justice at the workplace. Organisational justice augments organisational citizenship behaviours and lowers employee intention to leave. Though maintaining organisational justice is difficult at the Malaysian workplace, partly due to ethnic diversity as well as high power distance (Hofstede 1984), it is crucial if organisations wish to retain their key skilled employees. Greater efforts may be necessary, as research shows that no matter what, employees perceived that not everything is fair. For example, though there is no conclusive consensus on the fairness in promotion procedures, evidence of discontentment is present. Injustice in promotion procedures in the manufacturing sector has an effect on organisational commitment, intent to leave, career satisfaction and employee performance (Hooi et al. 2012). To remain resilient and competitive in the current uncertain global economic environment, enhancing organisational citizenship behaviours is of utmost importance.

Furthermore, retention of talents and skilled workers is necessary for the sustainability of the industry. To remain competitive, it may be necessary to promote and retain the best talents, but the need to comply with certain government regulations may hinder this move. Hence, employees who are eligible, but not promoted, may perceive organisational injustice and endure in silence. Unlike employees of developed nations, most employees in Malaysia tend to accept decisions made at the top. Sometimes, employees choose to remain silent for fear of unfavourable repercussions. This is consistent with the findings of Milliken et al. (2003), where 85 % of the managers and professionals chose to remain silent about at least some of their work concerns. Therefore, for most employees, the solution to any discontentment is to leave the organisation when opportunity arises (Bagdadli et al. 2006; Dailey and Kirk 1992; Hooi 2002).

Moreover, interpersonal relationship with decision-makers is indeed crucial as merit may not be given much emphasis in some organisations. In most cases, there is no added value in gaining a higher academic qualification, though there are some who resort to 'dodgy degrees' to boost their credentials (The Star 2009). It may be a case of who you know rather than what you know (Hooi et al. 2012). The in-group–out-group phenomenon is obviously prevalent in the Malaysian organisational context. In some organisations, this has led to unhealthy corporate practices that cater more for personal gain and individual development rather than organisational or national development. Company politics and conflict inhibit team spirit and further worsen the situation (Hooi et al. 2012). Hence, regardless of performance, without the right politics, an employee's chance of being rewarded accordingly may be jeopardised. The absence of a proper database system for employees has also aggravated the situation. Therefore, understanding the quality of leader–member exchange is important for mitigating employee perceptions of injustice, which in turn may affect organisational citizenship behaviour.

Furthermore, foreigners in top management in multinational companies may not be aware of certain cultures among the ethnic community in the country. Inadequate understanding of intercultural differences, in particular intercultural communication differences, may strain business and social relationships (Salleh 2005) that can jeopardise rational decision-making. Decision-making may be affected depending on the cultural context the expatriate is from. Besides, there are certain government policies that need to be adhered to which may affect rational decisions. As irrational decisions are likely to be perceived as unfair, employees' job satisfaction and the quality of their relationship with their superiors may be affected. In organisations where there is no proper yardstick to measure the contributions of the employees, subjectivity further strains the superior–subordinate relationship, and, hence, intensifies its impact on organisational citizenship behaviour.

Additionally, employees are unanimous in asserting that commitment to the organisation is likely to be affected if organisational injustice prevails (Hooi et al. 2012). Loyal employees who have sacrificed for the company would perceive that the organisation is not looking after their welfare. Job satisfaction and performance are also likely to be affected if decisions are perceived as unfair. There is less commitment and minimal effort is expected, as it is unlikely that dissatisfied employees will be motivated. Motivating dissatisfied employees to improve performance would be a mammoth task, and, thus, productivity is expected to fall. If recognition and rewards are not forthcoming after much hard work, most employees do not feel the need to strive for the organisation. It is apparent that employees will do enough to keep the job, but not necessary to do their utmost to contribute to organisational effectiveness. Intention to leave will probably increase. Employees, especially the younger ones, will not hesitate to switch jobs whenever there is an opportunity. Therefore, justice at the workplace, job satisfaction and quality leader–member exchange are essential for promoting organisational citizenship behaviour.

The Objectives of This Study

Given the high power distance in the Malaysian workplace, this study attempts to explore if organisational justice is indeed the core antecedent of organisational citizenship behaviour in the manufacturing sector in Malaysia. Indisputably, a wealth of research on organisational justice and organisational citizenship behaviour has been carried out in other countries, but the impact on the manufacturing sector in Malaysia is still ambiguous. Thus, this study hopes to test if what is observed in justice literature will be applicable in the Malaysian manufacturing environment. Generally, the study seeks to establish the relationship between employee perceptions of organisational justice and organisational citizenship behaviour. Organisational justice in this study encompasses distributive justice, procedural justice and interactional justice. Specifically, the main aim of the study is to examine the effect of each component of organisational justice on the five dimensions of organisational citizenship behaviour, namely, altruism, courtesy, conscientiousness, sportsmanship and civic virtue.

As employee perceptions of organisational justice are likely to affect job satisfaction and leader–member exchange, study is conducted to understand the relationship between these constructs. Subsequently, this study hopes to explore if job satisfaction and leader–member exchange have an influence on organisational citizenship behaviour. It is hypothesised that the impact of the different dimensions of organisational justice on organisational citizenship behaviour, job satisfaction and leader–member exchange would vary. Thus, the study will examine the link between the different facets of organisational justice on the dimensions of organisational citizenship behaviour, job satisfaction and leader–member exchange. Additionally, the study will establish if job satisfaction and leader–member exchange mediate the relationship between organisational justice and organisational citizenship behaviour. The findings from the study will likely fill the gaps in present knowledge and help resolve some of the inconsistencies in previous research.

In a nutshell, the objectives of this study are:

(a) To examine the relationship between employee perceptions of organisational justice and organisational citizenship behaviour
(b) To verify if employee perceptions of organisational justice influence job satisfaction
(c) To determine if employee perceptions of organisational justice influence leader–member exchange
(d) To establish if job satisfaction and leader–member exchange affect organisational citizenship behaviour
(e) To assess if job satisfaction and leader–member exchange mediate the relationship between organisational justice and organisational citizenship behaviour

Methodology

Based on observations, the broad problem area of organisational justice and organisational citizenship behaviour in the manufacturing sector was identified. Preliminary data gathering through literature review and unstructured interviews with some employees in the manufacturing sector in Malaysia helped define the problem that was to be investigated more specifically. After completing a literature survey and defining the problem, the theoretical framework was developed to

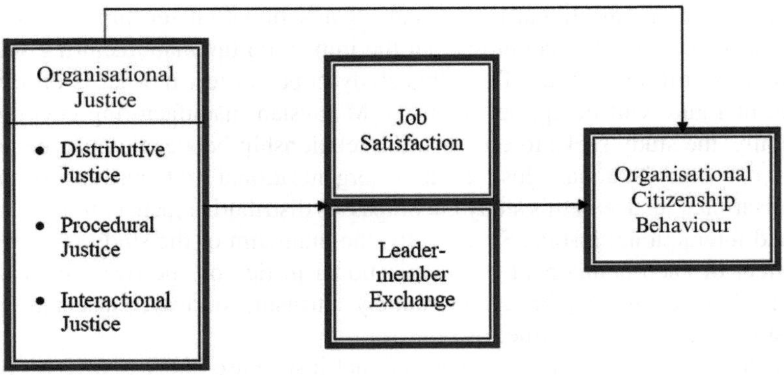

Fig. 1.1 Conceptual model of the study

identify the network of relationships among the variables considered integral to the dynamics of the problem to be investigated. The conceptual framework was developed to help postulate and test the relationships and, thus, enhanced the understanding of the dynamics of the situation. The conceptual model for the study is shown in Fig. 1.1.

Figure 1.1 shows the first model (Model 1) evaluated. It contains paths from organisational justice to organisational citizenship behaviour, organisational justice to job satisfaction, organisational justice to leader–member exchange, job satisfaction to organisational citizenship behaviour and leader–member exchange to organisational citizenship behaviour. From this saturated model, five nested models will be evaluated:

1. Model 2, which restricted the paths from organisational justice to organisational citizenship behaviour, will be used to test Hypothesis 1.
2. Model 3, which restricted the paths from organisational justice to job satisfaction and organisational justice to leader–member exchange, will be used to test Hypothesis 2 and Hypothesis 3.
3. Model 4, which restricted the paths from job satisfaction to organisational citizenship behaviour and leader–member exchange to organisational citizenship behaviour, will be used to test Hypothesis 4 and Hypothesis 5.
4. Model 5, which restricted the paths from organisational justice to job satisfaction and leader–member exchange to organisational citizenship behaviour, will be used to test Hypothesis 6.

From the theoretical framework, testable hypotheses were developed to examine the validity of the theory formulated. Integrating logical beliefs with published research and taking into consideration the boundaries and constraints governing the situation, six hypotheses for the study were developed. The development of these hypotheses is discussed in Chap. 2. Thereafter, these hypotheses would be tested through appropriate statistical analyses. The ability to test and replicate the findings would enhance one's belief in the rigour of the study.

The saturated model developed for this study required a reasonably large sample size to augment generalisability. In line with past research, questionnaire survey was the justified method of data collection, as this study required much information on the attitudes and behaviours from a wide spectrum of respondents. Besides, questionnaire surveys were modestly established in studying and predicting behaviour (Dillman 1991). Since most of the instruments were adopted from past similar studies, the questionnaire survey design provided an opportunity to test the validity and reliability of the instruments and allowed modification of the instruments for future research. Nonetheless, this cross-sectional study did not limit the sample to a single organisation, but rather attempted to extend the sample to include more organisations. The administering of questionnaires at the workplace was carried out with the help of the HR staff and distributed at their convenience.

Data for the study was collected from a sample of manufacturing companies listed in the Federation of Malaysian Manufacturers Directory 2010 (FMM). There were 2,571 companies registered with FMM as of 30 July 2010, and of these 100 companies were selected for the study. The sample was selected using stratified random sampling based on location, namely, the northern, central and southern region of Peninsular Malaysia. The northern region covered Perlis, Kedah, Penang, Kelantan, Terengganu and Perak; the central region Kuala Lumpur, Selangor and Pahang; and the southern region Johore, Malacca and Negri Sembilan. As the problem statement centred on organisational citizenship behaviour in the manufacturing sector, the study was interested in individual employees in the organisation. Therefore, the unit of analysis for this study was the individual or employee of the organisations. Specifically, all management staff of the manufacturing companies that were sampled was the sampling frame for the study. Ten management staffs from each of the 100 companies were randomly selected as respondents. Though the sample included a wide range of industries in the manufacturing sector, only companies that had been in operation for at least 2 years were selected in order to gauge the relationship between employee perceptions of organisational justice and organisational citizenship behaviour, job satisfaction and the quality of leader–member exchange.

The hypotheses for the study were tested using multi-item scales adopted from prior studies. Based on the research's objectives, the questionnaires were designed to collect a combination of attitudinal and behavioural data. Single direct questions were used to tap demographic data such as age, sex, marital status, race, education level, education background, position, working experience and length of service with the organisation. Nominal scale was used for most of the questions where a range of response options was provided. A set of questionnaire was used to tap on a five-point scale data on perceptions on organisational justice, namely, distributive justice (four questions), procedural justice (seven questions) and interactional justice (nine questions); job satisfaction (five questions); the quality of leader–member exchange relationship (seven questions); and organisational citizenship behaviour, namely, altruism (five questions), courtesy (five questions), sportsmanship (five questions), conscientiousness (five questions) and civic virtue (five questions).

To assess each component of organisational justice, this study employed measures developed by Colquitt (2001) as cross-pollination of items has been accounted for. The four-item scale for distributive justice reflected Leventhal's (1976) conceptualisation of the equity rule to maximise generalisability. The seven-item procedural justice scale measured the degree to which fair procedures were used in the organisations. Items for assessing interactional justice were based on Greenberg's (1993) designation of interpersonal and informational justice. Items for interpersonal justice developed by Bies and Moag (1986) focused on the personal behaviour of the supervisor. The informational justice items originated from the work of Shapiro et al. (1994) and examined factors that improved the perceived adequacy of explanations. Brayfield and Rothe's (1951) Job Satisfaction Scale was used to measure job satisfaction, while Graen and Uhl-Bien's (1995) seven-item LMX measure assessed the quality of the leader–member exchange relationship. The scales developed by Podsakoff et al. (1990) were used to assess the five dimensions of organisational citizenship behaviour.

To screen items for appropriateness, the respondents for the pilot survey were those from the population to be studied. For the purpose of this study, 162 responses from 20 organisations were used in the pilot survey. In addition to the response, participants were required to indicate items that were ambiguous and highlight words that were difficult to comprehend. Some participants were contacted for further clarification, and feedbacks received were used to improve the intelligibility of the items. The questionnaires were rephrased and refined to remove any ambiguity. Empirical testing of the pretest results was done in a manner identical to the final model analysis.

For the assessment of reliability and validity, the results were discussed in five parts – sampling results, data screening, reliability and validity of measures, exploratory factor analysis and confirmatory factor analysis. Sampling results provided an insight of the site and subjects of the study – the selection criteria, sampling procedure, response rate, profile of the companies and demographic data of the respondents. Data screening outlined the procedure involved in detecting missing data and outliers. The assessment of reliability covered Cronbach's alpha, while validity assessment concerned content validity, convergent validity and discriminant validity. The results of the exploratory factor analysis were based on the principal component method to identify the minimum number of factors needed, while confirmatory factor analysis assessed the validity of the measures.

Structural equation modelling was used to test the hypotheses of this study, as it involved relationships among multiple variables. As the three types of organisational justice seemed to have different impact on the dimensions of organisational citizenship behaviour, this study observed the correlation between each dimension of the two constructs. It also assumed that organisational justice would influence job satisfaction and the quality of leader–member exchange relationship and subsequently their impact on organisational citizenship behaviour. It further hypothesised that each dimension of organisational justice has varying degrees of impact on organisational citizenship behaviour, job satisfaction and the quality of leader–member exchange relationship. Thus, structural equation modelling was considered the appropriate statistical approach to examine the structure of interrelationships.

For the structural equation modelling analysis, the discussion was delineated into six parts. The first part focused on checking the assumptions on sample size; normality, linearity and homoscedasticity; multicollinearity; and correlation analysis. Then, the discussion converged on the validity and reliability of the measurement models – discriminant validity and convergent validity. Next, it deliberated on the results of the mediation analysis to confirm the significance of the relationships. This was followed by examining the structural model based on the goodness-of-fit indices. The direct, indirect and total effects were also discussed. Finally, the findings of the hypothesised relationships were explained.

Significance of the Study

Organisational justice is believed to have an impact on organisational citizenship behaviour, job satisfaction and leader–member exchange, which in turn will affect job performance. However, the significance of each justice component on each dimension of organisational citizenship behaviour in the manufacturing sector in Malaysia is still inconclusive. With globalisation and increased career mobility of young talented workers, perceived unfair processes will likely enhance the intent to leave. Thus, organisational justice is of paramount importance if organisations were to retain these workers. Furthermore, it may be crucial to retain these workers to gain competitive advantage. Studying the effect of organisational justice on organisational citizenship behaviour among managerial staff is deemed important as competition is rather intense in terms of career mobility of managerial staff.

This is further aggravated as promotion of managerial staff in the manufacturing sector in Malaysia is ad hoc and very much dependent on the availability of vacancies (Hooi 2002; Hooi et al. 2012). Furthermore, there is no guarantee that one may be promoted even if a vacancy becomes available, as it is not uncommon for companies in Malaysia to opt for external recruitment. Moreover, in some organisations, information on employees' performance is gathered through hearsay from peers, previous and current superiors and for some, customers and suppliers as well. The degree of accuracy of such information is much at the discretion of the person receiving it. Such subjectivity can result in discontentment among employees. Furthermore, in some organisations, there is no system at all. Organisational justice, then, is very much dependent on the good judgement of the decision-makers (Hooi et al. 2012). Hence, this study is of significance to the manufacturing sector in Malaysia.

The strongest significance of this study is probably providing indicators that influence organisational citizenship behaviours. Understanding the direct and indirect factors that affect organisational citizenship behaviours will help the organisation to increase its focus on those factors that encourage organisational citizenship behaviours. The inclusion of all three types of organisational justice in the study will probably enlighten organisations on the relative importance of each and its effects on the employees. A corollary of this is that organisations in the manufacturing sector will be able to see the effects of each type of organisational justice on each dimension of organisational citizenship behaviour. This helps the organisation to decide which aspect of justice to work on to improve citizenship behaviour among their employees. In essence, it provides the groundwork for organisations to study the dynamics through which fairness perceptions render organisational citizenship behaviours appropriate (Moorman 1991). Organisations may choose to cultivate a culture of fairness and influence employees' perception of a quality relationship between organisational justice and organisational citizenship behaviour (Tansky 1993).

As the study looks at job satisfaction and leader–member exchange as well, organisations will have an insight of whether these two factors are primary antecedents of organisational citizenship behaviours. If these two variables are indeed strongly related to organisational citizenship behaviours, then measures may be taken to improve job satisfaction and leader–member exchange. Studies by Tansky (1993) provide evidence that job satisfaction is directly related to some dimensions of organisational citizenship behaviour. The study will also give an indication of the importance of organisational justice on job satisfaction and leader–member exchange. Furthermore, by comparison, one will be able to see which type of organisational justice has a greater impact on organisational citizenship behaviour, job satisfaction and leader–member exchange. Knowing which type of organisational justice is salient for each construct allows the management of organisations to take appropriate actions to improve conditions at the workplace.

The results of the study are likely to suggest that organisations need to pay more attention to programmes and policies that encourage fairness if job satisfaction, leader–member exchange and organisational citizenship behaviour are the priority of management. Specifically, organisations may need to focus on overall justice to enhance job satisfaction, leader–member exchange and organisational citizenship behaviour. Employees will not demonstrate organisational citizenship behaviours even if management attempts to keep them satisfied if employees do not perceive organisational justice (Nadiri and Tanova 2010). Thus, it is crucial for organisations to manage fairness effectively. Yilmaz and Tasdan (2009) suggest that a positive organisational justice perception may increase a positive citizenship perception, and the more positive the organisational citizenship perception is, the more positive the organisational justice perception will be.

Organisation of Chapters

This study is organised into 12 chapters. Chap. 1 introduces the research topic and outlines the areas of research. It presents a simplified overview of the study on the effect of organisational justice on organisational citizenship behaviour. The objectives, research framework and methodology for the research are clearly stated and laid the groundwork for this study. It also highlights the implications of a sustainable Malaysian workforce. The significance of the study justifies the importance of conducting the study. The organisation of chapters is to help the audience follow through the research process and provides a profound understanding of the development of the research study. The chapter concludes with defining the key terms to develop an understanding of the concepts and terminology used in the study.

Chapter 2 gives a comprehensive overview of the manufacturing sector in Malaysia. This chapter provides an overview of the manufacturing sector initially and then outlines the production performance of the manufacturing sector, private and foreign investment in the manufacturing sector, exports of manufactured goods, employment in the manufacturing sector and financing for the manufacturing sector. After analysing the contribution of the manufacturing sector to the Malaysian economy, the importance of studying the relationship between organisational justice and organisational citizenship behaviour in the manufacturing sector is discussed.

Chapter 3 focuses on the literature review of the main constructs of the study. Specifically, this chapter focuses on related literature on organisational justice, job satisfaction, leader–member exchange and organisational citizenship behaviour. It outlines the different dimensions of organisational justice, job satisfaction, leader–member exchange and organisational citizenship behaviour. Specifically, discussion on organisational justice centres on distributive justice, procedural justice and interactional justice – interpersonal justice and informational justice. As for organisational citizenship behaviour, the discussion identifies the five dimensions of organisational citizenship behaviour that contribute to effectiveness – altruism, courtesy, conscientiousness, sportsmanship and civic virtue.

Chapter 4 encompasses a set of theories that is related to the constructs of the study. Some of the justice theories covered in this chapter include equity theory, justice judgement theory, psychological theories of justice and the more contemporary 'integrative' theories (fairness heuristic theory, uncertainty management theory, fairness theory). Theories of job satisfaction include the facet model, Herzberg's motivator-hygiene theory, the discrepancy model and the steady-state theory, while theories on leader–member exchange focus on the leader–member exchange theory, the role theory and the social exchange theory. The chapter concludes by justifying the adoption of the theory of reasoned action as the underpinning for this study.

Chapter 5 provides a critical review of the empirical association that may exist between perceptions of organisational justice, job satisfaction, leader–member exchange and organisational citizenship behaviour. The main aim is to provide a profound understanding of the interactions between the constructs in the study. Based on the arguments in the literature, a theoretical framework for the study is proposed and research hypotheses developed. The proposed framework is shown in this chapter. This review proposes the underpinning for testing the hypotheses in an attempt to answer the research questions and provides the basis for further analysis in the following chapters.

Chapter 6 highlights the importance of organisational citizenship behaviour for the sustainability of organisations in the new millennium. This chapter begins with a discussion on the importance of organisational citizenship behaviour in general, and then the impact of rewarding organisational citizenship behaviour. It then focuses on research on organisational citizenship behaviour in Malaysia. Next, it emphasises on ways to improve organisational citizenship behaviour and recommends some best practices to enhance organisational citizenship behaviour that are salient for manufacturing organisations in Asia in general and specifically in Malaysia.

Chapter 7 provides the preliminary data analysis and interpretation of the findings. First, the chapter outlines the sampling results covering data collection procedures, demographic data of the companies and demographic data of the respondents. Sampling results provide an insight of the site and subjects of the study – the selection criteria, sampling procedure, response rate, profile of the companies and demographic data of the companies and respondents. It then proceeds with screening the data to detect errors, missing data and outliers. Next, the discussion focuses on the refining of measures to assess the reliability and validity of the scales. Then, results of the exploratory and confirmatory factor analysis are discussed. This is followed by the assessment of conformity with structural equation modelling assumptions to check if the data satisfied the assumptions of sample size; normality, linearity and homoscedasticity; and multicollinearity. Finally, the chapter delineates the assessment of the measurement model to establish convergent and discriminant validity.

Chapter 8 delineates the research findings of the hypothesised relationship between organisational justice and organisational citizenship behaviour. A summary of the research findings of the hypothesised relationships from the empirical analysis reveals the effects of each type of organisational justice on each dimension of organisational citizenship behaviour. Understanding these effects is imperative for organisational effectiveness due to the significance of the relationships. Implications of the findings are discussed extensively to answer the research question identified for the hypothesised relationship.

Chapter 9 outlines the research findings of the hypothesised relationships between organisational justice, job satisfaction and organisational citizenship behaviour. The findings establish if job satisfaction affects the dimensions of organisational citizenship behaviour as well as ascertain the relationship between organisational justice and job satisfaction. An in-depth discussion on the outcomes of the findings provides indicators that practitioners could consider when implementing policies to enhance performance in general and organisational citizenship behaviours, in particular.

Chapter 10 summarises the research findings of the hypothesised relationships between organisational justice, leader–member exchange and organisational citizenship behaviour. The findings give an indication of whether leader–member exchange is an antecedent of organisational citizenship behaviour. It further enlightens practitioners of the significance of each type of justice on leader–member exchange. Discussions on the theoretical and practical implications of the findings offer an insight of what is best for the organisations.

Chapter 11 analyses the mediating role of job satisfaction and leader–member exchange in the organisational justice–organisational citizenship behaviour relationship. For the purpose of this study, the fully mediated model, the partially mediated model and the non-mediated model are examined. Based on the above models, a sequence of test performed using structural equation modelling establishes if job satisfaction and leader–member exchange are mediators in the relationship between organisational justice and organisational citizenship behaviour. The theoretical and practical implications of the findings suggest what is paramount for advancing organisational citizenship behaviour.

Chapter 12 encapsulates the entire study. The chapter meticulously discusses if the findings are consistent with previous studies and identifies contributions to extant literature. Justification for insignificant correlations and supportive arguments for significant relationships are detailed. It establishes the linkage between the findings and the research gaps in the literature review. Implications for research and practice are also outlined. Finally, limitations of the study and directions for future research are highlighted. The conclusion of the chapter recapitulates the contributions of this study to the existing wealth of knowledge in the domain.

Definition of Key Terms

Organisational justice is concerned with the ways in which employees determine if they have been treated fairly in their jobs and the ways in which those determinations influence other work-related variables (Moorman 1991).

Distributive justice refers to the perceived fairness of decision outcomes an employee receives and is assessed by determining whether rewards are proportional to costs (Homans 1961), whether outcomes adhere to expectations (Blau 1964), and whether outcome-input ratios match those of a comparison other (Adams 1965).

Procedural justice refers to the perceived fairness of decision-making procedures and is judged by gauging whether procedures are accurate, consistent, unbiased and correctable (Leventhal 1980).

Interactional justice refers to the perceived fairness of the enactment or implementation of procedures (Bies and Moag 1986).

Interpersonal justice captures the sincerity and respectfulness of authority communication (Colquitt 2001; Greenberg 1993).

Informational justice concerns the use of honest and adequate explanations for decisions (Colquitt 2001; Greenberg 1993).

Organisational citizenship behaviour concerns work-related behaviours that are discretionary, not related to the formal organisational reward system, and, taken together, promotes the effective functioning of the organisation (Organ 1988a).

Altruism is a voluntary behaviour of helping coworkers in the organisation in work-related matters.

Courtesy concerns undertaking and carrying out the obligation of cooperation with others (Organ 1988a).

Conscientiousness refers to employees' sincere devotion to the organisation and respect for company rules beyond the organisation's requirements.

Sportsmanship concerns employees' efforts in avoiding negative behaviours and not complaining in case of problems.

Civic virtue means having a thorough knowledge of things happening in the organisation with certain interest in new developments, work methods and company policies and self-improvement efforts (Yilmaz and Tasdan 2009).

Job satisfaction is a pleasant feeling resulting from the perception that one's job fulfils or allows for the fulfilment of one's important job values.

Leader–member exchange refers to the degree of emotional support and exchange of valued resources between the leader and members (Kang and Stewart 2007).

Behavioural intent refers to people's willingness and effort exerted to perform the behaviour. It is a function of both attitudes towards a behaviour and subjective norms towards that behaviour.

Attitude is the degree to which the person has a favourable or unfavourable evaluation of a particular behaviour.

Subjective norms concern the influence of important others in one's behavioural intention.

Behavioural beliefs are beliefs about the behaviour.

Normative beliefs are beliefs about what important others think about the behaviour.

Conclusion

With rapid technological changes, rising productivity demands and changing employee expectations, companies need to be proactive in contributing to employees' well-being, satisfaction and motivation to ensure they have a stable, engaged workforce in an increasingly competitive and challenging business environment. Implementing fair practices that enhance job satisfaction, the quality of leader–member exchange and organisational citizenship behaviour will be a step towards this. Understanding which justice factor is salient for each construct allows the management of organisations to take appropriate actions to improve conditions at the workplace and design a winning employee value proposition. Perceived organisational injustice can lead to loss of dedicated high performers that may affect organisational effectiveness and productivity. Breaching organisational justice means not only just the withdrawal of citizenship behaviours but also negative behaviours that are detrimental to organisational sustainability. Specifically, dissatisfied employees may retaliate with disruptive measures to punish the organisation and its authorities. Albeit the benefits of acting fairly, authorities find it really difficult to produce this behaviour in real time, especially when they are stressed out. Despite knowing what constitutes fairness, sustaining organisational justice is a challenging task for most people. Hence, this study is timely as it is critical that organisations manage their human capital well to enhance sustainability. Furthermore, limited research has studied the impact of individual justice dimensions on job satisfaction, the quality of leader–member exchange and organisational citizenship behaviour. This study is judicious considering its theoretical contributions and practical implications. The strongest significance of this study is probably providing indicators to facilitate the formulation of remedial policy actions that drive performance of manufacturing organisations.

This chapter introduces the research topic and outlines the areas of research. It presents a simplified overview of the study on the effect of organisational justice on organisational citizenship behaviour. The sustainability of the Malaysian workplace and the importance of studying the manufacturing industry in Malaysia are considered to justify the rationale of the study. The research objectives are clearly stated and laid the groundwork for hypotheses testing. The methodology of the study is to help the audience follow through the research process and provide a profound understanding of the development of the research study. Significance of the research highlights the contributions of the study. The next chapter will outline some data on the manufacturing sector in Malaysia.

References

Adams, J. S. (1965). Inequity in social exchange. In L. Berkowitz (Ed.), *Advances in experimental social psychology* (pp. 267–299). New York: Academic Press.

Alexander, S., & Ruderman, M. (1987). The role of procedural and distributive justice in organisational behaviour. *Social Justice Research, 1*(2), 177–198.

Bagdadli, S., Roberson, Q., & Paoletti, F. (2006). The mediating role of procedural justice in responses to promotion decisions. *Journal of Business and Psychology, 21*(1), 83–102.

Bies, R. J., & Moag, J. F. (1986). Interactional justice: Communication criteria of fairness. In R. J. Lewicki, B. H. Sheppard, & M. H. Bazerman (Eds.), *Research on negotiations in organisations* (pp. 43–55). Greenwich: JAI Press.

Blau, P. (1964). *Exchange and power in social life*. New York: Wiley.

Bogler, R., & Somech, A. (2005). Organisational citizenship behaviour in school: How does it relate to participation in decision making? *Journal of Educational Administration, 43*(5), 420–438.

Brayfield, A. H., & Rothe, H. F. (1951). An index of job satisfaction. *Journal of Applied Psychology, 35*(5), 307–311.

Christ, O., Van Dick, R., Wagner, U., & Stellmacher, J. (2003). When teachers go to extra mile: Foci or organisational identification as determinants of different forms of organisational citizenship behaviour among schoolteachers. *British Journal of Educational Psychology, 73*(3), 329–341.

Cohen-Charash, Y., & Spector, P. E. (2001). The role of justice in organisations: A meta-analysis. *Organisational Behaviour & Human Decision Processes, 86*(2), 278–321.

Colquitt, J. A. (2001). On the dimensionality of organisational justice: A construct validation of a measure. *Journal of Applied Psychology, 86*(3), 386–400.

Colquitt, J. A., Conlon, D. E., Wesson, M. J., Porter, C. O. L. H., & Ng, K. Y. (2001). Justice at the millennium: A meta-analytic review of 25 years of organisational justice research. *Journal of Applied Psychology, 86*(3), 425–445.

Cropanzano, R., & Greenberg, J. (1997). Progress in organisational justice: Tunneling through the maze. In C. L. Cooper & I. T. Robertson (Eds.), *International review of industrial and organisational psychology* (pp. 317–372). Chichester: Wiley.

Dailey, R. C., & Kirk, D. J. (1992). Distributive and procedural justice as antecedents of job dissatisfaction and intent to turnover. *Human Relations, 45*(3), 305–317.

DeConinck, J. B. (2010). The effect of organisational justice, perceived organisational support, and perceived supervisor support on marketing employees' level of trust. *Journal of Business Research, 63*(12), 1349–1355.

Dillman, D. A. (1991). The design and administration of mail surveys. *Annual Review of Sociology, 17*, 225–249.
DiPaola, M. F., & Hoy, W. K. (2005). Organisational citizenship of faculty and achievement of high school students. *The High School Journal, 88*(3), 35–44.
DiPaola, M. F., & Tschannen-Moran, M. (2001). Organisational citizenship behaviour in schools and its relation to school climate. *Journal of School Leadership, 11*(5), 424–447.
Erturk, A. (2007). Increasing organisational citizenship behaviours of Turkish academicians: Mediating role of trust in supervisor on the relationship between organisational justice and citizenship behaviours. *Journal of Managerial Psychology, 22*(3), 257–270.
Eskew, D. E. (1993). The role of organisational justice in organisational citizenship behaviour. *Employee Responsibilities and Rights Journal, 6*(3), 185–194.
Farh, J., Podsakoff, P. M., & Organ, D. W. (1990). Accounting for organisational citizenship behaviour: Leader fairness and task scope versus satisfaction. *Journal of Management, 16*(4), 705–721.
Fields, D., Pang, M., & Chiu, C. (2000). A comparative field study of the effects of distributive and procedural justice in Hong Kong. *Journal of Organisational Behaviour, 21*(5), 547–562.
Folger, R., & Konovsky, M. A. (1989). Effects of procedural and distributive justice on reactions to pay raise decisions. *Academy of Management Journal, 32*(1), 115–130.
Graen, G. B., & Uhl-Bien, M. (1995). Development of leader-member exchange (LMX) theory of leadership over 25 years: Applying a multi-level multi-domain perspective. *The Leadership Quarterly, 6*(2), 219–247.
Greenberg, J. (1988). Equity and workplace status: A field experiment. *Journal of Applied Psychology, 73*(4), 606–613.
Greenberg, J. (1989). Cognitive reevaluation of outcomes in response to underpayment inequity. *Academy of Management Journal, 32*(1), 174–184.
Greenberg, J. (1990). Looking fair vs. being fair: Managing impressions of organisational justice. In B. M. Shaw & L. L. Cummings (Eds.), *Research in organisational behaviour* (pp. 111–157). Greenwich: JAI Press.
Greenberg, J. (1993). The social side of fairness: Interpersonal and informational classes of organisational justice. In R. Cropanzano (Ed.), *Justice in the workplace: Approaching fairness in human resource management* (pp. 79–103). Hillsdale: Lawrence Erlbaum.
Hofstede, G. (1984). *Culture's consequences: International differences in work-related Values* (2nd ed.). Beverly Hills: Sage.
Homans, G. C. (1961). *Social behaviour: Its elementary forms*. London: Routledge/Kegan Paul.
Hooi, L. W. (2002). The impact of Japanese promotion practices on Malaysian enterprises. *Asia Pacific business Review, 9*(1), 21–38.
Hooi, L. W., Sulaiman, M., & Omar, A. (2012). Procedural justice in promotion decisions of managerial staff in Malaysia. *Asia Pacific Business Review, 18*(1), 99–121.
Hoy, W. K., & Tarter, C. J. (2004). Organisational justice in schools: No justice without trust. *International Journal of Educational Management, 18*(4), 250–259.
Kang, D. S., & Stewart, J. (2007). Leader-member exchange (LMX) theory of leadership and HRD: Development of units of theory and laws of interaction. *Leadership and Organisation Development Journal, 28*(6), 531–551.
Kim, W. C., & Mauborgne, R. (1997). Fair process: Managing in the knowledge economy. *Harvard Business Review, 75*(4), 65–75.
Konovsky, M. A., Folger, R., & Cropanzano, R. (1987). Relative effects of procedural and distributive justice on employee attitudes. *Representative Research in Social Psychology, 17*(1), 15–24.
Koopmann, R. (2002). The relation between perceived organisation justice and organisational citizenship behaviours: A review of the literature. *Journal of Student Research*. Retrieved March 15, 2010, from www.uwstout.edu/rs/uwsjsr/table.htm
Lee, C., Pillutla, M., & Law, K. S. (2000). Power distance, gender and organisational justice. *Journal of Management, 26*(4), 685–704.

Leventhal, G. S. (1976). The distribution of rewards and resources in groups and organisations. In L. Berkowitz & W. Walster (Eds.), *Advances in experimental social psychology* (pp. 91–131). New York: Academic.

Leventhal, G. S. (1980). What should be done with equity theory? In K. J. Gergen, M. S. Greenberg, & R. H. Willis (Eds.), *Social exchange: Advances in theory and research* (pp. 27–54). New York: Plenum Press.

Milliken, F. J., Morrison, E. W., & Hewlin, P. F. (2003). An exploratory study of employee silence: Issue that employees don't communicate upward and why. *Journal of Management Studies, 40*(6), 1453–1476.

Moorman, R. H. (1991). Relationship between organisational justice and organisational citizenship behaviour: Do fairness perceptions influence employee citizenship? *Journal of Applied Psychology, 76*(6), 845–855.

Nadiri, H., & Tanova, C. (2010). An investigation of the role of justice in turnover intentions, job satisfaction, and organisational citizenship behaviour in hospitality industry. *International Journal of Hospitality Management, 29*(1), 33–41.

Niehoff, B. P., & Moorman, R. H. (1993). Justice as a mediator of the relationship between methods of monitoring and organisational citizenship behaviour. *Academy of Management Journal, 36*(3), 527–556.

Oplatka, I. (2006). Going beyond role expectations: Toward an understanding of the determinants and components of teacher organisational behaviour. *Educational Administration Quarterly, 42*(3), 385–423.

Organ, D. W. (1988a). *Organisational citizenship behaviour: The good solider syndrome.* Lexington: Lexington Books.

Organ, D. W. (1988b). A restatement of the satisfaction-performance hypothesis. *Journal of Management, 14*(4), 547–557.

Organ, D. W. (1990). The motivational basis of organisational citizenship behaviour. *Research in Organisational Behaviour, 12*(1), 43–72.

Organ, D. W. (1997). Organisational citizenship behaviour: It's construct clean-up time". *Human Performance, 10*(2), 85–97.

Organ, D. W., & Konovsky, M. A. (1989). Cognitive versus affective determinants of organisational citizenship behaviour. *Journal of Applied Psychology, 74*, 157–164.

Phillips, J. M. (2002). Antecedent and consequences of procedural justice perceptions in hierarchical decision-making teams. *Small Group Research, 31*(1), 32–64.

Podsakoff, P. M., MacKenzie, S. B., Moorman, R. H., & Fetter, R. (1990). Transformational leader behaviours and their effects on followers' trust in leader, satisfaction, and organisational citizenship behaviours. *The Leadership Quarterly, 1*(2), 107–142.

Ramamoorthy, N., & Flood, P. (2004). Gender and employee attitudes: The role of organisational justice perceptions. *British Journal of Management, 15*(3), 247–258.

Robinson, S. L., & Morrison, E. W. (1995). Psychological contracts and the OCB: The effect of unfulfilled obligations on civic virtue behaviour. *Journal of Organisational Behaviour, 16*(3), 289–298.

Salleh, L. M. (2005). High/low context communication: the Malaysian Malay style. In: *Proceedings of the 2005 Association for Business Communication Annual Convention* (pp. 1–11). Arvine: Association for Business Communication.

Shapiro, D. L., Buttner, E. H., & Barry, B. (1994). Explanations: What factors enhance their perceived adequacy? *Organisational Behaviour and Human Decision Processes, 58*(3), 346–368.

Skarlicki, D. P., & Latham, G. (1995). Organisational citizenship behaviour and performance in a university setting. *Canadian Journal of Administrative Sciences, 12*(3), 175–181.

Somech, A., & Drach-Zahavy, A. (2000). Understanding extra-role behavior in schools: The relationships between job satisfaction, sense of efficacy, and teachers' extra-role behavior. *Teaching and Teacher Education, 16*(5–6), 649–659.

Tansky, J. W. (1993). Justice and organisational citizenship behaviour: What is the relationship? *Employee Responsibilities and Rights Journal, 6*(3), 195–207.

The Star. (2009, August 23). Dodgy degrees. *The Star*. p. 1.

Thibaut, J., & Walker, L. (1975). *Procedural justice: A psychological analysis*. Hillsdale: Erlbaum.

Tschannen-Moran, M. (2001). Collaboration and the need for trust. *Journal of Educational Administration, 39*(4), 308–331.

Yilmaz, K., & Tasdan, M. (2009). Organisational citizenship and organisational justice in Turkish primary schools. *Journal of Educational Administration, 47*(1), 108–126.

Chapter 2
The Manufacturing Sector in Malaysia

Abstract This chapter outlines data on the manufacturing sector in Malaysia. Data for this chapter comes mainly from government reports published by the Department of Statistics, the Central Bank of Malaysia (Bank Negara Malaysia), the Economic Report 2014/2015, newspaper articles and relevant journal articles. Specifically, this chapter focuses on data related to the economic performance and prospects of the manufacturing sector in Malaysia. The chapter begins with an overview of the manufacturing sector in Malaysia, followed by a description of the performance of the manufacturing sector. It then outlines the production performance of the industries in the manufacturing sector, namely, electrical and electronic products; chemicals, chemical products and petroleum products; wood and wood products; textiles, apparel and footwear; construction-related materials; transport equipment; and food products, beverages and tobacco products. The subsequent subsections focus on private and foreign investment in the manufacturing sector, exports of manufactured goods, employment in the manufacturing sector and financing for the manufacturing sector. The chapter concludes with a discussion on the importance of studying the manufacturing industry in Malaysia.

Introduction

As this study focuses on the manufacturing sector in Malaysia, this chapter will provide an overview of the performance, growth and contribution of the sector to the economy of Malaysia. The importance of the manufacturing sector to the economy is evidenced in its contribution to the gross domestic product (GDP), external trade and job creation. The manufacturing sector experienced moderate growth over the years and has contributed 7.3 % to the Malaysian economy in the second quarter of 2014 (Bank Negara Malaysia 2014). Performance of the manufacturing sector between January and November 2014 shows an increase in the sales value by 6.1 % to register RM600.1 billion. In the same period, the number of employees increased by 1.5 % to 1,030,383 persons, while productivity increased by 4.6 % to RM582,421. The overall manufacturing index expanded 5.9 % compared with the same period in the previous year and grew by 3.7 % in November 2014 compared with the same month in the previous year (Department of Statistics 2015c). Boosted by resilient

L.W. Hooi, *Organisational Justice and Citizenship Behaviour in Malaysia*,
Governance and Citizenship in Asia, DOI 10.1007/978-981-10-0030-0_2

domestic demand and recovery in the external sector, the manufacturing sector is expected to record a better performance. Moreover, Malaysia has been ranked as the world's top manufacturing location in new suitability index by Cushman and Wakefield (Business Circle 2014).

To sustain the sector's contribution to the economy, workforce engagement as well as the retention of talent workers in the manufacturing sector is indispensable. As the working environment in the manufacturing industry is comparatively more hazardous in nature, it is inevitable that employees will leave if they are not happy. However, it is imperative that organisations have an engaged and loyal workforce to remain resilient and competitive. Therefore, it is crucial that organisations in the manufacturing sector promote citizenship behaviour as part of its organisational culture. Boosted by business opportunities from the implementation of the Economic Transformation Programme (ETP) initiatives, domestic finance and strong inflows of foreign direct investment, the manufacturing sector is expected to expand further. To capitalise on this continuous growth, it is imperative that organisations in the manufacturing sector have a better insight of what influences organisational citizenship behaviour, as the workforce is the quality machine that drives organisational growth. In this study, the emphasis is on organisational justice with job satisfaction and leader–member exchange as potential mediators. After analysing the contribution of the manufacturing sector to the Malaysian economy, the importance of studying the relationship between organisational justice and organisational citizenship behaviour in the manufacturing sector is discussed.

Performance of the Manufacturing Sector

The manufacturing sector grew at a faster pace, driven by the strong performance of the electronic and electrical cluster as external demand improves, particularly global semiconductor demand. The manufacturing sector recorded a strong growth of 7.3 % in the second quarter of 2014 (1Q 2014: 6.8 %) and 3.7 % in November 2014 (3.2 % in October 2014). The subsectors which contributed to the increase in November 2014 were electrical and electronic products (10.2 %); petroleum, chemical, rubber and plastic products (1.8 %); and non-metallic mineral products, basic metal and fabricated metal products (2.7 %). On a seasonally adjusted month-on-month basis, manufacturing output increased by 1.3 % in November 2014 (Department of Statistics 2015c).

The sales value of the manufacturing sector in November 2014 rose 2.5 % (RM1.3 billion) to record RM54.3 billion. On a seasonally adjusted month-on-month, the sales value in November 2014 increased by 3.5 %. Sales and exports of personal computers and related parts rebounded strongly due to improved global demand and diminishing inventory. Better performance of the domestic-oriented cluster, particularly the manufactures of transport equipment and food, beverage and tobacco, further enhanced the performance of the manufacturing sector. Overall capacity utilisation rate in the manufacturing sector was sustained at 78 % (1Q

2014: 78 %) –79 % in export-oriented industries (1Q 2014: 79 %) and 77 % in the domestic-oriented industries (1Q 2014: 75 %). In line with resilient domestic consumption and robust private investment, growth of the domestic-oriented industries such as food and beverage as well as transportation equipment and machinery is expected to remain favourable (Bank Negara Malaysia 2014).

Production Performance of the Manufacturing Sector

Data obtained from the Economic Report 2014/2015 showed that generally, growth in the domestic-oriented industries remained strong due to higher exports and continued strength in private domestic demand. Real exports of goods grew at a faster pace, while growth in real imports of goods moderated, resulting in a significant improvement in net exports. Driven by private and government initiatives, domestic demand grew by 5.7 % in the second quarter of 2014 (1Q 2014: 7.4 %). Government initiatives such as the Bantuan Rakyat 1Malaysia (BR1M) gave out RM300 to individuals earning RM2,000 or less, RM650 to households earning RM3,000 or less, RM450 to households earning between RM3,001 and RM4,000 and the RM200 book voucher to university and college students, as well as the RM100 book voucher to primary and secondary school students. Private sector activity remained the key driver of growth during the quarter amid strong investment and consumption.

To provide an in-depth insight of the production performance of the industries in the manufacturing sector, the following section will outline the performance of each industry during the first 7 months of 2014. For the export-oriented industries, the focus is on electrical and electronic products; chemicals, chemical products and petroleum products; wood and wood products; and textiles, apparel and footwear. Subsectors in the domestic-oriented industries that will be discussed include construction-related materials; transport equipment; and food products, beverages and tobacco products. Data for the discussion are based on the information provided in the Economic Report 2014/2015.

Production of Electrical and Electronic Products

Driven by electronic components, communication equipment and domestic appliances, production in the electrical and electronic products subsector grew strongly by 13.3 % during the first 7 months of 2014 (January–July 2013: 6.9 %). The global sales of semiconductors increased 10.3 % during the first 7 months of 2014 to about USD188 billion. This was mainly due to the encouraging global trend in semiconductor sales in the USA, Asia Pacific, Japan and Europe since October 2013. Moreover, the output of printed circuit boards and semiconductor devices rose 53.9 % and 10.5 %, respectively (January–July 2013: 26.2 %; 18.5 %) as a result of growing demand for consumer electronics, particularly mobile devices, as well as improving global PC sales. The replacement of PCs with a new operating system and falling prices of PCs contributed to increased global PC sales, albeit on a moderating trend. However, production of general-purpose machinery decreased 8.8 % (January–July 2013: −1.8 %) due to lower output of air-conditioning machines (−17.9 %) as well as lifting and handling equipment (−8.2 %).

Production of Chemicals, Chemical Products and Petroleum Products

During the first 7 months of 2014, production of petroleum increased 2 % (January–July 2013: 0.9 %), largely supported by higher export production of refined petroleum (23.2 %) and residual petroleum products (124.4 %). However, production of rubber products contracted 0.3 % in the first 7 months of 2014 (January–July 2013: 8.9 %) due to slower external and domestic demand for rubber gloves and rubber tyres. External demand from the automotive industry for rubber tyres was weaker, particularly from China. Moreover, following the product shift from rubber-based to plastics, silicones and metal alloys in the manufacture of medical devices, output of other rubber products declined 3.8 % (January–July 2013: 14.8 %).

Production of Wood and Wood Products

During the first 7 months of 2014, production of wood products rebounded by 5.1 % (January–July 2013: −2.7 %) with higher output in the sawmilling and planing of wood segment at 25.9 % (January–July 2013: 22.7 %). The positive performance was attributed to vibrant residential and commercial construction activities as well as increased demand for Malaysian-made furniture. Demand for timber frame and glued-laminated timber from the construction sector increased due to cost savings compared to the use of concrete and steel. Moreover, demand from major export destinations such as the USA, Japan and Australia for Malaysian-made furniture further contributed to the higher output, particularly wooden and cane furniture which rebounded by 2.2 % (January–July 2013: −12.7 %).

Production of Textiles, Apparel and Footwear

Production of textiles, wearing apparel, leather products and footwear rebounded significantly by 11.5 % during the first 7 months of 2014 (January–July 2013: −2.5 %), mainly through higher output of spinning, weaving and finishing of textiles by 11.6 % and wearing apparel by 13.5 %, respectively (January–July 2013: −17.6 %; 1.6 %). This was due to increasing demand for textiles from Malaysia's top three export destinations, namely, Turkey, China and the Republic of Korea. Sales increased 14.5 % to RM5.5 billion (January–July 2013: 0.9 %; RM4.8 billion), attributed mainly to companies embarking into technical textile. Technical textile such as geotextile with safety elements embedded into the material was suitable for the construction industry. The apparel sector also benefited from contract manufacturing arrangement with producers of high-end international brands. Moreover, the rising affluence and household income as well as quality designs and variety of products boosted demand.

Production of Construction-Related Materials

During the first 7 months of 2014, the construction-related industries registered growth of 3.5 % (January–July 2013: 5.7 %). Precast concrete expanded 21.1 % (January–July 2013: 9.1 %). Though fabricated and basic metal products experienced a lower growth of 2.9 % and 1.9 %, respectively (January–July 2013: 17.2 %; 2.9 %), the subsector was cushioned by the turnaround in production of non-metallic mineral and other related products at 5.4 % (January–July 2013: −2 %) as well as glass products by 11.7 % (January–July 2013: −15.6 %). Robust housing construction activities and ongoing implementation of civil engineering projects contributed to the growth of the construction-related materials' subsector. New orders for construction-related materials increased, mainly driven by ongoing public works and infrastructure projects, such as MRT and LRT, extension of Duta-Ulu Kelang Expressway (DUKE) and widening of Lebuhraya Utara-Selatan (PLUS). Aided by government initiatives such as the Economic Transformation Programme (ETP), the Government Transformation Programme (GTP) and Programme Perumahan 1Malaysia (PR1MA) and the 10th Malaysian Plan (10MP) projects, production in this subsector is expected to remain resilient.

Production of Transport Equipment

Production and exports of transport equipment grew significantly by 22.9 % and 11.3 %, respectively, during the first 7 months of 2014 (January–July 2013: 9.8 %; 4.8 %). This is attributed to higher production in the shipbuilding segment (59 %), manufacture of motor vehicles (12.9 %) as well as parts and accessories (10.1 %). The automotive segment is the largest in the transport equipment subsector, with 11 car producers and 9 motorcycle manufacturers as well as 35,000 parts and accessories' manufacturers. With the aggressive sales campaign and launch of new models by industry players, total vehicle sales during the first 7 months of 2014 grew 3 % to 393,409 units comprising 350,357 passenger vehicles and 43,052 commercial vehicles. Vehicle sales are expected to expand further to 675,000 units in 2014

(2013: 655,793 units), making Malaysia the third biggest car manufacturer in the Association of Southeast Asian Nations (ASEAN) region.

Production of Food Products, Beverages and Tobacco Products

Malaysia's strength as a food producer is gaining momentum. During the first 7 months of 2014, total sales rose 2.5 % to RM20.6 billion (January–July 2013: 0.1 %; RM20.1 billion), while food exports increased significantly by 15.7 % to RM9.3 billion (January–July 2013: 6 %; RM8.1 billion). Output of food products grew 8.6 % (January–July 2013: 8.2 %) mainly from the increased production in refined palm oil (18.2 %), rice (17.6 %) as well as biscuits and cookies (8.7 %). Output of beverage recorded a growth of 19.3 % compared to −6.5% in the same period. All beverage segments registered higher gains as a result. The FIFA World Cup 2014 season, festivities and school holidays to some extent contributed to the improved performance of food and beverage subsectors. However, output of tobacco dropped 9.5 % (January–July 2013: −10.6 %). This is due to declining local leaf production and the contraband market for cigarettes, higher tax on tobacco as well as government initiatives to discourage smoking. Initiatives such as banning smoking in shopping complexes, government premises and other vicinities with central air-conditioning have impacted the production of tobacco.

Private and Foreign Investment in the Manufacturing Sector

In line with strengthening domestic demand and support from an improving external sector following the recovery in advanced economies, private and foreign investment remained relatively strong. Private investment, in particular, surged 13 % to RM78.7 billion during the first half of 2014 with its share to total investment increasing to 68.9 %. Overall, private investment grew strongly by 12 % in 2014 (2013: 13.1 %), especially in the services and manufacturing sectors. Government initiatives, higher export earnings, stable labour market conditions, positive consumer sentiment and improved business prospects further accelerated private sector participation. Meanwhile, private investment in the manufacturing sector is anticipated to contribute 17.7 % to real GDP in 2014 (2013: 16.7 %). Investment in the manufacturing sector will be supported by export and domestic-oriented industries. While expenditure in the domestic-oriented industries will be sustained, investment in the export-oriented industries is expected to increase. This is especially in electrical and electronic products, particularly in medical device, telecommunication equipment and fibre optic cable segments. Expenditure in the domestic-oriented industries will be mainly supported by transport equipment as well as food and beverage subsectors.

In consonance with upbeat business confidence in the domestic investment ecosystem, the manufacturing sector continued to attract domestic and foreign investment with investment approved by Malaysian Investment Development Authority (MIDA) totalling RM47.4 billion during the first 6 months of 2014 (January–June 2013: RM22.7 billion), mainly from Japan, China and Germany. Of the total investments approved by the Malaysian Investment Development Authority, foreign investment, which accounted for 58.9 %, increased 96 % to RM27.9 billion (January–June 2013: 62.7 %; 11.8 %; RM14.3 billion). The main source of foreign investment was from Japan, followed by China, Germany and Singapore which together accounted for 79.4 % of the total foreign investment. Meanwhile, various continuous probusiness initiatives launched by the government to attract private investment yielded positive results. Approved projects for domestic investment increased significantly to RM19.5 billion (January–June 2013: RM8.5 billion), mainly in the petroleum and petrochemical, chemical, electrical and electronic as well as basic metal industries.

Following the improvement in global foreign direct investment as well as increasing investors' confidence, Malaysia remains an attractive investment destination despite stiff competition from other emerging economies. Additionally, Malaysia as an investment destination is expected to strengthen further with Malaysia's improved ranking in various global business benchmarks. Malaysia was ranked the 7th top FDI recipient in Asia, recording a net FDI inflow of RM17.2 billion during the first half of 2014 (January–June 2013: RM17.7 billion) with 10.5 % of the investment in manufacturing. In the World Bank's Doing Business 2014 Report, Malaysia's ranking improved to 6th position from 12th position in 2013, scoring in getting credit (1st), protecting investors (4th) and doing trade across borders (5th). Furthermore, Malaysia improved to 15th from 25th position in the 2014 Foreign Direct Investment Confidence Index by A.T. Kearney. The report highlighted Malaysia's efforts in enhancing competitiveness in electronic, automotive, and machinery manufacturing to move up the value chain into high-technology and skill-intensive segments. Malaysia also improved to 12th position from 15th in the 2014 IMD World Competitiveness Yearbook, scoring in business efficiency (5th), economic performance (9th), government efficiency (15th) and infrastructure (25th). Moreover, the Global Competitiveness Report 2014–2015 ranked Malaysia among the top 20 most competitive economies out of 144 countries surveyed. Of significance is Malaysia's advancement of nine positions in the institutions pillar comprising financial market development, efficiency of goods and services market as well as business-friendly institutional framework.

Exports of Manufactured Goods

The manufacturing sector contributed 76.2 % to total exports in 2013, from 58.7 % in 1990 (Economic Report 2014/2015). During the first 7 months of 2014, manufactured exports rose at a double-digit pace of 11.4 % to RM337.2 billion

(January–July 2013: –0.3 %; RM302.8 billion), buoyed by the strengthening demand from advanced economies. Manufactured exports expanded as a result of a higher growth of both electrical and electronic and non-electrical and electronic products and a low base from the second quarter of 2013. Electrical and electronic exports were driven by strong demand for semiconductors, while non-electrical and electronic exports were supported by stronger demand for resource-based products. Non-electrical and electronics (non-E&E) manufactured exports accounted for 56.8 % in 2013 (1990: 47.3 %), while electrical and electronic products accounted for a third of total exports (Economic Report 2014/2015). On a year-on-year basis, electrical and electronic products, which accounted for 34.4 % of total exports, expanded RM3.0 billion or 14.9 % to RM23.3 billion (Department of Statistics 2015b). In 2014, gross exports of manufactured products are anticipated to expand 6.1 % (2013: 5.1 %) in line with improving external demand, albeit at a more moderate pace, in the second half of the year.

The strength in exports was broad-based with robust growth in both electrical and electronic and non-electrical and electronic subsectors. Receipts from electrical and electronic products grew at an impressive 10.6 % (January–July 2013: –2.9 %) as a result of a surge of 20.1 % in exports of semiconductor devices (January–July 2013: 0.8 %). Semiconductor devices accounted for 49.4 % of total electrical and electronic exports during the first 7 months of 2014. Increasing demand for semiconductor devices from major markets such as China, Singapore, Hong Kong and the USA boosted the export of electronic integrated circuits and photosensitive semiconductor devices by 24.1 % and 18.5 %, respectively. Semiconductor devices accounted for about 70 % of electrical and electronic exports to China, while semiconductors and petroleum products accounted for 66 % of exports to Singapore. During the period, semiconductor devices accounted for 30.6 % of total electrical and electronic exports to the USA. Additionally, telecommunication equipment and parts accelerated 30.9 % (January–July 2013: –9.4 %), largely supported by robust demand from the USA, the Netherlands, Singapore and Mexico to cater for the increasing demand for mid- to low-end smartphones and tablets, notably in emerging markets.

Non-electrical and electronic exports increased significantly by 11.9 % to RM193.2 billion (January–July 2013: 1.8 %; RM172.6 billion) attributable to stronger receipts across major subsectors except rubber and jewellery exports. Exports earnings of petroleum products expanded significantly by 23.4 % (January–July 2013: 12.4 %) mainly due to rising demand for refined petroleum products (23.2 %) from Singapore, Indonesia and Australia. Similarly, chemicals and chemical products expanded 6.7% (January–July 2013: –0.2 %) mainly due to higher receipts from Singapore, India, Indonesia and the USA. The increase came primarily from organic chemicals (6.3 %), soap, cleansing and polishing preparations (14.3 %) as well as dyeing, tanning and colouring materials (12.8 %). Additionally, exports of plastic products expanded 14 % (January–July 2013: 1.5 %), particularly for packaging. This is attributed largely to increase demand from ASEAN, Australia, Republic of Korea and China for plastic plates, sheets, film, foil and strip products, which grew 22.2 %.

Furthermore, exports of machinery, appliances and parts recorded a double-digit growth of 12.5 % (January–July 2013: 1.4 %), while exports of optical and scientific equipment rebounded strongly by 18.6 % during the first 7 months of 2014 (January–July 2013: −12.3 %). The growth in exports of machinery, appliances and parts was largely due to strong demand for specialised machinery for specific industries (16.3 %) and general industrial machinery and equipment (9.2 %) from Singapore, the USA, China and Australia. Likewise, exports of optical and scientific equipment accelerated as a result of strong external demand from the USA, Singapore and China, particularly for measuring, checking, analysing and controlling instruments and apparatus.

Correspondingly, fuelled by higher export demand for non-ferrous metal (12.4 %), particularly copper and nickel to China, India, Singapore and Australia, manufactures of metal rose 4.7 % (January–July 2013: 21.7 %). Similarly, iron and steel products registered a strong rebound of 28.2 % (January–July 2013: −28.4 %). The strong performance is because of robust demand for tubes, pipes, hollow profiles and fittings to Norway, Thailand and Indonesia. Likewise, exports of non-metallic mineral products surged 4.5 % (January–July 2013: −9.9 %), attributed mainly to construction-related materials such as lime, cement, clay and fabricated materials.

However, shipments of rubber products contracted 7.2 % (January–July 2013: −6.5 %) due to slower exports of rubber gloves and rubber materials. Demand for rubber gloves dropped 1.7 % (January–July 2013: 0.4 %), while exports of rubber materials declined significantly (−28 %). The drop in the receipts from rubber gloves was mainly attributed to lower sales of medical rubber gloves to Germany, the UK and Brazil as well as lower average selling prices of rubber gloves amid intensified competition, particularly from China. Exports of surgical rubber gloves remained stable at 2.4 %. Meanwhile, the significant decline in exports of rubber materials (−28 %) was chiefly due to lower shipments to China, the USA and Australia. Nonetheless, exports of articles of rubber remained strong at 16.1 % (January–July 2013: −2.5 %).

Higher export earnings were also recorded for processed food at 15.7 % (January–July 2013: 6 %), with exports to ASEAN accelerating 7.3 %. The growth was backed by growing demand for edible products and preparations (18.5 %) as well as cocoa and cocoa preparations (17.7 %). Similarly, beverage and tobacco exports remained steady at 8.4 % (January–July 2013: 6.9 %). The better performance was primarily attributable to higher exports of beverage to Singapore, Indonesia, Thailand and Vietnam as well as tobacco products to Taiwan, Thailand and Vietnam.

Driven by stronger export growth of wooden furniture (13.4 %) to the USA, Japan and Australia, shipments of wood products rebounded by 4.7 % in the first 7 months of 2014 (January–July 2013: −5.9 %). Exports of bedroom furniture and seats with wooden frame, in particular, increased significantly by 21.6 % and 15.2 %, respectively. On the contrary, veneers and plywood decreased marginally by 2.7 %. While increased new housing activity in Japan during the earlier part of 2014 boosted greater demand for plywood products, lower receipts from the

Republic of Korea, Taiwan and the Philippines dampened the growth of these products in general.

Likewise, exports of textiles, clothing and footwear surged 18.7 % (January–July 2013: 2.3 %) attributed mainly to textile as well as articles of apparel and clothing accessory segments, which expanded 14.1 % and 28 %, respectively. There was a robust demand for textile products such as textile yarn and woven fabrics, particularly from Turkey (10.3 %), followed by China (8.7 %), Republic of Korea (7.9 %) and Japan (7.6 %). The significant performance in the articles of apparel and clothing accessory segments, especially men's clothing (19.8 %), was the result of stronger global demand, particularly from the USA, Singapore and Belgium.

Meanwhile, shipments of transport equipment accelerated 11.3 % (January–July 2013: 4.8 %), primarily attributable to higher exports of aircraft and associated equipment (14.8 %) as well as ships, boats and floating structures (25 %) to the USA, Japan and Thailand. In contrast, jewellery exports plummeted sharply by 15.7 % (January–July 2013: 6.6 %). The drop was significant, notably during the second quarter of 2014 largely due to declining gold investment demand globally. Specifically, the significant contraction was attributed to a decline in jewellery exports of gold, silver, platinum (–14 %) and other articles of precious metals (–40.1 %) to the United Arab Emirates, Singapore and Thailand.

Employment in the Manufacturing Sector

In terms of employment, the manufacturing sector contributed 16.4 % to total employment. The total number of employees engaged in the manufacturing sector in November 2014 was 1,030,383 persons, an increase of 0.1 % compared with the preceding month. Meanwhile, year-on-year basis, the number of employees increased by 1.5 % (15,036 persons) as compared to 1,015,347 persons in November 2013 (Department of Statistics 2015a). The manufacturing sector has the highest number of job vacancies recording 259,831 out of 757,031 total vacancies during the first 8 months of 2014 (January–August 2013: 905,882).

Though retrenchment declined 17.6 % to 6,811 persons during the same period (January–August 2013: 29.6 %; 8,261), the manufacturing sector registered the highest number of retrenchments, accounting for 65 % of total retrenchments. In the same period, the manufacturing sector absorbed 13,910 jobseekers. During the first half of 2014, 722,750 of the two million foreign workers (January–June 2013: 2.1 million) were largely concentrated in the manufacturing sector. In the same period, of the 105,238 expatriates (2013: 81,991), 11,045 were in the manufacturing sector (Economic Report 2014/2015).

Aggregate real wages in the manufacturing sector increased by 4.5 % (1Q 2014: 3.6 %), supported by higher wage growth in the export-oriented industries (Bank Negara Malaysia 2014). During the first 7 months of 2014, average wage per employee and productivity improved to RM2,772 per month and 5.9 %, respectively (January–July 2013: RM2,608; 2.4 %). Month-on-month basis, salaries and wages paid in November 2014 were RM2,837.8 million, an increase by 0.1 % (RM1.8 million). Meanwhile, the total amount paid in November 2014 has increased by 4.3 % (RM117.9 million) compared to November 2013.

Financing for the Manufacturing Sector

The resilience and stability of the financial system provided support across all sectors of the economy. During the first 7 months of 2014, the manufacturing sector continued to receive the largest share of the loan disbursements at 20.6 % (2013: 20.8 %). As at end-July 2014, the manufacturing sector accounted for 7.7 % of total business loans outstanding (2013: 7.9 %) or RM98.3 billion of the impaired loans (2013: RM96.6 billion). In supporting the development of the strategic economic sectors, the development financial institutions continued to play a significant role. During the first 7 months of 2014, development financial institutions continued to provide financing totalling RM5.5 billion (2013: RM4.8 billion) to support the manufacturing sector. This represented 4.4 % share of total financing (2013: 7.9 %) by development financial institutions between January and July 2014.

Additionally, funds raised by the private sector through private debt security amounted to RM450 million accounting for 0.9 during the first 7 months of 2014 (January–July 2014: RM945 million; 2.4 %). Meanwhile, the venture capital industry continued to play an important role as a source of early stage funding for innovation especially for start-up companies and expansion, providing 12 % of total investments to the manufacturing sector as at end-July 2013. Additionally, as at end-July 2014, the manufacturing sector accounted for 4.9 % or RM19.4 billion of Islamic financing (end 2013: 4.7 %, RM17.3 billion). Apart from the banking system, five revolving funds administered by Bank Negara Malaysia also provided financing for SMEs. Microenterprises continued to receive financing support from ten participating financial institutions under Skim Pembiayaan Mikro 2006.

The Importance of Studying the Manufacturing Industry in Malaysia

This study, which used samples from the manufacturing industry in Malaysia, is deemed important due to the magnitude of the sector's impact on the Malaysian economy. The manufacturing sector, bolstered by strong domestic- and export-oriented industries, is expected to grow 5.5 % in 2015 (2014: 6.4 %). In addition, the manufacturing sector has contributed significantly (76.4 %) to total export earnings. Export earnings are expected to further increase from improved global trade, while domestic-oriented industries continue to expand in line with better business confidence and consumer sentiment. Spurred by higher demand for global electronics, particularly semiconductors, electronic components, communication and computer peripherals, the electrical and electronic subsector is expected to grow further. In line with the upward swing of demand for petroleum, rubber and chemical products, the resource-based industry is anticipated to grow steadily. Meanwhile, with better job prospects and higher disposable income, the transport equipment subsector, particularly the passenger car segment, is expected to expand further. In addition, the construction-related industry is likely to expand, attributed primarily to ongoing infrastructure projects such as MRT and extension of LRT.

Besides, the manufacturing sector created huge employment and skill enhancement opportunities in Malaysia (Chew 2005a). In line with the country's economic growth, employment has expanded, with the manufacturing sector contributing the highest number of job vacancies among other sectors during the first 8 months of 2014. The expected increase in global demand, particularly for electrical and electronic as well as for wood products, will further contribute to employment growth. Given the current positive trend in the manufacturing sector, production is expected to expand generating more career opportunities. With the growth in demand for labour exceeding supply, the competition for skilled and talented workers will be more intense. Workers may job hop for better salaries or career advancement (Chin 2003; Hooi 2002, 2008; Kawabe 1991). Chew (2005b) asserts that in Malaysia, new graduates who perform well tend to get their first promotion after 3 years of service, and given the changing social values of the workforce, high performers left for firms that reward rapid advancement. This scenario has not changed in the last 10 years. Most of the excellent managers that left for better career development elsewhere are currently directors of well-established companies through a fast-track upward advancement (Chew 2005b; Hooi 2008). As such, aggressive workers will move on, and with their experience, the next company is more than willing to take them. Labour mobility is rather high especially among young workers who do not hesitate to leave. They will 'search and hop' until they feel that it is irrational to change jobs anymore (Hooi 2008). Besides, Chin (2003) notes that, as materialism gains dominance, the social bonds that have made for a cohesive society are beginning to crumble. Therefore, to secure a highly competent pool of workforce for sustaining a competitive edge, organisations in the manufacturing sector have to undertake measures to instill organisational citizenship behaviour.

Similarly, organisations in the manufacturing sector may risk losing employees to other sectors if employees perceive that their organisations are not performing. Job insecurity in their current organisations may force employees to look for jobs in other sectors. Particularly, for middle age workers, with family commitments and children's education to consider, job security and stability are more important than the slight increase in pay (Hooi 2008). As mentioned earlier, the manufacturing sector has the highest number of retrenched workers in the first 8 months of 2014, accounting for 65 % of total retrenchments (Economic Report 2014/2015). To some extent, it affects employees psychologically, as laying-off employees and sudden dismissals during sluggish times are inevitable. Workers who have better opportunities elsewhere are likely to leave if they foresee imminent bankruptcy in their organisations. To avoid losing key workers, organisations in the manufacturing sector have to take measures to enhance sustainability and ensure that workers exhibit citizenship behaviours to further boost productivity.

In the same period, the manufacturing sector recorded a significant number of foreign workers (722,750 persons). Additionally, the manufacturing sector has 11,045 highly skilled expatriates as at end-August 2014. The presence of foreign workers in the manufacturing sector affects local employees in several ways if organisational justice is not in place. For example, significant responsibilities delegated to expatriates at the expense of local employees may affect their career advancement in the organisation and, hence, their job satisfaction. Hooi et al. (2012) affirm that perceived procedural injustice in promotion decisions intensify the intent to leave, especially among young managerial staff. Similarly, special privileges and benefits received by expatriates may further aggravate the situation if local employees perceive organisational injustice. Additionally, the presence of foreign labour from diverse cultures may create difficulties for supervisors managing them. These foreign workers may be a burden, as local employees have to understand not only their habits and cultures but also the laws that cover these foreign workers. Diversity management becomes an important competence of managers and supervisors, as they have to ensure harmony at the workplace. Where different nationalities have to work side-by-side, tension does set in over sensitive issues. Intention to leave among local employees would probably increase if the working environment were no longer conducive or fair.

Besides, due to rapid changes in technological innovations, it may be imperative for organisations in the manufacturing sector to arm their employees with a high level of broad skills and techniques. However, organisations cannot optimally reap the benefits of investment on training if the tendency of job hopping and turnover is high (Hooi 2008). Therefore, citizenship behaviours that promote a long-term employment system are necessary, though it is not the norm for Malaysian employees to remain with the same organisation in their entire career. However, as the system emphasises job security, employees may welcome it if organisations in the manufacturing sector ensure transparency and fairness at the workplace. Good quality leader–member exchange and enhanced job satisfaction further provide support for the system. Additionally, due to the increasing uncertainty in the global market, job security may be the priority of most employees. As such, establishing employment security as a core employment policy in manufacturing organisations may enhance citizenship behaviours in the manufacturing sector in Malaysia, making it worthwhile to invest in employee development. Additionally, for organisational success, it is imperative to acknowledge the value of the employees who devote their professional lives to the organisation through fair practices.

Furthermore, for manufacturing organisations, the quality of their products is essential for competitive advantage. The quality of the products is much dependent on the workers, as organisations have nothing, in terms of technology, that any other organisations cannot have. Essentially, besides competencies, the practices at the workplace affect the quality of work. Specifically, the negative effects of unhealthy work practices of the management staffs will spill over to the production staffs and, hence, the quality of the products. Therefore, besides continuous training, workers' commitment and loyalty need to be enhanced through organisational citizenship behaviours. However, it is difficult for organisations to create loyalty without first creating satisfied employees. It is unlikely that employees will display loyalty if they are dissatisfied at the workplace. Among other factors, research shows that organisational justice significantly affects job satisfaction and intent to leave (e.g. Alexander and Ruderman 1987; Ball et al. 1994; Cohen-Charash and Spector 2001; Colquitt et al. 2001; Hendrix et al. 1999; Konovsky and Cropanzano 1991; Latham and Pinder 2005; McFarlin and Sweeney 1992); employee loyalty (Lind and Tyler 1988) and organisational commitment (Schappe 1996). Murphy et al. (2006) further affirm that organisational justice affects team loyalty.

Thus, to sustain the sector's contribution to the economy, workforce engagement as well as the retention of talent workers in the manufacturing sector is indispensable. As the working environment in the manufacturing industry is comparatively more hazardous in nature, it is inevitable that employees will leave if they were not happy. However, it is imperative that organisations have an engaged and loyal workforce to remain resilient and competitive. Therefore, it is crucial that organisations in the manufacturing sector promote citizenship behaviour as part of its organisational culture. Boosted by business opportunities from the implementation of the Economic Transformation Programme (ETP) initiatives, domestic finance and strong inflows of foreign direct investment, the manufacturing sector is expected to expand further. To capitalise on this continuous growth, it is critical that organisations examine the relationships that may exist between employee perceptions of organisational justice, organisational citizenship behaviour, job satisfaction and leader–member exchange to have a better insight of what influences organisational citizenship behaviour, as an organisation's human capital is the quality machine that steers organisational growth. In this study, the emphasis is on organisational justice with job satisfaction and leader–member exchange as potential mediators.

Conclusion

For 2015, the manufacturing sector is envisaged to expand, spurred by robust domestic demand and export-oriented industries. Resilient domestic demand and favourable external demand support the growth of investment activities amid continued recovery in the advanced economies and better growth prospects in the region. As external demand improves, the manufacturing sector is anticipated to grow at a faster pace on higher shipments of electrical and electronic products. Improvement in the demand for electrical and electronic products, particularly global semiconductor demand as well as resilient regional trade, is expected to boost further the performance of the sector. Malaysia is likely to benefit from these developments, in particular demand for semiconductor devices – electronic integrated circuits and photosensitive semiconductor. Additionally, production of domestic-oriented industries is expected to expand further due to increasing domestic consumption and investment. Similarly, demand for construction-related materials remains robust, as projects under the 10th Malaysian Plan and National Key Economic Areas (NKEAs) gain momentum.

In essence, domestic demand, particularly private sector expenditure is expected to play a more significant role in driving economic expansion. Specifically, probusiness initiatives launched by the government, and incentives to promote new sources of growth and encourage manufacturers to move up the value chain, are expected to consolidate and strengthen the resilience and competitiveness of the manufacturing sector. To benefit from this, it is imperative that organisations in the manufacturing sector ensure that a pool of dedicated and knowledgeable staff is continuously available to support organisational growth. With the increase in private and foreign investment, strong financing through the banking system and government initiatives, there are many opportunities for growth. Organisations in the manufacturing sector can exploit these opportunities by enhancing workforce engagement, professionalism and staff retention through fair policies and practices, as employees may reciprocate by displaying organisational citizenship behaviours (Moorman 1991).

In the subsequent chapters, the research will be discussed in detail. The next chapter will focus on the literature review on organisational justice, job satisfaction, leader–member exchange and their effects on organisational citizenship behaviour. The chapter will outline the different dimensions of the main constructs of the study. A profound understanding of related literature helps justify the necessity and credibility of this study. The main aim is to expose contemporary research issues and narrow the gap in the domain.

References

Alexander, S., & Ruderman, M. (1987). The role of procedural and distributive justice in organisational behaviour. *Social Justice Research, 1*(2), 177–198.

Ball, G. A., Trevino, L. K., & Sims, H. P., Jr. (1994). Just and unjust punishment: Influences on subordinate performance and citizenship. *Academy of Management Journal, 37*(2), 299–322.

Bank Negara Malaysia. (2014). Developments in the Malaysian economy. *Quarterly Bulletin.* Second Quarter 2014.

Business Circle. (2014). *High-value manufacturing – Malaysia's next frontier* (14 May 2014). Available at http://www.businesscircle.com.my/high-value-manufacturing-malaysias-next-frontier/

Chew, Y. T. (2005a). Achieving organisational prosperity through employee motivation and retention: A comparative study of strategic HRM practices in Malaysian institutions. *Research and Practice in Human Resource Management, 13*(2), 87–104.

Chew, Y. T. (2005b). The changing HRM practices of Japanese firms and the impacts on compensation practices of Japanese affiliates in Malaysia. *Forum of International Development, 28*(1), 55–80.

Chin, T. (2003). Future directions. In Malaysia Institute of Management's *Management in Malaysia* (pp. 383–390). Selangor Darul Ehsan: Percetakan Printpack Sdn. Bhd.

Cohen-Charash, Y., & Spector, P. E. (2001). The role of justice in organisations: A meta-analysis. *Organisational Behaviour & Human Decision Processes, 86*(2), 278–321.

Colquitt, J. A., Conlon, D. E., Wesson, M. J., Porter, C. O. L. H., & Ng, K. Y. (2001). Justice at the millennium: A meta-analytic review of 25 years of organisational justice research. *Journal of Applied Psychology, 86*(3), 425–445.

Department of Statistics. (2015a). *Monthly manufacturing statistics*. November 2014.
Department of Statistics. (2015b). *Malaysia external trade statistics*. December 2014.
Department of Statistics. (2015c). *Index of industrial production, Malaysia*. November 2014.
Hendrix, W., Robbins, T., Miller, J., & Summers, T. P. (1999). *Procedural and distributive justice effects on turnover*. Paper presented at the Annual Meeting of the Society for Industrial and Organisational Psychology, Atlanta, GA.
Hooi, L. W. (2002). The impact of Japanese promotion practices on Malaysian enterprises. *Asia Pacific Business Review, 9*(1), 21–38.
Hooi, L. W. (2008). Current remuneration practices in the multinational companies in Malaysia: A case study analysis. *Research and Practice in Human Resource Management, 16*(1), 78–103.
Hooi, L. W., Sulaiman, M., & Omar, A. (2012). Procedural justice in promotion decisions of managerial staff in Malaysia. *Asia Pacific Business Review, 18*(1), 99–121.
Kawabe, N. (1991). Japanese management in Malaysia. In S. Yamashita (Ed.), *Transfer of Japanese technology and management to the ASEAN countries*. Tokyo: University of Tokyo Press.
Konovsky, M. A., & Cropanzano, R. (1991). Justice considerations in employee drug testing. In R. Cropanzano (Ed.), *Justice in the work place: Approaching fairness in human resource management* (pp. 171–192). Hillsdale: Lawrence Erlbaum.
Latham, G., & Pinder, C. (2005). Work motivation theory and research at the dawn of the twenty-first century. *Annual Review of Psychology, 56*(1), 485–516.
Lind, E. A., & Tyler, T. R. (1988). *The social psychology of procedural justice*. New York: Plenum Press.
McFarlin, D. B., & Sweeney, P. D. (1992). Distributive and procedural justice as predictors of satisfaction with personal and organisational outcomes. *Academy of Management Journal, 35*(3), 626–637.
Moorman, R. H. (1991). Relationship between organisational justice and organisational citizenship behaviour: Do fairness perceptions influence employee citizenship? *Journal of Applied Psychology, 76*(6), 845–855.
Murphy, C., Ramamoorthy, N., Flood, P. C., & MacCurtain, S. (2006). Organisational justice perceptions and employee attitudes among Irish blue collar employees: An empirical test of the main and moderating roles of individualism/collectivism. *Management Revue, 17*(3), 328–343.
Schappe, S. P. (1996). Bridging the gap between procedural knowledge and positive employee attitudes: Procedural justice as keystone. *Group & Organisation Management, 21*(3), 337–364.

Chapter 3
Organisational Justice, Organisational Citizenship Behaviour, Job Satisfaction and Leader–Member Exchange

Abstract This chapter focuses on the literature review of the main constructs of the study. Specifically, this chapter focuses on related literature on organisational justice, job satisfaction, leader–member exchange and organisational citizenship behaviour. It outlines the different dimensions of organisational justice, job satisfaction, leader–member exchange and organisational citizenship behaviour. Specifically, discussion on organisational justice centres on distributive justice, procedural justice and interactional justice – interpersonal justice and informational justice. As for organisational citizenship behaviour, the discussion identifies the five dimensions of organisational citizenship behaviour that contribute to effectiveness – altruism, courtesy, conscientiousness, sportsmanship and civic virtue. Similarly, it highlights the various dimensions of job satisfaction and leader–member exchange. Albeit a wealth of knowledge in the field of organisational justice with regard to specific organisational phenomena, meticulous forethought is imperative to institute a compelling reasoning for the study. An exhaustive literature review would unearth current research issues that could be explored further to explicate matters that merit further attention. Identifying the gap and then research on it contributes to theory and practice.

Introduction

Research on organisational justice has focused more on job attitudes rather than on organisational behaviours (Greenberg 1990a). As organisational citizenship behaviour makes an organisation more effective over time and across people (Organ 1988a), this study intends to explore the effects of organisational justice on organisational citizenship behaviour, taking into consideration job satisfaction and leader–member exchange as mediators. Specifically, this chapter focuses on related literature on organisational justice, job satisfaction, the quality of leader–member exchange relationship and organisational citizenship behaviour. Relationships that may exist between perceptions of fairness, organisational citizenship behaviour, job satisfaction and the quality of leader–member exchange relationship will be discussed in Chap. 5. Discussion on organisational justice concerns literature on distributive justice, procedural justice and interactional justice, while discussion on organisational citizenship behaviour focuses on altruism, courtesy, sportsmanship, civic virtue and conscientiousness. Finally, it examines some theoretical aspects of

L.W. Hooi, *Organisational Justice and Citizenship Behaviour in Malaysia*, Governance and Citizenship in Asia, DOI 10.1007/978-981-10-0030-0_3

job satisfaction and leader–member exchange. In-depth discussion will be made on each of the constructs as well as their effects on various organisational outcomes. Albeit a wealth of knowledge in the field of organisational justice with regard to specific organisational phenomena, such as organisational commitment, organisational citizenship behaviour, job satisfaction and intent to leave, meticulous forethought is imperative to institute a compelling reasoning for the study.

Organisational Justice

What Is Organisational Justice?

The term 'organisational justice' was coined by French (1964) to describe individuals' perceptions of fairness in organisations. Essentially, organisational justice refers to people's perceptions of justice and equality in organisations (Greenberg 1990a, 1996) – the extent to which employees view outcomes, procedures and interactions with organisational representatives as just. It is a concept that expressed employees' perceptions of organisational fairness and its effect on organisational outcomes (Greenberg 1996) and is related to employees' perceptions about the decisions and practices of organisational management (Witt 1993). Eskew (1993) opines that it is employees' perceptions of equity in work-related issues such as employees' work-related attitudes and behaviours. Folger and Cropanzano (1998) affirm that organisational justice is concerned with the rules developed to distribute or to take decisions on distribution of acquisitions that constitute the basis for these rules. Generally, organisational justice refers to the fairness in decisions organisations make, the procedures they used in making decisions and the interpersonal treatment employees received.

Organisational justice gained prominence in the 1970s as one of the social justice dimensions to fulfil all organisational values and principles. As fulfilment of social justice is impossible without fulfilment of organisational justice, organisational justice is, thus, a basis for strategic thinking and value management (Chegini 2009). Maslow asserts that justice is an essential need – a basic precondition for fulfilling needs. Greenberg (1990a) affirms the correlation between organisational justice and perceived fairness at work. Accordingly, organisational injustice is the basis of all organisational harms and destroys organisational integrity (Gholipour and Ezzat 2008). Injustice affects staff morale and progress of staff, which influences organisational growth. In general, organisational justice encompasses the principle of equality, perception, polyphony, interpersonal justice, consistency, political and social equality and correction (Hoy and Tarter 2004).

Dimensions of Organisational Justice

Research on organisational justice and its impact on effective organisational functioning have taken various dimensions. Greenberg (1990b) focused on a two-factor conceptualisation of organisational justice integrating distributive and procedural justice. According to Adams (1965) equity theory, distributive justice is fostered as long as outcomes are consistent with implicit norms for allocation (Colquitt 2001). Procedural justice concerns the perceived fairness of the processes used for determining these outcomes (Lind and Tyler 1988). Thibaut and Walker (1975) assert that voice during a decision-making process or influence over the outcome constitutes procedural justice. Procedural justice is fostered by adherence to fair justice rules such as consistency (there is consistency in allocation procedures across people and over time), bias-suppression (decision-makers suppress their own bias and self-interests during the allocation process), accuracy (accurate information is used in determining allocations), correctability (opportunities exists for changing unfair decisions), representativeness (the process represents the needs, values and perspectives of all affected parties) and ethicality (the allocation process meets moral and ethical values or codes) (Leventhal 1980; Leventhal et al. 1980).

Gilliland (1993) expanded these rules to ten and grouped them under three categories – formal characteristics (job-relatedness, chance to perform, reconsideration opportunity and consistency of information), explanation (feedback, information known and openness) and interpersonal treatment (treatment, two-way communication and propriety of questions). Violating these rules may tarnish the reputation of the organisation, lower motivation and an unsettling psychological contract, which may reduce cost effectiveness and increase turnover. Other dimensions of justice include adequate notice about performance expectations, clear communications of these standards, involvement of the supervisors and subordinates in the setting of performance standards, periodic reviews of task accomplishment, accurate performance feedback and an opportunity to resolve grievances with supervisors (Murphy et al. 2006).

Sweeney and McFarlin (1993) maintain that distributive justice is related to personal reference outcomes (e.g. pay satisfaction), while procedural justice is related to organisational reference outcomes (e.g. organisational commitment, lower level of trust, evaluation of supervision, job satisfaction, unwillingness to help other employees). Similar findings have been reported by other research in the domain (e.g. Fields et al. 2000; Folger and Konovsky 1989; Masterson et al. 2000; McFarlin and Sweeney 1992; Williams et al. 2002; Zellars et al. 2004) and discussed in literature reviews (e.g. Greenberg 1990b; Lind and Tyler 1988). However, only distributive justice is related to turnover intentions (Hendrix et al. 1999) or intent to stay (Cohen-Charash and Spector 2001).

Further to this, Bies and Moag (1986) introduce interactional justice in their three-factor model on organisational justice. Colquitt et al. (2005) described interactional justice as the 'third wave' in the conceptualisation of organisational justice, with the 'first wave' consisting of distributive justice and the 'second wave' consisting of procedural justice (Roch and Shanock 2006). Interactional justice defined as the interpersonal treatment people received as procedures is enacted, is fostered when decision-makers treat people with respect and sensitivity and 'the quality of the interpersonal treatment people receive when procedures are implemented' (Colquitt et al. 2001: 425). The rationale for decisions is explained thoroughly (Shapiro et al. 1994). Thus, interactional justice focuses on the perceived fairness of communications and interpersonal treatment by managers or other organisational representatives (Gillespie and Parry 2006). Similarly, past research shows that interactional justice has been considered as a third type of justice (e.g. Aquino 1995; Barling and Phillips 1993; Bies 2001; Bies and Shapiro 1987; Harlos and Pinder 1999; Skarlicki and Folger 1997; Tata and Bowes-Sperry 1996) or a subset of procedural justice (e.g. Moorman 1991; Nierhoff and Moorman 1993; Tyler and Bies 1990; Tyler et al. 1996). Others have combined them because of high intercorrelations even though separate measures have been used (e.g. Mansour-Cole and Scott 1998; Skarlicki and Latham 1997). Whether organisational justice is best depicted by two or three factors is still inconclusive (Colquitt 2001).

Greenberg (1987) breaks down organisational justice into four categories by combining two dimensions of organisational justice – the process–content dimension and the reactive–proactive dimension. The process approach analyses the methods used to determine outcomes in organisations and assesses procedural fairness in decision-making, while the content approach concerns distributive justice of outcomes. Both of these approaches focus on the relative fairness of the outcomes that are received by various employees. In a later four-factor model, Greenberg (1993b) makes clear distinctions between interpersonal justice and informational justice. He argues that the respect and sensitivity aspects of interactional justice (interpersonal justice) can alter reactions to decisions outcomes. Thus, it might best be viewed as an interpersonal facet of distributive justice because it can make people feel better about an unfavourable outcome. Accordingly, the explanation aspect of interactional justice (informational justice) can be viewed as an interpersonal facet of procedural justice because explanations often provide the information needed to evaluate structural aspects of the procedure. Though limited research has been conducted using the four-factor model, Colquitt (2001) proposes splitting interactional justice into interpersonal and informational justice as collapsing them would mask important differences. The measure used in his study was able to discriminate four different organisational justice factors. Colquitt et al. (2001: 425) define interpersonal justice as 'the degree to which people are treated with politeness, dignity and respect by authorities or third parties involved in executing procedures or determining outcomes' and informational justice as 'the explanations provided to people that convey information about why procedures were used in a certain way or why outcomes were distributed in a certain fashion'.

Rego et al. (2009) introduce a five-factor model by subdividing the distributive justice dimension into two facets – task distributive justice and reward distributive justice. Results of three studies with Portuguese public university teachers reveal that a five-factor model of justice (distribution of tasks, distribution of rewards, procedural, interpersonal, informational) is adequate, although factor analyses are not categorical in distinguishing interpersonal and informational justice. They emphasise that with regard to distributive justice, a distinction could be made between rewards and tasks allocation when some conditions are observed. The distinction is made based on the proposal that justice perceptions may be associated with a type as well as a focus or source (Byrne and Cropanzano 2000) and that people can distinguish justice according to the source of the justice experience (Blader and Tyler 2003). As the sources reflect the origins of the experiences that shape employees' justice evaluations, the differentiation of distributive justice into two dimensions is deemed necessary.

Nabatchi et al. (2007) suggest splitting the procedural justice factor into two distinct components – the procedural justice-process component and the procedural justice–mediator component. Erdogan et al. (2001) call it system procedural justice and rater procedural justice. This six-factor model, which includes distributive justice, procedural justice-process, procedural justice–mediator, informational justice, disputant–disputant interpersonal justice and disputant–mediator interpersonal justice, distinguishes between perceptions of justice relating to the procedure and the individual third party neutral or decision-maker who enacts that procedure. The first component captures information about the individuals' perceptions of the fairness of the process itself (perceived fairness of the process and procedures used by the organisation), while the second component captures the instrumental aspects of procedural justice (how the rater executes or implements the system, that is, the fairness of the procedures the rater uses). Thus, a clear distinction is made between the procedural aspects of the mediation process and the objective assessment of the mediator's performance as a professional. One construct captures information about perceptions of the mediation process as an organisationally designed decision-making process, and the other captures information about perceptions of the procedural enactment by the mediator. They argue that direct comparisons of the perceived fairness of the process, and of the person who enacts the process, would be possible with this distinction.

Ambrose and Schminke (2009) suggest considering overall justice instead of focusing on specific types of justice (distributive, procedural and interactional). Accordingly, overall justice judgements mediate the relationship between specific justice facets and outcomes. The study shows that overall justice judgements mediate the relationship between specific justice judgements and employee attitudes as well as for supervisor ratings of employee behaviour. Although there are various justice typologies in the literature, organisational justice in this study will examine distributive justice, procedural justice and interactional justice. Each of these types of justice will be discussed to link fairness principles to employees' perceptions. This is shown in Fig. 3.1.

As shown in Fig. 3.1, organisational justice comprises of distributive justice, procedural justice and interactional justice. Distributive justice rules include equity, equality and needs, while procedural justice focuses on fairness in policies, procedures and processes. The main concern of interactional justice is the interpersonal treatment that employees received from the employers – the organisation and the superiors. It comprises of informational justice and interpersonal justice. Distributive justice will affect employees' satisfaction with decisions and outcomes, procedural justice with system satisfaction and interactional justice with relationship satisfaction.

Fig. 3.1 Types of organisational justice

Studies on Organisational Justice

A number of studies have been conducted linking organisational outcomes to organisational justice. Prior studies show that generally, employees' perception of fairness is influenced by career outcomes. Positive career outcomes enhance employees' perception of fairness in decision-making. Fairness also influences decision acceptance. Organisational fairness in decision-making is likely to augment employees' acceptance and encourage positive reactions to organisational decisions (Bagdadli et al. 2006). Organisational decisions may include decisions on compensation and benefits (Folger and Konovsky 1989), layoffs and terminations (Brockner et al. 1994), performance appraisals (Greenberg 1986; Taylor et al. 1995) and employee selection processes (Gilliland 1993, 1994; Singer 1993). On the contrary, when organisational decisions and managerial actions are perceived as unfair, employees experience feelings of anger, outrage and resentment (Bies 1987; Folger 1993; Greenberg 1989, 1990b; Sheppard et al. 1992). As a result, employees may engage in acts of retribution or retaliation (Greenberg and Scott 1996; Sheppard et al. 1992; Skarlicki and Folger 1997). Procedural justice has strong emotional consequences (Tyler and Smith 1998), and injustice is particularly believed to educe feelings of anger and resentment (Folger and Cropanzano 1998).

However, little research has been done to identify antecedents of organisational justice (Cohen-Charash and Spector 2001), and the correlation between individual variables and justice perceptions remains ambiguous (Gillespie and Parry 2006) and inconsistent (Kausto et al. 2005). Demographic variables do not directly affect perceptions of fairness, but has a mediating effect (Cohen-Charash and Spector 2001). Sweeney and McFarlin (1997) notice that the effects of procedural justice on organisational outcomes such as organisational commitment and job satisfaction are stronger for females than for males and the converse for the effects of distributive justice on the same outcomes. Kausto et al. (2005) disclose that job insecurity moderated the effect of interactional justice on well-being only among female employees, but there were no gender differences for procedural justice. Some studies reveal a positive relationship between procedural justice and self-esteem (De Cremer and Sedikides 2005; Tyler 1999). This is probably due to lower occupational status of women compared to men and socialisation to gender roles. Nonetheless, research on the correlation between personality traits and perceived justice is much restrained.

It is important to note that previous studies have provided ambiguous findings on the relation of organisational justice and intent to leave. Studies show that intent to leave was more strongly related to distributive justice (Alexander and Ruderman 1987) as compared to procedural justice (Dailey and Kirk 1992). When procedural justice was separated from interactional justice, intent to leave was more strongly related to the latter (Barling and Phillips 1992; Masterson and Taylor 1996). Thus, procedural and interactional justice strongly affects attitudes and affective reactions towards the organisation (Cohen-Charash and Spector 2001). Judge and Colquitt (2004) emphasise that organisational justice has an effect on stress. Lack of control (Thibaut and Walker 1975) or social exclusion (Lind and Tyler 1988; Tyler and Lind 1992) may result and, thus, be a source of psychological stress at work, intensifying to a health risk (Elovainio et al. 2002; Kivimaki et al. 2003; Schmitt and Dorfel 1999; Tepper 2001). These studies substantiate that low levels of procedural and interactional justice correlate with subsequent psychological distress, psychosomatic symptoms, poor self-rated health and sickness absence. Concomitantly, perceived procedural and interactional justice may be an important organisational resource for employees facing challenges of the job. Studies (e.g. Kivimaki et al. 2003) implicate that perceived procedural and interactional injustice contributes to employee ill health and lack of well-being. Similarly, Kausto et al. (2005) recapitulate this, emphasising the effect on emotional exhaustion and stress. Some of the studies on organisational justice are shown in Table 3.1.

Table 3.1 Studies on organisational justice

Areas	Studies
Organisational commitment	Konovsky et al. (1987), Folger and Konovsky (1989), McFarlin and Sweeney (1992), Ball et al. (1994), Hendrix et al. (1999), Cohen-Charash and Spector (2001), Colquitt et al. (2001), Hassan (2002), Latham and Pinder (2005) and Murphy et al. (2006)
Management satisfaction	Alexander and Ruderman (1987) and Fryxell and Gordon (1989)
Pay satisfaction	Greenberg (1987), Konovsky et al. (1987), Folger and Konovsky (1989), Miceli and Lane (1991), Sheppard et al. (1992), Sweeney and McFarlin (1993), Welbourne (1998), St Onge (2000) and Tremblay et al. (2000)
Leadership evaluation	Tyler and Caine (1981) and Alexander and Ruderman (1987)
Job performance	Ball et al. (1994), Alder and Tompkins (1997), and Nasurdin and Soon (2011)
Job satisfaction and intent to quit	Alexander and Ruderman (1987) McFarlin and Sweeney (1992), Ball et al. (1994), Hendrix et al. (1999), Cohen-Charash and Spector (2001), and Colquitt et al. (2001)
Reactions to layoffs	Brockner and Greenberg (1990a) and Konovsky and Brockner (1993)
Reaction to criticism	Baron (1993)
Reactions to organisational grievance systems	Gordon and Fryxell (1993)
Employee theft	Greenberg (1990b)
Job design	Earley and Lind (1987) and Lowe and Vodanovich (1995)
Selection	Gilliland (1994), Ployhart and Ryan (1998), and Harris (2000)
Performance appraisal	Greenberg (1986), Greller (1975), and Williams (2000)
Training	Witt and Broach (1993), Skarlicki and Latham (1996), and Cole and Latham (1997)
Prosocial behaviour	Colquitt et al. (2001) and Murphy et al. (2006)
Team loyalty	Murphy et al. (2006)

Types of Organisational Justice

Distributive Justice

Distributive justice refers to the perceived fairness of the amounts of compensation employees receive (Folger and Konovsky 1989). Distributive justice is concerned with the outcomes of distributive decisions (Homans 1961) and emphasises on how decision-makers allocate resources and the reactions of individuals to the outcomes from those decisions. It determines employees' perceptions of equity in payment, promotion and similar resource distribution comparatively. Distributive justice assumes the fair distribution of organisational resources (Eskew 1993). Historically, the equity theory (Adams 1963, 1965) has been the focus of organisational justice scientists. This is because most distributive justice research focused on maximising productivity (Colquitt 2001). However, other theories on distributive justice have since been adopted, and these include the justice judgement model (Leventhal 1976, 1980), distributive justice theory (Homans 1961) and allocation preference theory (Leventhal et al. 1980). Organ (1988a) argues that criteria for determining salary such as status, seniority, productivity, effort and need are related to distributive justice. Outcomes can be individual related (pay raises, job security, promotions and layoffs, workplace retaliation and organisational citizenship behaviour) or group related (subsidiary performance, partner commitment, profit sharing in entrepreneur–investor relations and resource allocation in mergers and acquisitions) depending on the group of individuals or entities involved (Luo 2007). Organ (1988a) contends that distributive justice comprises of three rules of distribution, namely, equity, equality and need (Deutsch 1985; Koopmann 2002; Tyler 1994).

The equity rule of distribution presupposes that rewards should be contingent on the level of contribution (Yilmaz and Tasdan 2009). For example, a full-time employee deserves higher compensation than a part-time worker does, if all other aspects are equal. The equity rule is violated if contributions made to the organisation are not in proportion to income (Koopmann 2002). The equality rule of distribution insists that decisions should be taken according to personal interests independently (Hoy and Tarter 2004). Every individual should have an equal opportunity for attaining rewards, regardless of individual characteristics (such as, sex, age, ability and race). This rule is rarely used in practice, as it is illogical to reward people blindly for random behaviours. Instead, some measures would be used to determine the reward, which is then equally distributed. For example, the organisation may promote a male and a female employee if two similar vacant positions are available. One gender promoted to both positions constitutes inequality (Koopmann 2002). The need rule of distribution states that less well-to-do people deserve (i.e. need) the rewards more comparatively. Thus, other things being equal, a single mother of two would deserve a pay increase more than one with no children in a double income home (Koopmann 2002).

Research that focuses on employees' reaction to actual promotion decisions (Gilliland 1993, 1994; Johnston et al. 1993; Lyness and Judiesh 2001; Schwarzwald et al. 1992) conclude that non-promoted employees demonstrated lower levels of organisational commitment, higher levels of absenteeism and higher intent to leave. Research findings also show that non-promoted employees response negatively and this is further aggravated if employees perceive that the promotion process is unfair. Heneman et al. (2001) reveal that non-promoted internal candidates are more likely than external candidates are, to perceive the promotion process as unfair. Employees' perceptions of unfairness in promotion may result in unfavourable consequences for an organisation. Prior research shows that the lack of equity in promotion has led to discrimination suits (Cole and Latham 1997; Peterson and Danehower 1994), intent to leave (Dailey and Kirk 1992), increased absenteeism and on-the-job accidents (Sashkin and Williams 1990).

Procedural Justice

Procedural justice refers to the perceived quality of decision-making procedures (Leventhal 1980) or the perceived fairness of the procedures concerned with making and implementing decisions (Folger and Greenberg 1985; Lind and Tyler 1988) through which outcomes are allocated (Kim and Mauborgne 1997; Leventhal 1976; Thibaut and Walker 1975). Welbourne (1998) refers procedural justice as the perceived fairness of the procedures used in making promotions, while Folger and Greenberg (1985) describe it as equity of the procedures used in making decisions regarding the distribution of rewards. Similarly, Folger and Konovsky (1989) suggest that procedural justice is the perceived fairness of the means used to determine the amounts of compensation employees receive. The procedural justice perspective focuses on the fairness of the process that is used to make decisions on promotion, performance assessment, rewards and sharing other organisational opportunities (Roch and Shanock 2006) and compensation or other managerial judgements (Alexander and Ruderman 1987; Cropanzano and Folger 1991). How outcomes are determined may be more important than the actual outcome because procedural justice focuses on the perceived fairness of the means used to determine the amount of punishment or reward (Folger and Cropanzano 1998). Employees are also more likely to accept the authority's decision when the process is considered fair (Lind et al. 1993). Generally, organisational-level practices such as organisational support contribute to perceptions of procedural justice (Cohen-Charash and Spector 2001).

Indubitably, individuals perceive fair outcomes if they perceive that the structural characteristics of the decision-making process is fair (Eskew 1993). Numerous studies on this have verified the link between perceived equity on the structural characteristics of procedural justice on perceived fair outcomes. This includes research on performance appraisal contexts (Greenberg 1986), day-to-day managerial operations (Sheppard and Lewicki 1987) and compensation systems (Folger and Konovsky 1989). Procedural justice is more strongly related than distributive justice to positive organisational outcomes such as performance (Gilliland 1994; Welbourne et al. 1995), organisational commitment (Konovsky and Cropanzano 1991), commitment to organisational decisions (Greenberg 1994) and trust in management (Konovsky and Cropanzano 1991). Procedural justice is also negatively related to undesirable organisational activity such as turnover intentions (Olson-Buchanan 1996; Schaubroeck et al. 1994), theft behaviour (Greenberg 1994) and retaliation against an organisation (Skarlicki and Folger 1997).

Procedural justice is perceived as a precaution against dysfunction and improves the effectiveness of formalised and routinised policies in a particular relationship (Brockner 2002; Skarlicki and Folger 1997). Procedural formalisation may not improve alliance performance if it is perceived as unfair (Luo 2007). If procedures are perceived as unfair, people will pursue activities that advance their own self-interest (Fuller and Hester 2007). However, fair decision-making procedures would encourage cooperative behaviours, and people would pursue activities that promote group interests; they respond to 'group mode' rather than 'individual mode' (Lind

2001: 67). Additionally, perceived fairness in procedures helps employees receive better outcomes (Lind and Tyler 1988; Thibaut and Walker 1975; 1978) and enhances employees' faith in organisational systems, and minimises uncertainty about future distribution of income. In short, it helps advance the self-interest of employees in achieving positive outcomes (Posthuma et al. 2007).

Procedural justice is also conceptualised as process control (Gillespie and Parry 2006); the more control one has of a process (the ability to voice one's views and arguments during a procedure), the more likely the person will perceive the process as fair (Greenberg 1990a; Lind et al. 1990; Lind and Tyler 1988; Organ and Moorman 1993; Thibaut and Walker 1975; Tyler and Lind 1992). People will make procedural fairness judgements by assessing their direct or indirect control within a procedure (Chen and Park 2005). Fair procedures such as adequate notice, fair hearing, consistent application of rules and suppression of bias provide the employees a certain level of control over the process (Murphy et al. 2006). Based on observations of courtroom settings, Thibaut and Walker (1975) advocate decision control (the ability to influence the actual outcome) as well. They argue that people typically want to maximise their control over decisions that determine their outcomes when interacting with others.

Leventhal et al. (1980), on the contrary, promote the procedural justice concept to non-legal settings. The process one experiences is compared to several generalisable procedural rules. The procedure is fair if it conforms to the justice rules of consistency, bias-suppression, accuracy, correctability, representativeness and ethicality. Leventhal's criteria and Thibaut and Walker's process control tend to be highly correlated, but Leventhal's criteria have a significantly stronger correlation with procedural fairness perceptions (Colquitt et al. 2001). Gilliland (1993) synthesises ten different procedural justice rules within the context of selection decisions. A meta-analysis by Colquitt et al. (2001) confirms the usefulness of the multiple dimensions of procedural justice explicated by Leventhal (1980). Muchinsky (2000) opines that a decision that is consistent, without personal bias and accurate with an outcome that could be modified is procedurally just. Lind and Tyler (1988), however, did not include representativeness in their study as it subsumes process and decision control. Instead, Tyler (1989) proposes three additional criteria (neutrality, trust and standing) which Lind (1995) revises as neutrality, benevolence and status recognition.

Most research on procedural justice tends to be associated with attitudes towards overall organisational outcomes, such as organisational commitment (Bagdadli et al. 2006; Dailey and Kirk 1992; Folger and Konovsky 1989; Konovsky and Folger 1987; Korsgaard et al. 1995; Quarles 1994; Sweeney and McFarlin 1993), intent to leave (Carson et al. 1994; Porter and Steers 1973; Price 1977; Stroh et al. 1996), employees' identification with their organisations (O'Reilly and Chatman 1986) and trust in management/supervisor (Folger and Konovsky 1989). Similarly, Lind and Tyler (1988) believe fair procedures really determine employee behaviour and commitment. Overall, these studies have found that people perceive the process as fairer when they are given a 'voice' in the process as against a 'mute' condition where participation is not permitted (Folger and Cropanzano 1998; Lind et al. 1997). Thus, employees allowed to participate as assessors or as interviewers would likely be more accepting of the person chosen for the position in question. This can be especially important when the employee chosen for the promotion obtains legitimate power over former coworkers through the new position. The former coworkers should be more cooperative if they had participated in the promotion decision (Deutschman 1994).

Lind and Tyler (1988) reiterate that procedural justice is important in determining factors that are inherent to organisational citizenship behaviour, in particular individual's perceptions of system or institutional characteristics. For example, organisational commitment and trust in supervisors (Folger and Konovsky 1989) and trust in management and rating supervision (Alexander and Ruderman 1987) were better predicted by procedural justice. Konovsky and Cropanzano (1991) advocate that procedural justice not only positively influence organisational commitment and loyalty but also the possibility of fair treatment from that organisation in the future. Succinctly, positive perceptions of procedural justice augment a reciprocal relationship with the organisation.

Despite a plethora of literature on organisational decision-making on employees' attitude (Schappe 1998; Schwarzwald et al. 1992), very few researchers have focused on the link between procedural justice and promotion decisions (Gilliland 1993, 1994; Lemons and Jones 2001; Saal and Moore 1993). Some attempts made show that employees' perceptions of fairness are influenced by criteria used in promotion (Kaplan and Ferris 2001; McEnrue 1989; Pearce et al. 1994; Saal and Moore 1993). The studies reveal that there is a significant relationship between promotion criteria and perceived fairness of promotion decisions. Though little research has been conducted to investigate the importance of procedural justice perceptions in promotion decisions so far, there has been an increased interest. This is illustrated by frequent discussion of the glass ceiling – the invisible barrier that prevents women and minorities from advancing to higher levels in organisations (Morrison et al. 1987).

As far as the effect of procedural justice on promotion decisions is concerned, much of the research focused on the effects on organisational commitment (Fields et al. 2000; Folger and Konovsky 1989; Konovsky and Cropanzano 1991; Schaubroeck et al. 1994; Sweeney and McFarlin 1993) and intent to leave (Bagdadli et al. 2006; Lemons and Jones 2001). Employees' perceptions of procedural justice in promotion decisions are likely to result in positive perceptions of their organisation and higher levels of organisational commitment (Arvey and Sackett 1993; Beehr et al. 1980; De Souza 2002; Halaby and Sobel 1979; Lemons and Jones 2001). These studies showed a direct relationship between procedural justice and organisational commitment (Bagdadli et al. 2006; Folger and Konovsky 1989; Konovsky et al. 1987; Lemons and Jones 2001) and an inverse relationship with intent to leave (Carson et al. 1994; Porter and Steers 1973; Price 1977; Stroh et al. 1996).

Pillai et al. (2001) reveal that procedural justice principles may differ as a result of one's individualism versus collectivism orientation. Their study shows that procedural justice principles did not affect commitment and tenure intent among collectivistic Indians compared to individualistic Germans or US employees. However, Brockner et al. (1992) stress that individuals react more adversely to injustice when they are more committed to their institutions. McEnrue's (1989) study on the perceived justice of promotion decisions revealed that employees who perceived that they had future advancement opportunity perceived the promotion process as fair. Table 3.2 shows some empirical studies carried out on procedural justice.

Table 3.2 Studies on procedural justice

Areas	Studies
Organisational citizenship behaviour	Moorman (1991), Niehoff and Moorman (1993), Ball et al. (1994), Konovsky and Organ (1996), MacKenzie et al. (2001), and De Cremer and van Knippenberg (2002)
Turnover	Konovsky and Cropanzano (1991), Dailey and Kirk (1992), Aquino et al. (1997), Roberts et al. (1999), and Zellars et al. (2004)
Job satisfaction	Fields et al. (2000)
Organisational commitment	Flaherty and Pappas (2000) and Rhoades et al. (2001)
Altruism	Moorman (1991) and Spector and Fox (2002)
Trust	Korsgaard et al. (1995), Aquino et al. (1997), Kim and Mauborgne (1998) and Naumann and Bennett (2000)
Prosocial behaviour	Masterson et al. (2000) and Williams et al. (2002)
Evaluation of supervision	Tyler and Lind (1992), van Den Bos et al. (1998), and Fields et al. (2000)
Job performance	Sosik et al. (1997), Cohen-Charash and Spector (2001), and Mohd Nasurdin and Soon (2011)
Compliance with authorities	Lind and Tyler (1988)
Employee self-esteem	Tyler and Lind (1992) and Smith and Tyler (1997)
Emotions	Folger and Cropanzano (1998), Tyler and Smith (1998), Weiss et al. (1999), van Den Bos and Miedema (2000), and De Cremer (2004)
Leadership	De Cremer (2006)
Organisational change and strategic planning	Folger and Konovsky (1989) and Mishra and Spreitzer (1998)

Interactional Justice

Interactional justice is the perception of fairness on how people are treated, the courtesy and respect the decision-maker shows by informing the decision receiver of how the decision is made (Greenberg 1993a). It reflects the perceived fairness of the interpersonal treatment individuals received from others (the perceived fairness of the communication and the level of respect between the rater and the ratee). Bies and Moag (1986: 44) defined interactional justice as 'the quality of interpersonal treatment they (employees) receive during the enactment of organisational procedures'. It denotes individual's concerns about the quality of interpersonal treatment they receive during the enactment of organisational procedures – whether the individuals affected by a decision were treated in a courteous and civil manner (Bies 2001; Bies and Moag 1986; Cropanzano et al. 2002). Bies (2001: 106) contend that 'people are concerned about interpersonal treatment in their everyday encounters in organisations … interactional concerns transcend formal decision-making contexts'. This definition proposed four dimensions of interactional justice – derogatory judgements, deception, invasion of privacy and disrespect. McDowall and Fletcher (2004) associate interactional justice with the fairness of interpersonal communication relating to organisational procedures. It is broader than verbal aggression as perceived unfair behaviour need not be accompanied by anger

(Holmvall and Sidhu 2007). Cohen-Charash and Spector (2001: 4) define it as 'the human side of organisational practices, that is, the way the management (or those controlling rewards and resources) is behaving towards the recipient of justice'.

Interactional justice is considered by some as a social aspect of procedural justice (Folger and Cropanzano 1998; Skarlicki and Folger 1997). It influences cognitive, affective and behavioural reactions towards another party's representative (Tyler and Bies 1990). Others view interactional justice as either a form of distributive or procedural justice (Greenberg 1993a; Tyler and Bies 1990). Bies and Moag (1986), however, maintain that interactional justice can be distinguished from procedural justice. Nonetheless, interactional justice is very important in determining fairness (Eskew 1993). Bies and Moag (1986) identify four attributes for interactional justice – justification, truthfulness, respect and propriety. Perception of fairness is comparatively higher when reasonable justifications are given for decisional outcomes (Bies and Shapiro 1987, 1988). When decision-makers communicate a justification for the decision reached and the decision-maker is considered sincere, participants view the process as fairer (Bies 1987; Folger and Bies 1989). Bies and Moag (1986) posit that reasonable justifications and honest information concerning recruitment decisions enhance perceptions of fairness. Likewise, the inclusion of written descriptions of how the appraisal was made enhances performance appraisal fairness (Greenberg 1991). Shaw et al. (2003) report that providing an adequate explanation for a decision decreases potential retaliatory behaviour of employees by 43 %.

Greenberg (1993b) researched the four attributes along two dimensions – explanations (based on justification and truthfulness) and sensitivity (based on respect and propriety). These two dimensions, designated as interpersonal justice and informational justice, have independent effects. Other researchers (e.g. Brockner and Wiesenfeld 1996; Cropanzano and Greenberg 1997; Folger and Cropanzano 1998) substantiated the two-dimensional proposition. Colquitt (2001) formalised the division, thus, proposing the four-factor justice typology (distributive, procedural, interpersonal and informational). These researchers suggest that informational justice is distinct from interpersonal justice and studies have shown that interpersonal and informational justice can have differing antecedents and unique relationships with outcomes (e.g. Colquitt 2001; Judge and Colquitt 2004; Kernan and Hanges 2002).

Interpersonal justice refers to people's perception of fairness of the matter in which they are treated. Colquitt et al. (2001: 427) define it as the 'degree to which people are treated with politeness, dignity and respect by authorities or third parties involved in executing procedures or determining outcomes'. People perceive interpersonal justice when authorities or parties involved in executing procedures or determining outcomes abstain from inappropriate comments (politeness) and treat them with respect and dignity (Colquitt 2001; Greenberg 1993a). People may feel better about an unfavourable outcome if they experience interpersonal justice and, thus, can alter reactions to decision outcomes (Colquitt et al. 2001; Greenberg 1993a, 1994). Concisely, employees feel affirmed if the procedures that are implemented treat them with respect and dignity, making it easier to accept even outcomes they do not like (Deutsch 2000). Some common interpersonal treatment at the workplace includes interpersonal communication (Bies and Moag 1986; Folger and Cropanzano

1998); truthfulness, respect, propriety of questions and justification (Bies and Moag 1986); and honesty, courtesy, timely feedback and respect for rights (Bies 1986).

Informational justice refers to people's perception of the fairness of the information used as the basis for making decisions, the enactment and explanation of decision-making procedures (Giap et al. 2005). In informational justice, there is a free flow of information as the decision recipient is given the rationale behind the decision. Explanations for decision-making procedures and outcomes are given adequately and honestly (Colquitt 2001; Cropanzano and Greenberg 1997; Greenberg 1993a). Perceived level of informational justice is higher if explanation about the procedures used to determine outcomes is adequate (Bies 1987; Bies and Shapiro 1988; Greenberg 1990b; Shapiro 1993; Tyler and Bies 1990) as explanations provide the necessary information to evaluate the structural attributes of the procedures and its enactment (Colquitt et al. 2001; Greenberg 1993a, b, 1994). However, explanations must be communicated honestly and sincerely to be perceived as fair (Bies et al. 1988). It should be based on sound reasoning with logically relevant information (Shapiro and Buttner 1988) and determined by legitimate rather than arbitrary factors (Folger et al. 1983).

Research on interactional justice focuses predominantly on higher authorities as sources of justice or injustice during the communication of outcome-allocation decisions (Holmvall and Sidhu 2007). However, this is considered too narrow (Bies 2001, 2005; Cropanzano et al. 2001) as people's concern about interactional justice extend into day-to-day interactions as well (Colquitt et al. 2005; Mikula et al. 1990). Moreover, people's perceptions of interactional justice are not only limited to treatment received from authorities but also from treatment received from others both within (Donovan et al. 1998) and outside the organisation (Mikula et al. 1990; Holmvall and Sidhu 2007). Eskew (1993) affirms that perceived fairness in decision-making systems augments actions that benefit the organisation and impact organisational effectiveness as interactional justice has a significant impact on both satisfaction and performance (Fernandes and Awamleh 2006). Social exchange theorists posit that interactional justice satisfies needs for self-esteem and self-identity, thus, reducing role conflict and role ambiguity. Team working is expected to strengthen and better decisions may result. As interactional injustice tends to trickle from higher management due to displaced aggression at the top (Marcus-Newhall et al. 2000), it is imperative to address displaced aggression in order to enhance interactional justice. Krings and Facchin (2009) show that low interactional justice increases sexual harassment proclivities, suggesting that sexual harassment likelihood may increase as a response to perceived injustice.

Organisational Citizenship Behaviour

Organisational citizenship behaviour is defined as 'cooperative behaviour that has positive consequences for the organisation, but is not required or formally rewarded' (Van Dyne et al. 2000: 3). Robbins and Judge (2007: 30) define it as 'discretionary behaviour that is not part of an employee's formal job requirements, but that nevertheless promotes the effective functioning of the organisation'. In general, it refers to work-related behaviours that go beyond that which is dictated by organisational policy and one's job description (Wong et al. 2006). It is a specific type of behaviour that benefits the organisation and promotes organisational effectiveness (Bateman and Organ 1983). Typically, it includes helping others in work-related matters, volunteering for special projects, being considerate and punctual and participating in problem-solving (Meyer and Allen 1997). These discretionary behaviours are neither expected nor required from the employees and, thus, cannot be formally rewarded or punished for the presence or lack of by the organisation (Barnard 1938; Katz 1964; Koopmann 2002; Organ 1988a; Smith et al. 1983). It is an individual's personal choice to display organisational citizenship behaviour since it is not required by the individual's job description. It occurs freely to help others achieve the task at hand (Bateman and Organ 1983) and goes beyond the formal obligations of their positions (Giap et al. 2005). Organ (1988a: 4) defines organisational citizenship behaviour as

> … individual behaviour that is discretionary, not directly or explicitly recognised by the formal reward system, and that in the aggregate promotes the effective functioning of the organisation. By discretionary, we mean that the behaviour is not an enforceable requirement of the role or the job description, that is, the clearly specifiable terms of the person's employment contract with the organisation; the behaviour is rather a matter of personal choice, such that its omission is not generally understood as punishable.

Organ (1990) maintains that organisational citizenship behaviour embraces both the enactment of positive behaviours that enhance organisational functioning and refraining from negative behaviours that are damaging to organisational functioning. Subsequently, as the focus of organisational citizenship behaviour shifted to contextual performance, organisational citizenship behaviour was conceived as activities which provide the social and psychological support to core organisational behaviours designed to transform inputs to outputs (Borman and Motowidlo 1993; Motowidlo 2000; Van Scotter and Motowidlo 1996). In accordance with this theoretical trend, Organ (1997) redefines organisational citizenship behaviour as actions designed to assist in 'the maintenance and enhancement of the social and psychological context that supports task performance' (Organ 1997: 91). Nonetheless, all frameworks of organisational citizenship behaviour describe behaviours that do not represent routine job functions, contribute in some way to organisational functioning and are discretionary.

Since its initial formulation, Smith et al. (1983) suggest a two-dimensional construct comprising of altruism and general compliance. Williams (1988) identifies a two-dimensional structure of organisational citizenship behaviour – benefits directed at the organisation in general (OCBO-behaviours) and benefits directed at individuals within the organisation (OCBI-behaviours). Employees exhibit OCBO-behaviours when they perform beyond formal duties that enhance organisational image and performance (Erturk 2007) such as conserving and protecting organisational property and giving advance notice when unable to come to work (Williams and Anderson 1991). Though OCBI-behaviours benefit specific individuals directly, indirectly these behaviours contribute to the organisation. Altruism, helping colleagues who have heavier workload (Erturk 2007), going all out to help new employees and passing along information to coworkers (Williams and Anderson 1991) are some OCBI-behaviours in organisations. Studies show that this two-dimensional structure of organisational citizenship behaviour is present in the university setting (Skarlicki and Latham 1995) and in schools (Tschannen-Moran 2001). Others have suggested that the construct be more broadly formulated as prosocial organisational behaviour (Brief and Motowidlo 1986) or extra-role behaviour (Van Dyne et al. 1995).

Graham (1989) proposes a four-dimensional model consisting of interpersonal helping (helping colleagues in their jobs when such help is needed), individual initiative (communication at the workplace to enhance individual and group performance), personal industry (performing beyond the call of duty) and loyal boosterism (promotion of organisational image to others). Organ (1988a) identifies five dimensions of organisational citizenship behaviour that contribute to effectiveness – altruism, courtesy, conscientiousness, sportsmanship and civic virtue. It generally shows employees' altruism-directed helping behaviour towards other coworkers, courtesy in averting problems and offering practical information, conscientiousness in time usage and extra effort to enhance individual and organisational efficiency, sportsmanship in allaying complaints and enhancing organisational endeavours, and civic virtue in promoting organisational interests (Organ 1988a).

Altruism is associated with how an employee helps others on the job – employees display prosocial, helpful behaviours and neighbourliness with little or no interest in being rewarded for the effort. It includes all discretionary behaviours that have the effect of helping colleagues with work-related tasks or problems (Tansky 1993). Workers help each other to avoid distracting and showing supervisors their lack of competence. Altruism is also related to determining how to help others (Organ 1988a, 1990). Podsakoff and Mackenzie (1994) assert that displaying self-sacrifice and extra-role behaviours are two of the most important organisational citizenship behaviours. Examples of altruism include taking time to help newcomers learn their way around or being accommodating to new employees, sitting in for a sick coworker, assisting supervisors and others and helping or cooperating with other employees on organisationally relevant issues.

Courtesy represents helpful behaviours that involve checking with colleagues about actions that could affect their responsibilities. It is associated with undertaking and carrying out the obligation of cooperation with others (Organ 1988a). This helps prevent the occurrence of a work-related problem or taking precautions to mitigate the severity of a foreseen problem. Giving advance notices, reminders and consultation is a sign of courtesy (Koopmann 2002). Other examples include making innovative suggestions, treating others with respect and thwarting problems encountered by other coworkers or the organisation, such as protecting the organisation from fire, theft, vandalism and other misfortunes (George and Jones 2008).

Conscientiousness expresses certain role behaviours displayed by employees that are beyond organisation's requirements (Organ 1988a, 1990), but nonetheless necessary for organisational survival and effectiveness (George and Jones 2008). It is the dutiful respect of organisational rules, procedures and regulations (Eskew 1993; Koopmann 2002; Tansky 1993) and sincere devotion to the organisation

(Organ 1988a). Developing one's skills and capabilities, punctuality, good attendance record, arriving to work on time, working late or coming in early when necessary, not leaving early, not taking too many coffee breaks, taking only the required lunch time, willingly contributes beyond formal job requirements and adherence to organisational expectations are characteristics of conscientiousness.

Sportsmanship relates to negative behaviours employees refrain from doing (Tansky 1993). Having a positive attitude and tolerating less-than-desirable situations without complaining or 'making federal cases out of small potatoes' (Organ 1988a: 11) are some examples of sportsmanship. It demonstrates 'employees' willingness to disregard and not complain about impositions and minor inconveniences that arise in the workplace' (Fassina et al. 2008: 163).

Finally, civic virtue refers to the 'responsible participation in the political life of the organisation' (Organ 1988a: 12) – responsible political involvement in an organisation. It involves having a thorough knowledge of things happening in the organisation. It concerns how employees respond appropriately and responsibly to how the organisation governs. It shows the extent of employee interest to stay up-to-date with important issues of the organisation, such as in new developments, company policies, work methods and self-improvement efforts (Yilmaz and Tasdan 2009). Examples include voluntarily serving in committees and attending functions as well as spreading goodwill in the larger community.

Organisational citizenship behaviour is, therefore, crucial to the survival of an organisation (Murphy et al. 2002). It is instrumental in maximising efficiency and promotes effective functioning of the organisation (George and Brief 1992; Organ 1988a). Wagner and Rush (2000: 379) posit that organisational citizenship behaviours have 'an accumulative positive effect on organisational functioning'. Indubitably, organisational citizenship behaviours benefit both the organisation and its employees in numerous ways (Koopmann 2002). Organisations benefit from dedicated workers, lower turnover rate, greater productivity and better work environment, which in turn generate greater employee dedication and help the organisation in many other ways (Chen et al. 1998). Employee's persistent performance of organisational citizenship behaviour may augment management's affective response (Allen and Rush 1998). Moorman (1991: 846) states that, 'OCB appears to be a reasonable and likely way in which an employee can exchange the social rewards brought on by perceptions of fairness'.

Albeit propositions for integrating the dimensions of organisational citizenship behaviour (LePine et al. 2002), conceptual differences among the dimensions suggest that the dimensions may have different predictors or relate to outcomes differently (Moorman and Blakely 1995; Organ et al. 2006; Podsakoff et al. 1990). Hence, researchers continue to study Organ's (1988a) five organisational citizenship behaviour dimensions separately (e.g. Greenberg 1990a; Lazar et al. 2007; Moorman 1991; Skarlicki and Folger 1997; Williams et al. 2002) and provide evidence among predictors on different dimensions of organisational citizenship behaviour (e.g. Farh et al. 1990; Masterson et al. 2000; Moorman 1991; Organ and Konovsky 1989). Perceptions of procedural justice may relate more significantly to altruism than to other organisational citizenship behaviour dimensions (e.g. Farh et al. 1990;

Konovsky and Folger 1991) and to altruism, courtesy, sportsmanship and conscientiousness (Moorman 1991; Niehoff and Moorman 1993). Hooi (2011, 2012) shows that interpersonal justice is significantly related to courtesy, altruism and conscientiousness, and informational justice significantly predicted courtesy and procedural justice civic virtue. In addition, Tansky (1993) found that job satisfaction on its own related positively to courtesy, civic virtue, altruism and sportsmanship, but was non-significant in predicting altruism and sportsmanship when tested incrementally to overall fairness. Smith et al. (1983) found a correlation between job satisfaction and altruism as well as conscientiousness, while Hooi (2012) argued that job satisfaction explained more variance in civic virtue than courtesy, altruism or conscientiousness. Hooi (2011) further asserts that leader–member exchange accounts for more variance in civic virtue than altruism, conscientiousness or courtesy. Table 3.3 highlights some of the major studies on organisational citizenship behaviour.

Job Satisfaction

Job satisfaction consists of feelings and attitudes one has about one's job. All definitions of job satisfaction agree that it is a multidimensional concept (Koustelios 1991; Locke 1976; Rice et al. 1989; Shouksmith et al. 1990). Herzberg (1968) asserts that job satisfaction is the outcome of a good match between intrinsic and extrinsic motivation. Locke (1976) defines job satisfaction as a pleasurable or positive emotional state, resulting from the appraisal of one's job or job experience. Smith et al. (1969) suggest that job satisfaction is a feeling or affective response to facets of the situation. Dawis and Lofquist (1984) define job satisfaction as the result of the worker's appraisal of the degree in which the work environment fulfils the individual's needs. Pool (1997) posits that job satisfaction is an attitude that individuals maintain about their jobs based on their perceptions of their jobs. These definitions, as Lease (1998) points out, are similar to other definitions where job satisfaction is viewed as the degree of an employee's affective orientation towards the work role occupied in the organisation. Hence, job satisfaction is an affective response by an employee resulting from an overall comparison of actual outcomes with those that are expected, needed, wanted, desired or perceived to be fair or just (Cranny et al. 1992).

Job satisfaction is a complex concept, difficult to measure objectively and is influenced by a myriad of variables relating to individual, social, cultural, organisational and environmental factors (Mullins 2011). All these factors affect the job satisfaction of specific individuals in certain circumstances. As job satisfaction is associated with an individual's positive emotional reaction to particular job (Oshagbemi 2000), high job satisfaction is important to managers (Robbins 2001). Job satisfaction is linked to positive worker attitudes and behaviours that enhance productivity, creativity, innovation, receptivity to change and extra efforts (Clegg and Dunkerley 1980; Mathieu and Zajac 1990; Witt and Wilson 1991). As job satisfaction is instrumental to organisational strength and effectiveness, it is, therefore,

Table 3.3 Studies on organisational citizenship behaviour

Areas	Studies
Organisational citizenship behaviour	Organ (1977)
Organisational justice	Moorman (1991), Sheppard et al. (1992), Eskew (1993), Greenberg (1993a), Moorman et al. (1993), Tansky (1993), Ball et al. (1994), Konovsky and Pugh (1994), Skarlicki and Latham (1996), Allen and Rush (1998), Masterson et al. (2000), and Williams et al. (2002)
Procedural justice	Van Dyne et al. (2000)
Perception of fairness	Moorman et al. (1993), Organ and Ryan (1995), and Tepper and Taylor (2003)
Commitment and organisational commitment	O'Reilly and Chatman (1986), Eisenberger et al. (1990), Organ (1990), Becker (1992), Organ and Ryan (1995), and Truckenbrodt (2000)
Job satisfaction	Bateman and Organ (1983), Smith et al. (1983), Motowidlo (1984), Graham (1986), Motowidlo et al. (1986), Puffer (1987), Scholl et al. (1987), Organ (1988b, 1990), Organ and Konovsky (1989), Williams and Anderson (1991), Moorman (1993), Organ and Ryan (1995), Kemery et al. (1996), Wagner and Rush (2000), abd Murphy et al. (2002)
Interpersonal trust	Podsakoff et al. (1990), Deluga (1995), and Podsakoff et al. (1996)
Supervisor support	Van Yperen et al. (1999)
Leadership, leader supportiveness and leadership behaviour	Farh et al. (1990), Podsakoff et al. (1990), Schnake et al. (1993), Wayne and Green (1993), Organ and Ryan (1995), Podsakoff et al. (1996), and Truckenbrodt (2000)
Psychological contract	Coyle-Shapiro (2002) and Turnley et al. (2003)
Motivation	Folger (1993)
Definition	Smith et al. (1983)
Role definition	Morrison (1994)
Job involvement	Diefendorff et al. (2002)
Characteristics of work	Smith et al. (1983), Farh et al. (1990), Niehoff and Moorman (1993), and Van Dyne et al. (1994)
Attitude towards job	Smith et al. (1983), Organ (1988a), Podsakoff et al. (1990), (1993), Moorman (1991), Schnake (1991), Niehoff and Moorman (1993), Organ and Ryan (1995), and Schnake et al. (1995)
Hierarchical position	Aquino and Bommer (2003)
Job performance	Organ (1988a), Ball et al. (1994), and Piercy et al. (2006)
Employee mood	Williams and Wong (1999)
Employee age	Wagner and Rush (2000)
Labour union	Skarlicki and Latham (1996)
Personality	Smith et al. (1983), Van Dyne et al. (1994), Organ and Lingl (1995), and Holmes et al. (2002)
Needs	Schnake (1991)
Values	Burton (2003)
Determinants	Organ and Konovsky (1989), Moorman (1993), and Deluga (1995)
Construct validity	George and Brief (1992) and Becker and Vance (1993)
Classification	Morrison (1994)

important to delineate the potential causes of job dissatisfaction in order to suppress the negative consequences of discontentment at the workplace. A profound understanding of what causes job satisfaction and dissatisfaction of employees helps in eliciting positive outcomes from the employees. Axiomatically, understanding the contributory factors of job satisfaction is of paramount importance.

An employee's level of job satisfaction is determined by four main factors – personality, values, work situation and social influence. Personality affects the way people think and feel about their jobs. Extroverts, for example, tend to have positive feelings about their jobs and, therefore, are likely to have a higher level of job satisfaction. On the contrary, people who have negative personality are usually less satisfied with their jobs (Robbins and Judge 2007). As genetic factors account for 30 % of the differences in the level of satisfaction, managers can possibly influence 70 % of the variance in job satisfaction (George and Jones 2008). Hence, even though managers cannot change personalities in the short run, it is within their power to influence and change the level of job satisfaction. Similarly, employees with strong intrinsic work values or strong extrinsic work values are more likely to be satisfied with their jobs.

The work situation or job conditions affect job satisfaction too. It is perhaps the most important source of job satisfaction. Any aspect of the job and the employing organisation is part of the work situation. It includes the work itself, compensation, interpersonal relations, supervision, coworkers, job security, advancement opportunities, working environment, fairness at the workplace, autonomy and flexibility, among others. Research suggests that dissatisfaction with work situations can result in a more supportive environment due to management's commitment to change and improvement in the organisation (George and Jones 2008). Lastly, social influence, that is, the influence that individuals or groups have on a person's attitudes and behaviour, can influence job satisfaction. This includes the influence of the culture employees grow up and live in, coworkers, team members and the group employees belong. The family and culture in which employees grow up, for example, can affect their level of job satisfaction as an adult. Employees who are surrounded by people, particularly, coworkers who are dissatisfied with their jobs, are more likely to be dissatisfied themselves. A wide variety of groups that employees belong to, such as unions and religious groups, can have a profound effect on employees' job satisfaction.

What are the potential consequences of job satisfaction? High levels of job dissatisfaction may be costly to both the employees and the organisations. Job dissatisfaction has been associated with employee well-being (Schmiit and Bedeian 1982), anxiety (Spector et al. 1988) and depression (Bluen et al. 1990). For organisations, studies show that job dissatisfaction results in lower affective organisational commitment (Meyer et al. 2002), poorer in-role performance (Judge et al. 2001), contextual performance (Podsakoff et al. 2000), organisational citizenship behaviour (Bateman and Organ 1983; George and Brief 1992; Organ 1988a; Podsakoff et al. 2000; Smith et al. 1983), customer satisfaction (Griffith 2001; Koys 2001; Naumann and Jackson 1999; Schneider and Bowen 1985; Weaver 1994), absenteeism (Hackett and Guion 1985; Hardy et al. 2003; Locke 1976; McShane 1984; Scott and Taylor 1985; Steel and Rentsch 1995), turnover (Hom and Griffeth

1995; Griffeth et al. 2000; Mobley 1977) and workplace deviance (Hanisch et al. 1998; Hulin 1991). Furthermore, organisations may incur increased recruitment and training costs and lost productivity due to employee turnover (Sagie et al. 2002). In essence, whether or not an employee is satisfied with his or her job affects not only the employee but also coworkers, managers, groups, teams and the organisation as a whole. Intuitively, many people believe that its impact on job performance is crucial (George and Jones 2008), as it ultimately affects the bottomline and competitiveness of the organisation. Thus, understanding the contributory factors of job satisfaction is of paramount importance.

Does job satisfaction affect job performance? Many organisations believe that investment in employees' morale will pay off in better job performance (Gannon and Noon 1971). Enhancing job satisfaction would be a step towards improving employees' morale. Favourable work environment, managerial skills and quality leadership are the catalyst. Given that satisfied employees contribute to the bottom line, organisations, therefore, need to be proactive in ensuring that the workplace is employee friendly and human capital management practices are rewarding. If employees perceive that the organisation is concerned about their interests and well-being, employees are likely to reciprocate with positive behaviours. Nonetheless, prior studies examining this management myth and the conventional wisdom that job satisfaction affects job performance reveal that there is no appreciable relationship between job satisfaction and job performance (e.g. Brayfield and Crockett 1955). Vroom (1964) affirms that levels of job satisfaction accounted for only 14 % of the variance in job performance, while the study by Iaffaldano and Muchinsky (1985) shows 17 %. On average, job satisfaction accounted for 3 % of the variance in job performance across employees (Judge et al. 2001).

One explanation for this discrepancy is that managers and researchers are focused on different types of job performance (Organ 1988a). Organ asserts that practicing managers think that 'satisfied people are more willing to do the little 'extras' spontaneously or when requested, and in general are easier to work with in a day-to-day relationship' (Organ 1988a: 50). On the contrary, researchers focus on conventional measures of job performance such as employee productivity, material output or accomplishment of a challenging task. Another probable credible rationalisation is that an employee's level of satisfaction may not be relevant for his or her performance. Besides, strong situational pressures in organisations leave employees with little choice, but to perform dependably regardless of whether they are satisfied or not. Nonetheless, organisations with more satisfied employees tend to be more effective than organisations with fewer satisfied employees (Harter et al. 2002; Ostroff 1992; Ryan et al. 1996).

The Exit–Voice–Loyalty–Neglect Framework

One framework that is helpful in understanding the impact of employee job dissatisfaction on the workplace is the exit–voice–loyalty–neglect framework. Dissatisfied employees can choose to leave the organisation (exit), actively and constructively

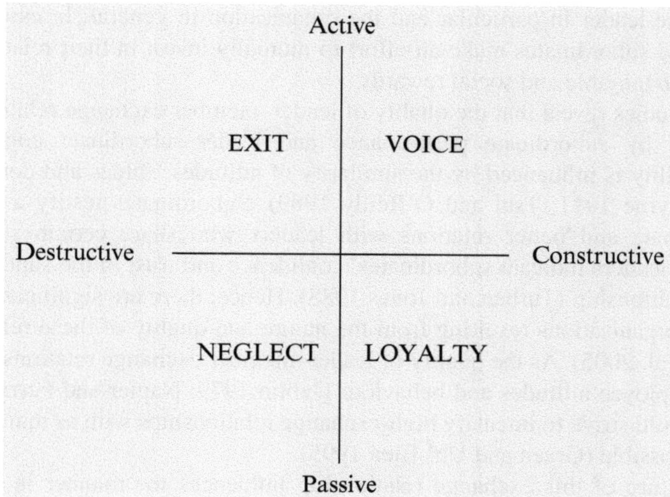

Fig. 3.2 Responses to job dissatisfaction (Source: Robbins and Judge 2007)

attempt to improve conditions (voice), passively, but optimistically waiting for conditions to improve (loyalty) or passively allowing conditions to worsen (neglect). Figure 3.2 illustrates the framework's four responses along two dimensions – constructive/destructive and active/passive. Employees that choose to exit or neglect affect productivity, absenteeism and turnover, while employees that fall under voice and loyalty display constructive behaviours. These employees though dissatisfied patiently tolerate unpleasant conditions or proactively attempt to revive deplorable working conditions.

Leader–Member Exchange

The leader–member exchange theory attempts to diagnose how leaders use their power and organisational resources to develop different social exchange relationships with their subordinates (Deluga and Perry 1994; Le Blanc et al. 1993). Graen et al. (1982) referred to the dynamic inherent in this dyadic relationship as leader–member exchange. Graen and Scandura (1987) posit that leader–member exchange reflects the quality of the leader–subordinate relationship. These relationships between leaders and subordinates can range from high to low quality (Deluga and Perry 1991). High-quality leader–member exchange relationships lead subordinates to engage in behaviours that are directly related to their leaders, such as in-role behaviour and organisational citizenship behaviours (Masterson et al. 2000; Settoon et al. 1996; Wayne et al. 1997). Specifically, leaders progressively foster exchange relationships with their subordinates to enhance employee performance that benefits the leader in particular and the organisation in general. In essence, both leaders and subordinates make an effort to mutually invest in their relationship to garner both tangible and social rewards.

Prior studies reveal that the quality of leader–member exchange relationships is influenced by subordinate performance and leader–subordinate compatibility. Compatibility is influenced by the similarity of attitudes, values and demographic factors (Byrne 1971; Tsui and O'Reilly 1989). Subordinates testify a rewarding work climate and better relations with leaders who share certain similarities. Likewise, leaders indicate subordinates' confidence and trust in the supervisor and a good relationship (Turban and Jones 1988). Hence, there are significant implications for organisations resulting from the nature and quality of these relationships (Varma et al. 2005). As the quality of leader–member exchange relationship is crucial to employee attitudes and behaviour (Jablin 1979; Napier and Ferris 1993), a leader should strive to intensify high-exchange relationships with as many subordinates as possible (Graen and Uhl-Bien 1995).

The nature of this exchange relationship influences the manner in which the leader treats each individual employee. The theory affirms that leaders exhibit different styles of leadership depending on the kind of leader's relationship with the different subordinates within work groups (Dansereau et al. 1975; Graen and Cashman 1975; Graen et al. 1982; Graen and Scandura 1987; Scandura and Graen 1984; Wayne et al. 1994). Graen and Uhl-Bien (1995) argue that this differentiation of the relationship between leaders and subordinates is the result of resource limitations. Leaders offer their limited resources, such as time, attention, energy, etc., to certain subordinates, termed the in-group, in exchange for trust, support, influence and loyalty (Varma et al. 2005). Those in the out-group only receive standard benefits (Erdogan et al. 2006). Subordinates are designated as in-group or out-group based on the leader's personal discretion of subordinates individual characteristics that are often unrelated to performance (Dansereau et al. 1975; Dienesch and Liden 1986; Graen et al. 1982; Graen and Scandura 1987; Graen and Schiemann 1978; Liden and Graen 1980; Scandura et al. 1986).

Podsakoff et al. (1990) opine that the in-group subordinates (higher-quality exchanges) perceive greater fairness from their leaders than members of the out-group (lower-quality exchanges) do. In-group members enjoy greater job latitude, increased access communication and rewards (Dienesch and Liden 1986) as well as leader's support, confidence and consideration (Dansereau et al. 1975). On the contrary, out-group members receive limited support and resources from the leaders and fewer rewards outside the employment contract (Dienesch and Liden 1986; Dockery and Steiner 1990; Gerstner and Day 1997; Steiner 1988; Wilhelm et al. 1993). As long as these subordinates fulfil their formal tasks and responsibilities, they receive standard benefits (Deluga and Perry 1991; Le Blanc et al. 1993). In essence, the quality of the leader–member exchange relationship usually differs from one subordinate to another (Yukl et al. 2009).

The leader–member exchange relationship develops steadily over time and is reciprocally strengthen by the behaviour of the leader and the subordinates. Leaders and subordinates work in tandem to determine the quality of leader–member exchange relationships (Dienesch and Liden 1986; Engle and Lord 1997; Ferris et al. 2009; Lapierre et al. 2006; Lord and Maher 1991; Martin et al. 2005; Schyns and von Collani 2002). These 'reciprocal interdependence' (Cropanzano and Mitchell 2005; Molm 1994) in social exchange relationships tends to be greater for subordinates than leaders because of the inherent power differential (Snodgrass et al. 1998). Both leaders and subordinates assess each other to ascertain how they think that their dyadic partner feels about them (Snodgrass et al. 1998). Hence, the quality of leader–member exchange relationships is the dual process of leaders and subordinates mutually assessing each other (Dienesch and Liden 1986; Graen and Scandura 1987; Lord and Maher 1991; Maslyn and Uhl-Bien 2001; Sin et al. 2009).

Past research treats leader–member exchange relationship as a unidimensional construct, but some empirical studies propose a multidimensional focus. Leader–member exchange as a unidimensional construct focuses on latitude or supervisor attention (Yammarino and Dubinsky 1990), social exchange relationships (Deluga and Perry 1991), maturity of the relationship (Graen and Uhl-Bien 1991; Graen and Wakabayashi 1992), negotiating latitude (McClane 1991a, b), incremental influence (Fairhurst 1993) and individualised leadership (Dansereau 1995). Cashman et al. (1976) posit the exchange relationship as two-dimensional based on attention and sensitivity, while Bhal and Ansari (2007) focus on contributions on-the-job and affective interactions off-the-job. Dienesch and Liden (1986) propose a three-dimensional model comprising of mutual affect, contribution and loyalty, while Maslyn and Uhl-Bien (2001) advocate affect, loyalty and professional respect dimensions. Graen (1976) considers competence, interpersonal skill and trust as the main dimensions. Graen and Ginsburgh (1977) added support, reward and satisfaction with the leader, exchange pattern and leader acceptance. Graen et al. (1977) later expanded it to include influence and latitude. Graen and Scandura (1987) present a three-phase model of leader–member exchange development, namely, role-taking, role-making and role-routinisation, and suggest two higher order dimensions, quality (the extent of loyalty, support and trust between dyad members) and coupling (addressing influence, delegation, latitude and innovativeness). Graen and his associates' (Graen and Wakabayashi 1992; Graen and Uhl-Bien 1995) three-dimensional conceptualisation of leader–member exchange quality consists of respect, trust and obligation and that a high leader–member exchange relationship will be characterised by mutual respect, reciprocal trust and obligations to each other.

Schiemann (1977) argues that the leader–member exchange subdomain includes trust, sensitivity, support and attention. Graen and Schiemann (1978) later added information as an additional element to the set proposed by Schiemann (1977) while excluding trust. Liden and Maslyn (1998) suggest contribution, affect, loyalty and professional respect, while Dansereau et al. (1975) maintain that leader–member exchange relationships are characterised by mutual trust, respect, liking and reciprocal influence. High-quality exchange relationships are expounded by high level of trust, liking and respect as well as expectations of mutual exchange (Yukl et al. 2009). In exchange for desired outcomes provided by the leader, subordinates reciprocate by being committed to the work and loyal to the leader. On the contrary, in low-quality exchange relationships, subordinates are only expected to perform the formal requirements of their jobs. In a similar vein, Ansari et al. (2007) assert that employees look for mutual trust. Mutual leader–member interpersonal trust and support is vital for maximum business results. Ansari et al. (2007) propose a four-dimensional construct – affect, loyalty, contribution and professional respect. Their findings suggest that affect and professional respect dimensions of leader–member exchange are significant to attitude-related outcomes in the Malaysian context.

The variations and evolutionary changes to the dimensions of leader–member exchange continued over the years. Graen and colleagues added 18 additional sub-dimensions which include trust, competence, motivation, assistance and support, understanding, latitude, authority, information, influence in decision-making, communications, confidence, consideration, talent, delegation, innovativeness, expertise, control of organisational resources and mutual control. Six dimensions appear to be predominant in a majority of the studies, namely, mutual support, trust, liking, latitude, attention and loyalty (Schriesheim et al. 1999). However, LMX-7, the seven-item measure detailed by Scandura and Graen (1984), is the most commonly adopted one (Yukl 2006) as it is the soundest measure of leader–member exchange (Erdogan and Liden 2002; Gerstner and Day 1997; Graen and Uhl-Bien 1995; Schriesheim et al. 1999). Regardless of the number of dimensions, these relationships become increasingly vital for organisations to foster mutual leader–subordinates interpersonal trust and support relations to enhance commitment from the subordinates. Moreover, prior studies (e.g. Dansereau et al. 1975; Graen and Cashman 1975) reveal that the quality of exchange relationships accounts for almost 90 % of the differentiation in all work units. Hence, management needs to pay attention to the quality of leader–member exchange.

Much empirical research links the quality of leader–member exchange with positive employee attitudes such as organisational commitment (Duchon et al. 1986; Gerstner and Day 1997; Kee et al. 2004; Kinicki and Vecchio 1994; Liden et al. 2000; Martin et al. 2005; Nystrom 1990; Schriesheim et al. 1999; Settoon et al. 1996; Wayne et al. 1997; Yukl 2006), intention to stay (Ansari et al. 2000; Ferris 1985; Gerstner and Day 1997; Graen et al. 1982; Griffeth et al. 2000; Harris et al. 2004, 2005; Mardanov et al. 2008; Vecchio and Gobdel 1984; Wayne et al. 1997), increased job performance (Gerstner and Day 1997; Schriesheim et al. 1999; Yukl 2006), contextual performance (e.g. Ilies et al. 2007), motivation (Tierney et al. 1999), lower job stress and greater workplace safety (Erdogan and Liden 2002) and overall job satisfaction (Epitropaki and Martin 2005; Gerstner and Day 1997; Graen et al. 1982; Yukl 2006). Other studies have shown it to be positively associated with organisational citizenship behaviour (Deluga 1998; Settoon et al. 1996; Yukl 2006), content-specific citizenship, leadership, satisfaction with supervision (Duchon et al. 1986; Gerstner and Day 1997), satisfaction with work, supervisory ratings of job performance (Liden et al. 1993), safety commitment, frequency of promotions, role clarity (Gerstner and Day 1997), innovation (Scott and Bruce 1994), employee well-being (Schyns and Wolfram 2008) and industrial/organisational psychology. However, Morrow et al. (2005) argue that both 'bad' LMX and 'good' LMX are associated with higher levels of turnover. Similarly, Harris et al. (2004), using push–

pull dynamics, reason that poor LMX employees are 'pushed' out of the organisation and good LMX employees are 'pulled' out by attractive competitors.

Graen and Uhl-Bien (1995) outlined four stages in the development of leader–member exchange research. Stage 1 (vertical dyad linkage or VDL stage) emphasises on the differentiation process within work units between the leader–member dyad. Dansereau et al. (1975) noted that studies at this stage focus on unit differentiation process in which subordinates are designated as in-groups (trusted lieutenants, assistants and advisors) or out groups (hired hands). The unit differentiation process typically occurs within 3 months of the formation of the group, sometimes based on social categorisation processes and stereotypes, and not performance (Traindis 1974). Studies on leader–member exchange did not examine this issue. Stage 2 (LMX stage) centres on the effect of leader–member exchange relationships on individual and organisational outcomes. Studies at this stage attempt to link outcomes of importance to organisations. The impact of the relationship on outcomes for individuals (e.g. promotions, role stress, employee grievances and job satisfaction) was established, as well as the organisation (employee turnover, improved socialisation, productivity, organisational citizenship behaviour). Studies at this stage did not address diversity issues – no differential relationships between leader–member exchange and work outcomes for diverse leader–member dyads were examined (Scandura 1996).

Stage 3 (leadership-making stage) concentrates on dyadic relationship development – relationship building, issues of reciprocity, time and incremental influence. The emphasis was on how the relationships between supervisors and subordinates evolved over time. A leader–member exchange development model of role-taking (strangers) through role-making (acquaintanceship) to role-routinisation (maturity) emerged, specifically focusing on the development process between leaders and members who are of diverse backgrounds. Finally, Stage 4 (team-making competence network stage) investigates how the assembly of dyads that are differentiated may be integrated to form high-functioning work teams and networks. Research at this stage examines team-making models and possible training interventions as well as attempts to link team-making and outcomes (e.g. team output and organisational effectiveness) at multiple levels of analysis. Since research on workforce diversity is relatively sparse during Stages 1 and 2, diversity issues need to be addressed too. Moreover, studies that address diversity in the leader–member exchange literature do not make full use of current research and theory on diversity (Scandura 1996).

Conclusion

This chapter has delineated a comprehensive review of related literature on the variables in the organisational justice–organisational citizenship behaviour relationship. An exhaustive literature review is imperative in developing the research questions and subsequent hypotheses for the study. The chapter begins with a review of the three components of organisational justice, organisational citizenship behaviour, job satisfaction and leader–member exchange, meticulously analysing studies in the domain. In accordance with the study, literature review of the three components of organisational justice, namely, distributive justice, procedural justice and interactional justice, has been laboriously elaborated to provide a holistic view of justice literature. Past research on job satisfaction and the quality of leader–member exchange relationship further highlights the link between these constructs with organisational justice and organisational citizenship behaviour. The next chapter focuses on the theories related to the study and helps identify the theory of reasoned action as the focus of the study.

References

Adams, J. S. (1963). Toward an understanding of inequity. *Journal of Abnormal and Social Psychology, 67*(5), 422–436.

Adams, J. S. (1965). Inequity in social exchange. In L. Berkowitz (Ed.), *Advances in experimental social psychology* (Vol. 2, pp. 267–299). New York: Academic.

Alder, S. A., & Tompkins, P. K. (1997). Electronic performance monitoring: An organizational justice and concretive control perspective. *Management Communications Quarterly, 10*(3), 259–289.

Alexander, S., & Ruderman, M. (1987). The role of procedural and distributive justice in organisational behavior. *Social Justice Research, 1*(2), 177–198.

Allen, T. D., & Rush, M. C. (1998). The effects of organizational citizenship behavior on performance judgements: A field study and a laboratory experiment. *Journal of Applied Psychology, 83*(2), 247–260.

Ambrose, M. L., & Schminke, M. (2009). The role of overall justice judgments in organizational justice research: A test of mediation. *Journal of Applied Psychology, 94*(2), 491–500.

Ansari, M. A., Kee, D. M. H., & Aafaqi, R. (2000). Fairness of human resource management practices, leader-member exchange, and intention to quit. *Journal of International Business and Entrepreneurship, 8*, 1–19.

Ansari, M. A., Mui Hung, D. K., & Aafaqi, R. (2007). Leader-member exchange and attitudinal outcomes: Role of procedural justice climate. *Leadership and Organization Development Journal, 28*(8), 690–709.

Aquino, K. (1995). Relationships among pay inequity, perceptions of procedural justice, and organizational citizenship. *Employee Responsibilities and Rights Journal, 8*(1), 21–33.

Aquino, K., & Bommer, W. H. (2003). Preferential mistreatment: How victim status moderates the relation between organizational citizenship behavior and workplace victimization. *Organization Science, 14*(4), 374–385.

Aquino, K., Griffeth, R. W., Allen, D. G., & Hom, P. W. (1997). Integrating justice constructs into the turnover process: A test of a referent cognitions model. *Academy of Management Journal, 40*(5), 1208–1227.

Arvey, R. D., & Sackett, P. R. (1993). Fairness in selection: Current developments and perspectives. In N. Schmitt & W. C. Borman (Eds.), *Personnel selection in organizations*. San Francisco: Jossey Bass.

Bagdadli, S., Roberson, Q., & Paoletti, F. (2006). The mediating role of procedural justice in responses to promotion decisions. *Journal of Business and Psychology, 21*(1), 83–102.

Ball, G. A., Trevino, L. K., & Sims, H. P., Jr. (1994). Just and unjust punishment: Influences on subordinate performance and citizenship. *Academy of Management Journal, 37*(2), 299–322.

Barling, J., & Phillips, M. (1992). Interactional, formal, and distributive justice in the workplace: An exploratory study. *The Journal of Psychology, 127*(6), 649–656.

Barling, J., & Phillips, M. (1993). Interactional, formal, and distributive justice in the workplace: An exploratory study. *Journal of Psychology, 127*(6), 649–656.

Barnard, C. I. (1938). *The functions of the executive*. Cambridge: Harvard University Press.

Baron, R. A. (1993). Criticism (informal negative feedback) as a source of perceived unfairness in organizations: Effects, mechanisms, and countermeasures. In R. Cropanzano (Ed.), *Justice in the workplace: Approaching fairness in human resource management* (pp. 155–170). Hillsdale: Lawrence Erlbaum Associates.

Bateman, T. S., & Organ, D. W. (1983). Job satisfaction and the good soldier: The relationship between affect and employee citizenship. *Academy of Management Journal, 26*(4), 587–595.

Becker, T. E. (1992). Foci and bases of commitment: Are they distinctions worth making? *Academy of Management Journal, 35*(1), 232–244.

Becker, T. E., & Vance, R. J. (1993). Construct validity of three types of organizational citizenship behavior: An illustration of the direct model with refinements. *Journal of Management, 19*(3), 663–682.

Beehr, T. A., Taber, T. D., & Walsh, J. T. (1980). Personnel mobility channels: Criteria for intra-organizational mobility. *Organizational Behavior and Human Performance, 26*, 250–260.

Bhal, K. T., & Ansari, M. A. (2007). Leader-member exchange-subordinate outcomes relationship: Role of voice and justice. *Leadership and Organization Development Journal, 28*(1), 20–35.

Bies, R. J. (1986). *Identifying principles of interactional justice: The case of corporate recruiting*. Paper presented at the Annual Meeting of the Academy of Management, Chicago, IL.

Bies, R. J. (1987). Beyond "voice": The influence of decision-maker justification and sincerity on procedural fairness judgments. *Representative Research in Social Psychology, 17*(1), 3–14.

Bies, R. J. (2001). Interactional (in)justice: The sacred and the profane. In J. Greenberg & R. Cropanzano (Eds.), *Advances in organizational justice* (pp. 89–118). Stanford: Stanford University Press.

Bies, R. J. (2005). Are procedural justice and interactional justice conceptually distinct? In J. Greenberg & J. A. Colquitt (Eds.), *Handbook of organizational justice* (pp. 85–112). Mahwah: Lawrence Erlbaum Associates.

Bies, R. J., & Moag, J. F. (1986). Interactional justice: Communication criteria of fairness. In R. J. Lewicki, B. H. Sheppard, & M. H. Bazerman (Eds.), *Research on negotiations in organizations* (pp. 43–55). Greenwich: JAI Press.

Bies, R. J., & Shapiro, D. L. (1987). Interactional fairness judgments: The influence of causal accounts. *Social Justice Research, 1*(2), 199–218.

Bies, R. J., & Shapiro, D. L. (1988). Voice and justification: Their influence on procedural fairness judgments. *Academy of Management Journal, 31*(3), 676–685.

Bies, R. J., Shapiro, D. L., & Cummings, L. L. (1988). Causal accounts and managing organizational conflict: Is it enough to say it's not my fault. *Communication Research, 15*(4), 381–399.

Blader, S., & Tyler, T. R. (2003). What constitutes fairness in work settings? A four-component model of procedural justice. *Human Resource Management Review, 13*(1), 107–126.

Bluen, S. D., Barling, J., & Burns, W. (1990). Predicting sales performance, job satisfaction, and depression by using the achievement strivings and impatience-irritability dimensions of Type A behavior. *Journal of Applied Psychology, 75*(2), 212–216.

Borman, W. C., & Motowidlo, S. J. (1993). Expanding the criterion domain to include elements to contextual performance. In N. Schmitt & W. C. Borman (Eds.), *Personnel selection in organizations* (pp. 71–98). San Francisco: Jossey-Bass.

Brayfield, A. H., & Crockett, W. H. (1955). Employee attitudes and employee performance. *Psychological Bulletin, 52*(5), 396–424.

Brief, A. P., & Motowidlo, S. J. (1986). Prosocial organizational behaviours. *Academy of Management Review, 11*(4), 710–725.

Brockner, J. (2002). Making sense of procedural fairness: How high procedural fairness can reduce or heighten the influence of outcome favorability. *Academy of Management Review, 27*(1), 58–76.

Brockner, J., & Greenberg, J. (1990). The impact of layoffs on survivors: An organizational justice perspective. In J. S. Carroll (Ed.), *Applied social psychology and organizational settings* (pp. 45–75). Hillsdale: Lawrence Erlbaum Associates.

Brockner, J., & Wiesenfeld, B. M. (1996). An integrative framework for explaining reactions to decisions: Interactive effects of outcomes and procedures. *Psychological Bulletin, 120*(2), 189–208.

Brockner, J., Tyler, T. R., & Cooper-Schneider, R. (1992). The influence of prior commitment to an institution on reactions to perceived unfairness: The higher they are, the harder they fall. *Administrative Science Quarterly, 37*, 241–261.

Brockner, J., Konovsky, M. A., Cooper-Schneider, R., Folger, R., Martin, C., & Bies, R. J. (1994). Interactive effects of procedural justice and outcome negativity on victims and survivors of job loss. *Academy of Management Journal, 37*(2), 397–409.

Burton, C. H. (2003). *An empirical investigation of the interrelations of organizational culture, managerial values, and organizational citizenship behavior*. Unpublished PhD thesis, The George Washington University, Washington, DC.

Byrne, D. (1971). *The attraction paradigm*. New York: Academic.

Byrne, Z. S., & Cropanzano, R. S. (2000, April 14–15). *To which source do I attribute this fairness? Differential effects of multi-foci justice on organizational work behaviors*. Paper presented at the 15th annual conference of the Society for Industrial and Organizational Psychology, New Orleans, LA.

Carson, P. P., Carson, K. D., Griffeth, R. W., & Steel, R. P. (1994). Promotion and employee turnover. Critique, meta-analysis, and implications. *Journal of Business and Psychology, 8*(4), 455–466.

Cashman, J., Dansereau, F., Jr., Graen, G. B., & Haga, W. J. (1976). Organizational understructure and leadership: A longitudinal investigation of role-making process. *Organizational Behavior and Human Decision Processes, 15*(2), 278–296.

Chegini, M. G. (2009). The relationship between organizational justice and organizational citizenship behavior. *American Journal of Economics and Business Administration, 1*(2), 171–174.

Chen, J. V., & Park, Y. (2005). The role of control and other factors in the electronic surveillance workplace. *Information, Communication and Ethics in Society, 3*(2), 79–91.

Chen, X., Hui, C., & Sego, D. J. (1998). The role of organizational citizenship behavior in turnover: Conceptualization and preliminary tests of key hypotheses. *Journal of Applied Psychology, 83*(6), 922–931.

Clegg, S., & Dunkerley, D. (1980). *Organization, class and control*. Boston: Routledge and Kegan Paul.

Cohen-Charash, Y., & Spector, P. E. (2001). The role of justice in organizations: A meta-analysis. *Human Decision Processes, 86*(2), 278–321.

Cole, N. D., & Latham, G. P. (1997). Effects of training in procedural justice on perceptions of disciplinary fairness by unionised employees and disciplinary subject matter experts. *Journal of Applied Psychology, 82*(5), 699–705.

Colquitt, J. A. (2001). On the dimensionality of organizational justice: A construct validation of a measure. *Journal of Applied Psychology, 86*(3), 386–400.

Colquitt, J. A., Conlon, D. E., Wesson, M. J., Porter, C. O. L. H., & Ng, K. Y. (2001). Justice at the millennium: A meta-analytic review of 25 years of organizational justice research. *Journal of Applied Psychology, 86*(3), 425–445.

Colquitt, J. A., Greenberg, J., & Zapata-Phelan, C. P. (2005). What is organizational justice?: A historical overview. In J. Greenberg & J. A. Colquitt (Eds.), *The handbook of organizational justice* (pp. 3–56). Mahwah: Erlbaum.

Coyle-Shapiro, J. (2002). A psychological contract perspective on organizational citizenship behavior. *Journal of Organizational Behavior, 23*(8), 927–946.

Cranny, C. J., Smith, P. C., & Stone, E. F. (1992). *Job satisfaction: How people feel about their jobs and how it affects their performance*. New York: Lexington Books.

Cropanzano, R., & Folger, R. (1991). Procedural justice and worker motivation. In R. M. Steers & L. W. Porter (Eds.), *Motivation and work behavior* (pp. 131–143). New York: McGraw-Hill.

Cropanzano, R., & Greenberg, J. (1997). Progress in organizational justice: Tunneling through the maze. In C. L. Cooper & I. T. Robertson (Eds.), *International review of industrial and organizational psychology* (pp. 317–372). Chichester: Wiley.

Cropanzano, R., & Mitchell, M. (2005). Social exchange theory: An interdisciplinary review. *Journal of Management, 31*(6), 874–900.

Cropanzano, R., Byrne, Z. S., Bobocel, D. R., & Rupp, D. E. (2001). Moral virtues, fairness heuristics, social entities, and other denizens of organizational justice. *Journal of Vocational Behavior, 58*(2), 164–209.

Cropanzano, R., Prehar, C. A., & Chen, P. Y. (2002). Using social exchange theory to distinguish procedural from interactional justice. *Group and Organizational Management, 27*(3), 324–351.

Dailey, R. C., & Kirk, D. J. (1992). Distributive and procedural justice as antecedents of job dissatisfaction and intent to turnover. *Human Relations, 45*(3), 305–317.

Dansereau, F. (1995). A dyadic approach to leadership: Creating and nurturing this approach under fire. *Leadership Quarterly, 6*(4), 479–490.

Dansereau, F. J., Graen, G., & Haga, W. J. (1975). A vertical dyad linkage approach to leadership within formal organizations – A longitudinal investigation of the role making process. *Organizational Behavior and Human Performance, 13*(1), 46–78.

Dawis, R., & Lofquist, L. (1984). *A psychological theory of work adjustment.* Minneapolis: University of Minnesota Press.

De Cremer, D. (2004). The influence of accuracy as a function of leader's bias: The role of trustworthiness in the psychology of procedural justice. *Personality and Social Psychology Bulletin, 30*(3), 293–304.

De Cremer, D. (2006). When authorities influence followers' affect: The interactive effect of procedural justice and transformational leadership. *European Journal of Work and Organizational Psychology, 15*(3), 322–351.

De Cremer, D., & Sedikides, C. (2005). Self-uncertainty and responsiveness to procedural justice. *Journal of Experimental Social Psychology, 41*(2), 157–173.

De Cremer, D., & van Knippenberg, D. (2002). How do leaders promote cooperation? The effects of charisma and procedural fairness. *Journal of Applied Psychology, 87*(5), 858–866.

De Souza, G. (2002). A study of the influence of promotions on promotion satisfaction nd expectations of future promotions among managers. *Human Resource Development Quarterly, 13*(3), 325–340.

Deluga, R. J., & Perry, J. T. (1991). The relationship of subordinate upward influencing behaviour, satisfaction and perceived superior effectiveness with leader-member exchanges. *Journal of Occupational and Organisational Psychology, 64*(3), 239–252.

Deluga, R. J. (1995). The relation between trust in the supervisor and subordinate organizational citizenship behavior. *Military Psychology, 7*(1), 1–16.

Deluga, R. J. (1998). Leader-member exchange quality and effectiveness ratings: The role of subordinate-supervisor conscientiousness similarity. *Group and Organization Management, 23*(2), 189–216.

Deluga, R. J., & Perry, J. T. (1994). The role of subordinate performance and ingratiation in leader-member exchanges. *Group and Organization Management, 19*(1), 67–86.

Deutsch, M. (1985). *Distributive justice.* New Haven: University Press.

Deutsch, M. (2000). Justice and conflict. In M. Deutsch & P. T. Coleman (Eds.), *The handbook of conflict resolution: Theory and practice* (pp. 41–64). San Francisco: Jossey Bass.

Deutschman, A. (1994). How H-P continues to grow and grow. *Fortune, 129*(9), 90–92.

Diefendorff, J., Brown, D., Kamin, A., & Lord, B. (2002). Examining the roles of job involvement and work centrality in predicting organizational citizenship behaviours and job performance. *Journal of Organizational Behaviour, 23*(1), 93–108.

Dienesch, R. M., & Liden, R. C. (1986). Leader-member exchange model of leadership: A critique and further development. *Academy of Management Review, 11*(3), 618–634.

Dockery, T. M., & Steiner, D. D. (1990). The role of the initial interaction in leader-member exchange. *Group & Organization Studies, 15*(4), 395–413.

Donovan, M. A., Drasgow, F., & Munson, L. J. (1998). The perceptions of fair interpersonal treatment scale: Development and validation of a measure of interpersonal treatment in the workplace. *Journal of Applied Psychology, 83*(5), 683–692.

Duchon, D., Green, S. G., & Taber, T. D. (1986). Vertical dyad linkage: A longitudinal assessment of antecedents, measures, and consequences. *Journal of Applied Psychology, 71*(1), 56–60.

Earley, P. C., & Lind, E. A. (1987). Procedural justice and participation in task selection: The role of control in mediating justice judgments. *Journal of Personality and Social Psychology, 52*(6), 1148–1160.

Eisenberger, R., Fasolo, P., & Davis-LaMastro, V. (1990). Perceived organizational support and employee diligence, commitment, and innovation. *Journal of Applied Psychology, 75*(1), 51–59.

Elovainio, M., Kivimaki, M., & Vahtera, J. (2002). Organizational justice: Evidence of a new psychosocial predictor of health. *American Journal of Public Health, 92*(1), 105–108.

Engle, E. M., & Lord, R. G. (1997). Implicit theories, self-schemas, and leader-member exchange. *Academy of Management Journal, 40*(4), 988–1010.

Epitropaki, O., & Martin, R. (2005). From ideal to real: A longitudinal study of the role of implicit leadership theories on leader-member exchanges and employee outcomes. *Journal of Applied Psychology, 90*(4), 659–676.

Erdogan, B., & Liden, R. C. (2002). Social exchanges in the workplace: A review of recent developments and future research directions in leader-member exchange theory. In L. L. Neider & C. A. Schriesheim (Eds.), *Leadership* (pp. 65–114). Greenwich: Information Age Publishing.

Erdogan, B., Kraimer, M. L., & Liden, R. C. (2001). Procedural justice as a two-dimensional construct. *Journal of Applied Behavioral Science, 37*(2), 205–222.

Erdogan, B., Liden, R. C., & Kraimer, M. L. (2006). Justice and leader-member exchange: The moderating role of organizational culture. *Academy of Management Journal, 49*(2), 395–406.

Erturk, A. (2007). Increasing organizational citizenship behaviors of Turkish academicians: Mediating role of trust in supervisor on the relationship between organizational justice and citizenship behaviours. *Journal of Managerial Psychology, 22*(3), 257–270.

Eskew, D. E. (1993). The role of organizational justice in organizational citizenship behavior. *Employee Responsibilities and Rights Journal, 6*(3), 185–194.

Fairhurst, G. T. (1993). The leader-member exchange patterns of women leaders in industry: A discourse analysis. *Communication Monographs, 60*(4), 321–351.

Farh, J., Podsakoff, P. M., & Organ, D. W. (1990). Accounting for organizational citizenship behavior: Leader fairness and task scope versus satisfaction. *Journal of Management, 16*(4), 705–721.

Fassina, N. E., Jones, D. A., & Uggerslev, K. L. (2008). Relationship clean-up time: Using meta analysis and path analysis to clarify relationships among job satisfaction, perceived fairness, and citizenship behaviors. *Journal of Management, 34*(2), 161–188.

Fernandes, C., & Awamleh, R. (2006). Impact of organisational justice in an expatriate work environment. *Management Research News, 29*(11), 701–712.

Ferris, G. R. (1985). Role of leadership in the employee withdrawal process: A constructive replication. *Journal of Applied Psychology, 70*, 777–781.

Ferris, G. R., Liden, R. C., Munyon, T. P., Summers, J. K., Basik, K. J., & Buckley, M. R. (2009). Relationships at work: Toward a multidimensional conceptualization of dyadic work relationships. *Journal of Management, 35*(6), 1379–1403.

Fields, D., Pang, M., & Chiu, C. (2000). A comparative field study of the effects of distributive and procedural justice in Hong Kong. *Journal of Organizational Behaviour, 21*(5), 547–562.

Flaherty, K. E., & Pappas, J. M. (2000). The role of trust in salesperson-sales manager relationship. *Journal of Personal Selling and Sales Management, 20*(4), 271–278.

Folger, R. (1993). Justice, motivation, and performance beyond role requirements. *Employee Responsibilities and Rights Journal, 6*(3), 239–248.

Folger, R., & Bies, R. J. (1989). Managerial responsibilities and procedural justice. *Employee Responsibilities and Rights Journal, 2*(2), 79–90.

Folger, R., & Cropanzano, R. (1998). *Organisational justice and human resource management*. Beverly Hills: Sage.

Folger, R., & Greenberg, J. (1985). Procedural justice: An interpretive analysis of personnel systems. *Research in Personnel and Human Resources Management, 3*, 141–183.

Folger, R., & Konovsky, M. A. (1989). Effects of procedural and distributive justice on reactions to pay raise decisions. *Academy of Management Journal, 32*(1), 115–130.

Folger, R., Rosenfield, D., & Robinson, T. (1983). Relative deprivation and procedural justification. *Journal of Personality and Social Psychology, 45*(2), 268–273.

French, W. (1964). *The personnel management process: Human resources administration*. Boston: Houghton Mifflin.

Fryxell, G. E., & Gordon, M. E. (1989). Workplace justice and job satisfaction as predictors of satisfaction with union and management. *Academy of Management Journal, 32*, 851–856.

Fuller, J. B., & Hester, K. (2007). Procedural justice and the cooperative worker: An interactional model of union participation. *Journal of Labor Research, 28*(1), 189–202.

Gannon, M. J., & Noon, J. P. (1971). Management's critical deficiency. *Business Horizons, 14*(1), 49–56.

George, J. M., & Brief, A. P. (1992). Feeling good, doing good: A conceptual analysis of the mood at work-organizational spontaneity relationship. *Psychological Bulletin, 112*(2), 310–329.

George, J., & Jones, G. (2008). *Understanding and managing organizational behavior* (5th ed.). Upper Saddle River: Pearson Prentice Hall.

Gerstner, C. R., & Day, D. V. (1997). Meta-analytic review of leader-member exchange theory: Correlates and construct issues. *Journal of Applied Psychology, 82*(6), 827–844.

Gholipour, A., & Poor Ezzat, A. (2008). *Injustice consequences in organization*. Tehran: Bardasht E Dovvom Publications, Imam Sadegh University Research Center.

Giap, B. N., Hackermeier, I., Jiao, X., & Wagdarikar, S. P. (2005). Organizational citizenship behavior and perception of organizational justice in student jobs. In: *Research study, psychology of excellence instructional design, job analysis & job design* (pp. 1–14). Munich: Ludwig-Maximilians-University.

Gillespie, T. L., & Parry, R. O. (2006). Fuel for litigation? Links between procedural justice and multisource feedback. *Journal of Managerial Issues, 18*(4), 530–546.

Gilliland, S. W. (1993). The perceived fairness of selection systems: An organizational justice perspective. *Academy of Management Review, 18*(4), 694–734.

Gilliland, S. W. (1994). Effects of procedural and distributive justice on reactions to a selection system. *Journal of Applied Psychology, 79*(5), 691–701.

Gordon, M. E., & Fryxell, G. E. (1993). The role of interpersonal justice in organizational grievance systems. In R. Cropanzano (Ed.), *Justice in the workplace: Approaching fairness in human resource management* (pp. 231–256). Hillsdale: Lawrence Erlbaum Associates.

Graen, G. (1976). Role-making processes within complex organizations. In M. D. Dunnette (Ed.), *Handbook of industrial and organizational psychology* (pp. 1201–1245). Chicago: Rand-McNally.

Graen, G., & Cashman, J. F. (1975). A role-making model in formal organizations: A developmental approach. In J. G. Hunt & L. L. Larson (Eds.), *Leadership frontiers* (pp. 143–165). Kent: Kent State Press.

Graen, G., & Ginsburgh, S. (1977). Job resignation as a function of role orientation and leader acceptance: A longitudinal investigation of organizational assimilation. *Organizational Behavior and Human Performance, 19*, 1–17.

Graen, G. B., & Scandura, T. A. (1987). Toward a psychology of dyadic organizing. In B. M. Staw & L. L. Cummings (Eds.), *Research in organizational behavior* (pp. 175–208). Greenwich: JAI Press.

Graen, G., & Schiemann, W. (1978). Leader–member agreement: A vertical dyad linkage approach. *Journal of Applied Psychology, 63*, 206–212.

Graen, G. B., & Uhl-Bien, M. (1991). The transformation of professionals into self-managing and partially self-designing contributors: Toward a theory of leadership-making. *Journal of Management Systems, 3*, 25–39.

Graen, G. B., & Uhl-Bien, M. (1995). Development of leader-member exchange (LMX) theory of leadership over 25 years: Applying a multi-level multi-domain perspective. *The Leadership Quarterly, 6*(2), 219–247.

Graen, G. B., & Wakabayashi, M. (1992). Cross-cultural leadership making: Bridging American and Japanese diversity for team advantage. In H. C. Triandis, M. D. Dunnette, & L. M. Hough (Eds.), *Handbook of industrial and organizational psychology* (2nd ed., Vol. 4, p. 41546). Palo Alto: Consulting Psychologists Press.

Graen, G., Cashman, J. F., Ginsburgh, S., & Schiemann, W. (1977). Effects of linking-pin quality upon the quality of working life of lower participants: A longitudinal investigation of the managerial understructure. *Administrative Science Quarterly, 22*, 491–504.

Graen, G. B., Novak, M. A., & Sommerkamp, P. (1982). The effect of leader-member exchange and job design on productivity and satisfaction: Testing a dual attachment model. *Organization Behavior and Human Performance, 30*(1), 109–131.

Graham, J. W. (1986). *Organizational citizenship informed by political theory*. Paper presented at the meeting of Academy of Management, Chicago.

Graham, J.W. (1989). *Organizational citizenship behavior: Construct redefinition, operationalization, and validation*. Unpublished working paper, Loyola University of Chicago, Chicago, IL.

Greenberg, J. (1986). Determinants of perceived fairness of performance evaluations. *Journal of Applied Psychology, 71*(2), 340–342.

Greenberg, J. (1987). A taxonomy of organizational justice theories. *Academy of Management Review, 12*(1), 9–22.

Greenberg, J. (1989). Cognitive reevaluation of outcomes in response to underpayment inequity. *Academy of Management Journal, 32*(1), 174–184.

Greenberg, J. (1990a). Looking fair vs. being fair: Managing impressions of organizational justice. In B. M. Shaw & L. L. Cummings (Eds.), *Research in organizational behavior* (pp. 111–157). Greenwich: JAI Press.

Greenberg, J. (1990b). Employee theft as a reaction to underpayment inequity: The hidden cost of pay cuts. *Journal of Applied Psychology, 75*(5), 561–568.

Greenberg, J. (1991). Using explanations to manage impression of performance appraisal fairness. *Employee Responsibilities and Rights Journal, 4*(1), 51–60.

Greenberg, J. (1993a). The social side of fairness: Interpersonal and informational classes of organizational justice. In R. Cropanzano (Ed.), *Justice in the workplace: Approaching fairness in human resource management* (pp. 79–103). Hillsdale: Lawrence Erlbaum.

Greenberg, J. (1993b). Stealing in the name of justice: Informational and interpersonal moderators of theft reactions to underpayment inequity. *Organizational Behavior and Human Decision Processes, 54*(1), 81–103.

Greenberg, J. (1994). Using socially fair procedures to promote acceptance of a work site smoking ban. *Journal of Applied Psychology, 79*(2), 288–297.

Greenberg, J. (1996). *The quest for justice on the job*. Thousand Oaks: Sage.

Greenberg, J., & Scott, K. S. (1996). Why do workers bite the hand that feeds them? Employee theft as a social exchange process. In B. M. Shaw & L. L. Cummings (Eds.), *Research in organizational behavior* (pp. 111–156). Greenwich: JAI Press.

Greller, M. M. (1975). Subordinate participation and reactions to the appraisal review. *Journal of Applied Psychology, 60*(5), 544–549.

Griffeth, R. W., Hom, P. W., & Gaertner, S. (2000). A meta-analysis of antecedents correlates of employee turnover: Update, moderator tests, and research implications for the new millennium. *Journal of Management, 26*(3), 464–488.

Griffith, J. (2001). Do satisfied employees satisfy customers? Support-services staff morale and satisfaction among public school administrators, students, and parents. *Journal of Applied Social Psychology, 31*(8), 1627–1658.

Hackett, R. D., & Guion, R. M. (1985). A reevaluation of the absenteeism-job satisfaction relationship. *Organisational Behaviour and Human Decision Processes, 35*(3), 340–381.

Halaby, C. N., & Sobel, M. E. (1979). Mobility effects in the workplace. *American Journal of Sociology, 85*(2), 385–416.

Hanisch, K. A., Hulin, C. L., & Roznowski, M. (1998). The importance of individuals' repertoires of behaviours: The scientific appropriateness of studying multiple behaviours and general attitudes. *Journal of Organisational Behaviour, 19*(5), 463–480.

Hardy, G. E., Woods, D., & Wall, T. D. (2003). The impact of psychological distress on absence from work. *Journal of Applied Psychology, 88*, 306–314.

Harlos, K. P., & Pinder, C. C. (1999). Patterns of organizational injustice: A taxonomy of what employees regard as unjust. *Advances in Qualitative Organizational Research, 2*, 97–125.

Harris, L. (2000). Procedural justice and perceptions of fairness in selection practice. *International Journal of Selection and Assessment, 8*(3), 148–157.

Harris, K. J., Kacmar, K. M., & Witt, L. A. (2004). An examination of the curvilinear relationship between leader-member exchange and intent to turnover. *Journal of Organizational Behavior, 26*, 363–378.

Harris, K. J., Kacmar, K. M., & Witt, L. A. (2005). An examination of the curvilinear relationship between leader-member exchange and intent to turnover. *Journal of Organizational Behavior, 26*(4), 363–378.

Harter, J. K., Schmidt, F. L., & Hayes, T. L. (2002). Business-unit level relationship between employee satisfaction, employee engagement, and business outcomes: A meta-analysis. *Journal of Applied Psychology, 87*(2), 268–279.

Hassan, A. (2002). Organizational justice as a determinant of organizational commitment and intention to leave. *Asian Academy of Management Journal, 7*(2), 55–66.

Hendrix, W., Robbins, T., Miller, J., & Summers, T. P. (1999). *Procedural and distributive justice effects on turnover*. Paper presented at the annual meeting of the Society for Industrial and Organizational Psychology, Atlanta, GA.

Heneman, H. G., Judge, T. A., & Heneman, R. L. (2001). *Staffing organizations*. Middleton: Irwin McGraw-Hill.

Herzberg, F. (1968). One more time: How do you motivate employees? *Harvard Business Review, 46*(1), 53–62.

Holmes, S. A., Langford, M., Welch, O. J., & Welch, S. T. (2002). Associations between internal controls and organizational citizenship behavior. *Journal of Managerial Issues, 14*(1), 85–99.

Holmvall, C., & Sidhu, J. (2007). Predicting customer service employees' job satisfaction and turnover intentions: The roles of customer interactional injustice and interdependent self-construal. *Social Justice Research, 20*(4), 479–496.

Hom, W., & Griffeth, R. W. (1995). *Employee turnover*. Vincinnati: Southwestern.

Homans, G. C. (1961). *Social behaviour: Its elementary forms*. London: Routledge and Kegan Paul.

Hooi, L. W. (2011). The role of leader-member exchange in organisational justice-organisational citizenship behavior relationship. *Research and Practice in Human Resource Management, 19*(2), 71–91.

Hooi, L. W. (2012). Organisational justice, organisational citizenship behavior and job satisfaction: What is the relationship? *Journal for International Business and Entrepreneurship Development, 6*(3/4), 274–302.

Hoy, W. K., & Tarter, C. J. (2004). Organizational justice in schools: No justice without trust. *International Journal of Educational Management, 18*(4), 250–259.

Hulin, C. L. (1991). Adaptation, persistence, and commitment in organisations. In M. D. Dunnette & L. M. Hough (Eds.), *Handbook of industrial and organisational psychology* (2nd ed., Vol. 2, pp. 445–505). Palo Alto: Consulting Psychologists Press.

Iaffaldano, M. T., & Muchinsky, P. M. (1985). Job satisfaction and job performance: A meta-analysis. *Psychological Bulletin, 97*(2), 251–273.

Ilies, R., Nahrgang, J. D., & Morgeson, F. P. (2007). Leader-member exchange and citizenship behaviors: A meta-analysis. *Journal of Applied Psychology, 92*(1), 269–277.

Jablin, F. M. (1979). Superior-subordinate communication: The state of the art. *Psychological Bulletin, 86*(6), 1201–1222.

Johnston, M. W., Griffeth, R. W., Burton, S., & Carson, P. P. (1993). An exploratory investigation into the relationship between promotion and turnover: A quasi-experimental longitudinal study. *Journal of Management, 19*(1), 33–49.

Judge, T. A., & Colquitt, J. A. (2004). Organizational justice and stress: The mediating role of work-family conflict. *Journal of Applied Psychology, 89*(3), 395–404.

Judge, T. A., Thoresen, C. J., Bono, J. E., & Patton, G. K. (2001). The job satisfaction-job performance relationship: A qualitative and quantitative review. *Psychological Bulletin, 127*(3), 376–407.

Kaplan, D. M., & Ferris, G. R. (2001). Fairness perceptions of employee promotion systems: A two-study investigation of antecedents and mediators. *Journal of Applied Social Psychology, 31*(6), 1204–1222.

Katz, D. (1964). The motivational basis of organizational behavior. *Behavioral Science, 9*(2), 131–133.

Kausto, J., Elo, A. L., Lipponen, J., & Elovainio, M. (2005). Moderating effects of job insecurity in the relationships between procedural justice and employee well-being: Gender differences. *European Journal of Work and Organizational Behavior, 14*(4), 431–452.

Kee, D. M. H., Ansari, M. A., & Aafaqi, R. (2004). Fairness of human resource management practices, leader-member exchange, and organizational commitment. *Asian Academy of Management Journal, 9*, 99–120.

Kemery, E. R., Bedeian, A. G., & Zacur, S. R. (1996). Expectancy-based job cognitions and job affect as predictors of organizational citizenship behaviours. *Journal of Applied Social Psychology, 26*, 635–651.

Kernan, M. C., & Hanges, P. J. (2002). Survivor reactions to reorganization: Antecedents and consequences of procedural, interpersonal, and informational justice. *Journal of Applied Psychology, 87*, 916–928.

Kim, W. C., & Mauborgne, R. (1997). Fair process: Managing in the knowledge economy. *Harvard Business Review, 75*(4), 65–75.

Kim, W. C., & Mauborgne, R. A. (1998). Procedural justice, strategic-decision making, and the knowledge economy. *Strategic Management Journal, 19*(4), 323–338.

Kinicki, A. J., & Vecchio, R. P. (1994). Influences on the quality of supervisor-subordinate relations: The role of time-pressure, organizational commitment, and locus of control. *Journal of Organizational Behavior, 15*(1), 75–82.

Kivimaki, M., Elovainio, M., Vahtera, J., & Ferrie, J. E. (2003). Organisational justice and health of employees: Prospective cohort study. *Occupational and Environmental Medicine, 60*(1), 27–34.

Konovsky, M. A., & Brockner, J. (1993). Managing victim and survivor layoff reactions: A procedural justice perspective. In R. Cropanzano (Ed.), *Justice in the workplace: Approaching fairness in human resource management* (pp. 134–154). Hillsdale: Lawrence Erlbaum Associates.

Konovsky, M. A., & Cropanzano, R. (1991). Justice considerations in employee drug testing. In R. Cropanzano (Ed.), *Justice in the work place: Approaching fairness in human resource management* (pp. 171–192). Hillsdale: Lawrence Erlbaum.

Konovsky, M. A., & Folger, R. (1987). Relative effects of procedural and distributive justice on employee attitudes. *Representative Research in Social Psychology, 17*(1), 15–24.

Konovsky, M. A., & Folger, R. (1991). The effects of procedures, social accounts, and benefits level on victims' layoff reactions. *Journal of Applied Social Psychology, 21*(8), 630–650.

Konovsky, M. A., & Organ, D. W. (1996). Dispositional and contextual determinants of organizational citizenship behavior. *Journal of Organizational Behavior, 17*(3), 253–266.

Konovsky, M. A., & Pugh, S. D. (1994). Citizenship behavior and social exchange. *Academy of Management Journal, 37*(3), 656–669.

Konovsky, M. A., Folger, R., & Cropanzano, R. (1987). Relative effects of procedural and distributive justice on employee attitudes. *Representative Research in Social Psychology, 17*(1), 15–24.

Koopmann, R. (2002). The relation between perceived organization justice and organizational citizenship behaviors: A review of the literature. *Journal of Student Research*. Retrieved March 15, 2010, from www.uwstout.edu/rs/uwsjsr/table.htm

Korsgaard, M. A., Schweiger, D. M., & Sapienza, H. J. (1995). Building commitment, attachment, and trust in strategic decision-making teams: The role of procedural justice. *Academy of Management Journal, 38*(1), 60–84.

Koustelios, A. (1991). *The relationships between organizational cultures and job satisfaction in three selected industries in Greece*. PhD dissertation. University of Manchester, Faculty of Education, United Kingdom.

Koys, D. J. (2001). The effects of employee satisfaction, organisational citizenship behaviour, and turnover on organisational effectiveness: A unit-level, longitudinal study. *Personnel Psychology, 54*(1), 101–114.

Krings, F., & Facchin, S. (2009). Organizational justice and men's likelihood to sexually harass: The moderating role of sexism and personality. *Journal of Applied Psychology, 94*(2), 501–510.

Lapierre, L. M., Hackett, R. D., & Taggar, S. (2006). A test of the links between family interference with work, job enrichment and leader-member exchange. *Applied Psychology: An International Review, 55*(4), 489–511.

Latham, G., & Pinder, C. (2005). Work motivation theory and research at the dawn of the twenty-first century. *Annual Review of Psychology, 56*(1), 485–516.

Lazar, A., Zinger, A., & Lachterman, B. (2007). The influence of prefeedback selection juctice on perceptions of overall procedural justice and organizational attractiveness in a real-life selection procedure. *European Journal of Work and Organizational Psychology, 16*(1), 94–109.

Le Blanc, P. M., Jong, R. D., Geersing, J., Furda, J., & Komproe, I. H. (1993). Leader-member exchanges: Distinction between two factors. *European Work and Organizational Psychologist, 3*(4), 297–309.

Lease, S. H. (1998). Annual review, 1993–1997: Work attitudes and outcomes. *Journal of Vocational Behavior, 53*(2), 154–183.

Lemons, M. A., & Jones, C. A. (2001). Procedural justice in promotion decisions: Using perceptions of fairness to build employee commitment. *Journal of Managerial Psychology, 16*(4), 268–280.

Lepine, J. A., Erez, A., & Johnson, D. E. (2002). The nature and dimensionality of organizational citizenship behavior: A critical review and meta-analysis. *Journal of Applied Psychology, 87*(1), 52–65.

Leventhal, G. S. (1976). The distribution of rewards and resources in groups and organizations. In L. Berkowitz & W. Walster (Eds.), *Advances in experimental social psychology* (pp. 91–131). New York: Academic.

Leventhal, G. S. (1980). What should be done with equity theory? In K. J. Gergen, M. S. Greenberg, & R. H. Willis (Eds.), *Social exchange: Advances in theory and research* (pp. 27–54). New York: Plenum Press.

Leventhal, G. S., Karuza, J., & Fry, W. R. (1980). Beyond fairness: A theory of allocation preferences. In G. Mikula (Ed.), *Justice and social interaction* (pp. 167–218). New York: Springer.

Liden, R., & Graen, G. (1980). Generalisability of the vertical dyad linkage model of leadership. *Academy of Management Journal, 23*(3), 451–465.

Liden, R. C., Wayne, S. J., & Stilwell, D. (1993). A longitudinal study of the early development of leader-member exchanges. *Journal of Applied Psychology, 78*(4), 662–674.

Liden, R. C., Wayne, S. J., & Sparrowe, R. T. (2000). An examination of the mediating role of psychological empowerment on the relations between the job, interpersonal relationships, and work outcomes. *Journal of Applied Psychology, 85*, 407–416.

Lind, E. A. (1995). Justice and authority relations in organizations. In R. Cropanzano & K. M. Kacmar (Eds.), *Organizational politics, justice, and support: Managing the social climate of the workplace* (pp. 83–96). Westport: Quorum Books.

Lind, E. A. (2001). Fairness heuristic theory: Justice judgments as pivotal cognitions in organizational relations. In J. Greenberg & R. Cropanzano (Eds.), *Advances in organizational justice* (pp. 56–88). Stanford: Stanford University Press.

Lind, E. A., & Tyler, T. R. (1988). *The social psychology of procedural justice*. New York: Plenum Press.

Lind, E. A., Kanfer, R., & Earley, P. C. (1990). Voice, control, and procedural justice: Instrumental and non-instrumental concerns in fairness judgments. *Journal of Personality and Social Psychology, 59*(5), 952–959.

Lind, E. A., Kulik, C. T., Ambrose, M., & de Vera Park, M. V. (1993). Individual and corporate dispute resolution: Using procedural fairness as a decision heuristic. *Administrative Science Quarterly, 38*(2), 224–251.

Lind, E. A., Tyler, T. R., & Huo, Y. J. (1997). Procedural context and culture: Variation in the antecedents of procedural justice judgments. *Journal of Personality and Social Psychology, 73*(4), 767–780.

Locke, E. A. (1976). The nature and causes of job satisfaction. In M. D. Dunnette (Ed.), *Handbook of industrial and organizational psychology* (pp. 1297–1349). Chicago: Rand McNally.

Lord, R., & Maher, K. (1991). *Leadership and information processing: Linking perception and performance*. Boston: Unwin Hyman.

Lowe, R. H., & Vodanovich, S. J. (1995). A field study of distributive and procedural justice as predictors of satisfaction and organizational commitment. *Journal of Business and Psychology, 10*(1), 99–114.

Luo, Y. (2007). The independent and interactive roles of procedural, distributive and interactional justice in strategic alliances. *Academy of Management Journal, 50*(3), 644–664.

Lyness, K. S., & Judiesch, M. K. (2001). Are female managers quitters? The relationship of gender, promotions and family leaves of absence to voluntary turnover. *Journal of Applied Psychology, 86*(6), 1167–1178.

MacKenzie, S. B., Podsakoff, P. M., & Rich, G. A. (2001). Transformational leadership and transactional leadership and salesperson performance. *Journal of the Academy of Marketing Science, 29*(2), 115–134.

Mansour-Cole, D. M., & Scott, S. G. (1998). Hearing it through the grapevine: The influence of source, leader-relations, and legitimacy on survivors' fairness perceptions. *Personnel Psychology, 51*(1), 25–54.

Marcus-Newhall, A., Pedersen, W. C., Carlson, M., & Miller, N. (2000). Displaced aggression is alive and well: A meta-analytic review. *Journal of Personality and Social Psychology, 78*(4), 670–689.

Mardanov, I. T., Heischmidt, K., & Henson, A. (2008). Leader-member exchange and job satisfaction bond and predicted employee turnover. *Journal of Leadership & Organizational Studies, 15*(2), 159–175.

Martin, R., Thomas, G., Charles, K., Epitropaki, O., & McNamara, R. (2005). The role of leader-member exchanges in mediating the relationship between locus of control and work reactions. *Journal of Occupational and Organizational Psychology, 78*, 141–147.

Maslyn, J. M., & Uhl-Bien, M. (2001). Leader-member exchange and its dimension: Effects of self-effort and other's effort on relationship quality. *Journal of Applied Psychology, 86*(4), 697–708.

Masterson, S. S., & Taylor M. S. (1996). *The broadening of procedural justice: Should interactional and procedural components be separate theories?* Paper presented at annual meeting of the Academy of Management, Cincinnati.

Masterson, S. S., Lewis, K., Goldman, B. M., & Taylor, M. S. (2000). Integrating justice and social exchange: The differing effects of fair procedures and treatment of work relationships. *Academy of Management Journal, 43*(4), 738–748.

Mathieu, J. E., & Zajac, D. M. (1990). A review and meta-analysis of the antecedents, correlates, and consequences of organizational commitment. *Psychological Bulletin, 108*(2), 171–194.

McClane, W. E. (1991a). Implications of member role differentiation: Analysis of a key concept in the LMX model of leadership. *Group & Organization Studies, 16*(1), 102–113.

McClane, W. E. (1991b). The interaction of leader and member characteristics in the leader member exchange (LMX) model of leadership. *Small Group Research, 22*(3), 283–300.

McDowall, A., & Fletcher, C. (2004). Employee development: An organizational justice perspective. *Personnel Review, 33*(1), 8–29.

McEnrue, M. P. (1989). The perceived fairness of managerial promotion practices. *Human Relations, 42*(9), 815–827.

McFarlin, D. B., & Sweeney, P. D. (1992). Distributive and procedural justice as predictors of satisfaction with personal and organisational outcomes. *Academy of Management Journal, 35*(3), 626–637.

McShane, S. L. (1984). Job satisfaction and absenteesm: A meta-analytic re-examination. *Canadian Journal of Administrative Science, 1*(1), 61–77.

Meyer, J. P., & Allen, N. J. (1997). *Commitment in the workplace: Theory, research, and application*. Newbury Park: Sage.

Meyer, J., Stanley, D., Herscovich, L., & Topolnytsky, L. (2002). Affective, continuance, and normative commitment to the organization: A meta-analysis of antecedents, correlates, and consequences. *Journal of Vocational Behavior, 61*(1), 20–52.

Miceli, M. P., & Lane, M. C. (1991). Antecedents of pay satisfaction: A review and extension. In K. Rowland & G. R. Ferris (Eds.), *Research in personnel and human resource management* (pp. 235–309). Greenwich: JAI Press.

Mikula, G., Petri, B., & Tanzer, N. (1990). What people regard as unjust. Types and structures of everyday experiences of injustice. *European Journal of Social Psychology, 20*(2), 133–149.

Mishra, A. K., & Spreitzer, G. M. (1998). Explaining how survivors respond to downsizing: The role of trust, empowerment, justice, and work redesign. *Academy of Management Journal, 23*(3), 567–588.

Mobley, W. H. (1977). Intermediate linkages in the relationship between job satisfaction and employee turnover. *Journal of Applied Psychology, 62*, 237–240.

Mohd Nasurdin, A., & Soon, L. K. (2011). Organisational justice, age, and performance connection in Malaysia. *International Journal of Commerce and Management, 21*(3), 273–290.

Molm, L. D. (1994). Dependence and risk: Transforming the structure of social exchange. *Social Psychology Quarterly, 57*, 163–176.

Moorman, R. H. (1991). Relationship between organizational justice and organizational citizenship behavior: Do fairness perceptions influence employee citizenship? *Journal of Applied Psychology, 76*(6), 845–855.

Moorman, R. H. (1993). The influence of cognitive and affective based job satisfaction measures on the relation between satisfaction and organizational citizenship behavior. *Human Relations, 46*(6), 759–776.

Moorman, R. H., & Blakely, G. L. (1995). Individualism-collectivism as an individual difference predictor of organizational citizenship behavior. *Journal of Organizational Behavior, 16*(2), 127–142.

Moorman, R. H., Niehoff, B. P., & Organ, D. W. (1993). Treating employees fairly and organizational citizenship behavior: Sorting the effects of job satisfaction, organizational commitment, and procedural justice. *Employee Responsibilities and Rights Journal, 6*(3), 209–225.

Morrison, E. W. (1994). Role definition and organizational citizenship behavior: The importance of the employee's perspective. *Academy of Management Journal, 37*(6), 1543–1567.

Morrison, A. M., White, R. P., & Van Velsor, E. (1987). *Breaking the glass ceiling: Can women reach the top of America's largest corporations?* Reading: Addison-Wesley.

Morrow, P. C., Suzuki, Y., Crum, M. R., Ruben, R., & Pautsch, G. (2005). The role of leader-member exchange in high turnover work environments. *Journal of Managerial Psychology, 20*(8), 681–694.

Motowidlo, S. J. (1984). Does job satisfaction lead to consideration and personal sensitivity? *Academy of Management Journal, 27*(4), 910–915.

Motowidlo, S. J. (2000). Some basic issues related to contextual performance and organizational citizenship behavior in human resource management. *Human Resource Management Review, 10*(1), 115–126.

Motowidlo, S. J., Packard, J. S., & Manning, M. R. (1986). Occupational stress: Its causes and consequences for job performance. *Journal of Applied Psychology, 71*(4), 618–629.

Muchinsky, P. M. (2000). *Psychology applied to work: An introduction to industrial and organizational psychology* (6th ed.). Belmont: Wadsworth/Thomas Learning.

Mullins, L. J. (2011). *Essentials of organisational behaviour* (3rd ed.). Essex: Pearson Education Limited.

Murphy, G., Athanasou, J., & King, N. (2002). Job satisfaction and organizational citizenship behavior: A study of Australian human-service professionals. *Journal of Managerial Psychology, 17*(4), 287–297.

Murphy, C., Ramamoorthy, N., Flood, P. C., & MacCurtain, S. (2006). Organisational justice perceptions and employee attitudes among Irish blue collar employees: An empirical test of the main and moderating roles of individualism/collectivism. *Management Revue, 17*(3), 328–343.

Nabatchi, T., Bingham, L. B., & Good, D. H. (2007). Organizational justice and workplace mediation: A six-factor model. *International Journal of Conflict Management, 18*(2), 148–174.

Napier, B. J., & Ferris, G. R. (1993). Distance in organizations. *Human Resources Management Review, 3*(4), 321–357.

Naumann, S. E., & Bennett, N. (2000). A case for procedural justice climate: Development and test of a multilevel model. *Academy of Management Journal, 43*(5), 881–889.

Naumann, E., & Jackson, D. W., Jr. (1999). One more time: How do you satisfy customers? *Business Horizons, 42*(3), 71–76.

Niehoff, B. P., & Moorman, R. H. (1993). Justice as a mediator of the relationship between methods of monitoring and organizational citizenship behavior. *Academy of Management Journal, 36*(3), 527–556.

Nystrom, H. (1990). Organizational innovation. In M. A. West & J. L. Farr (Eds.), *Innovation and creativity at work* (pp. 143–161). New York: Wiley.

O'Reilly, C., & Chatman, J. (1986). Organizational commitment and psychological attachment: The effects of compliance, identification, and internalization on prosocial behavior. *Journal of Applied Psychology, 71*(3), 492–499.

Olson-Buchanan, J. B. (1996). Voicing discontent: What happens to the grievance filer after the grievance? *Journal of Applied Psychology, 81*(1), 52–63.

Organ, D. W. (1977). A reappraisal and reinterpretation of the satisfaction-causes-performance hypothesis. *Academy of Management Review, 2*(1), 46–53.

Organ, D. W. (1988a). *Organizational citizenship behavior: The good solider syndrome*. Lexington: Lexington Books.

Organ, D. W. (1988b). A restatement of the satisfaction-performance hypothesis. *Journal of Management, 14*(4), 547–557.

Organ, D. W. (1990). The motivational basis of organizational citizenship behavior. *Research in Organizational Behavior, 12*(1), 43–72.

Organ, D. W. (1997). Organizational citizenship behavior: It's construct clean-up time. *Human Performance, 10*(2), 85–97.

Organ, D. W., & Konovsky, M. A. (1989). Cognitive versus affective determinants of organizational citizenship behavior. *Journal of Applied Psychology, 74*, 157–164.

Organ, D. W., & Lingl, A. (1995). Personality, satisfaction, and organizational citizenship behavior. *The Journal of Social Psychology, 135*(3), 339–350.

Organ, D. W., & Moorman, R. H. (1993). Fairness and organizational citizenship behavior: What are the connections? *Social Justice Research, 6*(1), 5–18.

Organ, D. W., & Ryan, K. (1995). A meta-analytic review of attitudinal and dispositional predictors of organizational citizenship behavior. *Personnel Psychology, 48*(4), 775–802.

Organ, D. W., Podsakoff, P. M., & MacKenzie, S. B. (2006). *Organizational citizenship behavior: Its nature, antecedents, and consequences*. Beverly Hills: Sage.

Oshagbemi, T. (2000). Gender differences in the job satisfaction of university teachers. *Women in Management Review, 15*(7), 331–343.

Ostroff, C. (1992). The relationship between satisfaction, attitudes and performance: An organizational level analysis. *Journal of Applied Psychology, 77*(6), 963–974.

Pearce, J. L., Branyiczki, I., & Bakacsi, G. (1994). Person-based reward systems: A theory of organisational reward practices in reform-communist organisations. *Journal of Organisational Behavior, 15*(3), 261–282.

Peterson, R.C., & Danehower, V.C. (1994). *Judicial decisions in promotion selection in employment: An empirical study of discrimination cases*. Paper presented at the Southwest Academy of Management meeting in Dallas, TX.

Piercy, N. F., Cravens, D. W., Lane, N., & Vorhies, D. W. (2006). Driving organizational citizenship behaviors and salespersons in role behavior performance: The role of management control and perceived organizational support. *Journal of the Academy of Marketing Science, 34*(2), 244–262.

Pillai, R., Williams, S. E., & Tan, J. J. (2001). Are the scales tipped in favor of procedural or distributive justice? An investigation of the U.S., India, Germany, and Hong Kong (China). *Interrnational Journal of Conflict Management, 12*(3), 310–333.

Ployhart, R. E., & Ryan, A. M. (1998). Applicants' reactions to the fairness of selection procedures: The effects of positive rule violations and time of measurement. *Journal of Applied Psychology, 83*(1), 3–16.

Podsakoff, P. M., & MacKenzie, S. B. (1994). Organizational citizenship behaviors and sales unit effectiveness. *Journal of Marketing Research, 3*(1), 351–363.

Podsakoff, P. M., MacKenzie, S. B., Moorman, R. H., & Fetter, R. (1990). Transformational leader behaviors and their effects on followers' trust in leader, satisfaction, and organizational citizenship behaviors. *The Leadership Quarterly, 1*(2), 107–142.

Podsakoff, P. M., MacKenzie, S. B., & Fetter, R. (1993). Substitutes for leadership and the management of professionals. *Leadership Quarterly, 4*(1), 1–44.

Podsakoff, P. M., MacKenzie, S. B., & Bommer, W. H. (1996). Transformational leaders' behaviors and substitutes for leadership as determinants of employee satisfaction, commitment, trust, and organizational citizenship behaviours. *Journal of Management, 22*(2), 259–298.

Podsakoff, P. M., MacKenzie, S. B., Paine, J. B., & Bachrach, D. G. (2000). Organizational citizenship behaviors: A critical review of the theoretical and empirical literature and suggestions for future research. *Journal of Management, 26*(3), 513–563.

Pool, S. W. (1997). The relationship of job satisfaction with substitute of leadership, leadership behavior and work motivation. *The Journal of Psychology, 131*(3), 271–283.

Porter, L. W., & Steers, R. M. (1973). Organisational, work, and personal factors in employee turnover and absenteeism. *Psychological Bulletin, 80*(2), 151–176.

Posthuma, R. A., Maertz, C. P., & Dworkin, J. B. (2007). Procedural justice's relationship with turnover: Explaining past inconsistent findings. *Journal of Organizational Behavior, 28*(4), 381–398.

Price, J. L. (1977). *The study of turnover*. Ames: Iowa State University Press.

Puffer, S. M. (1987). Pro-social behavior, non-compliant behavior and work performance among commission sales people. *Journal of Applied Psychology, 53*, 422–443.

Quarles, R. (1994). An examination of promotion opportunities and evaluation criteria as mechanism for affecting internal auditor commitment, job satisfaction and turnover intentions. *Journal of Managerial Issues, 6*(2), 176–194.

Rego, A., Cunha, M. G. E., & Pinho, C. (2009). Exploring a five-factor model of organizational justice. *Management Research, 7*(2), 103–125.

Rhoades, L., Eisenberger, R., & Armeli, S. (2001). Affective commitment to the organization: The contribution of perceived organizational support. *Journal of Applied Psychology, 86*(5), 825–836.

Rice, R. W., McFarlin, D. B., & Bennett, D. E. (1989). Standards of comparison and job satisfaction. *Journal of Applied Psychology, 74*, 591–598.

Robbins, S. P. (2001). *Organizational behavior*. Upper Saddle River: Prentice-Hall.

Robbins, S. P., & Judge, T. A. (2007). *Organizational behavior* (12th ed.). Upper Saddle River: Pearson Prentice-Hall.

Roberts, J. A., Coulson, K. R., & Chonko, L. B. (1999). Salesperson perceptions of equity and justice and their impact on organizational commitment and intent to turnover. *Journal of Marketing Theory and Practice, 7*(1), 1–16.

Roch, G., & Shanock, L. R. (2006). Organizational justice in an exchange framework: Clarifying organizational justice distinctions. *Journal of Management, 32*(2), 299–322.

Ryan, A. M., Schmidt, M. J., & Johnson, R. (1996). Attitudes and effectiveness: Examining relations at an organisational level. *Personnel Psychology, 49*(4), 853–882.

Saal, F. E., & Moore, S. C. (1993). Perceptions of promotion fairness and promotion candidates' qualifications. *Journal of Applied Psychology, 78*(1), 105–110.

Sagie, A., Birati, A., & Tziner, A. (2002). Assessing the costs of behavioral and psychological withdrawal: A new model and an empirical illustration. *Applied Psychology: An International Review, 51*(1), 67–89.
Sashkin, M., & Williams, R. L. (1990). Does fairness make a difference? *Organisational Dynamics, 19*(2), 56–71.
Scandura, T. A. (1996). Developing diverse leaders: A leader-member exchange approach. *Leadership Quarterly, 7*(2), 243–263.
Scandura, T. A., & Graen, G. B. (1984). Moderating effects of initial leader-member exchange status on the effects of a leadership intervention. *Journal of Applied Psychology, 69*(3), 428–436.
Scandura, T. A., Graen, G. B., & Novak, M. A. (1986). When managers decide not to decide autocratically: An investigation of leader-member exchange and decision influence. *Journal of Applied Psychology, 71*, 579–584.
Schappe, S. P. (1998). The influence of job satisfaction, organizational commitment, and fairness perceptions on organizational citizenship behavior. *The Journal of Psychology, 132*(3), 277–290.
Schaubroeck, J., May, D. R., & Brown, F. W. (1994). Procedural justice explanations and reactions to economic hardship: A field experiment. *Journal of Applied Psychology, 79*(3), 455–460.
Schiemann, W.A. (1977). *The nature and prediction of organizational communication: A review of the literature and an empirical investigation*. UMf dissertation services. Ann Arbor: University Microfilms International, 7724747.
Schmiit, N., & Bedeian, A. G. (1982). A comparison of LISREL and two-stage least squares analysis of a hypothesized job satisfaction-life satisfaction reciprocal relationship. *Journal of Applied Psychology, 67*, 807–817.
Schmitt, M. J., & Dorfel, M. (1999). Procedural injustice at work, justice sensitivity, job satisfaction and psychosomatic well-being. *European Journal of Social Psychology, 29*(4), 443–453.
Schnake, M. (1991). Organizational citizenship: A review, proposed model, and research agenda. *Human Relations, 44*(7), 735–759.
Schnake, M., Dumler, M., & Cochran, D. S. (1993). The relation between traditional leadership, and super leadership, and organizational citizenship behavior. *Group and Organizational Management, 18*(3), 352–365.
Schnake, M., Cochran, D. S., & Dumler, M. P. (1995). Encouraging organizational citizenship: The effects of job satisfaction, perceived equity and leadership. *Journal of Managerial Issues, 7*(2), 209–221.
Schneider, B., & Bowen, D. E. (1985). Employee and customer perceptions of service in banks: Replication and extension. *Journal of Applied Psychology, 70*(3), 423–433.
Scholl, R. W., Cooper, E. A., & McKenna, J. F. (1987). Referent selection in determining equity perceptions: Differential effects on behavioral and attitudinal outcomes. *Personnel Psychology, 40*(1), 113–124.
Schriesheim, C. A., Castro, S. L., & Cogliser, C. C. (1999). Leader-member exchange (LMX): A comprehensive review of theory, measurement, and data-analytic practices. *Leadership Quarterly, 10*(1), 63–113.
Schwarzwald, J., Koslowsky, M., & Shalit, B. (1992). A field study of employees' attitudes and behaviors after promotion decisions. *Journal of Applied Psychology, 77*(4), 511–514.
Schyns, B., & Collani, G. v. (2002). A new occupational self-efficacy scale and its relation to personality constructs and organisational variables. *European Journal of Work and Organizational Psychology, 11*(2), 219–241.
Schyns, B., & Wolfram, H. (2008). The relationship between leader-member exchange and outcomes as rated by leaders and followers. *Leadership & Organization Development Journal, 29*(7), 631–646.
Scott, S. G., & Bruce, R. A. (1994). Determinants of innovative behavior: A path model of individual innovation in the workplace. *Academy of Management Journal, 38*(5), 1442–1465.
Scott, K. D., & Taylor, G. S. (1985). An examination of conflicting findings on the relationship between job satisfaction and absenteeism: A meta-analysis. *Academy of Management Journal, 28*(3), 599–612.

Settoon, R. P., Bennett, N., & Liden, R. (1996). Social exchange in organizations: Perceived organizational support, leader-member exchange and employee reciprocity. *Journal of Applied Psychology, 81*(3), 219–227.

Shapiro, D. L. (1993). Reconciling theoretical differences among procedural justice researchers by re-evaluating what it means to have one's views considered: Implications for third-party managers. In R. Cropanzano (Ed.), *Justice in the workplace: Approaching fairness in human resource management* (pp. 51–78). Hillsdale: Lawrence Erlbaum Associates.

Shapiro, D. L., & Buttner, H. B. (1988). *Adequate explanations: What are they, and do they enhance procedural justice under severe outcome circumstances?* Paper presented at the annual meeting of the Academy of Management, Anaheim, CA.

Shapiro, D. L., Buttner, E. H., & Barry, B. (1994). Explanations: What factors enhance their perceived adequacy? *Organizational Behavior and Human Decision Processes, 58*(3), 346–368.

Shaw, J. C., Wild, R. E., & Colquitt, J. A. (2003). To justify or excuse?: A meta-analytic review of the effects of explanations. *Journal of Applied Psychology, 88*(3), 444–458.

Sheppard, B. H., & Lewicki, R. J. (1987). Towards general principles of managerial fairness. *Social Justice Research, 1*(2), 161–176.

Sheppard, B. H., Lewicki, R. J., & Minton, J. W. (1992). *Organizational justice: The search for fairness in the workplace*. New York: Lexington Books.

Shouksmith, G., Pajo, K., & Jepsen, A. (1990). Construction of a multidimensional scale of job satisfaction. *Psychological Reports, 67*(2), 355–364.

Sin, H. P., Nahrgang, J. D., & Morgeson, F. P. (2009). Understanding why they don't see eye to eye: An examination of leader-member exchange (LMX) agreement. *Journal of Applied Psychology, 94*(4), 1048–1057.

Singer, M. (1993). *Fairness in personnel selection: An organizational justice perspective*. Avebury: Aldershot.

Skarlicki, D. P., & Folger, R. (1997). Retaliation in the workplace: The roles of distributive, procedural, and interactional justice. *Journal of Applied Psychology, 82*(3), 434–443.

Skarlicki, D., & Latham, G. (1995). Organizational citizenship behavior and performance in a university setting. *Canadian Journal of Administrative Sciences, 12*(3), 175–181.

Skarlicki, D. P., & Latham, G. P. (1996). Increasing citizenship behaviour within a labor union: A test of organizational justice theory. *Journal of Applied Psychology, 81*(2), 161–169.

Skarlicki, D. P., & Latham, G. P. (1997). Leadership training in organizational justice to increase citizenship behavior within a labor union: A replication. *Personnel Psychology, 50*(3), 617–633.

Smith, H. J., & Tyler, T. R. (1997). Choosing the right pond: The impact of group membership on self-esteem and group-oriented behavior. *Journal of Experimental Social Psychology, 33*(2), 146–170.

Smith, P. C., Kendall, L. M., & Hulin, C. L. (1969). *The measurement of satisfaction in work and retirement*. Chicago: Rand McNelly.

Smith, C. A., Organ, D. W., & Near, J. P. (1983). Organisational citizenship behaviour: Its nature and antecedents. *Journal of Applied Psychology, 68*(4), 653–663.

Snodgrass, S. E., Hecht, M. A., & Ploutz-Snyder, R. (1998). Interpersonal sensitivity: Expressivity or perceptivity? *Journal of Personality and Social Psychology, 74*(1), 238–249.

Sosik, J. J., Avolio, B. J., & Kahai, S. S. (1997). Effects of leadership style and anonymity on group potency and effectiveness in a group decision support system environment. *Journal of Applied Psychology, 82*(1), 89–103.

Spector, P. E., & Fox, S. (2002). An emotion-centered model of voluntary work behavior: Some parallels between counter conductive work behavior and organizational citizenship behavior. *Human Resource Management Review, 12*, 269–292.

Spector, P. E., Dwyer, D. J., & Jex, S. M. (1988). Relation of job stressors to affective, health, and performance outcomes: A comparison of multiple data sources. *Journal of Applied Psychology, 73*(1), 11–19.

St Onge, S. (2000). Variables influencing the perceived relationship between performance and pay in a merit pay environment. *Journal of Business and Psychology, 14*(3), 459–479.

Steel, R., & Rentsch, J. R. (1995). Influence of cumulation strategies on the long-range prediction of absenteeism. *Academy of Management Journal, 38*(6), 1616–1634.
Steiner, D. D. (1988). Value perceptions in leader-member exchange. *Journal of Social Psychology, 128*, 611–618.
Stroh, L. K., Brett, J. M., & Really, A. H. (1996). Family structure, glass ceiling, and traditional explanations for the differential rate of turnover of female and male manager. *Journal of Vocational Behaviour, 49*(1), 99–118.
Sweeney, P. D., & McFarlin, D. B. (1993). Workers' evaluations of the 'ends' and the 'means': An examination of four models of distributive and procedural justice. *Organisational Behavior and Human Decision Processes, 55*(1), 23–40.
Sweeney, P. D., & McFarlin, D. B. (1997). Process and outcome: Gender differences in the assessment of justice. *Journal of Organizational Behaviour, 18*(1), 83–98.
Tansky, J. W. (1993). Justice and organizational citizenship behavior: What is the relationship? *Employee Responsibilities and Rights Journal, 6*(3), 195–207.
Tata, J., & Bowes-Sperry, L. (1996). Emphasis on distributive, procedural and interactional justice: Differential perspectives of men and women. *Psychological Reports, 79*(3), 1327–1330.
Taylor, M. S., Tracy, K. B., Renard, M. K., Harrison, J. K., & Carroll, S. J. (1995). Procedural justice in performance appraisal: A field test of the due process metaphor for performance appraisal systems. *Administrative Science Quarterly, 40*(3), 495–523.
Tepper, B. J. (2001). Health consequences of organizational injustice: Test of main and interactive effects. *Organizational Behavior and Human Decision Processes, 86*(2), 197–215.
Tepper, B. J., & Taylor, E. C. (2003). Relation among supervisors' and subordinates' procedural justice perceptions and organizational citizenship behaviours. *Academy of Management Journal, 46*(1), 97–105.
Thibaut, J., & Walker, L. (1975). *Procedural justice: A psychological analysis*. Hillsdale: Erlbaum.
Thibaut, J., & Walker, L. (1978). A theory of procedure. *California Law Review, 66*(3), 541–566.
Traindis, H. C. (1974). Psychologists on culture and thought. *Reviews in Anthropology, 1*(4), 484–492.
Tierney, P., Farmer, S. M., & Graen, G. B. (1999). An examination of leadership and employee creativity: The relevance of traits and relationships. *Personnel Psychology, 52*(3), 591–620.
Tremblay, M., Sire, B., & Balkin, D. B. (2000). The role of organizational justice in pay and employee benefit satisfaction, and its effects on work. *Group and Organizational Management, 25*(3), 269–290.
Truckenbrodt, Y. B. (2000). The relation between leader-member exchange and commitment and organizational behavior. *Acquisition Review Quarterly, 7*(3), 233–244.
Tschannen-Moran, M. (2001). Collaboration and the need for trust. *Journal of Educational Administration, 39*(4), 308–331.
Tsui, A. S., & O'Reilly, C. A., III. (1989). Beyond simple demographic effects: The importance of relational demography in supervisor-subordinate dyads. *Academy of Management Journal, 23*, 402–423.
Turban, D. B., & Jones, A. P. (1988). Supervisor-subordinate similarity: Types, effects and mechanisms. *Journal of Applied Psychology, 73*, 228–234.
Turnley, W. H., Bolino, M. C., Lester, S. W., & Bloodgood, J. M. (2003). The impact of psychological contract fulfillment on the performance of in-role and organizational citizenship behaviors. *Journal of Management, 29*(2), 187–206.
Tyler, T. R. (1989). The psychology of procedural justice: A test of the group value model. *Journal of Personality and Social Psychology, 57*(5), 830–838.
Tyler, T. R. (1994). Psychological models of the justice motive: Antecedents of distributive and procedural justice. *Journal of Personality and Social Psychology, 67*(5), 850–853.
Tyler, T. R. (1999). Why people cooperate with organizations: An identity-based perspective. *Research in Organizational Behavior, 21*, 201–246.
Tyler, T. R., & Bies, R. J. (1990). Beyond formal procedures: The interpersonal context of procedural justice. In J. S. Carroll (Ed.), *Applied social psychology in business settings* (pp. 77–98). Hillsdale: Erlbaum.

Tyler, T. R., & Caine, A. (1981). The influence of outcomes and procedures on satisfaction with formal leaders. *Journal of Personality and Social Psychology, 41*(4), 642–655.

Tyler, T. R., & Lind, E. A. (1992). A relational model of authority in groups. In M. P. Zanna (Ed.), *Advances in experimental social psychology* (pp. 115–191). San Diego: Academic.

Tyler, T. R., & Smith, H. J. (1998). Social justice and social movements. In D. T. Gilbert, S. T. Fiske, & G. Lindzey (Eds.), *The handbook of social psychology* (pp. 595–629). New York: McGraw-Hill.

Tyler, T., Degoey, P., & Smith, H. (1996). Understanding why the justice of group procedures matters: A test of the psychological dynamics of the group-value model. *Journal of Personality and Social Psychology, 70*(5), 913–930.

Van den Bos, K., & Miedema, J. (2000). Toward understanding why fairness matters: The influence of mortality salience on reactions to procedural fairness. *Journal of Personality and Social Psychology, 79*(3), 355–366.

Van den Bos, K., Wilke, H. A. M., & Lind, E. A. (1998). When do we need procedural fairness? The role of trust in authority. *Journal of Personality and Social Psychology, 75*(6), 1449–1458.

Van Dyne, L., Graham, J. W., & Dienesch, R. M. (1994). Organizational citizenship behavior: Construct redefinition, measurement, and validation. *Academy of Management Journal, 37*(4), 765–802.

Van Dyne, L., Cummings, L. L., & McLean Parks, J. (1995). Extra-role behaviors: In pursuit of construct and definitional clarity. *Research in Organizational Behavior, 17*(1), 215–285.

Van Dyne, L., Vandewalle, D., Kostova, T., Latham, M. E., & Cummings, L. L. (2000). Collectivism, propensity to trust and self-esteem as predictors of organizational citizenship in a nonwork setting. *Journal of Organizational Behavior, 21*(1), 3–23.

Van Scotter, J. R., & Motowidlo, S. J. (1996). Interpersonal facilitation and job dedication as separate facets of contextual performance. *Journal of Applied Psychology, 81*(5), 525–531.

Van Yperen, N. W., den Berg, A. E., & Willering, B. M. (1999). Towards a better understanding of the link between participation in decision-making and organizational citizenship behavior: A multilevel analysis. *Journal of Occupational and Organizational Psychology, 72*, 377–392.

Varma, A., Pichler, S., & Srinivas, E. S. (2005). The role of interpersonal affect in performance appraisal: Evidence from two samples – The US and India. *International Journal of Human Resource Management, 16*(11), 2029–2044.

Vecchio, R. P., & Gobdel, B. C. (1984). The vertical dyad linkage model of leadership: Problems and perspectives. *Organizational Behavior and Human Performance, 34*(1), 5–20.

Vroom, V. H. (1964). *Work and motivation*. New York: Wiley.

Wagner, S. L., & Rush, M. (2000). Altruistic organizational citizenship behavior: Context, disposition and age. *The Journal of Social Psychology, 140*(3), 379–391.

Wayne, S. J., & Green, S. A. (1993). The effects of leader-member exchange on employee citizenship and impression management behavior. *Human Relations, 46*(12), 1431–1440.

Wayne, S. J., Liden, R. C., & Sparrowe, R. T. (1994). Developing leader member exchanges: The influence of gender and ingratiation. *American Behavioral Scientist, 37*, 697–714.

Wayne, S. J., Shore, L. M., & Liden, R. C. (1997). Perceived organizational support and leader-member exchange: A social exchange perspective. *Academy of Management Journal, 40*(1), 82–111.

Weaver, J. J. (1994). Want customer satisfaction? Satisfy your employees first. *HR Magazine, 39*(2), 110–112.

Weiss, H. M., Suckow, K., & Cropanzano, R. (1999). Effects of justice conditions on discrete emotions. *Journal of Applied Psychology, 84*(5), 786–794.

Welbourne, T. M. (1998). Untangling procedural and distributive justice. *Group and Organizational Management, 23*(4), 325–346.

Welbourne, T. M., Balkin, D. B., & Gomez-Mejia, L. R. (1995). Gainsharing and mutual monitoring: A combined agency-organizational justice interpretation. *Academy of Management Journal, 38*(3), 881–899.

Wilhelm, C. C., Herd, A. M., & Steiner, D. D. (1993). Attributional conflict between managers and subordinates: An investigation of leader-member exchange effects. *Journal of Organizational Behavior, 14*(6), 531–544.

Williams, L. (1988*). Affective and non-affective components of job satisfaction and organizational commitment as determinants of organizational citizenship and in-role behaviours*. Unpublished doctoral dissertation, Indiana University, Bloomington, IN.

Williams, S. (2000). The effects of distributive and procedural justice on performance. *Journal of Psychology, 133*(2), 183–193.

Williams, L. J., & Anderson, S. E. (1991). Job satisfaction and organizational commitment as predictors of organizational citizenship and in-role behaviours. *Journal of Management, 17*(3), 601–617.

Williams, S., & Wong, T. S. (1999). Mood and organizational citizenship behavior: The effects of positive affect on employee organizational citizenship behavior intensions. *Journal of Psychology, 133*(6), 656–668.

Williams, S., Pitre, R., & Zainuba, M. (2002). Justice and organizational citizenship behavior intentions: Fair rewards versus fair treatment. *The Journal of Social Psychology, 142*(1), 33–44.

Witt, L. A. (1993). Reactions to work assignment as predictors of organizational commitment: The moderating effect of occupational identification. *Journal of Business Research, 26*(1), 17–30.

Witt, L. A., & Broach, D. (1993). Exchange ideology as a moderator of the procedural justice-satisfaction relationship. *Journal of Social Psychology, 133*(1), 97–103.

Witt, L. A., & Wilson, J. (1991). Moderating effect of job satisfaction on the relationship between equity and extra-role behaviors. *Journal of Social Psychology, 13*(2), 247–252.

Wong, Y. T., Ngo, H. Y., & Wong, C. S. (2006). Perceived organizational justice, trust, and OCB: A study of Chinese workers in joint ventures and state-owned enterprises. *Journal of World Business, 41*(4), 344–355.

Yammarino, F. J., & Dubinsky, A. J. (1990). Salesperson performance and managerially controllable factors: An investigation of individual and work group effects. *Journal of Management, 16*(1), 87–106.

Yilmaz, K., & Tasdan, M. (2009). Organizational citizenship and organizational justice in Turkish primary schools. *Journal of Educational Administration, 47*(1), 108–126.

Yukl, G. (2006). *Leadership in organizations* (6th ed.). Upper Saddle River: Pearson Prentice Hall.

Yukl, G., O'Donnell, M., & Taber, T. (2009). Influence of leader behaviors on the leader-member exchange relationship. *Journal of Managerial Psychology, 24*(4), 289–299.

Zellars, K., Briu, Y., Bratton, V., Brymer, R., & Perrewe, P. (2004). An examination of the dysfunctional consequences of organizational injustice and escapist coping. *Journal of Managerial Issues, 16*(4), 528–544.

Chapter 4
Theories on Organisational Justice, Job Satisfaction, Leader–Member Exchange and Organisational Citizenship Behaviour

Abstract This chapter encompasses a set of theories that is related to the constructs of the study. Some of the justice theories covered in this chapter include equity theory, justice judgement theory, psychological theories of justice and the more contemporary 'integrative' theories that examine the effects of multiple justice dimensions in concert – fairness heuristic theory, uncertainty management theory and fairness theory. Job satisfaction theories include the facet model of job satisfaction, Herzberg's motivator-hygiene theory of job satisfaction, the discrepancy model of job satisfaction and the steady-state theory of job satisfaction. The discussion on the leader–member exchange theory encompasses the role theory and social exchange theory as well. The chapter concludes by outlining the theory of reasoned action in detail providing justification for the adoption of the theory as the underpinning for this study.

Introduction

Many competing theories or models attempt to explain the nature of organisational justice, job satisfaction, leader–member exchange and organisational citizenship behaviour. These theories help explicate the differences in people behaviour and, therefore, are important to the managers as there is no ready-made solution or single answer to what motivates people to display organisational citizenship behaviour. Collectively, the different theories enhance knowledge on the various aspects of organisational justice, job satisfaction, leader–member exchange and organisational citizenship behaviour by providing an insight of the factors and issues that managers need to consider. It provides a framework within which organisations can direct attention to how best to promote organisational justice, job satisfaction, leader–member exchange and organisational citizenship behaviour in manufacturing organisations in Malaysia. However, it is important to emphasise that these various theories are not conclusive.

This chapter discusses the most influential theories on organisational justice, job satisfaction, leader–member exchange and organisational citizenship behaviour. By the end of this chapter, one will have a good appreciation of the range of thoughts and feelings central for understanding and managing organisational behaviour. The justice theories include equity theory, justice judgement theory, psychological

L.W. Hooi, *Organisational Justice and Citizenship Behaviour in Malaysia*, Governance and Citizenship in Asia, DOI 10.1007/978-981-10-0030-0_4

theories of justice and the more contemporary 'integrative' theories that examine the effects of multiple justice dimensions in concert. The prominent theories of job satisfaction including the facet model, Herzberg's motivator-hygiene theory, the discrepancy model and the steady-state theory enlighten managers on how best to enhance satisfaction levels in organisations. The leader–member exchange theory, the role theory and the social exchange theory highlight the different kinds of relationship between a leader and a follower. Theories that are closely related to organisational citizenship behaviour, such as the theory of reasoned action and social exchange theory, provide an insight of the relevance of these theories in enhancing organisational citizenship behaviour. The chapter concludes by justifying the adoption of the theory of reasoned action as the underpinning for this study. This study adopted the theory of reasoned action, as organisational citizenship behaviour (behavioural intention), is much dependent on attitudes and subjective norms. Perceptions of fairness will influence attitudes towards organisational citizenship behaviour. Additionally, important other positive perceptions of organisational citizenship behaviour will motivate employees to display organisational citizenship behaviour.

Organisational Justice Theories

A number of theories on organisational justice have evolved over the years. But, generally these theories either focus on only one type of justice (e.g. equity theory, Adams 1965) or examine the effects of multiple justice dimensions (e.g. justice judgement theory, Leventhal 1976, 1980; fairness heuristic theory, Lind 2001 and Van den Bos 2001a; uncertainty management theory, Lind and Van den Bos 2002 and Van den Bos and Lind 2002; fairness theory, Folger and Cropanzano 2001). Leventhal (1976) criticises the validity of the equity theory while Colquitt et al. (2006) support the more contemporary 'integrative' theories that examine the effects of multiple justice dimensions in concert. It is hypothesised that these integrative theories 'capture much of the current thinking on why justice matters to people and why it impacts their behaviour' (Colquitt et al. 2006: 111).

Generally, organisational justice theory is concerned with employees' perceptions of justice in work-related issues (Greenberg 1990). Bies et al. (1988) study on organisational justice theory places much emphasis on the beliefs that individuals used to guide judgements concerning the fairness of a decision. It is assumed that individuals hold on to a set of fairness beliefs to test if the decision made is perceived as being just. By evaluating both the outcome and procedural fairness of those judgements, individuals react accordingly. Positive judgements of these decisions increase employee loyalty (Lind and Tyler 1988) and job satisfaction (Konovsky and Cropanzano 1991; McFarlin and Sweeney 1992), and improve organisational commitment (Schappe 1996). To study the effect of organisational justice on organisational citizenship behaviour, some of the theories introduced in the justice literature are discussed.

Equity Theory

The equity theory introduced by Adams (1965) focused on the fairness of outcomes, such as pay and promotion decisions, as perceived by employees. The theory assumes that individuals judge the fairness of rewards based on a merit principle. It has an asymptotic relation between rewards and perceived equity or fairness (Gilliland 2008). It emphasises on the fair distribution of resources and outcomes in exchange relationships and affirms the link between sharing returns and actual contribution and responsibility (Lou 2007). Precisely, fairness exists when rewards are proportional to contribution. The theory asserts that people with greater contributions should receive higher outcomes. Equity is the basic norm of distributive justice and people expect that rewards will commensurate with their efforts (Walker and Pettigrew 1984). Equity theory stresses on employee's beliefs of the treatment received in relation to others. Perceived equity is likely to result in positive work attitudes and reduce the potential hazard of opportunistic behaviour.

Thus, according to Adams equity theory, fairness is achieved to the extent outcomes are proportional to contributions. The distribution of reward is said to be fair, just or equitable, if this ratio is perceived to be proportional (Homans 1976). When this ratio becomes disproportional (over rewarded or under rewarded), inequity distress would result. To reduce distress, people will try to alter their contributions, outcomes or both (Chen and Park 2005). Thus, the theory advocates that perceived inequity creates a psychological tension that motivates individuals to restore justice. The psychological tension that motivates action increases as perceived inequity increases. Nonetheless, the theory has outgrown its usefulness (Leventhal 1976) and formulations that are more comprehensive have emerged. The justice judgement model, for example, adopts a multidimensional approach and insists that perceptions of fairness is based not only on the contribution rule but also on a needs rule and an equality rule.

Justice Judgement Theory

The justice judgement theory advocated by Leventhal (1976) assumes that an individual's perception of fairness is based on justice rules. A justice rule is defined as 'an individual's belief that a distribution of outcomes, or procedure for distributing outcomes, is fair and appropriate when it satisfies certain criteria' Leventhal 1976: 4). The two categories of justice rules in the justice judgement theory are distribution rules and procedural rules. Distribution rules refer to perceived fairness when rewards, punishments or resources are distributed in accordance with certain criteria. Among the major distributive rules are contributions rule, needs rule and equality rule. According to the theory, individuals apply distribution rules selectively and criteria for evaluating fairness may vary with circumstances. Procedural rules are associated with an individual's belief that allocative procedures that satisfy certain criteria are fair and appropriate. The theory adopts a four-stage justice judgement sequence, namely, weighting, preliminary estimation, rule combination and outcome evaluation in evaluating fairness.

Psychological Theories of Justice

There are two broad psychological theories pertaining to perceptions of justice – the self-interest or control model of justice and the relational model of justice. Though both models provide different explanations of why justice affects people's behaviour, they both envisage that perceptions of equity in decision-making motivate employees to support the organisation (Fuller and Hester 2007). The self-interest model of justice approach based on the social exchange theory emphasised that people are concerned about fair procedures because they aimed to maximise their personal outcomes (Tyler 1989). In the self-interest model of distributive justice, people satisfy self-interest by maximising their own resources based on justice rules (Tyler 1994). To enhance perceptions of distributive justice, individuals exert as much control as possible over outcomes. Procedures are perceived as fair when individuals believed that they have some control over the decision-making process. Individuals are more likely to perceive justice in distributive rules that favour their own circumstances and are concerned with their own individual needs to the exclusion of those of other employees (Tyler and Hastie 1991). The relational model of distributive justice based on social identity theory concerns maintaining the social relationships within a group; control becomes less important. Tyler (1989: 831) reiterates that 'the basic assumption of the group-value model is that people value membership in social groups'. People use organisational membership 'to create and maintain a favourable identity' (Tyler 1999: 203). Concerns about the long-term interests of the group, bias-suppression and trust in the honesty of decision makers may offset self-interest.

The self-interest model of procedural justice (Thibaut and Walker 1975) posits that when individuals' self-interest is enhanced, perceptions of procedural justice increase. Indirect control of outcomes through process control such as voice, consistency of procedures, use of accurate information for decision-making (Leventhal 1980), the favourability of the procedure to the perceiver and the amount of control over outcomes (Lind and Tyler 1988) augment individuals' self-interest. The relational model of procedural justice, called the group value model (Lind and Tyler 1988; Tyler and Lind 1992), emphasises strong social bonds among group members. Individuals gain status and a positive identity if treated fairly by organisational authorities (Fuller and Hester 2007). Thus, maintaining one's position and relationships within the group is more important than control over outcomes. Procedures are perceived to be fair if in the long run the interests of all group members will be served. The affective tone of interpersonal interactions tends to be positive (Naumann and Bennett 2000; Roberson and Colquitt 2005) and facilitative of open communication. It connects the ideas expressed in social identity theory with research on justice.

The relational models posit that people are concerned about fair treatment as it reflects their social identity. Lind (2001) asserts that fairness indicates value and respect by others (belongingness), whereas unfairness represents disrespect and exclusion. The relational model in justice theory proposes that justice initiates neutrality and standing, which accordingly heightens reciprocation and communication (Allen and Meyer 1990; Brockner and Siegel 1996). Tyler (1989) identified the three relational concerns regarding procedural justice – neutrality, trust and standing. Neutrality involves individual perceptions of honesty and lack of bias in decision makers. All affected parties benefit fairly from a decision process (Taylor et al. 1995). Neutral decisions are based on facts, not opinions. Trust concerns beliefs about the benevolence of decision makers. Individuals trust that benevolent authorities will treat them in a fair and reasonable way, and work to serve their long-term interests. Standing refers to recognition of individual status by group authorities – treating them with politeness, respect and dignity. Ultimately, these procedural aspects will lead to reasonable allocation of resources by the group. The model assumes that it is psychologically rewarding for individuals to belong to a group (Tyler 1989) and that groups are important because membership offers an individual an identity (Tyler and Blader 2001), and, thus, a sense of self-worth (Huo et al. 1996). Members are provided with information about their self-worth by the fair treatment of group authorities (Lind and Tyler 1988; Tyler and Lind 1992).

Contemporary Integrative Justice Theories

Integrative theories onsider multiple forms of justice in concert. Three integrative theories in the justice literature, namely, fairness heuristic theory (Lind 2001; Van den Bos 2001a), uncertainty management theory (Lind and Van den Bos 2002; Van den Bos and Lind 2002) and fairness theory (Folger and Cropanzano 2001) encapsulate why justice significantly affects people and their behaviour (Colquitt et al. 2006). Fairness heuristic theory contends that individuals in organisations use a 'fairness heuristic' to deal with the 'fundamental social dilemma' (Lind 2001; Van den Bos 2001a) of whether to cooperate with the superiors. Unlike trust which can be difficult to judge, perceptions of distributive, procedural and interactional justice depend on relatively more observable phenomena. Hence, individuals use justice instead of trust to guide their daily actions in the system, associating fair treatment with a trustworthy authority (Lind 2001; Van den Bos 2001a). The fairness heuristic theory suggests that the fairness heuristic formed during a 'judgemental phase' guides the individuals in the 'use phase'(Lind 2001) until a 'phase shifting event' causes the individual to reassess fairness levels and return to the judgemental phase (Roberson and Colquitt 2005). Succinctly, fairness heuristic theory emphasises on cooperation, and, hence, is more associated with prosocial behaviours (Lind 2001).

Uncertainty management theory, a successor to fairness heuristic theory, asserts that general forms of uncertainty rather than uncertainty about trust per se have a stronger influence on individuals' reaction to authorities. Van den Bos (2001b) affirms that justice has a stronger effect on reactions when uncertainty is high than when uncertainty is low. The theory maintains that as long as justice is in place, there is no trust-related uncertainty and concerns associated with other forms of uncertainty is minimised. In essence, uncertainty about trust per se is deemphasised. Instead, individuals use justice to manage their reactions to more general forms of uncertainty which may have nothing to do with the authorities.

Fairness theory argues that individuals' reactions typically depend on counterfactual thinking – would, could and should. Specifically, an individual assesses what would have happened under similar situations, what could have happened if the events were or were not under the discretion of an authority and what should have happened if the authority's behaviour were or were not morally appropriate. In a decision-making event, individuals engage in counterfactual thinking to determine its fairness and whether interests have been jeopardised. The next question is whether authorities should be blamed if the welfare has been reduced or threatened (Folger and Cropanzano 2001). Folger and Cropanzano (2001) assert that authorities can only be blamed if some ethical principal of social conduct has been violated. Authorities cannot be blamed if they have no control over their choice of actions. The fairness theory emphasises on blame and, therefore, is ideal in explaining counterproductive reactions (Folger and Cropanzano 2001).

Job Satisfaction Theories

There are many theories or models of job satisfaction. These theories take into consideration the different determinants of job satisfaction, such as personality, values, the work situation and social influence, and specify, in more detail the reasons for an employee to be satisfied or dissatisfied with a job. A profound knowledge of these theories is essential for all managers as job satisfaction has consequences not just for the employee but also for other stakeholders and the organisation as a whole. Though prior research indicate that job satisfaction is not meaningfully associated with job performance (e.g., Iaffaldano and Muchinsky 1985; Judge et al. 2001), new research suggests that it is related to organisational citizenship behaviour (e.g., Hooi 2012; Moorman 1991; Murphy et al. 2002; Organ 1988, 1990; Smith et al. 1983). As job satisfaction has the potential to significantly affect behaviours at the workplace and contribute to employees' level of well-being, four complementary theories of job satisfaction are discussed to help managers comprehend the different facets of job satisfaction.

The Facet Model of Job Satisfaction

The facet model of job satisfaction focuses primary on the effect of job facets on employee satisfaction. It looks at how satisfied employees are with each job facet. The employee's satisfaction with each facet is summed up to determine the overall job satisfaction of the employee. Some job facets that influence job satisfaction are ability utilisation, achievement, activity, advancement, authority, company policies and practices, compensation, coworkers, creativity, independence, moral values, recognition, responsibility, security, social service, social status, human relations supervision, technical supervision, variety and working conditions (Weiss et al. 1967). As numerous aspects of the job influence employee satisfaction, managers have to acknowledge that jobs affect employees in multiple ways. Therefore, managers have to be cautious not to exclude an important facet that strongly influences job satisfaction. Managers have to be aware too that some job facets are more important than others for any given employee (Rice et al. 1991).

Herzberg's Motivator-Hygiene Theory of Job Satisfaction

The motivator-hygiene or the two-factor theory of job satisfaction was proposed by Frederick Herzberg in 1959. It focuses on the effects of certain types of job facets on job satisfaction. The theory proposes that two set of factors affect job satisfaction. One set of factors, the hygiene or maintenance factors, are those when absent cause dissatisfaction. These are factors associated with the physical and psychological context in which the work is performed. They are necessary to avoid unpleasantness at work and serve to prevent dissatisfaction. Some examples of hygiene factors are working conditions, salary, job security, interpersonal relations with peers and subordinates, status, personal life, level and quality of supervision, and company policy and administration. The other set of factors, motivators or growth factors, are those, that if present, motivates superior performance. These factors are associated with how challenging the actual work is – the quality of human experience at work. The intensity of motivator factors cause feelings of satisfaction or no satisfaction, but not dissatisfaction. Some examples of motivators are job autonomy, interesting work, recognition, sense of achievement, personal growth and advancement, responsibility and nature of the work. Motivator factors satisfy motivator needs while hygiene factors satisfy hygiene needs of employees. Hence, the theoretical relationships between motivator needs, hygiene needs and job satisfaction are:

1. Employees will be satisfied when motivator needs are met and will not be satisfied when these needs are not met.
2. Employees will not be dissatisfied when hygiene needs are met and will be dissatisfied when these needs are not met.

In essence, Herzberg's proposition implies that unlike the traditional view of job satisfaction, satisfaction and dissatisfaction are two separate dimensions – one ranging from satisfaction to no satisfaction and the other ranging from dissatisfaction to no dissatisfaction. The traditional view contends that satisfaction and dissatisfaction are at opposite ends of a single continuum, and employees are either satisfied or dissatisfied with their jobs. On the contrary, Herzberg affirms that the opposite of satisfaction is not dissatisfaction. Factors that enhance job satisfaction are distinct from those that lead to job dissatisfaction. Eliminating dissatisfying characteristics from a job does not necessarily make the job satisfying. Employees will be neither dissatisfied nor satisfied. Herzberg asserts that employees can experience satisfaction and dissatisfaction with their jobs at the same time. An employee could be satisfied because motivator needs are being met, but dissatisfied because hygiene needs are not being met. The extent to which motivator needs are met determines an employee's location on the satisfaction continuum. Similarly, the extent to which hygiene needs are met determines an employee's location on the dissatisfaction continuum. Herzberg emphasises the importance of motivators to enhance effort and performance, but cautions that hygiene factors are equally important, but for different reasons. Nonetheless, managers need to be cognizant of the limited empirical support for the theoretical relationships Herzberg proposed. Herzberg's theory has been criticised among others, for its limited application to 'manual' workers, for ignoring situational factors, and that it is 'methodologically bound'. Whatever the validity of Herzberg's theory is, the theory has been widely read and is still relevant in motivating employees.

The Discrepancy Model of Job Satisfaction

The discrepancy model of job satisfaction uses a comparative approach to determine how satisfied employees are with their jobs. Employees compare their job to some ideal job, and when their expectations about their ideal job are met, employees will be satisfied. When employees' expectations about their ideal job are high, they will be dissatisfied when these expectations are not met. This ideal job could be what the employee thinks the job should be like, what the employee expected the job to be like, what the employee wants from a job or what the employee's former job was like. The discrepancy model of job satisfaction can be combined with the facet model to determine employees' level of satisfaction with their jobs. The difference between the facets employees currently have, and what they think their jobs should have, is the employees' level of satisfaction with the facets. The overall satisfaction score of the employee is determined by aggregating the scores for each job facet compared. Hence, to increase the level of job satisfaction, managers should ask their employees what their ideal job is. Understanding what employees want their jobs to be like helps managers take remedial initiatives to enhance job satisfaction.

The Steady-State Theory of Job Satisfaction

The steady-state theory suggests that every employee has a steady-state or equilibrium level of job satisfaction. This steady state when affected by different circumstances may change temporarily, but eventually will return to the equilibrium level, as job satisfaction tends to be rather stable over time. For example, positive outcomes may temporarily increase employees' level of satisfaction, but it ultimately will return to the equilibrium level. It is, therefore, imperative that managers determine whether the changes made will result in temporary or long lasting increases in job satisfaction. It is also important for managers to determine how long it takes employees to return to their former levels. These would help managers find ways to sustain an increase in job satisfaction.

The Leader–Member Exchange Theory

The leader–member exchange theory conceived by George Graen and Fred Dansereau stresses on the significance of variable relationships between leaders and each of their subordinates (Barling et al. 2010; Dansereau et al. 1975; Graen and Cashman 1975). Scandura et al. (1986: 580) posit that leader–member exchange is 'a system of components and their relationships involving both members of a dyad, involving interdependent patterns of behaviours, and sharing mutual outcome instrumentalities, and producing conceptions of environments, cause maps, and value'. The theory describes 'the different kinds of relationships that may develop between a leader and a follower and what the leader and follower give to and receive back from the relationship' (George and Jones 2008: 406). The theory emphasises on the leader-follower dyad or the 'vertical dyad' – the relationship between the leader and the follower. The idea originated from the fact that ratings given by the same leader differ from subordinate to subordinate. Graen and associates (e.g., Graen and Uhl-Bien 1995) assume that this variance is due to the quality of the relationship between leader and follower.

This relationship varies from subordinate to subordinate as leaders treat every subordinate differently depending on personal compatibility, the interactions between them, personality, attitude and subordinate competence. Leaders develop different kinds of relationships with different subordinates, and, therefore, every leader-follower relationship is unique and independent. The theory suggests that this relationship would determine if subordinates fall into the in-group or out-group (Dansereau et al. 1975; Truckenbrodt 2000). In-group subordinates are those employees who have created high-quality relationships with their supervisors, characterised by mutual trust, respect, liking and reciprocal influence (Liden and Maslyn 1998), commitment and involvement. Out-group subordinates are those employees who have low-quality or bad relationships (Morrow et al. 2005) with their immediate supervisors, characterised by 'limited reciprocal trust and support, and few rewards' (Truckenbrodt 2000). Their relationships with immediate supervisors are based on the formal authority of the leader and obedience to rules. Thus, a key feature in the leader–member exchange theory is whether the individual subordinate is in the leader's in-group or out-group. Leaders reward in-group subordinates and punish out-group subordinates (Liden and Graen 1980; Liden et al. 1993; Masterson et al. 2000; Wayne et al. 2002). Nonetheless, the leader and the subordinate must mutually invest in the relationship for the vertical dyad to sustain.

In-group subordinates and leaders mutually support and influence each other. Leaders commit much time in this relationship and empower subordinates to work autonomously. The in-group receives special duties and stronger support from the leader. They may be given special privileges and more rewards. They are more likely to know about forthcoming events before out-group subordinates and privy to sensitive information. In-group subordinates reciprocate by performing their best. Hence, in-group subordinates tend to have higher performance ratings, higher overall satisfaction and lower turnover intentions than out-group subordinates (Gerstner and Day 1997; Gomez and Rosen 2001; Kraimer et al. 2001; Maslyn and Uhl-Bien 2001). Out-group subordinates have much less influence over the leader and are expected to perform according to directives in an acceptable manner. The relationship is based on formal authority interactions. Out-group subordinates have less freedom to work autonomously and are likely to be assigned the more mundane tasks. They receive weaker support from the leader and have less of the leader's time and attention. They may also receive fewer rewards and perform at lower levels. The relationship in these dyads is impersonal, distant or cold. Generally, leaders who have high-quality relationship with their superiors are more likely to develop high quality relationships with their subordinates. The theory suggests that leaders should develop high-quality relationships with as many subordinates as possible as in-group subordinates are relatively more loyal and perform better than out-group subordinates (Klein and Kim 1998). Besides, out-group subordinates might resent their relatively inferior status and differential treatment (McClane 1991).

Role Theory

The formation of leader–member exchange is theoretically and empirically grounded originally in role theory (Katz and Kahn 1978), and then the social exchange theory (Blau 1964). The role theory argues that every employee is expected to play a specific role in the organisation (Katz and Kahn 1978) and work is accomplished through roles (Dienesch and Liden 1986). An employee's role developed gradually from informal exchanges between the leader and the employee (Graen 1976) through mutual acceptance and expectation that the roles assumed will be mutually beneficial (Dienesch and Liden 1986; Graen and Scandura 1987). The relational context of the exchange process involves the leader's expectations of the employee's role and the extent to which these expectations are met. This results in behavioural interdependency between the leader and the employee (Dansereau et al. 1975; Dienesch and Liden 1986; Graen and Cashman 1975) that ultimately enables the leader to precisely define an employee's assigned organisational role. Graen and Scandura (1987) proposed a three-phase leader–member exchange development model incorporating role taking, role making and role routinisation. These phases influence the type of leader–member exchange relationship formed through the extent to which the employee demonstrates compliance with a series of role episodes and a worthiness to be trusted. This determines the extent to which the leader reciprocates with work-related resources. The role relationship that evolves based on mutual dependencies between the leader and the employee plays a major part in this role-making process (Dienesch and Liden 1986), which is not restricted to only a formally designated leader but also with an entire role set of others (Sparrowe and Liden 1997).

Theories Related to Organisational Citizenship Behaviour

Social Exchange Theory

Social exchange theory is one of the most important paradigms for comprehending employees' attitudes (Colquitt 2001; Dirks and Ferrin 2002; Rhoades and Eisenberger 2002; Richard et al. 2009). Rather than focusing on the role of leaders and employees, social exchange theory focuses on the exchange between them. This exchange developed from an initial interaction between the leader and the employee. Through a sequence of exchanges, leaders and employees decide whether high-quality relationships can be developed. This normally centres around trust, respect and obligation (Uhl-Bien et al. 2000). If both parties are mutually satisfied with the exchange, the individuals continue the exchanges. On the contrary, if the expectation of the exchange and satisfaction with the exchange behaviours are not positive or if the exchange never occurs, it is likely that the quality of leader–member exchange and relationship will be lower.

The social exchange theory is based on studies carried out by sociologist (Blau 1964; Homans 1958) and social psychologist (Thibaut and Kelley 1959). Social exchange is defined as 'the voluntary actions of individuals that are motivated by the returns they are expected to bring and typically do in fact bring others' (Blau 1964: 91). Gouldner (1960) defines it as 'the norm of reciprocity, where reciprocity is a mutually contingent exchange of benefits between two or more units'. Thus, social exchange involves unspecified obligations and high levels of trust and obligation and far exceeds the employment contract (Gouldner 1960). Trust is gained through the reciprocal interactions of the parties involved in the relationship (Homans 1958). The social exchange theory envisages that, given certain conditions, people seek to reciprocate those who benefit them (Bateman and Organ 1983), and a behaviour that indicates this is organisational citizenship behaviour. Social exchange accounts for organisational citizenship behaviour by advocating employee behaviours that are not firmly directed by their employers (Rousseau and McLean Parks 1993). Similarly, social exchange augments organisational citizenship behaviour, as mutual trust that stimulates social exchange relationships assures that organisational citizenship behaviour will be reciprocated in the long run (Menguc 2000; Organ 1990). Dirks and Ferrin (2000) confirm that trust in organisation correlates positively with organisational citizenship behaviour.

According to the social exchange theory, the employment relationship consists of economic and social exchanges between the employer and employee (Aryee et al. 2002). While economic exchanges are quantifiable, social exchanges are intended to support the ongoing relationship (Shore and Shore 1995). A mutually beneficial social relationship is established once the employer initiates fair treatment of its employees, as employees feel obligated to reciprocate (Blau 1964; Homans 1961). Employees reciprocate by exhibiting extra-role behaviours (Robinson and Morrison 1995) such as organisational citizenship behaviours (Organ 1988). Much of the theory is used to explain organisational and interactional justice. Employees will have positive perceptions of social exchange they receive from the employer if perceptions of procedural and distributive justice are high. Fair treatment will enhance the social exchange relationship, and, thus, improves the level of trust between the employer and the employee. Social exchange theory underpins the reasoning of interactional justice, as interactional justice is incrementally embedded by the social norms prevalent in the society surrounding social relationships (Blau 1964; Granovetter 1985). Concurrently, under this social exchange relationship, the leader–member exchange model is also dependent on the theoretical framework of social exchange theory (Wayne and Green 1993). In essence, social exchange involves two important facets – trust and fairness.

Theory of Reasoned Action

The theory of reasoned action was developed in 1967 by Icek Ajzen and Martin Fishbein to examine the relationship between attitudes and behaviour. The theory was used to study human behaviour and argued that 'attitudes could explain human actions' (Ajzen and Fishbein 1980: 13). According to this theory, behavioural intentions are determined by individuals' attitudes toward a certain behaviour (personal factor) and norms representing their perception of other people's view of such behaviour (social factor). It is based on the assumption that people are usually quite rational and make systematic use of information available to them. People generally consider the implications of their actions before deciding to engage in a given behaviour. Thus, the theory of reasoned action is concerned with rational, volitional and systematic behaviour (Chang 1998; Fishbein and Ajzen 1975) in which the individual has control (Thompson et al. 1994). The theory works best when behaviours are fully under a person's volitional control (the actual willful control over behaviour). The lack of volitional control will constrain the individual from performing the action, despite being highly motivated by own attitudes and subjective norms. Realising the limitations of this theory, the concept of perceived behavioural control was included, resulting in the newer theory known as the theory of planned behaviour.

As a study of attitudes toward behaviours, behaviour intent has been identified as the most important determinant of a person's behaviour. The theory of reasoned action focuses on behavioural intentions as the main antecedents to behaviour. Behavioural intention measures a person's relative strength of intention to perform a behaviour. It is theorised that the stronger a person's intention to perform a particular behaviour, the more successful it is likely to be. In short, if a person intends to do a behaviour, then it is likely that the person will do it. The theory further hypothesises that the direct determinants of behavioural intention are the individual's attitude towards the behaviour (attitudes toward the expected outcome or result of a behaviour) and subjective norms (the influence other people have on a person's attitudes and behaviour) associated with the behaviour. Concisely, intentions are guided by salient beliefs and information that performing a particular behaviour will lead to a specific outcome. These beliefs called behavioural beliefs determined attitudes and are weighted by outcome evaluations. Positive evaluations of behavioural outcome will motivate an individual to perform a certain behaviour intentionally.

Subjective norm refers to whether these behavioural values are accepted by important others (referent individuals) and their motivation to comply with those referents. Normative beliefs underlie subjective norms. An individual will intend to execute a certain behaviour if it is perceived that important others expect the performance of that behaviour. Thus, important others strongly influence whether or not a person participates or intends to participate in any behaviour. People may also be inclined (or not inclined) to participate in a behaviour based upon their desire to comply with others. A positive subjective norm is expected if important others see performing the behaviour as positive and the individual is motivated to meet the expectations of important others. It would be a negative subjective norm for the individual if the important others see the behaviour as negative, and the individual wants to meet the expectations of these others. Hence, subjective norms is a combination of perceived expectations from important others along with intentions to comply with these expectations. It is the sum of the product of a person's normative belief and the person's motivation to comply. Nonetheless, behavioural intentions would be weak despite positive attitudes toward the behaviour and approval from important others if there is no volitional control, and resources or opportunities are constrained.

Although a person's attitude, combined with subjective norms, forms his/her behaviour, the attitudes and norms are not weighted equally in predicting behaviour. The effect on behavioural intention is dependent on the individual and the situation. Subjective norms are insignificant in predicting the behaviour of an individual who cares little for what others think (Miller 2005). According to Hale et al. (2003), the theory of reasoned action can be expressed as

$$BI = (AB)W1 + (SN)W2$$

BI = behavioural intention
(AB) = one's attitude toward performing the behaviour

W = empirically derived weights
SN = one's subjective norm related to performing the behaviour

The variables, attitude and subjective norm can be measured using both direct (generic) and indirect (belief based) measures. Thus, the direct measures can be applied across different behavioural domain, but the indirect measures are, and are specific to the behaviour under study. An individual's general evaluation of a behaviour constitutes the direct measure of attitude whilst an individual's behavioural beliefs related to the consequences of performing the behaviour is an indirect measure. The indirect measure of attitude is weighted by outcome evaluation, that is, the beliefs concerning the value the individual attaches to each consequence. An individual's belief about whether or not important others or referents would want him/her to perform the target behaviour is a direct measure of subjective norm whilst an individual's beliefs regarding the opinion of significant others or referents about the target behaviour (normative beliefs) is an indirect measure. The indirect measure of subjective norm is weighted by the individual's motivation to comply with the opinion of those referents (Khanna et al. 2009). A model for the theory of reasoned action is shown in Fig. 4.1.

Based on Fig. 4.1, the theory of reasoned action describes intention as the best predictor of whether a behaviour is performed. According to the theory of reasoned action, attitude towards the behaviour and subjective norm associated with the behaviour are the direct determinants of behavioural intention. Attitude refers to personal beliefs about the positive or negative significance of a behaviour and its

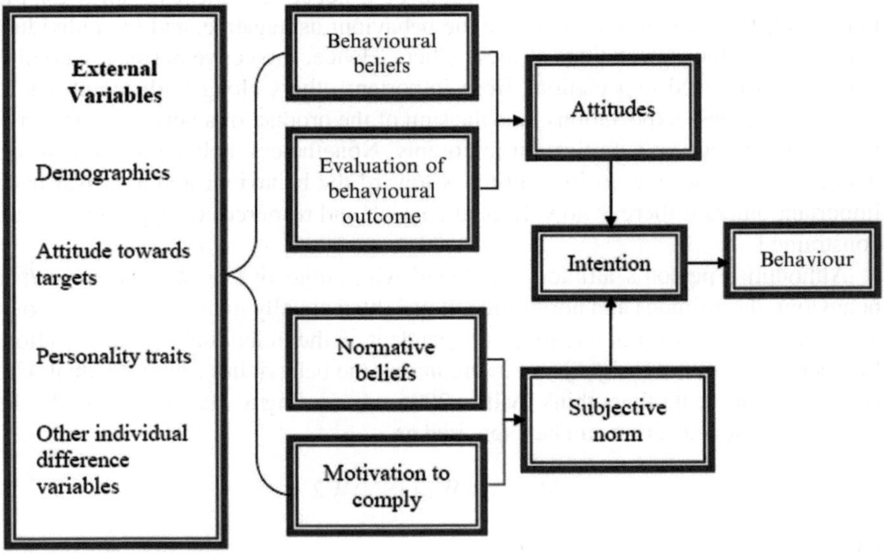

Fig. 4.1 Model of theory of reasoned action (Source: Montano and Kasprzyk (2008))

outcomes. Thus, attitude is affected by one's behavioural beliefs and evaluation of behavioural outcomes. People are likely to have a positive attitude towards performing a behaviour if a positive outcome is perceived from that behaviour. Subjective norm concerns a person's positive or negative value associated with a behaviour. It depends on whether or not the behaviour is endorsed by important others and their motivation to comply with those referents. Ultimately, interventions can be designed to change behavioural intention by affecting attitude and subjective norm to promote specific behaviours. These external variables may include demographics, attitude towards targets, personality traits and other individual difference variables.

Applying the theory of reasoned action to the current study, behavioural intention refers to employees' intention to exhibit organisational citizenship behaviour. The intention to demonstrate organisational citizenship behaviour is predicted by attitudes towards organisational citizenship behaviour and subjective norms regarding organisational citizenship behaviour. However, attitude and subjective norms might not be the most important predictor of organisational citizenship behaviour. It is likely that employee perceptions of organisational justice might act independently or in combination with attitudes and subjective norms to predict organisational citizenship behaviour. Employees are likely to exercise organisational citizenship behaviour if perception of organisational fairness is evaluated positively. Also, important others perception of the link between organisational justice and organisational citizenship behaviour will influence employees' intention to display organisational citizenship behaviour. Additionally, employees' attitude and subjective norms vis-à-vis organisational citizenship behaviour will indicate if organisational justice effects on job satisfaction and the quality of leader–member exchange relationship will result in organisational citizenship behaviour. It helps predict whether employees' and important others perceptions of organisational justice would determine employees' intention to exhibit organisational citizenship behaviour. The more positive the attitude and subjective norms, the more likely are employees to practise organisational citizenship behaviour.

Conclusion

This chapter outlines the various theories related to organisational justice, job satisfaction, leader–member exchange and organisational citizenship behaviour. An in-depth discussion of the theories provides the theoretical basis for this study. Among the theories, the theory of reasoned action seems to reflect organisational citizenship behaviour best and, therefore, is applied to study the effects of the different constructs on organisational citizenship behaviour. According to this theory, employee intention of displaying organisational citizenship behaviour is determined by attitude towards the behaviour and subjective norms. Although employee perceptions of organisational justice, job satisfaction and leader–member exchange may act independently to predict organisational citizenship behaviour, the possibility of these factors acting in tandem with attitudes and subjective norms cannot be dismissed. The next chapter examines the relationships between organisational justice, job satisfaction, leader–member exchange and organisational citizenship behaviour.

References

Adams, J. S. (1965). Inequity in social exchange. In L. Berkowitz (Ed.), *Advances in experimental social psychology* (Vol. 2, pp. 267–299). New York: Academic.

Ajzen, I., & Fishbein, M. (1980). *Understanding attitudes and predicting social behavior.* Englewood Cliffs: Prentice Hall.

Allen, N. J., & Meyer, J. P. (1990). The measurement and antecedents of affective, continuance and normative commitment to the organization. *Journal of Occupational Psychology, 63*(1), 1–18.

Aryee, S., Budhwar, P. S., & Chen, Z. X. (2002). Trust as a mediator of the relationship between organizational justice and work outcomes: Test of a social exchange model. *Journal of Organizational Behavior, 23*(3), 267–285.

Barling, J., Christie, A., & Hoption, C. (2010). Leadership. In S. Zedeck (Ed.), *Handbook of industrial and organisational psychology* (pp. 183–240). Washington, DC: American Psychological Association.

Bateman, T. S., & Organ, D. W. (1983). Job satisfaction and the good soldier: The relationship between affect and employee citizenship. *Academy of Management Journal, 26*(4), 587–595.

Bies, R. J., Shapiro, D. L., & Cummings, L. L. (1988). Causal accounts and managing organizational conflict: Is it enough to say it's not my fault. *Communication Research, 15*(4), 381–399.

Blau, P. (1964). *Exchange and power in social life*. New York: Wiley.

Brockner, J., & Siegel, P. (1996). Understanding the interaction between procedural and distributive justice: The role of trust. In R. M. Kramer & T. R. Tyler (Eds.), *Trust in organizations – Frontiers of theory and research* (pp. 390–413). Thousand Oaks: Sage Publications.

Chang, M. K. (1998). Predicting unethical behavior: A comparison of the theory of reasoned action and the theory of planned behavior. *Journal of Business Ethics, 17*(16), 1825–1834.

Chen, J. V., & Park, Y. (2005). The role of control and other factors in the electronic surveillance workplace. *Information, Communication and Ethics in Society, 3*(2), 79–91.

Colquitt, J. A. (2001). On the dimensionality of organizational justice: A construct validation of a measure. *Journal of Applied Psychology, 86*(3), 386–400.

Colquitt, J. A., Scott, B. A., Judge, T. A., & Shaw, J. C. (2006). Justice and personality: Using integrative theories to derive moderators of justice effects. *Organizational Behavior and Human Decision Processes, 100*(1), 110–127.

Dansereau, F. J., Graen, G., & Haga, W. J. (1975). A vertical dyad linkage approach to leadership within formal organizations – A longitudinal investigation of the role making process. *Organizational Behavior and Human Performance, 13*(1), 46–78.

Dienesch, R. M., & Liden, R. C. (1986). Leader-member exchange model of leadership: A critique and further development. *Academy of Management Review, 11*, 618–634.

Dirks, K. T., & Ferrin, D. L. (2000). The effects of trust in leadership on employee performance, behavior, and attitudes: A meta-analysis. In S. J. Havlovic (Ed.), *Academy of Management Best Papers Proceedings*. OB: H1.

Dirks, K. T., & Ferrin, D. L. (2002). Trust in leadership: Meta-analytic findings and implications for research and practice. *Journal of Applied Psychology, 87*(4), 611–628.

Fishbein, M., & Ajzen, I. (1975). *Belief, attitude, intention, and behavior*. Reading: Addison-Wesley.

Folger, R., & Cropanzano, R. (2001). Fairness theory: Justice as accountability. In J. Greenberg & R. Cropanzano (Eds.), *Advances in organizational justice* (pp. 89–118). Stanford: Stanford University Press.

Fuller, J. B., & Hester, K. (2007). Procedural justice and the cooperative worker: An interactional model of union participation. *Journal of Labor Research, 28*(1), 189–202.

George, J., & Jones, G. (2008). *Understanding and managing organizational behavior* (5th ed.). Upper Saddle River: Pearson Prentice Hall.

Gerstner, C. R., & Day, D. V. (1997). Meta-analytic review of leader-member exchange theory: Correlates and construct issues. *Journal of Applied Psychology, 82*(6), 827–844.

Gilliland, S. (2008). The tails of justice: A critical examination of the dimensionality of organizational justice constructs. *Human Resource Management Review, 18*(4), 271–281.

Gomez, C., & Rosen, B. (2001). The leader-member exchange as a link between managerial trust and employee empowerment. *Group & Organisation Management, 26*(1), 53–69.

Gouldner, A. (1960). The norm of reciprocity. *American Sociological Review, 25*(2), 165–167.

Graen, G. B. (1976). Role making processes within complex organizations. In M. D. Dunnette (Ed.), *Handbook of industrial and organizational psychology* (pp. 1201–1245). Chicago: Rand-McNally.

Graen, G., & Cashman, J. F. (1975). A role-making model in formal organizations: A developmental approach. In J. G. Hunt & L. L. Larson (Eds.), *Leadership frontiers* (pp. 143–165). Kent: Kent State Press.

Graen, G. B., & Scandura, T. A. (1987). Toward a psychology of dyadic organizing. In B. M. Staw & L. L. Cummings (Eds.), *Research in organizational behavior* (pp. 175–208). Greenwich: JAI Press.

Graen, G. B., & Uhl-Bien, M. (1995). Development of leader-member exchange (LMX) theory of leadership over 25 years: Applying a multi-level multi-domain perspective. *The Leadership Quarterly, 6*(2), 219–247.

Granovetter, M. (1985). Economic action and social structure: The problem of embeddedness. *American Journal of Sociology, 91*(3), 481–493.

Greenberg, J. (1990). Looking fair vs. being fair: Managing impressions of organizational justice. In B. M. Shaw & L. L. Cummings (Eds.), *Research in organizational behavior* (pp. 111–157). Greenwich: JAI Press.

Hale, J. L., Householder, B. J., & Greene, K. L. (2003). The theory of reasoned action. In J. P. Dillard & M. Pfau (Eds.), *The persuasion handbook: Developments in theory and practice* (pp. 259–286). Thousand Oaks: Sage.

Herzberg, F., Mausner, B., & Snyderman, B. (1959). *The motivation to work*. New York: Wiley.

Hofmann, D. A., Morgeson, F. P., & Gerras, S. J. (2003). Climate as a moderator of the relationship between leader-member exchange and content-specific citizenship: Safety climate as an exemplar. *Journal of Applied Psychology, 88*(1), 170–178.

Homans, G. C. (1958). Social behavior as exchange. *American Journal of Sociology, 63*(6), 597–606.

Homans, G. C. (1961). *Social behaviour: Its elementary forms*. London: Routledge and Kegan Paul.

Homans, G. C. (1976). Commentary. In M. P. Zanna (Ed.), *Advances in experimental social psychology* (pp. 231–232). San Diego: Academic.

Hooi, L. W. (2012). Enhancing employee satisfaction: An analysis of current promotion practices. *International Journal of Management Practice, 5*(3), 245–269.

Huo, Y. J., Smith, H. J., Tyler, T. R., & Lind, E. A. (1996). Superordinate identification, subgroup identification, and justice concerns: Is separatism the problem; is assimilation the answer? *Psychological Science, 7*(1), 40–45.

Iaffaldano, M. T., & Muchinsky, P. M. (1985). Job satisfaction and performance: A meta-analysis. *Psychological Bulletin, 97*(2), 251–273.

Judge, T. A., Thoresen, C. J., Bono, J. E., & Patton, G. K. (2001). The job satisfaction-job performance relationship: A qualitative and quantitative review. *Psychological Bulletin, 127*(3), 376–407.

Katz, D., & Kahn, R. L. (1978). *The social psychology of organizations* (2nd ed.). New York: Wiley.

Khanna, R., Kavookjian, J., Scott, V., Kamal, K. M., Miller, L. N., & Neal, W. A. (2009). Using the theory of reasoned action to determine physicians' intention to measure body mass index in children and adolescents. *Research in Social and Administrative Pharmacy, 5*(2), 170–181.

Klein, H. J., & Kim, J. S. (1998). A field study of the influence of situational constraints, leader-member exchange, and goals. *Academy of Management Journal, 41*, 88–96.

Konovsky, M. A., & Cropanzano, R. (1991). Perceived fairness of employee drug testing as a predictor of employee attitudes and job performance. *Journal of Applied Psychology, 76*(5), 698–707.

Kraimer, M. L., Wayne, S. J., & Jaworski, R. A. (2001). Sources of support and expatriate performance: The mediating role of expatriate adjustment. *Personnel Psychology, 54*(1), 71–99.

Leventhal, G. S. (1976). The distribution of rewards and resources in groups and organizations. In L. Berkowitz & W. Walster (Eds.), *Advances in experimental social psychology* (pp. 91–131). New York: Academic.

Leventhal, G. S. (1980). What should be done with equity theory? In K. J. Gergen, M. S. Greenberg, & R. H. Willis (Eds.), *Social exchange: Advances in theory and research* (pp. 27–54). New York: Plenum Press.

Liden, R., & Graen, G. (1980). Generalisability of the vertical dyad linkage model of leadership. *Academy of Management Journal, 23*(3), 451–465.

Liden, R. C., & Maslyn, J. M. (1998). Multidimensionality of leader-member exchange: An empirical assessment through scale development. *Journal of Management, 24*(1), 43–72.

Liden, R. C., Sparrowe, R. T., & Wayne, S. J. (1997). Leader-member exchange theory: The past and potential for the future. *Research in Personnel and Human Resources Management, 15*, 47–119.

Liden, R. C., Wayne, S. J., & Stilwell, D. (1993). A longitudinal study of the early development of leader-member exchanges. *Journal of Applied Psychology, 78*(4), 662–674.

Lind, E. A. (2001). Fairness heuristic theory: Justice judgments as pivotal cognitions in organizational relations. In J. Greenberg & R. Cropanzano (Eds.), *Advances in organizational behavior* (pp. 56–88). Stanford: Stanford University Press.

Lind, E. A., & Tyler, T. R. (1988). *The social psychology of procedural justice*. New York: Plenum Press.

Lind, E. A., & Van den Bos, K. (2002). When fairness works: Toward a general theory of uncertainty management. In B. M. Staw & R. M. Kramer (Eds.), *Research in organizational behavior* (pp. 181–223). Boston: Elsevier.

Lou, Y. (2007). The independent and interactive roles of procedural, distributive, and interactional justice in strategic alliances. *Academy of Management Journal, 50*(3), 644–664.

Maslyn, J. M., & Uhl-Bien, M. (2001). Leader-member exchange and its dimension: Effects of self-effort and other's effort on relationship quality. *Journal of Applied Psychology, 86*(4), 697–708.

Masterson, S. S., Lewis, K., Goldman, B. M., & Taylor, M. S. (2000). Integrating justice and social exchange: The differing effects of fair procedures and treatment of work relationships. *Academy of Management Journal, 43*(4), 738–748.

McClane, W. E. (1991). Implications of member role differentiation: Analysis of a key concept in the LMX model of leadership. *Group and Organisation Studies, 16*(1), 102–113.

McFarlin, D. B., & Sweeney, P. D. (1992). Distributive and procedural justice as predictors of satisfaction with personal and organisational outcomes. *Academy of Management Journal, 35*(3), 626–637.

Menguc, B. (2000). An empirical investigation of a social exchange model of organizational citizenship behaviors across two sales situations: A Turkish case. *Journal of Personal Selling and Sales Management, 20*(4), 205–214.

Miller, K. (2005). *Communications theories: Perspectives, processes, and contexts*. New York: McGraw-Hill.

Montano, D., & Kasprzyk, D. (2008). Theory of reasoned action, theory of planned behavior, and the integrated behavioral model. In K. Glanz, B. Rimer, & K. Vizwanath (Eds.), *Health behav-*

ior and health education: Theory, research, and practice (4th ed., pp. 67–96). San Francisco: Jossey-Bass.

Moorman, R. H. (1991). Relationship between organizational justice and organizational citizenship behavior: Do fairness perceptions influence employee citizenship? *Journal of Applied Psychology, 76*(6), 845–855.

Morrow, P. C., Suzuki, Y., Crum, M. R., Ruben, R., & Pautsch, G. (2005). The role of leadermember exchange in high turnover work environments. *Journal of Managerial Psychology, 20*(8), 681–695.

Murphy, G., Athanasou, J., & King, N. (2002). Job satisfaction and organizational citizenship behavior: A study of Australian human-service professionals. *Journal of Managerial Psychology, 17*(4), 287–297.

Naumann, S. E., & Bennett, N. (2000). A case for procedural justice climate: Development and test of a multilevel model. *Academy of Management Journal, 43*(5), 881–889.

Organ, D. W. (1988). *Organizational citizenship behavior: The good solider syndrome*. Lexington: Lexington Books.

Organ, D. W. (1990). The motivational basis of organizational citizenship behavior. *Research in Organizational Behavior, 12*(1), 43–72.

Rhoades, L., & Eisenberger, R. (2002). Perceived organizational support: A review of the literature. *Journal of Applied Psychology, 87*(4), 698–714.

Rice, R. W., Markus, K., Moyer, R. P., & McFarlin, D. B. (1991). Facet importance and job satisfaction: Two experimental tests of Locke's range of affect hypothesis. *Journal of Applied Social Psychology, 21*, 1977–1987.

Richard, O. C., Ismail, K. M., Bhuian, S. N., & Taylor, E. C. (2009). Mentoring in supervisor-subordinate dyads: Antecedents, consequences, and test of a mediation model of mentorship. *Journal of Business Research, 62*(11), 1110–1118.

Roberson, Q. M., & Colquitt, J. A. (2005). Shared and configural justice: A social network model of justice in teams. *Academy of Management Review, 30*, 595–607.

Robinson, S. L., & Morrison, E. W. (1995). Psychological contracts and the OCB: The effect of unfulfilled obligations on civic virtue behavior. *Journal of Organizational Behavior, 16*(3), 289–298.

Rousseau, D. M., & McLean Parks, J. (1993). The contracts of individuals and organizations. In B. M. Shaw & L. L. Cummings (Eds.), *Research in organizational behavior* (pp. 1–43). Greenwich: JAI Press.

Scandura, T. A., Graen, G. B., & Novak, M. A. (1986). When managers decide not to decide autocratically. *Journal of Applied Psychology, 71*, 106–126.

Schappe, S. P. (1996). Bridging the gap between procedural knowledge and positive employee attitudes: Procedural justice as keystone. *Group & Organization Management, 21*(3), 337–364.

Shore, L. M., & Shore, T. H. (1995). Perceived organizational support and organizational justice. In R. Cropanzano & K. M. Kacmar (Eds.), *Organizational politics, justice, and support: Managing the social climate of the workplace* (pp. 149–164). Westport: Quorum.

Smith, C. A., Organ, D. W., & Near, J. P. (1983). Organizational citizenship behavior: Its nature and antecedents. *Journal of Applied Psychology, 68*(4), 653–663.

Sparrowe, R. T., & Liden, R. C. (1997). Process and structure in leader-member exchange. *Academy of Management Review, 22*, 522–552.

Taylor, M. S., Tracy, K. B., Renard, M. K., Harrison, J. K., & Carroll, S. J. (1995). Procedural justice in performance appraisal: A field test of the due process metaphor for performance appraisal systems. *Administrative Science Quarterly, 40*(3), 495–523.

Thibaut, J. W., & Kelley, H. H. (1959). *The social psychology of groups*. New York: Wiley.

Thibaut, J., & Walker, L. (1975). *Procedural justice: A psychological analysis*. Hillsdale: Erlbaum.

Thompson, K. E., Haziris, N., & Alekos, P. J. (1994). Attitudes and food choice behavior. *British Food Journal, 96*(11), 9–17.

Truckenbrodt, Y. B. (2000). The relation between leader-member exchange and commitment and organizational behavior. *Acquisition Review Quarterly, 7*(3), 233–244.

Tyler, T. R. (1989). The psychology of procedural justice: A test of the group value model. *Journal of Personality and Social Psychology, 57*(5), 830–838.
Tyler, T. R. (1994). Psychological models of the justice motive: Antecedents of distributive and procedural justice. *Journal of Personality and Social Psychology, 67*(5), 850–853.
Tyler, T. R. (1999). Why people cooperate with organizations: An identity-based perspective. *Research in Organizational Behavior, 21*, 201–246.
Tyler, T. R., & Blader, S. L. (2001). Identity and cooperative behavior in groups. *Group Processes and Intergroup Relations, 4*(3), 207–226.
Tyler, T. R., & Hastie, R. (1991). The social consequences of cognitive illusions. In M. Bazerman, R. Lewicki, & B. Sheppard (Eds.), *Research on negotiations in organizations: Handbook of negotiation research* (pp. 69–98). Greenwich: JAI Press.
Tyler, T. R., & Lind, E. A. (1992). A relational model of authority in groups. In M. P. Zanna (Ed.), *Advances in experimental social psychology* (pp. 115–191). San Diego: Academic.
Uhl-Bien, M., Graen, G. B., & Scandura, T. (2000). Implications of leader–member exchange for strategic human resource management systems: Relationships as social capital for competitive advantage. In G. Ferris (Ed.), *Research in personnel and human resource management* (pp. 137–185). Greenwich: JAI Press.
Van den Bos, K. (2001a). Fairness heuristic theory: Assessing the information to which people are reacting has a pivotal role in understanding organizational justice. In S. W. Gilliland, D. D. Steiner, & D. P. Skarlicki (Eds.), *Theoretical and cultural perspectives on organizational justice* (pp. 63–84). Greenwich: Information Age Publishing.
Van den Bos, K. (2001b). Uncertainty management: The influence of uncertainty salience on reactions to perceived procedural fairness. *Journal of Personality and Social Psychology, 80*(6), 931–941.
Van den Bos, K., & Lind, E. A. (2002). Uncertainty management by means of fairness judgments. In M. P. Zanna (Ed.), *Advances in experimental social psychology* (pp. 1–60). Boston: Elsevier.
Walker, I., & Pettigrew, T. F. (1984). Relative deprivation theory: An overview and conceptual critique. *British Journal of Social Psychology, 23*(4), 301–310.
Wayne, S. J., & Green, S. A. (1993). The effects of leader-member exchange on employee citizenship and impression management behavior. *Human Relations, 46*(12), 1431–1440.
Wayne, S. J., Shore, L. M., Bommer, W. H., & Tetrick, L. E. (2002). The role of fair treatment and rewards in perceptions of organizational support and leadermember exchange. *Journal of Applied Psychology, 87*(3), 590–598.
Weiss, D. J., Dawis, R. V., England, G. W., & Lofquist, L. H. (1967). *Manual for the Minnesota satisfaction questionnaire* (Minnesota studies in vocational rehabilitation: XXII). Minneapolis: University of Minnesota Industrial Relations Center.

Chapter 5
Relationship Between Organisational Justice, Organisational Citizenship Behaviour, Job Satisfaction and Leader–Member Exchange

Abstract This chapter provides a critical review of the empirical association that may exist between perceptions of justice, job satisfaction, leader–member exchange and organisational citizenship behaviour. This chapter acts as a guide for academicians and, particularly practitioners, to understand the interactions between organisational justice, organisational citizenship behaviour, job satisfaction and leader–member exchange. It highlights the spiralling effects of these interactions that ultimately affect the bottom line of an organisation. This analysis designed to help human capital professionals understand current issues and global trends in the justice–citizenship relationship, aids in identifying best practices that can be applied in organisations in order to attain employer of choice status. Based on the arguments in the literature, a theoretical framework for the study is proposed and research hypotheses developed. This review proposes the underpinning for testing the hypotheses in an attempt to answer the research questions and provides the basis for further analysis in the following chapters.

Introduction

This chapter provides a critical review of the empirical association that may exist between perceptions of justice, job satisfaction, leader–member exchange and organisational citizenship behaviour. Building upon the ongoing stream of research, this chapter intends to shed light on conceptual debates over research on organisational justice, organisational citizenship behaviour, job satisfaction and leader–member exchange. Based on the theoretical foundations regarding these constructs in Chaps. 3 and 4, this chapter seeks to understand the relationships between organisational justice and organisational citizenship behaviour, organisational justice and job satisfaction, organisational justice and leader–member exchange, job satisfaction and organisational citizenship behaviour, leader–member exchange and organisational citizenship behaviour and the mediating role of job satisfaction and leader–member exchange in the organisational justice–organisational citizenship behaviour relationship. An exhaustive literature review would unearth current research issues that could be further explored to explicate matters that merit further attention. Identifying the gap and then researching on it contribute to theory and practice.

L.W. Hooi, *Organisational Justice and Citizenship Behaviour in Malaysia*,
Governance and Citizenship in Asia, DOI 10.1007/978-981-10-0030-0_5

By setting out to validate the link between organisational justice, organisational citizenship behaviour, job satisfaction and leader–member exchange, this chapter seeks to contribute to the literature by identifying the significance of each organisational justice component on each dimension of organisational citizenship behaviour, providing a clearer understanding of the association between organisational justice and organisational citizenship behaviour by testing job satisfaction and leader–member exchange as mediating variables and advancing empirical evidence on the use of organisational justice to develop job satisfaction and leader–member exchange as a key strategy for enhancing organisational citizenship behaviour. Furthermore, the study responds to calls for more consensus on the nature of the link between these constructs (Fassina et al. 2008; Organ 1988b, 1990). Scholars have repeatedly call for a better understanding of the link and propose that it is construct clean-up time for the organisational citizenship behaviour literature (e.g. Fassina et al. 2008; Organ 1997) though the black box in-between has received less attention. Specifically, the overall impact of organisational justice on organisational citizenship behaviour is expected to strengthen through its role in enhancing job satisfaction and leader–member exchange.

This chapter acts as a guide for academicians and, particularly practitioners, to understand the interactions between organisational justice, organisational citizenship behaviour, job satisfaction and leader–member exchange. It highlights the spiralling effects of these interactions that ultimately affect the bottom line of an organisation. Hence, this chapter aims at getting a better understanding of the organisational justice factors that influence organisational citizenship behaviour and the roles of job satisfaction and leader–member exchange in the relationship. This analysis designed to help human capital professionals understand current issues and global trends in the justice–citizenship relationship, aids in identifying best practices that can be applied in organisations in order to attain employer of choice status. Based on the arguments in the literature, a theoretical framework for the study is proposed and research hypotheses developed. This review proposes the underpinning for testing the hypotheses in an attempt to answer the research questions and provides the basis for further analysis in the following chapters. This would contribute towards theory building in organisational citizenship behaviour research in the manufacturing sector.

Organisational Justice and Organisational Citizenship Behaviour

One of the predictors of organisational citizenship behaviour is the perception of organisational justice (Cohen-Charash and Spector 2001; Colquitt et al. 2001; Hassan and Mohd Noor 2008; Organ and Paine 1999; Podsakoff et al. 2000). According to many studies, organisational justice seems to be a key determinant of work outcomes such as organisational citizenship behaviour (Abdullah and Mohd

Nasurdin 2008; Konovsky and Pugh 1994; Lo et al. 2006; Materson et al. 2000; Moorman 1991; Moorman et al. 1993, 1998; Niehoff and Moorman 1993; Organ and Ryan 1995; Williams et al. 2002). Moorman (1991) argues that employees may reciprocate by displaying organisational citizenship behaviour if employees perceive a culture of fairness that leads to global organisational evaluations.

Perceived organisational justice and organisational citizenship behaviours have frequently been studied separately (e.g. Allen and Rush 1998; Chen et al. 1998; Sheppard et al. 1992; Skarlicki and Folger 1997), as well as in conjunction with each other (e.g. Ball et al. 1994; Moorman 1991). Ball et al. (1994) in their study on the effects of perceived unjust punishment on organisational citizenship behaviour found that subordinates tend to engage in organisational citizenship behaviours and avoid anti-citizenship behaviours when perceived organisational justice (i.e. control over punishment procedures and imposed punishment) is high. Moorman (1991) finds a causal relationship between perceived organisational justice and organisational citizenship behaviour initially. However, upon further investigation, this was limited to interactional justice and organisational citizenship behaviour, akin to Skarlicki and Folger's (1997) findings. Thus, organisational justice and organisational citizenship behaviour are not completely separate and unrelated ideas. Indubitably, organisational justice is able to elicit citizenship behaviours in many cases, and citizenship behaviours are the mainstay in many organisations with high organisational justice.

Employee perceptions of organisational justice likely lead to organisational citizenship behaviour (Organ and Konovsky 1989) as employees may change their mindset with regard to their relationship with the organisation if they are treated fairly (Erturk 2007). Fair and unfair treatment, especially pertaining to interactional and procedural justice, helps employees to critically review the nature of their relationships with an organisation and its authorities (e.g. Moorman 1991; Organ 1988b). Tansky (1993) posits that procedural justice and fair treatment from managers and supervisors seem to be the most important component to the relationship between justice and organisational citizenship behaviour. Thus, organisational citizenship behaviour would probably be more enhanced if employees perceived that they received fair treatment from their organisations. Fair treatment would likely encourage employees to engage in unrewarded, extra-role behaviours that are beneficial to the organisation (Eskew 1993; Hassan and Mohd Noor 2008). Employees who perceive unfair treatment are much more likely to adhere to negative reciprocity norms and may withdraw their organisational citizenship behaviour. Based on economic exchange, employees restore equity through withdrawing organisational citizenship behaviour (Adams 1965) and restricting their effort to satisfying only the contractual obligations (Greenberg and Scott 1996; Organ 1988b). Generally, relative to procedural and interactional justice, distributive justice is more closely tied to economic, rather than social exchange (e.g. Konovsky and Pugh 1994).

Similarly, Organ and Ryan (1995) find that perceptions of fairness correlate with organisational citizenship behaviour. For example, fairness in pay is associated with both the altruism and generalised compliance factors of organisational citizenship behaviour (Organ and Konovsky 1989). Williams et al. (2002) obtain similar results that show that organisational justice components have strong positive effects on organisational citizenship behaviour. Likewise, Robinson and Morrison (1995) argue that employees are less likely to engage in civic behaviour if they perceive that their employer has failed to fulfil employment obligations. Fair procedures move people to support the needs of the group and augment organisational citizenship behaviour (Moorman and Blakely 1995). In addition, meta-analytic data show positive correlations between both procedural and distributive justice and organisational citizenship behaviour (Cohen-Charash and Spector 2001; Colquitt et al. 2001; Farh et al. 1997; Folger 1987; Konovsky and Organ 1996; LePine et al. 2002; Moorman and Byrne 2005; Nadiri and Tanova 2010).

Studies on perceptions of distributive justice on organisational citizenship behaviour focused mainly on professional employees (Giap et al. 2005). Past research ascertain that perceptions of job equity and pay equity are significantly correlated with extra-role discretionary behaviour (Dittrich and Carrell 1979; Scholl et al. 1987). Fassina et al. (2008) assert that distributive justice accounted for unique variance in only civic virtue. Studies on the relationship between procedural justice and organisational citizenship behaviour have found a robust relationship between perceptions of procedural justice and organisational citizenship behaviour. Konovsky and Folger (1991) reveal a correlation between procedural justice and altruism, while Farh et al. (1990) contend that procedural justice accounts for unique variance with respect to altruism dimension of organisational citizenship behaviour. Similarly, studies show a positive relationship between procedural justice and four organisational citizenship behaviour dimensions (Niehoff and Moorman (1993)). However, Fassina et al. (2008) posit that procedural justice did not account for incremental variance in altruism, conscientiousness and courtesy. Nadiri and Tanova (2010) further assert that distributive justice tended to be a stronger predictor of organisational citizenship behaviour compared to procedural justice. However, perceptions of fairness will affect organisational citizenship behaviour only after perceived inequity (Folger 1993). Additionally, Tepper et al. (2001) conceive that the correlation between procedural justice and organisational citizenship behaviour is stronger for people who define organisational citizenship behaviour as extra-role than for those who define organisational citizenship behaviour as in-role.

Likewise, perceptions of interactional justice are instrumental in predicting organisational citizenship behaviour (Hassan and Jubari 2010; Moorman 1991). Fassina et al. (2008) confirm that interactional justice accounted for incremental variance in all dimensions of organisational citizenship behaviour. In accordance with the agent-system model presented, Masterson et al. (2000) and Lazar et al. (2007) affirm that interactional justice is related to organisational citizenship behaviours directed at the supervisor. Williams et al. (2002) assert that organisational citizenship behaviour increased with higher interactional justice. Similarly, Greenberg (1990) posits that interactional justice is positively associated with organisational citizenship behaviour. He observes that employees resort to non-organisational citizenship behaviour (commit theft) to fulfil contractual obligations if no explanations or apologies were offered for the unfair treatment. Although most empirical studies show a positive relationship between perceptions of justice and fairness and the organisational citizenship behaviours of employees (Dittrich and Carrell 1979; Farh et al. 1990; Konovsky and Folger 1991; Moorman 1991; Scholl et al. 1987), Giap et al. (2005) stress that the only significant correlation is that between altruism and interpersonal justice. This indicates that individuals would like to do extra-role work to help when their supervisors treat them respectfully. Hence, managers might be able to induce most types of organisational citizenship behaviour through demonstrating interactional justice (Bies and Moag 1986) – by treating employees with dignity and respect and by providing explanations for decisions and events that affect them.

This study will extend prior research by testing a model that investigates the relationship between perceptions of organisational justice (in the form of distributive, procedural and interactional justice) and dimensions of organisational citizenship behaviour in the manufacturing industry in Malaysia. To verify if organisational justice does indeed have a greater influence on organisational citizenship behaviour, the study aims to test the following hypotheses:

H1: Employee perceptions of organisational justice positively influence the dimensions of organisational citizenship behaviour.
H1a: Employee perceptions of distributive justice positively influence the dimensions of organisational citizenship behaviour.
H1b: Employee perceptions of procedural justice positively influence the dimensions of organisational citizenship behaviour.
H1c: Employee perceptions of interactional justice positively influence the dimensions of organisational citizenship behaviour.

Organisational Justice and Job Satisfaction

Numerous studies have confirmed the relationship between organisational justice and satisfaction at the workplace. Employees' feelings of inequity are associated with dissatisfaction (Brief 1998). Similarly, perceptions of organisational justice affect employees' job satisfaction and organisational commitment (Price and Mueller 1986). McFarlin and Rice (1992: 51) using equity-based concepts report that 'psychological comparison processes play an important role in determining satisfaction with particular job facets'. Likewise, other studies attest that perceptions of fairness affect motivation and subsequently job satisfaction (Folger and Cropanzano 1998; Greenberg 1990). Research also shows that employees' perception of fair treatment in the allocation process enhances employees' satisfaction with supervisors (Alexander and Ruderman 1987; Fields et al. 2000; Folger and Konovsky 1989; Konovsky and Cropanzano 1991; Schaubroeck et al. 1994; Sweeney and McFarlin 1993).

Research in the justice domain revealed that perceptions of justice are related to organisational satisfaction. Studies include satisfaction with management (Alexander and Ruderman 1987; Fryxell and Gordon 1989), satisfaction with pay

(Folger and Konovsky 1989; Greenberg 1987; Konovsky et al. 1987; Miceli and Lane 1991; Roch and Shanock 2006; Sheppard et al. 1992; St. Onge 2000; Sweeney and McFarlin 1993; Tremblay et al. 2000; Welbourne 1998) and job satisfaction and intent to quit (Alexander and Ruderman 1987; Ball et al. 1994; Cohen-Charash and Spector 2001; Colquitt et al. 2001; Hendrix et al. 1999; Latham and Pinder 2005; McFarlin and Sweeney 1992). Additionally, perceptions of fairness of outcomes or procedures have contributed significantly to other organisational phenomena such as organisational commitment (Flaherty and Pappas 2000; Rhoades et al. 2001), job performance (Alder and Tompkins 1997; Ball et al. 1994) and prosocial behaviour (Colquitt et al. 2001; Masterson et al. 2000; Murphy et al. 2006; Williams et al. 2002) which may be related to job satisfaction.

Fields et al. (2000) posit a correlation between procedural justice and job satisfaction. Others affirm that procedural fairness enhances job satisfaction (Bartol 1979; Igbaria and Greenhouse 1992; Korsgaard et al. 1995; Nadiri and Tanova 2010; Quarles 1994). Ismail et al. (2011) maintain that interactional justice significantly correlates with job satisfaction. Additionally, considerable research links rude and disrespect treatment from authorities (interactional injustice) with job satisfaction (Cohen-Charash and Spector 2001; Colquitt et al. 2001). Others (e.g. Folger and Konovsky 1989; James 1993; McFarlin and Sweeney 1992; Sweeney and McFarlin 1993, 1997) assert that both distributive justice and procedural justice affect job satisfaction. Prior research indicates that distributive justice is a significant predictor of pay satisfaction. Distributive justice tends to have a stronger link with job satisfaction probably because of recent rewards and recognition. This relationship is stronger for males (Brockner and Adsit 1986; Sweeney and McFarlin 1997), while the effect of procedural justice on job satisfaction is more significant for women.

Although research shows a positive correlation between organisational justice and job satisfaction, the impact of the different components varies. In some studies, it is observed that the relationships with pay satisfaction and organisational satisfaction are stronger for distributive justice than for procedural justice (Sweeney and McFarlin 1993; Tremblay et al. 2000). On the contrary, other studies show that procedural justice is more strongly related than distributive justice is to job satisfaction (Schaubroeck et al. 1994). Cropanzano et al. (2002) confirm that procedural justice and not interactional justice was more strongly associated with performance appraisal system satisfaction. In a meta-analytic study, Colquitt et al. (2001) affirm that three types of organisational justice perceptions (including interactional justice) correlate with each other. The study shows that all the three justice dimensions are related to job satisfaction, organisational commitment, evaluation of authority, prosocial behaviours and employee withdrawal behaviours.

Prior research shows that the lack of equity in promotion has affected employees' satisfaction with the job (Dailey and Kirk 1992; McFarlin and Sweeney 1992) and pay (Folger and Konovsky 1989; McFarlin and Sweeney 1992). Promotion is a powerful source of motivation and satisfaction (Campbell et al. 1970; Igbaria and Greenhouse 1992; Rosenbaum 1984), and an employee's career mobility that is constrained by unfair practices is likely to result in job dissatisfaction, which will affect organisational commitment. Additionally, Lemons and Jones (2001) reiterate that employees are more likely to be satisfied with organisational outcomes when high procedural justice in promotion decisions exists. Promoted people who perceive high procedural justice in the decision will show a moderately higher level of job satisfaction than promoted people who do not perceive high procedural justice. This is probably because those who receive a promotion are unlikely to question if the procedures are fair or unfair. In contrast, non-promoted managers will ponder over the failure to secure a promotion. In doing so, non-promoted managers will try to understand the procedure by which promotion decisions were made. Those who perceive low procedural justice will be particularly dissatisfied with their career. Those not promoted are more likely to exhibit higher job satisfaction if they perceived that the procedure was fair (Lorsh and Takagi 1987). They might decide to stay and to maintain positive attitudes and behaviours. Thus, job satisfaction results clearly show that procedural justice plays a pivotal role in determining managers' attitudes. Non-promoted managers will decide to leave only if they perceive low procedural justice in their careers (Bagdadli et al. 2006; Dailey and Kirk 1992). If they decide to stay, it is likely they will be less committed, less productive and less accommodating and will demonstrate withdrawal behaviours. Hence,

H2: Employee perceptions of organisational justice positively influence job satisfaction.

H2a: Employee perceptions of distributive justice positively influence job satisfaction.

H2b: Employee perceptions of procedural justice positively influence job satisfaction.

H2c: Employee perceptions of interactional justice positively influence job satisfaction.

Organisational Justice and Leader–Member Exchange

In the workplace, superior's interaction with the subordinates is unavoidable, and it is imperative that both parties form a quality relationship to enhance harmony at the workplace and other organisational phenomena. Though little is known about the relationship between leader–member exchange and organisational justice (Pillai et al. 1999), studies have shown that leader–member exchange is positively related to procedural and interactional justice (e.g. Alexander and Ruderman 1987; Manogran et al. 1994). Additionally, Cropanzano et al. (2002) found that leader–member exchange was more strongly related to interactional justice than procedural justice. Masterson et al. (2000) affirm that interactional justice and leader–member exchange are closely related constructs as actions by the supervisor affect employee attitudes associated with exchanges with the supervisor. The quality of relationship between leader and members to a considerable extent is affected by perceived fairness of decisions made. Perceived equity improves the quality of leader–member exchange relationship and enhances employees' trust in superiors (Aquino et al. 1997; Kim and Mauborgne 1998; Korsgaard et al. 1995; Naumann and Bennett 2000). The results of past research indicate a significant relationship between each component of organisational justice and trust in the supervisor (Camerman et al. 2007; Konovsky and Pugh 1994; Stinglhamber et al. 2006). Some empirical studies found that procedural justice affects trust (Folger and Konovsky 1989; Lind and Tyler 1988; McFarlin and Sweeney 1992). Employees' trust in their superiors would probably be higher if their superiors were more procedurally fair (Brockner and Siegel 1996; Konovsky and Pugh 1994). Brockner et al. (1997) find that trust based on procedural justice interacts with outcome favourability to influence employees' reactions.

Likewise, it is important that interactional justice in a subordinate/supervisor relationship is high to combat counterproductive work behaviour. Perceived interactional injustice creates resentment towards the supervisor or institution (Aryee et al. 2007) and reduces the effectiveness of organisational communication (Baron and Neuman 1996). Interactional justice, which focuses on interaction with the supervisor, is linked to supervisory trust (Ambrose and Schminke 2003; Hopkins and Weathington 2006; Moorman et al. 1998; Roch and Shanock 2006; Stinglhamber et al. 2006). DeConnick (2010) reiterates the link between interactional justice and perceived supervisor support and supervisory trust. To enhance interactional justice, the supervisor has to explain the procedures involved, ascertain employee perceptions of the procedures, communicate with the employee, make timely decisions and tailor decisions to meet the specific needs of the employee. Roch and Shanock (2006) verify that informational justice, interpersonal justice and interactional justice affect leader–member exchange significantly. However, when considered simultaneously, only interactional justice is significantly related to leader–member exchange. Additionally, Hassan and Jubari (2010) affirm that distributive and interactional justice promote leader–member exchange – the latter stronger than the former. However, Cohen-Charash and Spector (2001) contend that interactional justice has a stronger relationship with leader–member exchange than procedural and distributive justice. Roch and Shanock (2006) assert that as informational justice is significantly related to leader–member exchange, there is a need for justice researchers to investigate this justice type in more depth. In response to this, this study attempts to determine if each justice dimension is indeed uniquely associated with leader–member exchange. Thus, it is argued that there might be a correlation between perceptions of organisational justice and the quality of leader–member exchange relationship. Accordingly,

H3: Employee perceptions of organisational justice positively influence leader–member exchange.

H3a: Employee perceptions of distributive justice positively influence leader–member exchange.

H3b: Employee perceptions of procedural justice positively influence leader–member exchange.

H3c: Employee perceptions of interactional justice positively influence leader–member exchange.

Job Satisfaction and Organisational Citizenship Behaviour

Job satisfaction is traditionally conceptualised as beliefs and feelings regarding one's job in general (Locke 1976) or specific facets of one's job (Smith et al. 1969). Building on social exchange theories (Bateman and Organ 1983), individuals may engage in organisational citizenship behaviour to reciprocate general job satisfaction (Nadiri and Tanova 2010; Podsakoff et al. 2000), which is influenced by satisfaction with aspects of the work environment (e.g. Smith et al. 1969) or task characteristics (e.g. Hackman and Oldham 1980). In essence, satisfied employee, due in part to favourable task characteristics or to other aspects of their work environment, may repay their employer through organisational citizenship behaviour. Moreover, satisfied employees experience more positive affect at work (Judge and Ilies 2004) and are more likely to engage in prosocial behaviour. Satisfied employees may also engage in organisational citizenship behaviour for instrumental motives – to protect their status as valued employees, thereby increasing their job security. Employees who go 'the extra mile' are more likely to survive layoffs or mergers.

Brown (1985) asserts that individuals with higher job satisfaction are more likely to experience positive mood states, and, hence, a greater inclination to engage in extra-role behaviour (Organ 1977). Positive mood states at work promote organisational citizenship behaviour above and beyond fairness perceptions (George 1991). Many other studies established an association between an employee's overall job satisfaction and organisational citizenship behaviour in a variety of research settings (Organ and Ryan 1995; Williams and Anderson 1991). Nonetheless, literature on the direct effect of job satisfaction on organisational citizenship behaviour does not suggest any consensus. Literature indicates that there might be a correlation between job satisfaction and organisational citizenship behaviour as well as a correlation between job dissatisfaction and organisational citizenship behaviour if dissatisfaction is expressed in an active matter (Appelbaum et al. 2004).

Prior empirical studies (e.g. Bateman and Organ 1983; Foote and Tang 2008; Graham 1986; Moorman 1993; Motowidlo 1984; Motowidlo et al. 1986; Organ and Konovsky 1989; Organ and Ryan 1995; Puffer 1987; Scholl et al. 1987; Smith et al. 1983; Wagner and Rush 2000) and the conceptual rationale proposed by Organ (1988a, 1990) reveal a positive relationship between job satisfaction and organisational citizenship behaviour. Similarly, other studies have indicated significant correlations between job satisfaction and organisational citizenship behaviour. Murphy et al. (2002) found a correlation of between 0.40 and 0.67 in the job satisfaction–organisational citizenship behaviour relationship, while Smith et al. (1983) established a correlation of 0.33 between job satisfaction and altruism and 0.29 between job satisfaction and compliance (conscientiousness). Robbins (2001) suggests there is a modest overall relationship between job satisfaction and organisational citizenship behaviour. Tansky (1993) confirms that job satisfaction on its own related positively to courtesy, civic virtue, altruism and sportsmanship. Fassina et al. (2008) concluded that job satisfaction consistently accounted for the unique variance in all dimensions of organisational citizenship behaviour. Further, Organ and his colleagues (Organ 1988a, 1990; Organ and Near 1985; Organ and Konovsky 1989) contend that it is the cognitive rather than the affective dimension of job satisfaction that significantly affects organisational citizenship behaviour. Essentially, how individuals cognitively determine why they are satisfied educe organisational citizenship behaviour though emotions or feelings induced by job satisfaction may stimulate citizenship behaviours as well.

However, some researchers maintain that job satisfaction (Organ 1988b; Smith et al. 1969) and job dissatisfaction (Herzberg et al. 1959) are significantly influenced by issues pertaining to fairness. Some literature suggests that if a lack of fairness is perceived, there is no correlation between job satisfaction and organisational citizenship behaviour (Appelbaum et al. 2004). Organ (1988a, b, 1990) asserts that determination of fairness is a key cognition in estimating job satisfaction. He argues that the relationship between job satisfaction and organisational citizenship behaviour reflects a relationship between perceptions of fairness and organisational citizenship behaviour. That is, the cognitive component of job satisfaction that appears to be related to organisational citizenship behaviour probably reflects the perceptions of fairness. Similarly, perceptions of fairness, and not job satisfaction, would be related to organisational citizenship behaviour if job satisfaction and perceptions of fairness were both measured (Moorman 1991; Nadiri and Tanova 2010). Moorman (1991) opines that the relationship between job satisfaction and organisational citizenship behaviour simply indicates the extent to which job satisfaction measures include job fairness.

Because of the conceptual distinctions between organisational justice and job satisfaction, it is perhaps better to consider these constructs separately in the prediction of organisational citizenship behaviour. Since justice and job satisfaction are likely distinguishable from each other and in their relationships to organisational citizenship behaviour, this study seeks to clarify the association between job satisfaction and organisational citizenship behaviour. Besides, there is a lack of consensus about the specific role of job satisfaction in predicting organisational citizenship behaviour in tandem with fairness perceptions (Fassina et al. 2008). Hence,

H4: Job satisfaction positively influences the dimensions of organisational citizenship behaviour.

Leader–Member Exchange and Organisational Citizenship Behaviour

Empirical research on the leader–member exchange–organisational citizenship behaviour relationship has received widespread interest in the past two decades (Wang et al. 2005; Wayne et al. 2002). Many other studies have also emphasised the importance of the leader–member exchange relationship on organisational citizenship behaviour (Basu and Green 1995; Deluga 1994; Hassan and Chandaran 2005; Hassan and Jubari 2010; Moorman 1991; Niehoff and Moorman 1993; Podsakoff et al. 1990, 2000; Wang et al. 2005; Wayne and Green 1993; Zhong et al. 2011). The social exchange theory posits that employees can develop a relationship between both the organisation and supervisor (Settoon et al. 1996). In social exchanges, trust is an important element for a continuous relationship. Feelings of trust in the leader–member exchange relationship will result in long-term reciprocal obligations (Rhoades and Eisenberger 2002). Trust in supervisors involves day-to-day interaction between supervisors and employees and is associated with organisational citizenship behaviours (Tan and Tan 2000). In addition to trust, the extent to which the superior values the employee's contributions also affects the quality of leader–member exchange relationship. If subordinates feel that they receive more than they give to the supervisors or organisations, they are likely to restore equity by engaging in organisational citizenship behaviour.

Moorman (1991) maintains that only interactional justice which focuses on interactions with superiors/supervisors relates significantly to organisational citizenship behaviour. His findings show that subordinates rated highly by their superiors on organisational citizenship behaviour perceive better quality of their relationship with their superiors. It is also likely that these subordinates will rate their superiors highly. Similarly, high-quality leader–member exchange can motivate the subordinates to engage in behaviours beyond job scope (Hui et al. 1999; Ilies et al. 2007; Zhong et al. 2011). Employees engage in discretionary organisational citizenship behaviour to reciprocate the support and mutual benefits from supervisors (Settoon et al. 1996; Zhong et al. 2011). Additionally, a meta-analytic study shows a mean correlation of 0.32 between leader–member exchange and overall organisational citizenship behaviour (Lapierre and Hackett 2007). Thus,

H5: Leader–member exchange positively influences the dimensions of organisational citizenship behaviour.

Mediators in the Justice–Citizenship Relationship

Prior empirical studies show that job satisfaction may relate to organisational citizenship behaviour directly (e.g. Organ and Ryan 1995) or mediates the relationship between organisational justice and organisational citizenship behaviour (e.g. Netemeyer et al. 1997; Tansky 1993). Other studies reveal that organisational justice is a common predictor of both job satisfaction and organisational citizenship behaviour (e.g. Farh et al. 1990). The notion that job satisfaction is influenced by perceived fairness (Herzberg et al. 1959; Organ 1988b; Smith et al. 1969) suggests that job satisfaction potentially mediates the relationship between organisational justice and organisational citizenship behaviour. However, prior studies on this show modest support for the mediating role of job satisfaction in the organisational justice–organisational citizenship behaviour relationship (e.g. Netemeyer et al. 1997; Tansky 1993). Moreover, these studies reveal that organisational justice rather than job satisfaction is a more important predictor of organisational citizenship behaviour (e.g. Alotaibi 2001; Farh et al. 1990; McNeely and Meglino 1994; Moorman 1991; Organ 1990; Organ and Konovsky 1989; Tansky 1993).

On the contrary, some studies have shown that job satisfaction accounted for the variance in some dimensions of organisational citizenship behaviour beyond that explained by organisational justice (e.g. Farh et al. 1990; McNeely and Meglino 1994). Tansky (1993) asserts that job satisfaction explains unique variance above and beyond perceived fairness in civic virtue and courtesy. Similarly, Organ and Ryan (1995: 794) reveal that the zero-order relationships between job satisfaction and organisational justice with organisational citizenship behaviour 'do not encourage any supposition that any one of them mediates the effects of the others, or that any one of them 'accounts for' the relationships between the others and organisational citizenship behaviour'. The reason for this is attributed to Adams's (1965) equity theory. Since unfairness will create tension within a person, changing of one's level of organisational citizenship behaviour is likely to be a response to inequity. Another explanation is based on Blau's (1964) social exchange theory where an individual's relationship with the organisation is one of social exchange. Employees may be more likely to demonstrate organisational citizenship behaviour if they favour social exchange.

Thus, there is a lack of consensus on the precise role of job satisfaction in predicting organisational citizenship behaviour in tandem with organisational justice. Moreover, empirical evidence within studies has been mixed on different dimensions of organisational citizenship behaviour (e.g. Farh et al. 1990; Tansky 1993). The lack of consensus has stymied theory and research development on organisational citizenship behaviour and its predictors and restricted guidance for managerial practice (Fassina et al. 2008). Hence, it is imperative to understand the specific role of job satisfaction in the organisational justice–organisational citizenship behaviour relationship. If job satisfaction directly predicts organisational citizenship behaviour or mediates the relationship between organisational justice and organisational citizenship behaviour, then managers may be able to promote organisational citizenship behaviour by attending to various antecedents of job satisfaction. Otherwise, managers may foster organisational citizenship behaviour by promoting perceived fairness if perceived fairness uniquely explains organisational citizenship behaviour and job satisfaction does not.

Additionally, perception of fairness promotes social exchange relationships between employees and their supervisors (Organ 1988a) and leads to employee citizenship behaviour. When an employee perceives that a decision is fair, the employee will assume that future decisions will be fair. Thus, mutual reciprocation over time will augment quality leader–member exchange relationship and may instigate organisational citizenship behaviours. Procedural justice increases employee's trust in supervisor, and, hence, organisational citizenship behaviour (Aycan 2001; Konovsky and Pugh 1994). Studies by Giap et al. (2005) and Erturk (2007) attest that trust in supervisors mediates the relationship between organisational justice and organisational citizenship behaviour. Similarly, Hassan and Jubari (2010) contend that leader–member exchange fully mediates the relationship between interactional justice and organisational citizenship behaviour. Moreover, Karriker and Williams (2009) establish that leader–member exchange is a mediator in the organisational justice–organisational citizenship behaviour relationship, in particular, agent-referenced distributive justice and agent-referenced procedural justice. Thus, the supervisor (justice source) determines the quality of leader–member exchange that promotes the employee's citizenship behaviours. Based on the norm of reciprocity (Gouldner 1960), employees are likely to reciprocate by engaging in organisational citizenship behaviour (Organ 1988a; Van Yperen et al. 1999) when employees perceive that their supervisors are treating them fairly and with respect. Similarly, Zhong et al. (2011) reiterate that to sustain a mutually beneficial relationship, subordinates are likely to engage in organisational citizenship behaviour to restore equity if they perceive that they receive more than they give to the supervisors. Nonetheless, the engagement of subordinates in organisational citizenship behaviour is affected by the quality of leader–member exchange they are engaged in. Accordingly,

H6: Job satisfaction and leader–member exchange mediate the relationship between organisational justice and organisational citizenship behaviour.

H6a: Job satisfaction mediates the relationship between organisational justice and organisational citizenship behaviour.

H6b: Leader–member exchange mediates the relationship between organisational justice and organisational citizenship behaviour.

Conclusion

This chapter has considered the relationships between organisational justice, job satisfaction, leader–member exchange and organisational citizenship behaviour. It provides an insight of the dynamics through which fairness perceptions affect organisational citizenship behaviour. A great deal of literature related to organisational citizenship behaviour has focused on the antecedents, while some studies integrated mediators in the justice–citizenship relationship. This chapter provides greater clarity around what these relationships involve and complements extant literature in contributing to the efforts towards building more comprehensive justice–citizenship behaviour models of organisations. An in-depth understanding of the various relationships enables management of organisations to decide more accurately on the appropriate actions to improve conditions at the workplace. This understanding is imperative as perceived organisational injustice, lower job satisfaction and poor quality leader–member exchange can lead to loss of dedicated high performers that may affect organisational sustainability.

Cohen and Vigoda (2000) insist that organisational citizenship behaviour is essential for practically all forms of organisations. Indubitably, for employees to reciprocate with organisational citizenship behaviours, employees' perception of justice is crucial. Breaching organisational justice not only hinders citizenship behaviours but also triggers negative behaviours that are detrimental to organisational effectiveness. Despite its significance, there is a dearth of research about the specific factors that promote organisational citizenship behaviours under differing organisational contexts (Erturk 2007). Considering the growing recognition in both professional and academic literature of management on the significance of discretionary behaviours on organisational effectiveness and performance, it is vital that practitioners understand the dynamics of organisational citizenship behaviours. This chapter has provided an in-depth review of related literature on justice–citizenship and some mediators that have been noted in past research. A thorough comprehension of all the four constructs of the current study is imperative to enhance managerial effectiveness. Generally, authorities find it really difficult to be impartial in real time, despite knowing what constitutes fairness. To sustain organisational citizenship behaviour, organisations may promote a culture of justice to improve job satisfaction and the quality of leader–member exchange.

References

Abdullah, M. H., & Mohd Nasurdin, A. (2008). Investigating the influence of organizational justice on hotel employees' organizational citizenship behavior intentions and turnover intentions. *Journal of Human Resources in Hospitality & Tourism, 7*(1), 1–23.

Adams, J. S. (1965). Inequity in social exchange. In L. Berkowitz (Ed.), *Advances in experimental social psychology* (Vol. 2, pp. 267–299). New York: Academic.

Alder, S. A., & Tompkins, P. K. (1997). Electronic performance monitoring: An organizational justice and concretive control perspective. *Management Communications Quarterly, 10*(3), 259–289.

Alexander, S., & Ruderman, M. (1987). The role of procedural and distributive justice in organisational behavior. *Social Justice Research, 1*(2), 177–198.

Allen, T. D., & Rush, M. C. (1998). The effects of organizational citizenship behavior on performance judgements: A field study and a laboratory experiment. *Journal of Applied Psychology, 83*(2), 247–260.

Alotaibi, B. N. (2001). *The use of constant time delay in the acquisition of incidental learning when teaching sight word recognition to students with moderate and severe disabilities*. PhD dissertation.

Ambrose, M. L., & Schminke, M. (2003). Organizations structure as a moderator of the perceived relationship between procedural justice, interactional justice, perceived organizational support, and supervisory trust. *Journal of Applied Psychology, 88*(2), 295–305.

Appelbaum, S., Bartolomucci, N., Beaumier, E., Boulanger, J., Corrigan, R., Doré, I., Girard, C., & Serroni, C. (2004). Organizational citizenship behavior: A case study of culture, leadership and trust. *Management Decision, 42*(1), 13–40.

Aquino, K., Griffeth, R. W., Allen, D. G., & Hom, P. W. (1997). Integrating justice constructs into the turnover process: A test of a referent cognitions model. *Academy of Management Journal, 40*(5), 1208–1227.

Aryee, S., Chen, Z. X., Sun, L. Y., & Debrah, Y. A. (2007). Antecedents and outcomes of abusive supervision: Test of a trickle-down model. *Journal of Applied Psychology, 92*(1), 191–201.

Aycan, Z. (2001). Human resource management in Turkey: Current issues and future challenges. *International Journal of Manpower, 22*(3), 252–260.
Bagdadli, S., Roberson, Q., & Paoletti, F. (2006). The mediating role of procedural justice in responses to promotion decisions. *Journal of Business and Psychology, 21*(1), 83–102.
Ball, G. A., Trevino, L. K., & Sims, H. P., Jr. (1994). Just and unjust punishment: Influences on subordinate performance and citizenship. *Academy of Management Journal, 37*(2), 299–322.
Baron, R. A., & Neuman, J. H. (1996). Workplace violence and workplace aggression: Evidence of their relative frequency and potential causes. *Aggressive Behavior, 22*(3), 161–173.
Bartol, K. (1979). Individual versus organizational predictors of job satisfactions and turnover among professionals. *Journal of Vocational Behavior, 15*(1), 55–67.
Basu, R., & Green, S. G. (1995). Subordinate performance, leader-subordinate compatibility, and exchange quality in leader-member dyads: A field study. *Journal of Applied Social Psychology, 25*(1), 77–92.
Bateman, T. S., & Organ, D. W. (1983). Job satisfaction and the good soldier: The relationship between affect and employee citizenship. *Academy of Management Journal, 26*(4), 587–595.
Bies, R. J., & Moag, J. F. (1986). Interactional justice: Communication criteria of fairness. In R. J. Lewicki, B. H. Sheppard, & M. H. Bazerman (Eds.), *Research on negotiations in organizations* (pp. 43–55). Greenwich: JAI Press.
Blau, P. (1964). *Exchange and power in social life*. New York: Wiley.
Brief, A. P. (1998). *Attitudes in and around organizations*. Thousand Oaks: Sage Publications.
Brockner, J., & Adsit, L. (1986). The moderating effect of sex on the equity-satisfaction relationship. *Journal of Applied Psychology, 71*(4), 585–590.
Brockner, J., & Siegel, P. (1996). Understanding the interaction between procedural and distributive justice: The role of trust. In R. M. Kramer & T. R. Tyler (Eds.), *Trust in organizations – Frontiers of theory and research* (pp. 390–413). Thousand Oaks: Sage Publications.
Brockner, J., Siegel, P. A., Daly, J. P., Tyler, T., & Martin, C. (1997). When trust matters: The moderating effect of outcome favorability. *Administrative Science Quarterly, 42*(3), 558–583.
Brown, R. (1985). *Social psychology*. New York: Free Press.
Camerman, J., Cropanzano, R., & Vandenberghe, C. (2007). The benefits of justice for temporary workers. *Group and Organizational Management, 32*(2), 176–207.
Campbell, J. P., Dunette, M. D., Lawler, E. E., & Weick, K. E. (1970). *Managerial behavior, performance, and effectiveness*. New York: McGraw Hill.
Chen, X., Hui, C., & Sego, D. J. (1998). The role of organizational citizenship behavior in turnover: Conceptualization and preliminary tests of key hypotheses. *Journal of Applied Psychology, 83*(6), 922–931.
Cohen, A., & Vigoda, E. (2000). Do good citizens make good organizational citizens? An empirical examination of the relationship between general citizenship and organizational citizenship behavior in Israel. *Administration and Society, 32*, 596–625.
Cohen-Charash, Y., & Spector, P. E. (2001). The role of justice in organizations: A meta-analysis. *Organizational Behavior & Human Decision Processes, 86*(2), 278–321.
Colquitt, J. A., Conlon, D. E., Wesson, M. J., Porter, C. O. L. H., & Ng, K. Y. (2001). Justice at the millennium: A meta-analytic review of 25 years of organizational justice research. *Journal of Applied Psychology, 86*(3), 425–445.
Cropanzano, R., Prehar, C. A., & Chen, P. Y. (2002). Using social exchange theory to distinguish procedural from interactional justice. *Group and Organizational Management, 27*(3), 324–351.
Dailey, R. C., & Kirk, D. J. (1992). Distributive and procedural justice as antecedents of job dissatisfaction and intent to turnover. *Human Relations, 45*(3), 305–317.
DeConinck, J. B. (2010). The effect of organizational justice, perceived organizational support, and perceived supervisor support on marketing employees' level of trust. *Journal of Business Research, 63*(12), 1349–1355.
Deluga, R. J. (1994). Supervisor trust building, leader-member exchange and organizational citizenship behaviour. *Journal of Occupational and Organizational Psychology, 77*, 315–326.

Dittrich, J. E., & Carrell, M. R. (1979). Organizational equity perceptions, employee job satisfaction and departmental absence and turnover rates. *Organizational Behavior and Human Performance, 24*(1), 29–40.

Erturk, A. (2007). Increasing organizational citizenship behaviors of Turkish academicians: Mediating role of trust in supervisor on the relationship between organizational justice and citizenship behaviours. *Journal of Managerial Psychology, 22*(3), 257–270.

Eskew, D. E. (1993). The role of organizational justice in organizational citizenship behavior. *Employee Responsibilities and Rights Journal, 6*(3), 185–194.

Farh, J., Podsakoff, P. M., & Organ, D. W. (1990). Accounting for organizational citizenship behavior: Leader fairness and task scope versus satisfaction. *Journal of Management, 16*(4), 705–721.

Farh, J. L., Earley, P. C., & Lin, S. C. (1997). Impetus for action: A cultural analysis of justice and organizational citizenship behavior in Chinese society. *Administrative Science Quarterly, 42*(3), 421–444.

Fassina, N. E., Jones, D. A., & Uggerslev, K. L. (2008). Relationship clean-up time: Using meta analysis and path analysis to clarify relationships among job satisfaction, perceived fairness, and citizenship behaviors. *Journal of Management, 34*(2), 161–188.

Fields, D., Pang, M., & Chiu, C. (2000). A comparative field study of the effects of distributive and procedural justice in Hong Kong. *Journal of Organizational Behaviour, 21*(5), 547–562.

Flaherty, K. E., & Pappas, J. M. (2000). The role of trust in salesperson-sales manager relationship. *Journal of Personal Selling and Sales Management, 20*(4), 271–278.

Folger, R. (1987). Distributive and procedural justice in the workplace. *Social Justice Research, 1*(2), 143–159.

Folger, R. (1993). Justice, motivation, and performance beyond role requirements. *Employee Responsibilities and Rights Journal, 6*(3), 239–248.

Folger, R., & Cropanzano, R. (1998). *Organisational justice and human resource management.* Beverly Hills: Sage Publications.

Folger, R., & Konovsky, M. A. (1989). Effects of procedural and distributive justice on reactions to pay raise decisions. *Academy of Management Journal, 32*(1), 115–130.

Foote, D. A., & Tang, T. L. (2008). Job satisfaction and organizational citizenship behavior (OCB): Does team commitment make a difference in self-directed teams? *Management Decision, 46*(6), 933–947.

Fryxell, G. E., & Gordon, M. E. (1989). Workplace justice and job satisfaction as predictors of satisfaction with union and management. *Academy of Management Journal, 32*, 851–856.

George, J. M. (1991). State or trait: Effects of positive mood on prosocial behaviors at work. *Journal of Applied Psychology, 76*, 299–307.

Giap, B. N., Hackermeier, I., Jiao, X., & Wagdarikar, S. P. (2005). Organizational citizenship behavior and perception of organizational justice in student jobs. In: *Research study, psychology of excellence instructional design, job analysis & job design* (pp. 1–14). Munich: Ludwig-Maximilians-University.

Gouldner, A. (1960). The norm of reciprocity. *American Sociological Review, 25*(2), 165–167.

Graham, J. W. (1986). *Organizational citizenship informed by political theory*. Paper presented at the meeting of Academy of Management, Chicago.

Greenberg, J. (1987). A taxonomy of organizational justice theories. *Academy of Management Review, 12*(1), 9–22.

Greenberg, J. (1990). Looking fair vs. being fair: Managing impressions of organizational justice. In B. M. Shaw & L. L. Cummings (Eds.), *Research in organizational behavior* (pp. 111–157). Greenwich: JAI Press.

Greenberg, J., & Scott, K. S. (1996). Why do workers bite the hand that feeds them? Employee theft as a social exchange process. In B. M. Shaw & L. L. Cummings (Eds.), *Research in organizational behavior* (pp. 111–156). Greenwich: JAI Press.

Hackman, J. R., & Oldham, G. R. (1980). *Work redesign.* Reading: Addison Wesley.

Hassan, A., & Al Jubari, I. H. A. (2010). Organizational justice and employee work engagement: LMX as mediator. *Journal of International Business and Entrepreneurship Development, 5*(2), 167–178.

Hassan, A., & Chandaran, S. (2005). Quality of supervisors-subordinate relationship and work outcome: Organizational justice as mediator. *IIUM Journal of Economics and Management, 13*(1), 33–52.

Hassan, A., & Mohd Noor, K. (2008). Organizational justice and extra-role behavior: Examining the relationship in the Malaysian cultural context. *IIUM Journal of Economics and Management, 16*(2), 187–208.

Hendrix, W., Robbins, T., Miller, J., & Summers, T. P. (1999). *Procedural and distributive justice effects on turnover*. Paper presented at the Annual Meeting of the Society for Industrial and Organizational Psychology, Atlanta.

Herzberg, F., Mausner, B., & Snyderman, B. B. (1959). *The motivation to work* (2nd ed.). New York: Wiley.

Hopkins, S. M., & Weathington, B. L. (2006). The relationship between justice perceptions, trust, and employee attitudes in a downsized organization. *Journal of Psychology, 140*(5), 477–498.

Hui, C., Law, K. S., & Chen, Z. X. (1999). A structural equation model of the effects of negative affectivity, leader-member exchange, and perceived job mobility on in-role and extra-role performance: A Chinese case. *Organizational Behavior & Human Decision Processes, 77*(1), 3–21.

Igbaria, M., & Greenhouse, J. H. (1992). The career advancement prospects of managers and professionals: Are MIS employees unique? *Decision Sciences, 23*, 478–499.

Ilies, R., Nahrgang, J. D., & Morgeson, F. P. (2007). Leader-member exchange and citizenship behaviors: A meta-analysis. *Journal of Applied Psychology, 92*(1), 269–277.

Ismail, M. T., Abdul Karim, S. A., & Alwadi, S. (2011). A study of structural breaks in Malaysian stock market. *African Journal of Business Management, 5*(6), 2418–2425.

James, K. (1993). The social context of organizational justice: Cultural, intergroup and structural effects on justice behaviors and perceptions. In R. Cropanzano (Ed.), *Justice in the workplace: Approaching fairness in human resource management* (pp. 21–50). Hillsdale: Erlbaum.

Judge, T. A., & Ilies, R. (2004). Affect and job satisfaction: A study of their relationship at work and at home. *Journal of Applied Psychology, 89*, 661–673.

Karriker, J., & Williams, M. (2009). Organizational justice and organizational citizenship behavior: A mediated multifoci model. *Journal of Management, 35*(1), 112–135.

Kim, W. C., & Mauborgne, R. A. (1998). Procedural justice, strategic-decision making, and the knowledge economy. *Strategic Management Journal, 19*(4), 323–338.

Konovsky, M. A., & Cropanzano, R. (1991). Perceived fairness of employee drug testing as a predictor of employee attitudes and job performance. *Journal of Applied Psychology, 76*(5), 698–707.

Konovsky, M. A., & Folger, R. (1991). The effects of procedures, social accounts, and benefits level on victims' layoff reactions. *Journal of Applied Social Psychology, 21*(8), 630–650.

Konovsky, M. A., & Organ, D. W. (1996). Dispositional and contextual determinants of organizational citizenship behavior. *Journal of Organizational Behavior, 17*(3), 253–266.

Konovsky, M. A., & Pugh, S. D. (1994). Citizenship behavior and social exchange. *Academy of Management Journal, 37*(3), 656–669.

Konovsky, M. A., Folger, R., & Cropanzano, R. (1987). Relative effects of procedural and distributive justice on employee attitudes. *Representative Research in Social Psychology, 17*(1), 15–24.

Korsgaard, M. A., Schweiger, D. M., & Sapienza, H. J. (1995). Building commitment, attachment, and trust in strategic decision-making teams: The role of procedural justice. *Academy of Management Journal, 38*(1), 60–84.

Lapierre, L. M., & Hackett, R. D. (2007). Trait conscientiousness, leader-member exchange, job satisfaction and organizational citizenship behaviour: A test of a integrative model. *Journal of Occupational and Organizational Psychology, 80*(3), 539–554.

Latham, G., & Pinder, C. (2005). Work motivation theory and research at the dawn of the twenty-first century. *Annual Review of Psychology, 56*(1), 485–516.
Lazar, A., Zinger, A., & Lachterman, B. (2007). The influence of prefeedback selection justice on perceptions of overall procedural justice and organizational attractiveness in a real-life selection procedure. *European Journal of Work and Organizational Psychology, 16*(1), 94–109.
Lemons, M. A., & Jones, C. A. (2001). Procedural justice in promotion decisions: Using perceptions of fairness to build employee commitment. *Journal of Managerial Psychology, 16*(4), 268–280.
Lepine, J. A., Erez, A., & Johnson, D. E. (2002). The nature and dimensionality of organizational citizenship behavior: A critical review and meta-analysis. *Journal of Applied Psychology, 87*(1), 52–65.
Lind, E. A., & Tyler, T. R. (1988). *The social psychology of procedural justice*. New York: Plenum Press.
Lo, M. C., Ramayah, T., & Hui, J. K. S. (2006). An investigation of leader member exchange effects on organizational citizenship behavior in Malaysia. *Journal of Business and Management, 12*, 5–23.
Locke, E. (1976). The nature and causes of job satisfaction. In M. D. Dunnette (Ed.), *Handbook of industrial and organizational psychology* (pp. 1297–1349). Chicago: Rand McNally.
Lorsh, J. W., & Takagi, H. (1987). Keeping managers off the shelf. *Harvard Business Review, 64*(4), 60–65.
Manogran, P., Stauffer, J., & Conlon, E. J. (1994). Leader-member exchange as a key mediating variable between employees' perceptions of fairness and organizational citizenship behavior. In *National Academy of Management Meeting Proceedings*, Dallas.
Masterson, S. S., Lewis, K., Goldman, B. M., & Taylor, M. S. (2000). Integrating justice and social exchange: The differing effects of fair procedures and treatment of work relationships. *Academy of Management Journal, 43*(4), 738–748.
McFarlin, D. B., & Rice, R. W. (1992). The role of facet importance as a moderator in job satisfaction processes. *Journal of Organizational Behavior, 13*(1), 41–54.
McFarlin, D. B., & Sweeney, P. D. (1992). Distributive and procedural justice as predictors of satisfaction with personal and organisational outcomes. *Academy of Management Journal, 35*(3), 626–637.
McNeely, B. L., & Meglino, B. M. (1994). The role of dispositional and situational antecedents in prosocial organizational behavior: An examination of the intended beneficiaries of prosocial behavior. *Journal of Applied Psychology, 79*, 836–844.
Miceli, M. P., & Lane, M. C. (1991). Antecedents of pay satisfaction: A review and extension. In K. Rowland & G. R. Ferris (Eds.), *Research in personnel and human resource management* (pp. 235–309). Greenwich: JAI Press.
Moorman, R. H. (1991). Relationship between organizational justice and organizational citizenship behavior: Do fairness perceptions influence employee citizenship? *Journal of Applied Psychology, 76*(6), 845–855.
Moorman, R. H. (1993). The influence of cognitive and affective based job satisfaction measures on the relation between satisfaction and organizational citizenship behavior. *Human Relations, 46*(6), 759–776.
Moorman, R. H., & Blakely, G. L. (1995). Individualism-collectivism as an individual difference predictor of organizational citizenship behavior. *Journal of Organizational Behavior, 16*(2), 127–142.
Moorman, R. H., & Byrne, Z. S. (2005). How does organizational justice affect organizational citizenship behavior? In J. Greenberg & J. A. Colquitt (Eds.), *Handbook of organizational justice* (pp. 355–380). Mahwah: Lawrence Erlbaum Associates.
Moorman, R. H., Niehoff, B. P., & Organ, D. W. (1993). Treating employees fairly and organizational citizenship behavior: Sorting the effects of job satisfaction, organizational commitment, and procedural justice. *Employee Responsibilities and Rights Journal, 6*(3), 209–225.

Moorman, R. H., Blakely, G. L., & Niehoff, B. P. (1998). Does perceived organizational support mediate the relationship between procedural justice and organizational citizenship behavior? *Academy of Management Journal, 41*(3), 351–357.
Motowidlo, S. J. (1984). Does job satisfaction lead to consideration and personal sensitivity? *Academy of Management Journal, 27*(4), 910–915.
Motowidlo, S. J., Packard, J. S., & Manning, M. R. (1986). Occupational stress: Its causes and consequences for job performance. *Journal of Applied Psychology, 71*(4), 618–629.
Murphy, G., Athanasou, J., & King, N. (2002). Job satisfaction and organizational citizenship behavior: A study of Australian human-service professionals. *Journal of Managerial Psychology, 17*(4), 287–297.
Murphy, C., Ramamoorthy, N., Flood, P. C., & MacCurtain, S. (2006). Organisational justice perceptions and employee attitudes among Irish blue collar employees: An empirical test of the main and moderating roles of individualism/collectivism. *Management Revue, 17*(3), 328–343.
Nadiri, H., & Tanova, C. (2010). An investigation of the role of justice in turnover intentions, job satisfaction, and organizational citizenship behavior in hospitality industry. *International Journal of Hospitality Management, 29*(1), 33–41.
Naumann, S. E., & Bennett, N. (2000). A case for procedural justice climate: Development and test of a multilevel model. *Academy of Management Journal, 43*(5), 881–889.
Netemeyer, R. G., Boles, J. S., McKee, D. O., & McMurrian, R. (1997). An investigation into the antecedents of organizational citizenship behaviors in a personal selling context. *Journal of Marketing, 61*(3), 85–98.
Niehoff, B. P., & Moorman, R. H. (1993). Justice as a mediator of the relationship between methods of monitoring and organizational citizenship behavior. *Academy of Management Journal, 36*(3), 527–556.
Organ, D. W. (1977). A reappraisal and reinterpretation of the satisfaction-causes-performance hypothesis. *Academy of Management Review, 2*(1), 46–53.
Organ, D. W. (1988a). *Organizational citizenship behavior: The good solider syndrome*. Lexington: Lexington Books.
Organ, D. W. (1988b). A restatement of the satisfaction-performance hypothesis. *Journal of Management, 14*(4), 547–557.
Organ, D. W. (1990). The motivational basis of organizational citizenship behavior. *Research in Organizational Behavior, 12*(1), 43–72.
Organ, D. W. (1997). Organizational citizenship behavior: It's construct clean-up time. *Human Performance, 10*(2), 85–97.
Organ, D. W., & Konovsky, M. A. (1989). Cognitive versus affective determinants of organizational citizenship behavior. *Journal of Applied Psychology, 74*, 157–164.
Organ, D. W., & Near, J. P. (1985). Cognitions vs. affect in measures of job satisfaction. *International Journal of Psychology, 20*(2), 241–253.
Organ, D. W., & Paine, J. B. (1999). A new kind of performance for industrial and organizational psychology: Recent contributions to the study of organizational citizenship behavior. In C. L. Cooper & I. T. Robertson (Eds.), *International review of industrial and organizational psychology* (pp. 338–368). Chichester: Wiley.
Organ, D. W., & Ryan, K. (1995). A meta-analytic review of attitudinal and dispositional predictors of organizational citizenship behavior. *Personnel Psychology, 48*(4), 775–802.
Pillai, R., Schriesheim, C. A., & Williams, E. S. (1999). Fairness perceptions and trust as mediators for transformational and transactional leadership: A two-sample study. *Journal of Management, 25*(6), 897–933.
Podsakoff, P. M., MacKenzie, S. B., Moorman, R. H., & Fetter, R. (1990). Transformational leader behaviors and their effects on followers' trust in leader, satisfaction, and organizational citizenship behaviors. *The Leadership Quarterly, 1*(2), 107–142.

Podsakoff, P. M., MacKenzie, S. B., Paine, J. B., & Bachrach, D. G. (2000). Organizational citizenship behaviors: A critical review of the theoretical and empirical literature and suggestions for future research. *Journal of Management, 26*(3), 513–563.

Price, J. L., & Mueller, C. W. (1986). *Handbook of organizational measurement.* Marshfield: Pittman.

Puffer, S. M. (1987). Pro-social behavior, non-compliant behavior and work performance among commission sales people. *Journal of Applied Psychology, 53*, 422–443.

Quarles, R. (1994). An examination of promotion opportunities and evaluation criteria as mechanism for affecting internal auditor commitment, job satisfaction and turnover intentions. *Journal of Managerial Issues, 6*(2), 176–194.

Rhoades, L., & Eisenberger, R. (2002). Perceived organizational support: A review of the literature. *Journal of Applied Psychology, 87*(4), 698–714.

Rhoades, L., Eisenberger, R., & Armeli, S. (2001). Affective commitment to the organization: The contribution of perceived organizational support. *Journal of Applied Psychology, 86*(5), 825–836.

Robbins, S. P. (2001). *Organizational behavior*. Upper Saddle River: Prentice-Hall.

Robinson, S. L., & Morrison, E. W. (1995). Psychological contracts and the OCB: The effect of unfulfilled obligations on civic virtue behavior. *Journal of Organizational Behavior, 16*(3), 289–298.

Roch, G., & Shanock, L. R. (2006). Organizational justice in an exchange framework: Clarifying organizational justice distinctions. *Journal of Management, 32*(2), 299–322.

Rosenbaum, J. E. (1984). *Career mobility in a corporate hierarchy*. Orlando: Academic.

Schaubroeck, J., May, D. R., & Brown, F. W. (1994). Procedural justice explanations and reactions to economic hardship: A field experiment. *Journal of Applied Psychology, 79*(3), 455–460.

Scholl, R. W., Cooper, E. A., & McKenna, J. F. (1987). Referent selection in determining equity perceptions: Differential effects on behavioral and attitudinal outcomes. *Personnel Psychology, 40*(1), 113–124.

Settoon, R. P., Bennett, N., & Liden, R. (1996). Social exchange in organizations: Perceived organizational support, leader-member exchange and employee reciprocity. *Journal of Applied Psychology, 81*(3), 219–227.

Sheppard, B. H., Lewicki, R. J., & Minton, J. W. (1992). *Organizational justice: The search for fairness in the workplace*. New York: Lexington Books.

Skarlicki, D. P., & Folger, R. (1997). Retaliation in the workplace: The roles of distributive, procedural, and interactional justice. *Journal of Applied Psychology, 82*(3), 434–443.

Smith, C. A., Organ, D. W., & Near, J. P. (1983). Organizational citizenship behavior: Its nature and antecedents. *Journal of Applied Psychology, 68*(4), 653–663.

Smith, P. C., Kendall, L. M., & Hulin, C. L. (1969). *The measurement of satisfaction in work and retirement*. Chicago: Rand McNally.

St. Onge, S. (2000). Variables influencing the perceived relationship between performance and pay in a merit pay environment. *Journal of Business and Psychology, 14*(3), 459–479.

Stinglhamber, F., De Cremer, D., & Mercken, L. (2006). Perceived support as a mediator of the relationship between justice and trust. *Group and Organizational Management, 31*(4), 442–468.

Sweeney, P. D., & McFarlin, D. B. (1993). Workers' evaluations of the 'ends' and the 'means': An examination of four models of distributive and procedural justice. *Organisational Behavior and Human Decision Processes, 55*(1), 23–40.

Sweeney, P. D., & McFarlin, D. B. (1997). Process and outcome: Gender differences in the assessment of justice. *Journal of Organizational Behavior, 18*(1), 83–98.

Tan, H. H., & Tan, C. S. (2000). Toward the differentiation of trust in supervisor and trust in organization. *Genetic, Social, and General Psychology Monographs, 126*(2), 241–260.

Tansky, J. W. (1993). Justice and organizational citizenship behavior: What is the relationship? *Employee Responsibilities and Rights Journal, 6*(3), 195–207.

Tepper, B. H., Lockhart, D., & Hoobler, J. (2001). Justice, citizenship, and role definition effects. *Journal of Applied Psychology, 86*(4), 789–796.

Tremblay, M., Sire, B., & Balkin, D. B. (2000). The role of organizational justice in pay and employee benefit satisfaction, and its effects on work. *Group and Organizational Management, 25*(3), 269–290.

Van Yperen, N. W., den Berg, A. E., & Willering, B. M. (1999). Towards a better understanding of the link between participation in decision-making and organizational citizenship behavior: A multilevel analysis. *Journal of Occupational and Organizational Psychology, 72*, 377–392.

Wagner, S. L., & Rush, M. (2000). Altruistic organizational citizenship behavior: Context, disposition and age. *The Journal of Social Psychology, 140*(3), 379–391.

Wang, H., Law, K. S., Hackett, R. D., Wang, D. X., & Chen, Z. X. (2005). Leader-member exchange as a mediator of the relationship between transformational leadership and follower' performance and organizational citizenship behavior. *Academy of Management Journal, 48*(3), 420–432.

Wayne, S. J., & Green, S. A. (1993). The effects of leader-member exchange on employee citizenship and impression management behavior. *Human Relations, 46*(12), 1431–1440.

Wayne, S. J., Shore, L. M., Bommer, W. H., & Tetrick, L. E. (2002). The role of fair treatment and rewards in perceptions of organizational support and leader-member exchange. *Journal of Applied Psychology, 87*(3), 590–598.

Welbourne, T. M. (1998). Untangling procedural and distributive justice. *Group and Organizational Management, 23*(4), 325–346.

Williams, L. J., & Anderson, S. E. (1991). Job satisfaction and organizational commitment as predictors of organizational citizenship and in-role behaviours. *Journal of Management, 17*(3), 601–617.

Williams, S., Pitre, R., & Zainuba, M. (2002). Justice and organizational citizenship behavior intentions: Fair rewards versus fair treatment. *The Journal of Social Psychology, 142*(1), 33–44.

Zhong, J. A., Lam, W., & Chen, Z. (2011). Relationship between leader–member exchange and organizational citizenship behaviors: Examining the moderating role of empowerment. *Asia Pacific Journal of Management, 28*(3), 609–626.

Chapter 6
Organisational Citizenship Behaviour for Organisational Sustainability

Abstract Chapter 6 highlights the importance of organisational citizenship behaviour for the sustainability of organisations in the new millennium. This chapter begins with a discussion on the importance of organisational citizenship behaviour in general, and then the impact of rewarding organisational citizenship behaviour. Empirical support provides justification for this assertion. It then focuses on research on organisational citizenship behaviour in Malaysia. Next, it outlines some ways to improve organisational citizenship behaviour and provides recommendations to enhance organisational citizenship behaviour. The main purpose is to spin out best practices in organisational citizenship behaviour that are salient for organisations in Asia in general, and Malaysia in particular, to enhance organisational sustainability in the new millennium.

Introduction

The sustainability of manufacturing organisations in the new millennium substantially relies on the competitiveness of its human capital. High-performance organisations should, therefore, make concerted efforts to increase the productivity and efficiency of the workforce. Becker (1993) asserts that the most successful companies are those that manage human capital in the most effective and efficient fashion. As competitiveness in the marketplace demands competitive human capital, management strategies must give due attention to building and sustaining a committed workforce. To remain sustainable, organisations must strategically design supportive work environments that promote desirable employee behaviours and outcomes. Axiomatically, organisations that provide high job satisfaction and cherish excellence and effectiveness of employees would likely motivate employees to give their best efforts to the organisation. In management research, there has been much emphasis on the importance of organisational citizenship behaviour as salient behaviours for organisations. Organisational citizenship behaviours are exceptionally good proactive behaviours above and beyond prescribed role requirements in which employees willingly choose to engage. Nemeth and Staw (1989) expound on the value of organisational citizenship behaviours in contributing to performance

L.W. Hooi, *Organisational Justice and Citizenship Behaviour in Malaysia*, Governance and Citizenship in Asia, DOI 10.1007/978-981-10-0030-0_6

and competitive advantage. Accordingly, for the prosperity and good functioning of every organisation, a 'good soldier syndrome' is essential (Organ 1988).

Extant research reveals that organisational citizenship behaviour is positively associated with individual, unit and organisational performance (Organ et al. 2006; Podsakoff et al. 1997; Podsakoff and MacKenzie 1994; Walz and Niehoff 2000; Werner 1994). Organ (1988) argues that organisational citizenship behaviour is vital for the survival of an organisation. Generally, there is consensus among contemporary organisational behaviour theorists that organisational citizenship behaviour can maximise efficiency and productivity that ultimately enhances the effective functioning of an organisation (Wagner and Rush 2000). Based on the above arguments, this chapter sets out to discuss the importance of organisational citizenship behaviour on organisational outcomes by providing empirical support to justify this assertion. It then discusses the impact of rewarding organisational citizenship behaviours and empirical works on organisational citizenship behaviour in Malaysia. Next, it provides suggestions for improving organisational citizenship behaviour and identifies best practices in organisational citizenship behaviour that are salient for organisations in Asia in general, and Malaysia in particular, to enhance organisational sustainability in the new millennium.

The Importance of Organisational Citizenship Behaviour

In the current volatile and turbulent global environment, it is pertinent that manufacturing organisations possess employees that perform beyond expectations. Generally, organisational citizenship behaviour is believed to have compelling effects on the individual and the success of an organisation. There is increasing consensus among organisational citizenship behaviour researchers that these proactive employee behaviours are associated with a broad set of desirable individual and organisational outcomes. Organisational citizenship behaviour has been proven to enhance employee productivity (Organ et al. 2006), employee commitment (Organ and Ryan 1995), organisational performance (Chahal 2010; Podsakoff and MacKenzie 1994; Podsakoff et al. 2000) and customer satisfaction (Morrison 1995), free up resources (Podsakoff and MacKenzie 1997), attract and retain good employees, and create social capital (Organ et al. 2006). Therefore, it can be leveraged to improve organisational effectiveness (e.g. George and Bettenhausen 1990; Podsakoff et al. 1997).

At the individual level, performance is expected to improve, which ultimately leads to better overall performance evaluation ratings by their managers (Podsakoff et al. 2009). This may be due to the 'halo effect' where employees who display organisational citizenship behaviours are viewed positively by their superiors for their commitment or managerial perception of the significant role of organisational citizenship behaviour in the organisation's overall success (Organ et al. 2006). Regardless of the reason, a better performance rating results in gaining higher rewards such as pay increments, bonuses, promotions or work-related benefits.

Moreover, during unfavourable economic conditions and organisational restructuring, these employees are less likely to be made redundant (Organ et al. 2006). Concisely, this not only provides an opportunity for employees engaging in organisational citizenship behaviour to advance in their career but also reaps the short- and long-term benefits offered. Seeing that organisational citizenship behaviours are positively related to evaluations of individuals' overall performance (e.g. Allen and Rush 1998; Whiting et al. 2008), employees may seize the opportunity to enhance their performance further as well as secure and establish their presence in the organisation. Moreover, as organisational citizenship behaviour has approximately equal weight as task performance in determining performance evaluations (Podsakoff et al. 2009), it is unlikely that employees will restrain organisational citizenship behaviours. Besides, managers apparently factor citizenship behaviours into their assessments of employee performance (Podsakoff et al. 2000).

Albeit informally, organisational citizenship behaviours are being evaluated in most performance appraisal systems (Becton et al. 2008). This indefinitely raises employee awareness of the need to embrace citizenship behaviours. Incorporating the dimensions of organisational citizenship behaviour in performance appraisal systems ultimately benefits both the employees and the organisation. For instance, an emphasis on civic virtue may result in increase feedback and innovative ideas from employees (Podsakoff and MacKenzie 1997), while rewarding proactive behaviours may encourage employees to take initiatives to accomplish objectives or to solve organisational problems. Nonetheless, organisations have to decide on the types of organisational citizenship behaviour to emphasise on in order to elicit the desire response from the employees.

Organisational citizenship behaviour has also been shown to increase the quality and quantity of unit-level production (Organ et al. 2006), contribute to organisational and group effectiveness (e.g. George and Bettenhausen 1990; Podsakoff et al. 1997) as well as increase productivity, efficiency and customer satisfaction, and reduce costs and rates of turnover and absenteeism (Podsakoff et al. 2009). In essence, organisations benefit from encouraging employees to engage in organisational citizenship behaviour. Moreover, high levels of organisational citizenship behaviour should enhance organisational efficiency and entice new resources (members, raw materials, company goodwill, branding) into the organisation (Organ 1988). As organisational citizenship behaviour significantly influences operational efficiency, customer perception of organisational effectiveness is a reflection of the intensity of organisational citizenship behaviour fostered.

A noticeable spillover effect of organisational citizenship behaviour on employees is job satisfaction. Organ (1988) affirms that the correlation between organisational citizenship behaviour and job satisfaction is approximately 0.4. Job satisfaction affects organisational effectiveness as it influences employee performance that is related to citizenship behaviour. Moreover, it has been empirically proven that satisfied workers perform better. Hence, higher job satisfaction translates to increased performance and lower rates of employee turnover and absenteeism. Besides, job satisfaction exerts a positive influence on employees' knowledge sharing behaviours (Teh and Sun 2012). At the organisational level, benefits that accrue include increased productivity, efficiency and customer satisfaction as well as reduced costs (Podsakoff et al. 2009). Ehrhart and Naumann (2004) contend that organisational citizenship behaviour in grocery stores/supermarkets explained approximately 20 % of the variance in store profitability. Additionally, organisational citizenship behaviour increases available resources and reduces formal and costly mechanisms of control (Organ 1988).

Teh and Sun (2012) further argue that organisational citizenship behaviour directly affects employees' knowledge sharing behaviour. This concurs with the notion that individuals with higher citizenship behaviours favour knowledge sharing as they are more willing to increase the welfare of others (Hsu and Lin 2008). Though knowledge sharing is instrumental in organisational survival, in reality creating and sustaining organisational knowledge sharing culture is a challenge as knowledge employees are less inclined to share their knowledge with coworkers (Ho et al. 2009; Lam and Lambermont-Ford 2010). Therefore, management may find it worthwhile to invest in developing leaders to actively promote organisational citizenship behaviour. Considering the contribution of knowledge sharing to organisational effectiveness, active constructive leadership skills can be exercised to encourage open sharing of knowledge through improving organisational citizenship behaviour. Enhancing employee positive perception of psychological and/or behavioural outcomes potentially improves organisational citizenship behaviour and encourages knowledge sharing behaviours. In the long run, coworker and managerial productivity are likely to improve.

Cohen and Vigoda (2000) contend that organisational citizenship behaviour affects organisational effectiveness through its influence on customers. The lack of organisational citizenship behaviour hinders innovative behaviours and may result in low-quality products and services. Consequently, customers develop negative perceptions towards the organisation beyond the immediate customer–provider contract (Vigoda and Beeri 2011). Axiomatically, this affects the bottom line and may jeopardise organisational efficiency and effectiveness. The importance of organisational citizenship behaviour on customers is further attest in its effectiveness in promoting a more positive social and working environment that enhances work performance (Chiun et al. 2006). Specifically, it enhances efficiency, productivity, human relations in the work unit, team work and learning (Battaglio and Condrey 2009; Coggburn 2006; Coggburn et al. 2010). Subsequently, the quality of products and services offered and customer relationship improve. This helps in ameliorating the image, reputation and branding of organisations. Therefore, organisational citizenship behaviour is important not only for employees and the organisation but also the customers of the organisation. Concisely, organisational citizenship behaviour enhances performance and strengthens the overall ethos of organisations, ultimately benefitting all stakeholders.

Podsakoff et al. (2000) provide evidence that organisational citizenship behaviour affects performance evaluation and other managerial decisions as well as organisational performance and success. The empirical evidence provided shows that reasons associated with norms of reciprocity and fairness (Blau 1964; Gouldner 1960; Homans 1961), implicit performance theories (Berman and Kenny 1976;

Bruner and Tagiuri 1954), schema-triggered affect (Fiske 1981, 1982; Fiske and Pavelchak 1986), behavioural distinctiveness and accessibility (DeNisi et al. 1984), attributional processes and accessibility (DeNisi et al. 1984), and illusory correlations (Chapman 1967; Chapman and Chapman 1967; Cooper 1981) significantly influence managerial evaluations of performance (Podsakoff et al. 1993). Across the 11 samples reported by Podsakoff et al. (2000), organisational citizenship behaviours uniquely accounted for 42.9 % of the variance in performance evaluations. Podsakoff et al. (2000) concluded that organisational citizenship behaviour accounted for substantially more variance in performance evaluations than objective performance. Comparatively, except for courtesy, all the other dimensions significantly affected performance evaluation in most of the studies in which it was included.

In another analysis across eight samples, Podsakoff et al. (2000) contend that organisational citizenship behaviour is a more important predictor of performance evaluation than in-role performance. Organisational citizenship behaviour uniquely accounted for 12 % of the variance in performance evaluation, while in-role performance uniquely accounted for only 9.3 %. Nonetheless, both in-role performance and organisational citizenship behaviour are significantly related to reward recommendations (Allen and Rush 1998). In summarising experimental studies that have examined the effects of organisational citizenship behaviour on performance evaluations or reward allocation decisions, Podsakoff et al. (2000) assert that both organisational citizenship behaviour and in-role performance have important influences on reward recommendations, such as salary and promotion recommendations. In essence, organisational citizenship behaviour influences several key managerial decisions, specifically performance evaluations and reward recommendations. Moreover, these empirical studies show that organisational citizenship behaviour is as important as in-role performance in influencing managerial decisions.

Indubitably, organisational citizenship behaviour affects organisational performance and success. Podsakoff et al. (2000) argue that organisational citizenship behaviour may contribute to organisational success by enhancing productivity, utilising resources productively, reducing the allocation of scarce resources to purely maintenance functions, improving coordination of work activities, strengthening recruitment and retention strategies, increasing the stability of organisational performance and facilitating organisations to adapt effectively to environmental changes. Concisely, organisational citizenship behaviour is correlated with organisational effectiveness. Podsakoff and his colleagues (MacKenzie et al. 1996; Podsakoff et al. 1997; Podsakoff and MacKenzie 1994) establish that organisational citizenship behaviour on average affects performance quantity (19 %), performance quality (18 %), financial efficiency indicators (25 %) and customer service indicators (38 %). Comparatively, altruism seems to be a more significant predictor of organisational performance. It significantly relates to almost every indicator of performance though its significance varies depending on the context. For example, altruism has no effect on customer complaints (Walz and Niehoff 1996) and a negative impact on the quantity of performance (Podsakoff and MacKenzie 1994). The other two dimensions that affect organisational performance are sportsmanship (quantity of performance, some aspects of financial efficiency and customer service) and civic virtue (quantity of performance, reduce customer complaints). Hence, organisational citizenship behaviour is indeed related to organisational performance (Organ 1988).

Impact of Rewarding Organisational Citizenship Behaviour

Organisational citizenship behaviour has been shown to have a considerable positive and negative impact at the organisational level (Zhang 2011). The positive impact shows that different dimensions of organisational citizenship behaviour enhance organisational effectiveness from 18 to 38 % (Ehrhart 2004; Podsakoff et al. 2000). Moreover, emphasising civic virtue in the performance appraisal system promotes valuable feedback and suggestions for improvement (Podsakoff and MacKenzie 1997), while emphasis on task citizenship behaviours encourages employees to be more supportive with concerns about organisational problems and impending solutions. It also increases occurrence of organisational citizenship behaviours in extrinsically motivated employees. Other benefits include improving self-efficacy and leader–member exchange and reducing role ambiguity (Becton et al. 2008).

On the contrary, too much emphasis on certain types of organisational citizenship behaviour, such as altruism and sportsmanship, could result in less accurate organisational diagnosis of organisational problems and issues. Emphasis on altruism in performance appraisal and reward system, for example, could mask critical human resource needs within the organisation. Moreover, promoting sportsmanship could discourage employees from bringing forth flawed organisational practices and processes to avoid being seen as bad organisational citizens. Hence, optimal organisational effectiveness is hindered as organisational issues may only be detected at a more serious stage (Becton et al. 2008). Other consequences include decreased occurrence in organisational citizenship behaviours in intrinsically motivated employees, emotional dissonance leading to emotional exhaustion and burnout, increased role conflict and overload, greater legal risk and impeded employee development.

Becton et al. (2008) suggested several ways to ameliorate the potential negative effects of rewarding organisational citizenship behaviour. Most of all, practitioners must ensure a balance between organisational citizenship behaviour and job performance. Hence, it is imperative that the level of emphasis given to each dimension of organisational citizenship behaviour is proportionate to its importance to overall job performance. This not only reduces the tendency for employees to focus more on citizenship behaviours than other important job behaviours but also discourages personally gratifying organisational citizenship behaviours. Organisations need to recognise that organisational citizenship behaviour is not a substitute for traditional job performance (Bolino and Turnley 2003).

Another precautionary measure is to focus on rater-error training and frame of reference training to mitigate rating errors. These trainings reduce halo error, recency error and employee impression management tactics. Inaccurately rewarding organisational citizenship behaviours potentially creates employee dissatisfaction and reduces task performance. Hence, implementing 360° feedback or multi-rater formats may be more appropriate for evaluating and rewarding organisational citizenship behaviour. Moreover, many citizenship behaviours might not be noticed by raters or exhibited only when the supervisor is present.

As rewarding organisational citizenship behaviour may increase job stress and work–family conflict, it is crucial that organisations help their employees balance work and family demands. Work–life balance policies and practices likely motivate employee performance, and, consequently, organisational effectiveness. As employee critical feedback is essential for organisations to improve organisational practices and processes, practitioners must also create ways to encourage employees to bring forward ideas to improve operations or practices. Additionally, it is important that organisations define organisational citizenship behaviour in observable and behavioural terms to minimise legal risks, improve the usefulness of performance feedback as well as promote employee development.

Research on Organisational Citizenship Behaviour in Malaysia

In the Malaysian context, a number of studies on organisational citizenship behaviour and organisational justice have been carried out (e.g. Abdullah and Mohd Nasurdin 2008; Ishak and Ahmad 2004; Hassan and Hashim 2011; Hassan and Noor 2008; Hooi et al. 2012; Khalid and Ali 2005; Lo et al. 2006; Mohd Nasurdin and Soon 2011; Othman et al. 2005) albeit not in the manufacturing sector. The reason for this is research in the manufacturing sector tends to focus on issues of performance and productivity or managing of human resources (e.g. Ahmad and Singh 2001; Chew 2005a, b; Chin and Maniam 2001; Chong and Jain 1987; Hooi 1997a, b, 1999, 2001a, b, 2002, 2006a, b, c, 2007a, b, c, 2008a, b, c, 2010a, b, c; Kawabe 1991; Lim 2001; Mirza and Juhary 1995; Putra 1993; Sheppard 2001; Thong 1991; Yong 2003). Furthermore, the question of organisational justice is not a major concern as the work culture in Malaysia is one of conformity and adherence to superior decisions. Confrontation over justice issues is restrained as employees accept injustice as a norm due to high power distance in most organisations. As there is no long-term employment policy, employees are free to switch jobs if they are dissatisfied with the system. Thus, employees are not too concern about organisational injustice as they have the liberty to move on.

However, as the job market becomes saturated, the ease of job hopping is constrained. Therefore, it is imperative that employees that stay on contribute significantly to the organisation. To fully capitalise on workforce capability and capacity for organisational effectiveness, organisational citizenship behaviour is crucial. As justice perceptions affect employee behaviour and attitude in Western societies (e.g. Cohen-Charash and Spector 2001; Colquitt et al. 2001), it is likely that local employees will be similarly affected. This aroused the interest of local scholars, and, in the new millennium, studies on organisational citizenship behaviour became apparent (Abdullah and Mohd Nasurdin 2008; Ishak and Ahmad 2004; Hassan and Hashim 2011; Hassan and Noor 2008; Hooi et al. 2012; Khalid and Ali 2005; Lo et al. 2006; Mohd Nasurdin and Soon 2011; Othman et al. 2005). Specifically, local scholars began examining not only the relationship between organisational justice and organisational citizenship behaviour as well as other organisational outcomes but also the antecedents of organisational citizenship behaviour in the local context.

Hooi et al. (2012) explored the effect of procedural justice in promotion decisions of managerial staff in Malaysia on managers' commitment, specifically organisational commitment, intent to leave, career satisfaction and job performance. A sample of 28 local managers from different industries with 12–25 years of working experience in multinational organisations of more than 1,000 employees were interviewed. The in-depth interviews revealed that perceived procedural injustice in promotion decisions has an unfavourable impact on employee commitment, job performance and career satisfaction. The intent to leave was also higher, especially among young managerial staff. Mohd Nasurdin and Soon (2011) examined the links between organisational justice (distributive justice and procedural justice) and job performance (task performance and contextual performance) as well as the moderating role of age in the above-mentioned relationship. Data gathered from a sample of 136 customer-contact employees within the telecommunications industry of Malaysia demonstrated that distributive justice had a significant and positive relationship with task performance while procedural justice was found to be significantly and positively related to contextual performance. Age, however, did not moderate the justice–performance relationships.

Hassan and Hashim (2011) analysed the role of organisational justice in determining work outcomes of national and expatriate academic staff in Malaysian institutions of higher learning. It also explored the role of organisational justice in shaping teaching faculties' attitude (job satisfaction and commitment) and behavioural intention (turnover intention). Sample drawn from four public universities in Malaysia revealed that except for job satisfaction, where Malaysians recorded significantly higher endorsement compared to expatriates, no significant difference was found between the two groups on perception of distributive, procedural and interactional aspects of organisational justice, as well as organisational commitment and turnover intention. However, Malaysians demonstrated significantly higher level of job satisfaction compared to expatriates. Different facets of organisational justice predicted work outcomes in the two groups. Whereas interactional and distributive justice promoted expatriates' organisational commitment and/or intention to stay with the organisation, it was mainly procedural justice that contributed to local employees' job satisfaction, organisational commitment and turnover intentions. Distributive justice also predicted turnover intentions of locals.

Additionally, Hassan and Noor (2008) studied the effect of organisational justice on extra role behaviour at a public university in Malaysia. Findings drawn from students enrolled in the MBA executive programme revealed that there was no significant relationship between procedural, distributive, informational and interpersonal justice and extra role behaviour. As hypothesised, in a high power distance and collectivistic society like Malaysia, organisational justice had no effect on extra role behaviour. However, Abdullah and Mohd Nasurdin (2008) assert that there is a significant relationship between organisational justice and organisational citizenship behaviour. The study carried out in the hotel industry in Malaysia showed that distributive and procedural justice significantly influenced organisational citizenship behaviour. Similarly, Khalid and Ali (2005) explored the hotel industry in Malaysia and compared supervisors' rating scores of employee organisational citizenship behaviours with self-rating scores of employees. Data obtained from 557 subordinates and 287 superiors showed a positive correlation with higher self-rating scores comparatively. Othman et al. (2005) considered the moderating role of organisational justice in the psychological contract violation–organisational citizenship behaviour relationship and found partial support for the model during organisational downsizing. Ishak and Ahmad (2004) investigated perceived justice in the distribution of organisational resources, and the findings indicated that, in general, merit was the most important norm for the distribution of organisational resources, followed by need of the recipient and equality in terms of merit and need. However, perception of minority ethnic groups differed from the majority on fairness of the allocation decisions.

A few other studies have also been conducted in the Malaysian context taking into consideration the effects of leader–member exchange. Kandan and Ali (2010) researched the correlation effects between leader–member exchange and organisational citizenship behaviour in a public sector organisation in Peninsular Malaysia and affirmed that both the variables were significantly correlated. Exploring the banking sector, Ishak and Alam (2009) examined the relationships of organisational justice, organisational citizenship behaviour and leader–member exchange among nonsupervisory employees and supervisors. Results indicated that interactional justice contributed to the performance of altruism and consideration through leader–member exchange while procedural justice and distributive justice did not contribute to subordinates performing organisational citizenship behaviour.

In a study among auditors serving in audit firms across Malaysia, who were registered with the Malaysian Institute of Accountants, Leow and Khong (2009) scrutinised the relationship and tested the interaction effects of organisational justice (distributive, procedural and interactional) and the dimensions of leader–member exchange (affect, contribution, professional respect and loyalty) on organisational commitment. The findings on direct effects revealed that predictor variables have a positive relationship with affective–normative commitment and only partial support for continuance commitment. Perceptions of organisational justice, reciprocity and leader–member exchange significantly influenced affective–normative commitment, while leader–member exchange significantly predicted continuance commitment. Partial support was found for the interaction effects of affective–normative and continuance commitment. One implication of the study is that to enhance employee commitment, human resources departments have to consider organisational justice and leader–member exchange when implementing human resource policies. Commitment to some extent promotes organisational citizenship behaviour.

Asgari et al. (2008) explored the mediating role of leader–member exchange, perceived organisational support and trust in the relationship between transformational leadership behaviours (transformational and transactional), organisational justice (distributive, procedural and interactional justice) and organisational citizenship behaviour. Data collected from a sample of 162 employees in five ministries in Putrajaya revealed that leader–member exchange, perceived organisational support and trust mediated the relationships between transformational leadership behaviours, organisational justice and organisational citizenship behaviour. Ansari et al. (2007) hypothesised the mediating impact of procedural justice climate on the relationship between leader–member exchange (contribution, affect, loyalty and professional respect) and two attitudinal outcomes: organisational commitment (affective, normative and continuance) and turnover intentions. Data was obtained from 224 managers in nine multinational companies located in northern Malaysia. Hypotheses for direct effects received low to moderate support, while substantial support was observed for the mediating role of procedural justice in the professional respect dimension of leader–member exchange. Further to this, Lo et al. (2006) assert that leader–member exchange contributes significantly in promoting organisational citizenship behaviour among executives and managers in Malaysia.

Improving Organisational Citizenship Behaviour

Improving organisational citizenship behaviour is perhaps the best way for businesses to enhance organisational effectiveness as it is a relatively cheap way of getting employees to willingly embrace good organisational values. Considering the instrumental role of organisational citizenship behaviour on organisational performance and success, it is imperative that organisations be supportive and committed to increasing organisational citizenship behaviour among their core employees. Empirical evidence suggests that organisations should focus on employee characteristics, task characteristics, organisational characteristics and leadership behaviours to promote organisational citizenship behaviour (Podsakoff et al. 2000). According to Organ and Ryan (1995), employee characteristics that significantly influence organisational citizenship behaviour are categorised as affective morale factor (job satisfaction, organisational commitment, organisational justice and leader support) and dispositional factors (agreeableness, conscientiousness, positive affectivity and negative affectivity). Task characteristics such as task feedback, task routinisation and intrinsically satisfying tasks have consistent relationships with citizenship behaviours. Organisational characteristics that affect organisational citizenship behaviour include organisational formalisation, organisational inflexibility, advisory/staff support, spatial distance, group cohesiveness and perceived organisational support. Leadership behaviours can be divided into transformational leadership behaviours, transactional leadership behaviours and behaviours identified with either the path or goal theory of leadership–the leader–member exchange theory of leadership.

Empirical evidence suggests that employee characteristics influence organisational citizenship behaviour. Podsakoff et al. (2000) assert that all the affective morale factors such as job satisfaction, organisational commitment, organisational justice and leader support have significant relationships with organisational citizenship behaviour of roughly comparable strength (ranging from 0.23 to 0.31). According to Organ et al. (2006), job satisfaction has the strongest correlation at 0.9, while the other three factors range between 0.72 and 0.76. Morale factors as a whole correlate with organisational citizenship behaviour at 0.69. Organisational support positively influenced organisational citizenship behaviour (Chang 2014; Somech and Ron 2007), while organisational inducements of perceived supervisor support and participation led to higher levels of perceived insider status, which in turn enhanced organisational citizenship behaviour (Hui et al. 2015). Similarly, Lloyd et al. (2015) argue that perceived supervisor listening significantly affects organisational citizenship behaviour directed towards the organisation. As for dispositional factors, conscientiousness (Organ and Ryan 1995), agreeableness (Konovsky and Organ 1993) and positive affectivity (George 1990; Van Dyne et al. 1995) have the strongest effects on organisational citizenship behaviour. Conscientiousness and agreeableness significantly affect both altruism and generalised compliance, while positive affectivity is related positively to altruism (Podsakoff et al. 2000). Organisational citizenship behaviour is, therefore, a powerful tool of free-will conduct that obviously makes a difference in organisational competitiveness. Nonetheless, managerial commitment is essential for making this a success.

As for task characteristics, prior research (e.g. Podsakoff and MacKenzie 1995; Podsakoff et al. 1996, 1993) reveals that task characteristics such as task feedback, task routinisation and intrinsically satisfying tasks have consistent relationships with all dimensions of organisational citizenship behaviour. Task feedback and intrinsically satisfying tasks positively influence citizenship behaviour, while task routinisation negatively relates to organisational citizenship behaviour. However, inconsistent relationships exist between organisational characteristics and organisational citizenship behaviour. The relationships between organisational formalisation, organisational inflexibility, advisory/staff support, and spatial distance and organisational citizenship behaviour are somewhat inconsistent. Nonetheless, group cohesiveness is significantly and positively related to all dimensions of organisational citizenship behaviour, while perceived organisational support significantly influences altruism. In addition, rewards outside the leader's control negatively affect altruism, courtesy, and conscientiousness.

As far as leadership behaviours are concerned, transformational leadership behaviour consistently affects all dimensions of organisational citizenship behaviour positively. Transformational leaders have the ability to get employees to put in extra effort and perform beyond expectations (Bass 1985; Burns 1978; Kouzes and

Posner 1987). Similarly, transactional leader behaviour has a significant influence on every form of organisational citizenship behaviour. Contingent reward behaviour has a positive effect, while noncontingent punishment behaviour has a negative effect. When leaders dispense rewards contingent upon performance (Park and Sims 1989; Allen and Rush 1998), organisational citizenship behaviour increases as employees engage in citizenship behaviour as a means of obtaining rewards (Morrison 1994). As for the path–goal leadership dimensions, supportive leader behaviour positively affects all dimensions of organisational citizenship behaviour, while leader role clarification positively influences altruism, courtesy, conscientiousness and sportsmanship. Leader–member exchange, however, relates positively to altruism and overall citizenship behaviours. Hence, leaders play a key role in influencing citizenship behaviours (Podsakoff et al. 2000).

As leadership behaviours have a primary effect on organisational citizenship behaviour (Organ et al. 2006; Podsakoff et al. 2000), leaders need to articulate a vision on organisational citizenship behaviour and enhance employees' belief that they are a valued part of the organisation. Lilly (2015) asserts that employees engage in higher levels of organisational citizenship behaviour when the supervisor exhibits high levels of leadership behaviour, regardless of whether that leader behaviour is relationship oriented or task oriented. Leadership styles can encourage organisational citizenship behaviour in various ways if deployed effectively (Organ et al. 2006). For example, supportive leader behaviour may influence organisational citizenship behaviour through the norm of reciprocity. Similarly, contingent reward behaviour of leaders may improve organisational citizenship behaviour as employee performance is partially contingent on these behaviours. Instrumental leadership behaviour facilitates role clarity, while transformational leadership behaviour facilitates motivation. These leadership behaviours not only inform employees clearly about organisational expectations of their performance but also provide support that inspires employees to achieve high performance expectations. Therefore, it is likely that these behaviours enhance organisational citizenship behaviour as these behaviours are critical for high performance.

Likewise, several studies (e.g. Fuller et al. 1996; Judge and Piccolo 2004; Lowe et al. 1996; Organ et al. 2006; Podsakoff et al. 2000) reveal that charismatic leadership significantly affects organisational citizenship behaviour. However, the effect of leadership behaviours on organisational citizenship behaviour may be contingent on country of origin as it significantly moderated the relationship. Cavazotte et al. (2014) found that charismatic leadership was positively associated with organisational citizenship behaviours in the US group, but not in the Brazilian group. Moreover, Vigoda-Gadot and Beeri (2011) assert that more charismatic transformational leaders are less likely to view employees as engaged in change-oriented organisational citizenship behaviour. Albeit a negative relationship between transformational leadership behaviours and change-oriented organisational citizenship behaviour, Vigoda-Gadot and Beeri (2011) affirm a direct positive relationship between transactional leadership behaviours and change-oriented organisational citizenship behaviour.

Further to this, Niehoff and Moorman (1993) argue that certain types of leadership monitoring behaviour on citizenship behaviours are mediated by justice. Effective leadership monitoring behaviour increases employees' perceptions of fair treatment, which subsequently enhances employees' trust in leadership and ultimately improves organisational citizenship behaviour. In a similar vein, Pillai et al. (1999) maintain that procedural justice and trust mediate the relationship between transformational leadership and organisational citizenship behaviour. Konovsky and Pugh (1994) further establish that trust significantly mediates the relationships between procedural and distributive justice and organisational citizenship behaviour. Other mediators include employees' trust in their leader and job satisfaction (Podsakoff et al. 1990). Additionally, Chang (2014) affirms that organisational justice perception has a positive moderating effect between organisational support and organisational citizenship behaviour. Therefore, leadership appears to have a strong influence on employee willingness to engage in organisational citizenship behaviour. Leadership behaviours also influence organisational citizenship behaviour indirectly via various attitudinal and organisational factors.

Numerous empirical studies show that leadership behaviours significantly influence employee perceptions of organisational justice, which may impact their job satisfaction. As discussed in Chaps. 3 and 5, both organisational justice and job satisfaction have been found to be positively related to organisational citizenship behaviour. The empirical results of the current study discussed in Chaps. 8 and 9 also support this assertion. Organ and Ryan (1995) reveal that attitudinal variables such as job satisfaction, organisational justice and organisational commitment have the strongest relationships with organisational citizenship behaviour. Similarly, other studies reinforce the significance of job satisfaction (e.g. Bateman and Organ 1983; Lee and Allen 2002; Organ 1997; Smith et al. 1983), organisational justice (e.g. Folger 1993; Hooi 2012; Moorman et al. 1993 and organisational commitment (e.g. VanYperen et al. 1999) in predicting organisational citizenship behaviour. Considering the spiralling effects of job satisfaction on job performance as well as employee absenteeism, turnover and psychological distress (Davis 1992), organisations ought to adopt job satisfaction enhancing strategies to improve organisational citizenship behaviour. In tandem, organisations need to mitigate role conflict and role ambiguity, as both significantly affect organisational citizenship behaviour negatively. Both role ambiguity and role conflict are significantly negatively related to altruism, courtesy and sportsmanship. Moreover, both role ambiguity and role conflict affect job satisfaction, which is related to organisational citizenship behaviour. Instead, role clarity and role facilitation, which positively affect organisational citizenship behaviour, should be encouraged (Podsakoff et al. 2000).

Based on the social exchange theory, career growth prospect and formal mentoring support may affect organisational citizenship behaviour. In an exchange relationship, employees tend to respond positively to favourable treatment received from their organisations (Eisenberger et al. 1997). Moreover, the extent that employees and employers are committed to meet each other's desires determines the strength of the relationship. If employers were committed to enhancing career growth prospect and formal mentoring support, it is likely that employees will reciprocate through citizenship behaviours (Ishak 2005; Organ and Konovsky 1989) to compensate the organisation (Organ 1988). Employees feel obligated to improve performance in response to career growth and mentoring support (Rousseau 1989, 1990). Okurame (2012) contends that career growth prospect significantly affects organisational citizenship behaviour, specifically sportsmanship, conscientiousness and civic virtue. This is probably because to enhance career growth prospect, employees tend to employ work behaviours that reflect organisational citizenship behaviour. Alternatively, favourable career growth prospect makes employees focus on their work responsibilities, thereby enhancing organisational citizenship behaviour.

Specifically, career growth prospect is likely to affect sportsmanship positively as employees may be more willing to tolerate inevitable inconveniences and impositions of work. Succinctly, employees maintain a positive attitude, do not complain, and are more willing to sacrifice their personal interest for the good of the work group. Career growth prospect is also expected to correlate positively with conscientiousness as employees may be motivated to go well beyond minimum role requirements in terms of attendance, punctuality, obeying rules and regulations, breaks, housekeeping, conserving resources and staying current on their work activities. Similarly, career growth prospect may positively affect altruism and courtesy, as employees are likely to engage in helping behaviours and behaviours aimed at preventing work-related problems with others if they perceive prospects of career growth. By the same token, career growth prospect probably influences civic virtue, as employees responsibly assume responsive, constructive involvement in the organisation to improve effectiveness. In essence, it represents employees' commitment to the organisation's governance, environment and interests even at great personal cost.

Linking mentoring support to organisational citizenship behaviour, employees are likely to judge mentors' actions as the organisation's care and concern for their welfare. In the social exchange exposition, mentor resources that fulfil the needs of employees should enhance reciprocation obligation. Mentees feel obliged to reciprocate a mentor's actions indirectly through prosocial behaviours such as organisational citizenship behaviour. Hence, mentors play an instrumental role in fostering organisational citizenship behaviour. Mentors facilitate positive work behaviour, inculcate skills (Allen et al. 2004; Kram 1985; Okurame 2009), provide proper orientation (Payne 2006), create opportunities and provide more incentives for employees (Dawley et al. 2008; Hunt and Michael 1983; Kram 1985). Besides, it promotes organisational trust, job satisfaction and organisational commitment (Fagenson 1989; Okurame 2008, 2009; Scandura 1992; Whitely et al. 1991). Prior studies (e.g. Allen et al. 2009; Donaldson et al. 2000; Kwan et al. 2011) revealed that overall mentoring functions enhanced organisational citizenship behaviour. However, Okurame (2012) asserts that though formal mentoring support significantly influences sportsmanship, courtesy and altruism, it has no effect on overall organisational citizenship behaviour.

Specifically, formal mentoring support may positively influence sportsmanship. Despite inconveniences, mentees are less likely to complain as work seems less challenging with mentor's support (Okurame 2011). Moreover, mentees keep a positive attitude despite difficult circumstances and uncomfortable working conditions and may even be willing to sacrifice the personal interest for group. Likewise, formal mentoring support is expected to positively affect conscientiousness. Mentees observe organisation's rules and procedures to compensate the organisation for providing mentoring resources. Mentees make it a point to arrive to work on time, have few coffee breaks, observe lunch hours and not leave the office early. In a similar vein, formal mentoring support may relate positively with altruism and courtesy. Mentees are more likely to be cooperative, helpful, friendly and accommodating though it is not normally expected of the employee. Moreover, mentees have a tendency to be polite and courteous, maintain the social order and reciprocating favours, prevent work-related problems and conflict with others and not abuse the rights of others. In the same way, formal mentoring support affects civic virtue because mentees responsibly keep abreast of organisational issues and assertively involve in organisational governance. Nonetheless, it should be noted that formal mentoring support should work in tandem with the quality of mentoring relationship to augment organisational citizenship behaviour.

A conducive office social environment that provides opportunities for employees to demonstrate organisational citizenship behaviour can improve organisational effectiveness. For example, a friendly, helpful and cooperative office environment may encourage altruism and expedite work processes. These helpful behaviours may reduce or lessen the severity of work-related problems, thus, promoting courtesy. Employees may derive satisfaction from the smooth workflow, motivating them to contribute more. This not only encourages knowledge sharing but also advances civic virtue as employees are likely to responsibly participate in the political life of the organisation (Organ 1988). This enhances employees' knowledge of things happening in the organisation. Employees will show an interest in organisational changes and initiate self-improvement efforts to keep up with the changes. This improves conscientiousness as employees sincerely devote to the organisation as well as conform to organisational rules, regulations and procedures beyond the organisation's requirements. Sportsmanship will follow as inspired employees are more likely to tolerate less-than-desirable situations without complaining and avoid negative behaviours. Hence, a conducive office social environment is worth considering, and organisations can promote this through increased staff participation in office social functions such as office-wide birthday celebrations.

There is little value in exhibiting organisational citizenship behaviour unless it is endorsed by the organisations. To promote organisational citizenship behaviour, awareness is crucial. Thus, educating staff on the benefits of organisational citizenship behaviour for personal advancement and organisational sustainability is central. Training can be provided to improve management awareness of organisational citizenship behaviour and assist leaders to identify employee displays of organisational citizenship behaviour. The benefits of displaying organisational citizenship behaviour may encourage management to include organisational citizenship behaviour in their performance appraisals. Once organisational citizenship behaviour is endorsed by the organisations and employees see it as instrumental in career advancement, employees will make an effort to display these behaviours. If, however, management chooses not to factor organisational citizenship behaviour in the performance appraisal, an alternative informal reward system can be considered.

Best Practices in Organisational Citizenship Behaviour in the New Millennium

As mentioned earlier, incorporating organisational citizenship behaviours in formal evaluation and reward systems might affect individuals and their display of organisational citizenship behaviours (Becton et al. 2008). It may give a positive or negative impact on organisational effectiveness (Zhang 2011). Hence, it is imperative that organisations incorporate the right dimensions of organisational citizenship behaviour in the formal evaluation and reward systems so as to improve organisational citizenship behaviour and, ultimately, organisational effectiveness. In addition, Zhang (2011) noted motivating employees, promoting high-quality leader–member exchange and looking out for traits related to organisational citizenship behaviour in hiring practices to encourage organisational citizenship behaviour at the workplace. New hires with positive attitudes can be utilised to motivate other staffs to exhibit organisational citizenship behaviours. Moreover, Cohen and Vigoda (2000) affirm that organisations may benefit from hiring employees with high citizenship values and encouraging the adoption of such values by their current employees. Organ et al. (2006) emphasise on creating a workplace environment that is conducive and supportive of organisational citizenship behaviour, while Zhang (2011) seeks management's understanding and consideration of organisational citizenship behaviour in performance evaluations to actively facilitate organisational citizenship behaviour among employees.

Cohen and Vigoda (2000) further assert that the organisation is instrumental in determining whether general citizenship behaviour contributes to organisational citizenship behaviour in the organisation. Contextual work attitudes (job satisfaction, organisational commitment and participation in decision-making) mediate the effect of general citizenship (political participation, community involvement, civility and faith in citizen involvement) on organisational citizenship behaviour. It argues that general citizenship equips the individual with positive attitudes and valuable civic skills that can be transferred to the work setting provided that the individual perceives a fair and satisfactory work setting. Community involvement and faith in citizen involvement significantly affect participation in decision-making, while civility enhances organisational commitment. Faith in citizen involvement also enhances job satisfaction. In essence, participation in nonwork activities in general, and in citizenship activities in particular, can enhance organisational citizenship behaviour. People who tend to perform more good general citizenship behaviour are also more likely to do so in the workplace (Pateman 1970; Peterson 1990).

Organisational citizenship behaviour could also be enhanced through motivating employees and giving them the opportunity to display organisational citizenship behaviours (Zhang 2011). Organ et al. (2006) contend that organisational citizenship behaviour is a function of ability, motivation and opportunity. Hence, organisations that provide a platform to promote ability, motivation and opportunity could possibly enhance organisational citizenship behaviour and consequently organisational performance. Jiang et al. (2012) emphasise on how the internal fit among human resource practices influences employee abilities, motivation and opportunities to contribute in a potentially harmonious manner (Becker and Huselid 1998; Delery and Shaw 2001; Guest 1997) to obtain desired employee performance which, conceptually, directly impacts organisational performance. Shih et al. (2006) identify training (e.g. on-the-job training, off-the-job training, online training and classroom training), involvement (e.g. empowerment, voice, employee participation and information sharing) and motivation as leading contributory factors to improved performance. Providing training, particularly when used as a reward, motivates employees (Liao et al. 2009), while empowerment provides employees with opportunities to contribute as well as motivation to perform (Delery and Shaw 2001). Hence, human resource policies may be oriented towards influencing the knowledge, skills, and abilities domain; the motivation and effort domain; and the opportunities to contribute domain, in order to maximise employee contributions (Lepak et al. 2006). All three human resource policy domains synergistically and simultaneously contribute to employee performance (Jiang et al. 2012). Additionally, Wang et al. (2011) established the relationship between value/identity-based motivation and sportsmanship, civic virtue, courtesy and altruism.

As organisational citizenship behaviour is influenced by positive job attitudes (Podsakoff et al. 2000), practitioners should recognise the importance of human resource management programmes to monitor and improve employees' job attitudes. Employees that are satisfied or committed to their jobs are more likely to exhibit organisational citizenship behaviour (e.g. Bateman and Organ 1983; Bolino et al. 2002; MacKenzie et al. 1998) and potentially promote knowledge sharing (Hsu and Lin 2008). Teh and Sun (2012) affirm that attitude factors such as job involvement and job satisfaction are positively related to knowledge sharing behaviour. Hence, management should focus on improving organisational citizenship behaviour through active constructive leadership to nurture a knowledge sharing culture. Management has to acknowledge the instrumentality of organisational citizenship behaviour for organisational effectiveness (Jiao et al. 2011).

The magnitude of employees' expectations about the importance of role requirements also has a significant influence on not only the performance of task activities but also on their ultimate enactment of citizenship (Dierdorff et al. 2010). Hence, management needs to define or negotiate role performance effectively as these affect employees' role perceptions (Naylor et al. 1980; Schaubroeck et al. 1993) as well as enhance individual-level motivation, satisfaction and effectiveness (Abramis 1994; Jackson and Schuler 1995). Other interventions such as 'on-boarding' or organisational socialisation and specific manager-to-employee feedback on employee role expectations may be equally effective. Additionally, it is critical to take into account the moderating effects of both the person and environment. Ambiguous environments will negatively affect citizenship, and, therefore, interventions should aim at helping employees examine prosocial elements of role performance and providing clarity around task-specific demands. Conversely, as social support positively affects citizenship, interventions aimed at training managers to create more supportive work environments are more likely to improve citizenship (Podsakoff et al. 1996; Tepper et al. 2004). It is also important that management creates a context to incorporate citizenship as part of overall role performance since autonomy has an effect on prosocial role expectations (Dierdorff et al. 2010).

Organisations with very high or very low power distance may leverage it to improve organisational citizenship behaviours. Although the literature is quite ambivalent regarding the implications of power distance for organisational citizenship behaviours, researchers have asserted an inverse relationship between employee's power distance beliefs and organisational citizenship behaviours (Kirkman et al. 2009). Employees with high power distance beliefs would engage less frequently in organisational citizenship behaviours since they would likely behave submissively to avoid disagreements. On the contrary, low power distance would create more opportunity, liberty and willingness to voice their opinions and engage in other discretionary behaviours (Hofstede 2001). However, the other school of thought believes that in high power distance countries, organisational citizenship behaviour is an implied requirement of the job, and, therefore, the tendency for organisational citizenship behaviour is higher than low power distance nations (Javidan et al. 2006; Lam et al. 1999; Paine and Organ 2000). This line of thought is evidenced in a comparative study between Malaysia and Germany where Malaysians display higher levels of organisational citizenship behaviours than Germans (Coyne and Ong 2007). Nonetheless, for distinct reasons, both very low and very high power distance beliefs favour organisational citizenship behaviours (Cavazotte et al. 2014).

Somech and Ron (2007) argue that collectivism is the most effective predictor of organisational citizenship behaviour when examined simultaneously with positive and negative affectivity. Collectivism is positively related to altruism, conscientiousness, sportsmanship, and civic virtue. A collectivistic orientation promotes in-group collaboration and social responsibility values unlike individualism which encourages competition and may be more inwardly focused (Bontempo et al. 1990; George and Jones 1997). Hence, variations in individualism–collectivism should influence personal tendencies to engage in organisational citizenship behaviour. The strong association between positive affectivity and organisational citizenship behaviour could be attributed to positive emotional state in general, and positive perception of situations and other workers, generally favourable outlook, and increased social awareness, in particular. On the contrary, negative affectivity increases the psychological distance between such individuals and others, who, hence, will less likely exhibit helping and prosocial acts (George 1990).

Perceived superior support is also valued as a predictor of organisational citizenship behaviour. Perceived superior support is positively and significantly related to altruism, conscientiousness, sportsmanship and civic virtue (Somech and Ron

2007). Superiors that appreciate the contributions of their subordinates, help them in their work and deal with stressful situations (Randall et al. 1999), care about their well-being, take pride in them and compensate them (Eisenberger et al. 2002) and evaluate them fairly are likely to be reciprocated favourably. Based on the principle of social exchange and reciprocity norms, individuals are obligated to repay superiors through positive, beneficial actions. Moreover, fair and supportive superiors can be trusted to protect their interests; this in turn engenders high-quality exchange relationships. Perceptions of fairness and perceived supervisor's support have significant relationships with organisational citizenship behaviour of roughly comparable strength (Podsakoff et al. 2000). Hence, organisational citizenship behaviour is the currency of reciprocity and is supported by literature (Organ and Ryan 1995; Schnake 1991).

Conclusion

As organisational citizenship behaviour promotes the effective functioning of the organisation (Robbins 1996), organisational citizenship behaviour should be actively encouraged at the organisational level (Zhang 2011). Besides classic organisational citizenship behaviour factors, organisations may wish to consider introducing change-oriented organisational citizenship behaviour as well. Change-oriented organisational citizenship behaviour that incorporates innovation, creativity and voice in good citizenship plays a major role in making some organisations better than others (Bettencourt 2004). Moreover, given the positive relationships between organisational citizenship behaviour and individual outcomes, Podsakoff et al. (2000) emphasise that organisations ought to encourage employees to engage in organisational citizenship behaviour. Organisations should, therefore, focus on identifying factors such as leadership style, employee attitudes, dispositions and work characteristics (Podsakoff et al. 2000) that promote organisational citizenship behaviour. Organisations may also consider the extent to which employees are motivated by their value and identity perceptions (Wang et al. 2011).

In essence, given that organisational citizenship behaviour potentially impacts productivity and efficiency of the organisation, organisational citizenship behaviour should be seriously considered in improving organisational profitability, reducing costs, increasing employee performance and well-being as well as enhancing the social environment in the workplace. Considering the long-term benefits of organisational citizenship behaviour in the workplace, organisational citizenship behaviour is indeed a worthy investment. Moreover, it may be essential for organisational sustainability in the new millennium. Hence, it is worthwhile to enhance employee awareness of organisational citizenship behaviour in the workplace. Having comprehensively discussed the theoretical aspects of the study, the remaining chapters will focus on data analysis and interpretation of the findings. The final chapter summarises the entire study and provides conclusions and recommendations.

References

Abdullah, M. H., & Mohd Nasurdin, A. (2008). Investigating the influence of organizational justice on hotel employees' organizational citizenship behavior intentions and turnover intentions. *Journal of Human Resources in Hospitality & Tourism, 7*(1), 1–23.

Abramis, D. J. (1994). Work role ambiguity, job satisfaction, and job performance: Meta-analyses and review. *Psychological Reports, 75*, 1411–1433.

Ahmad, A. K., & Singh, S. (2001). Leading and motivating a Malaysian workforce. In A. Abdullah & H. M. Low (Eds.), *Understanding the Malaysian workforce: Guidelines for managers* (pp. 43–60). Kuala Lumpur: Kinta Enterprise.

Allen, T. D., & Rush, M. C. (1998). The effects of organizational citizenship behavior on performance judgements: A field study and a laboratory experiment. *Journal of Applied Psychology, 83*(2), 247–260.

Allen, T. D., Eby, L. T., Poteet, M., Lima, L., & Lentz, E. (2004). Outcomes associated with mentoring proteges: A meta-analysis. *Journal of Applied Psychology, 89*(1), 127–136.

Allen, T. D., Smith, M. A., Mael, F. A., O'Shea, P. G., & Eby, L. T. (2009). Organisation-level mentoring and organisational performance within substance abuse centres. *Journal of Management, 35*(5), 1113–1128.

Ansari, M. A., Kee, M. H. D., & Aafaqi, R. (2007). Leader-member exchange and attitudinal outcomes: Role of procedural justice climate. *Leadership and Organization Development Journal, 28*(8), 690–709.

Asgari, A., Silong, A. D., Ahmad, A., & Bahaman, A. S. (2008). The relationship between transformational leadership behaviors, organizational justice, leader-member exchange, perceived organizational support. *European Journal of Scientific Research, 23*(2), 227–242.

Bass, B. M. (1985). *Leadership and beyond expectations*. New York: Free Press.

Bateman, T. S., & Organ, D. W. (1983). Job satisfaction and the good soldier: The relationship between affect and employee citizenship. *Academy of Management Journal, 26*(4), 587–595.

Battaglio, P. R., Jr., & Condrey, S. E. (2009). Reforming public management: Analyzing the impact of public service reform on organizational and managerial trust. *Journal of Public Administration Research and Theory, 19*, 689–707.

Becker, G. S. (1993). The economic way of looking at behaviour. *The Journal of Political Economy, 101*(3), 385–409.

Becker, B., & Huselid, M. A. (1998). High performance work systems and firm performance: A synthesis of research and managerial implications. *Research in Personnel and Human Resource Management, 16*(1), 53–101.

Becton, J. B., Giles, W. F., & Schraeder, M. (2008). Evaluating and rewarding OCBs. *Employee Relations, 30*(5), 494–514.

Berman, J. S., & Kenny, D. A. (1976). Correlational bias in observer ratings. *Journal of Personality and Social Psychology, 34*, 263–273.

Bettencourt, L. A. (2004). Change-oriented organizational citizenship behaviors: The direct and moderating influence of goal orientation. *Journal of Retailing, 80*(3), 165–180.

Blau, P. (1964). *Exchange and power in social life*. New York: Wiley.

Bolino, M. C., & Turnley, W. H. (2003). Going the extra mile: Cultivating and managing employee citizenship behavior. *Academy of Management Executive, 17*(3), 60–71.

Bolino, M. C., Turnley, W. H., & Bloodgood, J. M. (2002). Citizenship behavior and the creation of social capital in organizations. *Academy of Management Review, 27*, 505–522.

Bontempo, R., Lobel, S., & Triandis, H. (1990). Compliance and value internationalisation in Brazil and the United States. *Journal of Cross-Cultural Psychology, 21*(2), 200–213.

Bruner, J. S., & Tagiuri, R. (1954). The perception of people. In G. Lindzey (Ed.), *Handbook of social psychology* (Vol. 2, pp. 634–654). Cambridge: Addison-Wesley.

Burns, J. M. (1978). *Leadership*. New York: Harper & Row.

Cavazotte, F., Hartman, N. S., & Bahiense, E. (2014). Charismatic leadership, citizenship behaviors, and power distance orientation: Comparing Brazilian and U.S. workers. *Cross Cultural Research, 48*(1), 3–31.

Chahal, H. (2010). Antecedents and consequences of organisational citizenship behaviour (OCB): A conceptual framework in reference to health care sector. *Journal of Services Research, 10*(2), 25–44.

Chang, C. S. (2014). Moderating effects of nurses' organizational justice between organizational support and organizational citizenship behaviors for evidence-based practice. Worldviews on *Evidence-based Nursing, 11*(5), 332–340.

Chapman, L. J. (1967). Illusory correlation in observational reports. *Journal of Verbal Learning and Verbal Behavior, 6*, 151–155.

Chapman, L. J., & Chapman, J. P. (1967). Genesis of popular but erroneous psychodiagnostic observations. *Journal of Abnormal Psychology, 72*, 193–204.

Chew, Y. T. (2005a). Achieving organisational prosperity through employee motivation and retention: A comparative study of strategic HRM practices in Malaysian institutions. *Research and Practice in Human Resource Management, 13*(2), 87–104.

Chew, Y. T. (2005b). The changing HRM practices of Japanese firms and the impacts on compensation practices of Japanese affiliates in Malaysia. *Forum of International Development, 28*(1), 55–80.

Chin, T., & Maniam, M. (2001). The future Malaysian workforce. In A. Abdullah & H. M. Low (Eds.), *Understanding the Malaysian workforce: Guidelines for managers* (pp. 208–216). Kuala Lumpur: Kinta Enterprise.

Chiun, L. M., Ramayah, T., & Kueh, J. S. H. (2006). An investigation of leader member exchange effects on organizational citizenship behavior in Malaysia. *Journal of Business and Management, 12*, 5–23.

Chong, L. C., & Jain, H. C. (1987). Japanese management in Singapore: Convergence of human capital management practices. *Asia Pacific Journal of Management, 4*(2), 73–89.

Coggburn, J. D. (2006). At-will employment in government: Insights from the State of Texas. *Review of Public Personnel Administration, 26*, 158–177.

Coggburn, J. D., Battaglio, R. P., Jr., Bowman, J. S., Condrey, S. E., Goodman, D., & West, J. P. (2010). State government human resource professionals' commitment to employment at will. *American Review of Public Administration, 40*, 189–208.

Cohen, A., & Vigoda, E. (2000). Do good citizens make good organizational citizens?: An empirical examination of the relationship between general citizenship and organizational citizenship behavior in Israel. *Administration & Society, 32*(5), 596–624.

Cohen-Charash, Y., & Spector, P. E. (2001). The role of justice in organizations: A meta-analysis. *Organizational Behavior & Human Decision Processes, 86*(2), 278–321.

Colquitt, J. A., Conlon, D. E., Wesson, M. J., Porter, C. O. L. H., & Ng, K. Y. (2001). Justice at the millennium: A meta-analytic review of 25 years of organizational justice research. *Journal of Applied Psychology, 86*(3), 425–445.

Cooper, W. H. (1981). Ubiquitous halo. *Psychological Bulletin, 90*, 218–244.

Coyne, I., & Ong, T. (2007). Organizational citizenship behaviour and turnover intention: A cross-cultural study. *International Journal of Human Resource Management, 18*(6), 1085–1097.

Davis, R. V. (1992). Person-environment fit and job satisfaction. In C. J. Cranny, P. C. Smith, & E. F. Stone (Eds.), *Job satisfaction* (pp. 69–73). New York: Lexington Books.

Dawley, D. D., Andrews, M. C., & Bucklew, N. S. (2008). Mentoring, supervisor support and perceived organisational support: What matters most? *Leadership & Organisational Development Journal, 29*(3), 235–247.

Delery, J. E., & Shaw, J. D. (2001). The strategic management of people in work organizations: Review, synthesis, and extension. *Research in Personnel and Human Resources Management, 20*, 165–197.

DeNisi, A. S., Cafferty, T. P., & Meglino, B. M. (1984). A cognitive view of the performance appraisal process: A model and research propositions. *Organizational Behavior and Human Performance, 33*, 360–396.

Dierdorff, E. C., Surface, E. A., & Brown, K. G. (2010). Frame-of-reference training effectiveness: Effects of goal orientation and self-efficacy on affective, cognitive, skill-based, and transfer outcomes. *Journal of Applied Psychology, 95*(6), 1181–1191.

Donaldson, S. I., Ensher, E. A., & Grant-Vallone, E. J. (2000). Longitudinal examination of mentoring relationships on organizational commitment and citizenship behaviour. *Journal of Career Development, 26*(4), 233–249.
Ehrhart, M. G. (2004). Leadership and justice climate as antecedents of unit-level organizational citizenship behavior. *Personnel Psychology, 57*(1), 61–94.
Ehrhart, M. G., & Naumann, S. E. (2004). Organizational citizenship behavior in work groups: A group norms approach. *Journal of Applied Psychology, 89*(6), 960–974.
Eisenberger, R., Cummings, S., Armeli, S., & Lynch, P. (1997). Perceived organisational support, discretionary treatment and job satisfaction. *Journal of Applied Psychology, 82*(5), 812–820.
Eisenberger, S., Stinglhamber, F., Vandenberghe, C., Sucharski, I. L., & Rhoades, L. (2002). Perceived supervisor support: Contributions to perceived organizational support and employee retention. *Journal of Applied Psychology, 87*(3), 565–573.
Fagenson, E. A. (1989). The mentor advantage: Perceived career/job experiences of proteges versus non-proteges. *Journal of Organisational Behaviour, 10*(4), 309–320.
Fiske, S. T. (1981). Social cognition and affect. In J. Harvey (Ed.), *Cognition, social behavior, and the environment* (pp. 227–264). Reading: Addison-Wesley.
Fiske, S. T. (1982). Schema-triggered affect: Applications to social perception. In M. Clark & S. T. Fiske (Eds.), *Affect and cognition: The 17th annual Carnegie symposium on cognition* (pp. 55–78). Hillsdale: Erlbaum.
Fiske, S. T., & Pavelchak, M. (1986). Category-based versus piecemeal-based affective responses: Developments in schema-triggered affect. In R. M. Sorrentino & E. T. Higgens (Eds.), *The handbook of motivation and cognition: Foundations of social behavior* (pp. 167–203). New York: Guilford.
Folger, R. (1993). Justice, motivation, and performance beyond role requirements. *Employee Responsibilities and Rights Journal, 6*(3), 239–248.
Fuller, J. B., Patterson, C. E. P., Hester, K., & Stringer, D. Y. (1996). A quantitative review of research on charismatic leadership. *Psychological Reports, 78*, 271–287.
George, J. M. (1990). Personality, affect and behavior in groups. *Journal of Personality and Social Psychology, 75*, 462–474.
George, J. M., & Bettenhausen, K. (1990). Understanding prosocial behavior, sales performance, and turnover: A group-level analysis in a service context. *Journal of Applied Psychology, 75*, 698–709.
George, J. M., & Jones, G. R. (1997). Organizational spontaneity in context. *Human Performance, 10*(2), 153–170.
Gouldner, A. (1960). The norm of reciprocity. *American Sociological Review, 25*(2), 165–167.
Guest, D. (1997). Human resource management and performance: A review and research agenda. *International Journal of Human Resource Management, 8*(3), 263–276.
Hassan, A., & Hashim, J. (2011). Role of organizational justice in determining work outcomes of national and expatriate academic staff in Malaysia. *International Journal of Commerce and Management, 21*(1), 82–93.
Hassan, A., & Mohd Noor, K. (2008). Organizational justice and extra-role behavior: Examining the relationship in the Malaysian cultural context. *IIUM Journal of Economics and Management, 16*(2), 187–208.
Ho, C. T. B., Hsu, S. F., & Oh, K. B. (2009). Knowledge sharing: Game and reasoned action perspectives. *Industrial Management & Data Systems, 109*(9), 1211–1230.
Hofstede, G. (2001). *Culture's consequences: Comparing values, behaviors, institutions, and organizations across nations*. Thousand Oaks: Sage.
Homans, G. C. (1961). *Social behaviour: Its elementary forms*. London: Routledge and Kegan Paul.
Hooi, L. W. (1997a). Education and training in automanufacturing companies in Japan and Malaysia: A comparative analysis. In *Discussion papers in economics and business* (Discussion Paper 97–22, pp. 1–20). Osaka: Faculty of Economics and Osaka School of International Public Policy (OSIPP) Osaka University.

Hooi, L. W. (1997b). A comparative analysis of human resource management between Japan and Malaysia in automanufacturing companies. In *Discussion papers in economics and business* (Discussion Paper 97–23, pp. 1–20). Osaka: Faculty of Economics and Osaka School of International Public Policy (OSIPP) Osaka University.

Hooi, L. W. (1999). A comparative analysis of human resource management between Japan and Malaysia in auto manufacturing companies. *Journal of International Public Policy Studies, 3*(2), 153–174.

Hooi, L. W. (2001a). Education and training in the private sector: A comparative analysis between Japan and Malaysia. *Human Resource Development Journal, 3*(2), 39–46.

Hooi, L. W. (2001b). Education and training in the auto manufacturing industry: A comparative analysis between Japan and Malaysia. *Human Resources Health Development Journal, 5*(1–3), 39–46.

Hooi, L. W. (2002). The impact of Japanese promotion practices on Malaysian manufacturing companies. *Asia Pacific Business Review, 9*(1), 21–38.

Hooi, L. W. (2006a). Implementing E-HRM: The readiness of small and medium sized manufacturing companies in Malaysia. *Asia Pacific Business Review, 12*(4), 465–485.

Hooi, L. W. (2006b). Japanese remuneration system in Malaysia: A case study analysis. *Compensation & Benefits Review, 38*(6), 31–41.

Hooi, L. W. (2006c). Employee loyalty at the workplace: The impact of Japanese style of human resource management. *International Journal of Applied HRM, 3*(1), 1–17.

Hooi, L. W. (2007a). Remuneration practices in the chemical industry in Malaysia: The impact on employee satisfaction. *Compensation & Benefits Review, 39*(4), 56–67.

Hooi, L. W. (2007b). Human capital development policies: Enhancing employees' satisfaction. *Journal of European Industrial Training, 31*(4 & 5), 297–322.

Hooi, L. W. (2007c). Current recruitment trends in Malaysia: A case study analysis. *International Journal of Knowledge Culture and Change Management, 7*(6), 23–32.

Hooi, L. W. (2008a). Current remuneration practices in the multinational companies in Malaysia: A case study analysis. *Research and Practice in Human Resource Management, 16*(1), 78–103.

Hooi, L. W. (2008b). The adoption of Japanese recruitment practices in Malaysia. *International Journal of Manpower, 29*(4), 362–378.

Hooi, L. W. (2008c). Integrating global recruitment trends: The effect on employee satisfaction. *International Journal of Knowledge Culture and Change Management, 8*(4), 151–164.

Hooi, L. W. (2010a). Technical training in the MNCs in Malaysia: A case study analysis of the petrochemical industry. *Journal of European Industrial Training, 34*(4), 317–343.

Hooi, L. W. (2010b). Human capital management in Malaysia: Local and foreign perspectives. *St. Andrew's University Economic and Business Review, 52*(1), 20–32.

Hooi, L. W. (2012). Organisational justice, organisational citizenship behavior and job satisfaction: What is the relationship? *Journal for International Business and Entrepreneurship Development, 6* (3/4), 274–302.

Hooi, L. W., & Su, A. S. Y. (2010c). Motivational factors of shift workers in the chemical industry in Malaysia. *International Journal of Management Practice, 4*(2), 149–168.

Hooi, L. W., Sulaiman, M., & Omar, A. (2012). Procedural justice in promotion decisions of managerial staff in Malaysia. *Asia Pacific Business Review, 18*(1), 99–121.

Hsu, C. L., & Lin, J. C. C. (2008). Acceptance of blog usage: The roles of technology acceptance, social influence and knowledge sharing motivation. *Information & Management, 45*, 65–74.

Hui, C., Lee, C., & Wang, H. (2015). Organizational inducements and employee citizenship behavior: The mediating role of perceived insider status and the moderating role of collectivism. *Human Resource Management, 54*(3), 439–456.

Hunt, D. M., & Michael, C. (1983). Mentorship: A career training and development tool. *Academy of Management Review, 8*(3), 475–485.

Ishak, N. A. (2005). Promoting employees' innovativeness and organisational citizenship behaviour through superior-subordinate relationship in the workplace. *Research and Practice in Human Resource Management, 13*(92), 16–30.

Ishak, N. A., & Ahmad, Z. A. (2004). Organizational justice and organizational citizenship behaviour: The mediating impact of leader-member exchange. *Academy of World Business, Marketing and Management Development Conference Proceedings, 1*,1094–1102.
Ishak, N. A., & Alam, S. S. (2009). The effects of leader-member exchange on organisational justice and organisational citizenship behavior: Empirical study. *European Journal of Social Sciences, 8*(2), 324–334.
Jackson, S. E., & Schuler, R. S. (1995). Understanding human resource management in the context of organizations and their environments. In M. R. Rosenszweig, & L.W. Porter (Eds.), *Annual review of psychology, 46*, 237–264. Palo Alto: Annual Reviews.
Javidan, M., Dorfman, P. W., de Luque, M. S., & House, R. J. (2006). In the eye of the beholder: Cross cultural lessons in leadership from project GLOBE. *The Academy of Management Perspectives, 20*(1), 67–90.
Jiang, K., Lepak, D. P., Han, K., Hong, Y., Kim, A., & Winkle, A. (2012). Clarifying the construct of human resource systems: Relating human resource management to employee performance. *Human Resource Management Review, 22*, 73–85.
Jiao, C., Richards, D. A., & Zhang, K. (2011). Leadership and organizational citizenship behavior: OCB-specific meanings as mediators. *Journal of Business Psychology, 26*(1), 11–25.
Judge, T. A., & Piccolo, R. F. (2004). Transformational and transactional leadership: A meta-analytic test of their relative validity. *Journal of Applied Psychology, 89*, 755–768.
Kandan, P., & Ali, I. (2010). A correlation study of leader-member exchange and organisational citizenship behaviour in a public sector organisation. *Journal of Global Business and Economics, 1*(1), 62–78.
Kawabe, N. (1991). Japanese management in Malaysia. In S. Yamashita (Ed.), *Transfer of Japanese technology and management to the ASEAN countries*. Tokyo: University of Tokyo Press.
Khalid, S. A., & Ali, H. (2005). The effects of organizational citizenship behavior on withdrawal behavior: A Malaysian study. *International Journal of Management and Entrepreneurship, 1*(1), 30–40.
Kirkman, B., Chen, G., Farh, J., Chen, Z., & Lowe, K. (2009). Individual power distance orientation and follower reactions to transformational leaders: A cross-level, crosscultural examination. *Academy of Management Journal, 52*(4), 744–764.
Konovsky, M. A., & Organ, D. W. (1993). *Dispositional versus contextual determinants of organizational citizenship behavior* (Unpublished manuscript). New Orleans: Tulane University.
Konovsky, M. A., & Pugh, S. D. (1994). Citizenship behavior and social exchange. *Academy of Management Journal, 37*(3), 656–669.
Kouzes, J. M., & Posner, B. Z. (1987). *The leadership challenge: How to get extraordinary things done in organizations*. San Francisco: Jossey-Bass.
Kram, K. E. (1985). *Mentoring at work: Developmental relationships in organizational life*. Glenview: Scott, Foresman and Co.
Kwan, H. K., Liu, J., Liu, J., & Hong-Kit Yim, F. (2011). Effects of mentoring functions on receivers' organisational citizenship behaviour in a Chinese context: A two-study investigation. *Journal of Business Research, 64*(4), 363–370.
Lam, A., & Lambermont-Ford, J. P. (2010). Knowledge sharing in organisational contexts: A motivation-based perspective. *Journal of Knowledge Management, 14*(1), 51–66.
Lam, S. K., Hui, C., & Law, K. (1999). Organizational citizenship behavior: Comparing perspectives of supervisors and subordinates across four international samples. *Journal of Applied Psychology, 84*, 594–601.
Lee, K., & Allen, N. J. (2002). Organizational citizenship behavior and workplace deviance: The role of affect and cognitions. *Journal of Applied Psychology, 87*, 131–142.
Leow, K. L., & Khong, K. W. (2009). Mentoring and leader-member exchange (LMX) in Malaysia. *Sunway Academic Journal, 6*, 147–172.
Lepak, D. P., Liao, H., Chung, Y., & Harden, E. E. (2006). A conceptual review of human resource management systems in strategic human resource management research. *Research in Personnel and Human Resources Management, 25*, 217–271.

Liao, H., Toya, K., Lepak, D. P., & Hong, Y. (2009). Do they see eye to eye? Management and employee perspectives of high-performance work systems and influence processes on service quality. *Journal of Applied Psychology, 94*(2), 371–391.

Lilly, J. (2015). The impact of justice type on organisational citizenship behaviour: Do outcome favourability and leader behaviour matter? *Current Psychology, 34*(1), 26–49.

Lim, L. (2001). Work cultural values of Malays and Chinese Malaysians. *International Journal of Cross Cultural Management, 1*(2), 209–226.

Lloyd, K. J., Boer, D., Keller, J. W., & Voelpel, S. (2015). Is my boss really listening to me? The impact of perceived supervisor listening on emotional exhaustion, turnover intention, and organizational citizenship behaviour. *Journal of Business Ethics, 130*(3), 509–524.

Lo, M. C., Ramayah, T., & Hui, J. K. S. (2006). An investigation of leader member exchange effects on organizational citizenship behavior in Malaysia. *Journal of Business and Management, 12*, 5–23.

Lowe, K. B., Kroeck, K. G., & Sivasubramaniam, N. (1996). Effectiveness correlates of transformational leadership and transactional leadership: A meta-analytic review of the MLQ literature. *Leadership Quarterly, 7*, 385–425.

MacKenzie, S. B., Podsakoff, P. M., & Ahearne, M. (1996). *Unpublished data analysis.* Bloomington: Indiana University School of Business.

MacKenzie, S. B., Podsakoff, P. M., & Ahearne, M. (1998). Some possible antecedents and consequences of in-role and extra-role salesperson performance. *Journal of Marketing, 62*(3), 87–98.

Mirza, S. S., & Juhary, H. A. (1995). *Managerial training and development in Malaysia*. Kuala Lumpur: Malaysia Institute of Management.

Mohd Nasurdin, A., & Soon, L. K. (2011). Organizational justice, age, and performance connection in Malaysia. *International Journal of Commerce and Management, 21*(3), 273–290.

Moorman, R. H., Niehoff, B. P., & Organ, D. W. (1993). Treating employees fairly and organizational citizenship behavior: Sorting the effects of job satisfaction, organizational commitment, and procedural justice. Employee Responsibilities and Rights *Journal, 6*(3), 209–225.

Morrison, E. W. (1994). Role definition and organizational citizenship behavior: The importance of the employee's perspective. *Academy of Management Journal, 37*(6), 1543–1567.

Morrison, E. W. (1995). Organisational citizenship behaviour as a critical link between HRM practices and service quality. *Human Resource Management, 35*(4), 493–512.

Naylor, J. C., Pritchard, R. D., & Ilgen, D. R. (1980). *A theory of behavior in organizations.* New York: Academic.

Nemeth, C. J., & Staw, B. M. (1989). The tradeoffs of social control and innovation in small groups and organizations. In L. Berkowitz (Ed.), *Advances in experimental social psychology* (Vol. 22, pp. 175–210). New York: Academic.

Niehoff, B. P., & Moorman, R. H. (1993). Justice as a mediator of the relationship between methods of monitoring and organizational citizenship behavior. *Academy of Management Journal, 36*(3), 527–556.

Okurame, D. E. (2008). Effects of protege-mentor gender mix on organizational commitment. *Journal of International Women's Studies, 9*(3), 1–12.

Okurame, D. E. (2009). Mentoring and organizational constraints as predictors of attitudes to work in the Nigerian public health sector. *Journal of Health and Human Services Administration, 32*(3), 342–371.

Okurame, D. E. (2011). Linking work-family conflict to career commitment: The moderating effects of gender and mentoring among Nigerian civil servants. *Journal of Career Development, 39*(5), 423–442.

Okurame, D. E. (2012). Impact of career growth prospects and formal mentoring on organisational citizenship behaviour. *Leadership & Organization Development Journal, 33*(1), 66–85.

Organ, D. W. (1988). *Organizational citizenship behavior: The good solider syndrome*. Lexington: Lexington Books.

Organ, D. W. (1997). Organizational citizenship behavior: It's construct clean-up time. *Human Performance, 10*(2), 85–97.

Organ, D. W., & Konovsky, M. A. (1989). Cognitive versus affective determinants of organizational citizenship behavior. *Journal of Applied Psychology, 74*, 157–164.

Organ, D. W., & Ryan, K. (1995). A meta-analytic review of attitudinal and dispositional predictors of organizational citizenship behavior. *Personnel Psychology, 48*(4), 775–802.
Organ, D. W., Podsakoff, P. M., & MacKenzie, S. B. (2006). *Organizational citizenship behavior. Its nature, antecedents, and consequences*. Thousand Oaks: Sage.
Othman, R. A., Rashida, H., Noor, A., & Rosmah, M. (2005). Psychological contract violation and organizational citizenship behavior. *Gaja Mada International Journal of Business, 7*, 325–349.
Paine, J. B., & Organ, D. W. (2000). The cultural matrix of organizational citizenship behavior: Some preliminary conceptual and empirical observations. *Human Resource Management Review, 10*(1), 45–59.
Park, O. S., & Sims, H. P., Jr. (1989). *Beyond cognition in leadership: Pro-social behavior and affect in managerial judgement* (Working paper). Seoul National University and Pennsylvania State University.
Pateman, C. (1970). *Participation and democratic theory*. London: Cambridge University.
Payne, S. (2006). *Mentoring a smart business decision, research shows*. Available at: http://communications.tamu.edu/newsarchives/05/020705-10.html. Accessed 12 Dec 2006.
Peterson, S. A. (1990). *Political behavior*. Thousand Oaks: Sage.
Pillai, R., Schriesheim, C. A., & Williams, E. S. (1999). Fairness perceptions and trust as mediators for transformational and transactional leadership: A two-sample study. *Journal of Management, 25*(6), 897–933.
Podsakoff, P. M., & MacKenzie, S. B. (1994). Organizational citizenship behaviors and sales unit effectiveness. *Journal of Marketing Research, 3*(1), 351–363.
Podsakoff, P. M., & MacKenzie, S. B. (1995). An examination of substitutes for leadership within a levels of analysis framework. *Leadership Quarterly, 6*, 289–328.
Podsakoff, P. M., & MacKenzie, S. B. (1997). Impact of organizational citizenship behavior on organizational performance: A review and suggestions for future research. *Human Performance, 10*(2), 133–151.
Podsakoff, P. M., MacKenzie, S. B., Moorman, R. H., & Fetter, R. (1990). Transformational leader behaviors and their effects on followers' trust in leader, satisfaction, and organizational citizenship behaviors. *The Leadership Quarterly, 1*(2), 107–142.
Podsakoff, P. M., MacKenzie, S. B., & Fetter, R. (1993). Substitutes for leadership and the management of professionals. *Leadership Quarterly, 4*(1), 1–44.
Podsakoff, P. M., MacKenzie, S. B., & Bommer, W. H. (1996). A meta-analysis of the relationships between Kerr and Jermier's substitutes for leadership and employee job attitudes, role perceptions, and performance. *Journal of Applied Psychology, 81*, 380–399.
Podsakoff, P. M., Ahearne, M., & MacKenzie, S. B. (1997). Organizational citizenship behavior and the quantity and quality of work group performance. *Journal of Applied Psychology, 82*, 262–270.
Podsakoff, P. M., MacKenzie, S. B., Paine, J. B., & Bachrach, D. G. (2000). Organizational citizenship behaviors: A critical review of the theoretical and empirical literature and suggestions for future research. *Journal of Management, 26*(3), 513–563.
Podsakoff, N. P., Whiting, S. W., Podsakoff, P. M., & Blume, B. D. (2009). Individual- and organizational-level consequences of organizational citizenship behaviors: A meta-analysis. *Journal of Applied Psychology, 94*, 122–141.
Putra, R. (1993). *Survey report: Indonesia in Asian dynamism through human capital development*. Tokyo: Asian Productivity Organization.
Randall, M. L., Cropanzano, R., Borman, C. A., & Birjulin, A. (1999). Organizational politics and organizational support as predictors of work attitudes, job performance, and organizational citizenship behavior. *Journal of Organizational Behavior, 20*, 159–174.
Robbins, S. P. (1996). *Organisational Behaviour: Concepts, controversies, and applications* (7th ed.). Englewood Cliffs: Prentice Hall.
Rousseau, D. M. (1989). Psychological and implied contracts in organisations. *Employee Rights and Responsibilities Journal, 2*(2), 121–139.

Rousseau, D. M. (1990). New hire perceptions of their own and their employer's obligations: A study of psychological contracts. *Journal of Organisational Behaviour, 11*(5), 389–400.
Scandura, T. A. (1992). Mentorship and career mobility: An empirical investigation. *Journal of Organizational Behaviour, 13*(2), 169–174.
Schnake, M. (1991). Organizational citizenship: A review, proposed model, and research agenda. *Human Relations, 44*(7), 735–759.
Schaubroeck, J., Ganster, D. C., Sime, W., & Editman, D. (1993). A field experiment testing supervisory role clarification. *Personnel Psychology, 46*, 1–25.
Shih, H.-A., Chiang, Y.-W., & Hsu, C.-C. (2006). Can high performance work systems really lead to better performance? *International Journal of Manpower, 27*(8), 741–763
Sheppard, P. (2001). Making decisions. In A. Abdullah & H. M. Low (Eds.), *Understanding the Malaysian workforce: Guidelines for managers* (pp. 71–80). Kuala Lumpur: Kinta Enterprise.
Smith, C. A., Organ, D. W., & Near, J. P. (1983). Organizational citizenship behavior: Its nature and antecedents. *Journal of Applied Psychology, 68*, 653–663.
Somech, A., & Ron, I. (2007). Promoting organizational citizenship behavior in schools: Impact of individual and organizational characteristics. *Educational Administration Quarterly, 43*(1), 38–66.
Teh, P., & Sun, H. (2012). Knowledge sharing, job attitudes and organisational citizenship behaviour. *Industrial Management & Data Systems, 112*(1), 64–82
Tepper, B. J., Duffy, M. K., Hoobler, J., & Ensley, M. D. (2004). Moderators of the relationships between coworkers' organizational citizenship behavior and fellow employees' attitudes. *Journal of Applied Psychology, 89*(3), 455–465.
Thong, G. T. S. (1991). Foundations of human capital management practices in Japanese companies in Malaysia. In S. Yamashita (Ed.), *Transfer of Japanese technology and management to the ASEAN Countries* (pp. 135–152). Tokyo: University of Tokyo Press.
Van Dyne, L., Cummings, L. L., & McLean Parks, J. (1995). Extra-role behaviors: In pursuit of construct and definitional clarity. *Research in Organizational Behavior, 17*(1), 215–285.
Van Yperen, N. W., den Berg, A. E., & Willering, B. M. (1999). Towards a better understanding of the link between participation in decision-making and organizational citizenship behavior: A multilevel analysis. *Journal of Occupational and Organizational Psychology, 72*, 377–392.
Vigoda, E., & Beeri, I. (2011). Change-oriented organizational citizenship behavior in public administration: The power of leadership and the cost of organizational politics. *Journal of Public Administration Research and Theory, 22*, 573–596.
Wagner, S. L., & Rush, M. (2000). Altruistic organizational citizenship behavior: Context, disposition and age. *The Journal of Social Psychology, 140*(3), 379–391.
Walz, S. M., & Niehoff, B. P. (1996). Organizational citizenship behaviors and their effect on organizational effectiveness in limited-menu restaurants. In J. B. Keys & L. N. Dosier (Eds.), *Academy of management best papers proceedings* (pp. 307–311). Briarcliff Manor: Academy of Management.
Walz, S. M., & Niehoff, B. P. (2000). Organizational citizenship behaviors: Their relationship to organizational effectiveness. *Journal of Hospitality & Tourism Research, 24*, 301–319.
Wang, H., Tsui, A. S., & Xin, K. R. (2011). CEO leadership behaviors, organizational performance and employees' attitude. *Leadership Quarterly, 22*(1), 92–105.
Weiss, D. J., Dawis, R. V., England, G. W., & Lofquist, L. H. (1967). *Manual for the Minnesota satisfaction questionnaire. Minnesota studies in vocational rehabilitation* (Vol. 22, pp. 32–35). Minneapolis: University of Minnesota Industrial Relations Center.
Werner, J. M. (1994). Dimensions that make a difference: Examining the impact of in-role and extrarole behaviors on supervisory ratings. *Journal of Applied Psychology, 94*, 98–107.
Whitely, W., Dougherty, T. W., & Dreher, G. F. (1991). Relationship of career mentoring and socio-economic origin to managers' and professionals' early career progress. *Academy of Management Journal, 34*(2), 331–335.

Whiting, S. W., Podsakoff, P. M., & Pierce, J. R. (2008). Effects of task performance, helping, voice and organizational loyalty on performance appraisal ratings. *Journal of Applied Psychology, 93*, 125–139.

Yong, K. B. (2003). Human resource management. In Malaysian Institute of Management (Ed.), *Management in Malaysia* (pp. 230–250). Shah Alam: Percetakan Printpack Sdn. Bhd.

Yu, G. W., Ahmad, K. Z., & Yap, S. F. (2014). Organisational justice and its role in promoting citizenship behaviour among hotel employees in Malaysia. *Institutions and Economies, 6*(2), 79–104

Zhang, D. (2011). *Organisational citizenship behaviour* (White paper 2011, pp. 1–13). Auckland: University of Auckland.

Chapter 7
Preliminary Data Analysis and Interpretation

Abstract This chapter provides the preliminary data analysis and interpretation of the findings. First, the chapter outlines the sampling results covering data collection procedures, demographic data of the companies and demographic data of the respondents. It then proceeds with screening the data to detect errors, missing data and outliers. Next, the discussion focuses on refining of measures to assess the reliability and validity of the scales. The analysis involves Cronbach's alpha, variance extracted measure and construct reliability to confirm the reliability of the scales. To test the goodness of measures, the study draws on content validity, convergent validity and discriminant validity. Then, results of the exploratory and confirmatory factor analysis are discussed. This is followed by the assessment of conformity with structural equation modelling (SEM) assumptions to check if the data satisfied the assumptions of sample size; normality, linearity and homoscedasticity; and multicollinearity. Finally, the chapter delineates the assessment of the measurement model to establish convergent and discriminant validity.

Introduction

This chapter delineates the research findings on the assessment of reliability and validity of the study. For the assessment of reliability and validity, the results are discussed in five parts – sampling results, data screening, reliability and validity of measures, exploratory factor analysis (EFA) and confirmatory factor analysis (CFA). Sampling results provide an insight of the site and subjects of the study – the selection criteria, sampling procedure, response rate, profile of the companies and demographic data of the respondents. Data screening discusses the procedure involved in detecting missing data and outliers. The assessment of reliability covers Cronbach's alpha, variance extracted measure and construct reliability, while validity assessment concerns content validity, convergent validity and discriminant validity. The results of the exploratory factor analysis are based on the principal component method to identify the minimum number of factors needed, while confirmatory factor analysis relates to the assessment of the validity of the measures. For the SEM analysis, the discussion focused on checking the assumptions on sample size; normality, linearity and homoscedasticity; multicollinearity; correlation

L.W. Hooi, *Organisational Justice and Citizenship Behaviour in Malaysia*,
Governance and Citizenship in Asia, DOI 10.1007/978-981-10-0030-0_7

analysis; validity and reliability of the measurement models, namely, discriminant validity and convergent validity.

Sampling Results

Data Collection Procedures

Data for the study was collected from a sample of manufacturing companies listed in the Federation of Malaysian Manufacturers (FMM) Directory. There were 2,571 companies registered with FMM as of 30 July 2010, and of these 100 companies were selected for the study. To enhance generalisability of the results obtained, the sample was selected using stratified random sampling as it was more appropriate (Cooper and Schindler 2001) and wide geographic regions can be reached (Sekaran 2003). In this study, the stratification of the population was by location, namely, the northern, central and southern region of Peninsular Malaysia. The northern region covers Perlis, Kedah, Penang, Kelantan, Terengganu and Perak; the central region Kuala Lumpur, Selangor and Pahang; and the southern region Johore, Malacca and Negri Sembilan. The companies have to fulfil two criteria to be selected – manufacturing companies registered with FMM and in operation for not <2 years. Though the sample includes a wide range of industries in the manufacturing sector, only companies that had been in operation for at least 2 years were selected in order to gauge the relationship between employee perceptions of organisational justice and organisational citizenship behaviour, job satisfaction and the quality of leader–member exchange.

After sampling based on the above criteria, permission was obtained to conduct the survey from the companies. After approval from the CEO, the next step was to contact the HR department of each of the companies by telephone. The theme, purpose, general outline, method and details of this study were explained. Three requests were made – to randomly select respondents to complete the questionnaire, to distribute the questionnaire and to return the completed questionnaires. A general outline of the research's aim and methodology was mailed to them in advance of the call. Ten questionnaires together with a cover letter and postage-paid return envelope were either mailed or personally distributed to each of the 100 companies. The companies were given 3 weeks to return the questionnaires, and reminders were sent to those companies that have not responded after the due date. Some of the companies were also contacted by phone in an attempt to collect back the questionnaires. Personal visits were also made to some of the companies in the vicinity. The response rate was 26.7 %. As a 30 % rate was quite acceptable for mail questionnaires (Sekaran 2003), the 267 responses were deemed usable for further analysis.

Demographic Data of Companies

Although a sample size of 100 companies was targeted, only 43 companies responded to the survey. As the companies were from a wide range of industrial groups, variation in the samples well represented the population of the manufacturing industry. Three industrial groups, namely, electrical products and computer (20.2 %), chemical and plastics (18.4 %) and machinery, equipment and engineering (16.1 %), dominated the sample. Food, beverages and tobacco constituted 10.1 % of the total sample. The other industrial groups such as building and furnishing materials; household goods; printing and publishing; pharmaceutical products and cosmetics; textile, clothing and footwear; energy; mining; and vehicle and parts each contributed <10 % of the total sample. Another 19.5 % of the sample was from other industrial groups not listed in the questionnaire.

In terms of company size based on number of employees, the majority of the companies (20.6 %) employed more than 1000 employees. 20.2 % of the companies have between 101 and 250 employees, followed by 50–100 employees and 501–1000 employees (16.1 %), and 251–500 employees (15.4 %). About 11.6 % of the companies have <50 employees. The distribution showed that slightly more than a third of the sample (36.7 %) was from large-scale companies (more than 500 employees) and slightly more than half (51.7 %) was from medium-scale companies (51–500 employees) in the industry.

As far as length of operation is concerned, 93 % of the companies have been in operation for more than 20 years. The majority of the companies were established between 1991 and 2000 (53.5 %). Only three companies were established between 2001 and 2009 (7 %). Two companies were established before 1971 (4.6 %), eight companies between 1971 and 1980 (18.6 %) and seven companies between 1981 and 1990 (16.3 %). This implies that the majority of the respondent companies are relatively stable organisations and are very likely to have certain practices that may influence employee citizenship. Furthermore, the majority of the companies are medium- to large-size companies, indicating that procedures and interpersonal relations may be more formalised. As the size of the companies complemented the age of the organisations, these two criteria gave a positive implication to the results of this study. The demographic data of the sample companies is summarised in Tables 7.1 and 7.2.

Demographic Data of Respondents

The demographic data of the respondents include age, gender, marital status, race, highest education level, educational background, years of working experience, length of service with current organisation, position and the department of the respondents. As far as age is concerned, the majority of the respondents are between the 25 and 40 years of age. This age group makes up about two thirds of the total

Table 7.1 Demographic data of the companies

Demographic characteristics	No. of Cos.	*N*	%	Cum. %
Industry				
Electrical products and computer	8	54	20.2	20.2
Chemical and plastics	6	49	18.4	38.6
Machinery, equipment and engineering	6	43	16.1	54.7
Food, beverages and tobacco	4	27	10.1	64.8
Building and furnishing materials	4	21	7.9	72.7
Household goods	2	10	3.7	76.4
Printing and publishing	1	4	1.5	77.9
Pharmaceutical products and cosmetics	1	2	0.7	78.6
Textile, clothing and footwear	1	2	0.7	79.3
Energy	1	1	0.4	79.7
Mining	1	1	0.4	80.1
Vehicle and parts	1	1	0.4	80.5
Others	7	52	19.5	100
Total	43	267	100	
Number of employees				
Less than 50 employees	8	31	11.6	11.6
50–100 employees	8	43	16.1	27.7
101–250 employees	9	54	20.2	47.9
251–500 employees	5	41	15.4	63.3
501–1000 employees	6	43	16.1	79.4
More than 1000 employees	7	55	20.6	100
Total	43	267	100	
Year of establishment				
Before 1971	2	10	3.7	3.7
1971–1980	8	56	21	24.7
1981–1990	7	40	15	39.7
1991–2000	23	152	57	96.7
2001–2009	3	9	3.3	100
Total	43	267		

respondents. Of these, 23.6 % are between 31 and 35 years of age. The others equally represent the 25–30 age group and 36–40 age group (22.1 %). Not many of the respondents are below 25 years of age, between 46 and 50 years of age or above 50 years of age. Each of these groups represents <10 % of the total respondents. Six percent of the respondents are below 25 years of age, and 7.9 % are between 46 and 50 years of age, while 4.5 % are above 50. About 13.9 % of the respondents are aged between 41 and 45. Thus, in terms of age, the variation in the sample well represented the working population.

Similarly, in terms of gender, the sample portrays the current working ratio among men and women in the country. As expected, the number of male respondents exceeds female respondents though the difference is not obvious. Male

Table 7.2 Number of respondents by industry and size

Industry	<50	50–100	101–250	251–500	501–1000	>1000	Total
Electrical products and computer	13	0	3	10	7	21	54
Chemical and plastics	0	15	17	0	17	0	49
Machinery, equipment and engineering	2	10	13	0	0	18	43
Food, beverages and tobacco	1	0	10	0	0	16	27
Building and furnishing materials	6	2	0	13	0	0	21
Household goods	1	0	0	9	0	0	10
Printing and publishing	0	4	0	0	0	0	4
Pharmaceutical products and cosmetics	2	0	0	0	0	0	2
Textile, clothing and footwear	0	0	2	0	0	0	2
Energy	0	0	0	0	1	0	1
Mining	0	0	1	0	0	0	1
Vehicle and parts		1	0	0	0	0	1
Others	6	11	8	9	18	0	52
Total	31	43	54	41	43	55	267

respondents representing more than half of the total respondents (56.6 %) exceed female respondents by 13.2 %. Among the respondents, two thirds are married (66.7 %), while the others are either single (31.1 %), divorce or separated (1.9 %) or widowed (0.4 %). As far as race is concerned, the variation in the respondents is representative of the management workforce composition in the corporate sector. About half of the respondents are Chinese (46.8 %), about a third Bumiputera (34.5 %), 16.5 % Indians and the rest others.

More than two thirds of the respondents have tertiary education qualification with a majority of the respondents having a bachelor degree or an advanced diploma in their respective fields (56.2 %). About a quarter of the respondents have a diploma qualification (25.8 %). Few have postgraduate qualifications – only two respondents have a doctoral degree and 11.6 % have a masters degree. Likewise, <10 % of the respondents have never studied beyond secondary school (5.6 %). All the respondents come from diverse educational background. The majority of the respondents are from engineering, production, science or technology background (44.6 %). Almost a third of the respondents are finance, accounting, economics or business majors (32.6 %). Some specialise in human resource management (4.9 %) or marketing (5.2 %). Thus, the respondents well represented the population of the manufacturing industry.

More than 75 % of the respondents have more than 5 years of working experience, while <10 % have worked for not more than 2 years. This indicates that the majority of the respondents probably have many experiences at the workplace that help shape their perceptions and relationship at work. Additionally, 73.4 % of the respondents have been with their current organisations for at least 3 years. Three years are reasonably long enough for the respondents to form perceptions that may affect their behaviour at the workplace. Hence, the responses of the majority of the respondents are relatively reliable and valid for the study. Of these, 26.6 % have between 3 and 5 years of service with their current organisations, 21.7 % 6–10 years, 19.1 % 11–15 years and 6 % more than 15 years.

Much variance can be observed among the respondents in terms of position in the organisation. More than half of the respondents are either engineers or executives (51.3 %). Slightly more than a third of the respondents are at the managerial level (36.2 %) – CEO/general managers (2.2 %), managers (24.3 %) and assistant managers (9.7 %). The rest of the respondents are section heads (12.4 %). Likewise, the respondents are from various departments typical of a manufacturing company. Accordingly, the variation in the samples reflects the perceptions of the respondents precisely. As in most manufacturing companies, the majority of the respondents are from the manufacturing, operations or engineering department (45.3 %). The next major groups of respondents are with the accounting or finance department (18.7 %) and marketing department (12.4 %). About 5.6 % of the respondents either are in top management or are corporate heads. The rest of the respondents are from various departments such as human resource department (5.2 %), IT/MIS department (6 %), research and development department (5.6 %), purchasing department (0.4 %) and other smaller departments (0.7 %). Table 7.3 summarises the demography of the respondents of this study.

Table 7.3 Demographic data of the respondents

Demographic characteristics	*N*	%	Cum. %
Age			
Below 25 years	16	6.0	6.0
25–30 years	59	22.1	28.1
31–35 years	63	23.6	51.7
36–40 years	59	22.1	73.8
41–45 years	37	13.9	87.6
46–50 years	21	7.9	95.5
More than 50 years	12	4.5	100
Total	267	100	
Sex			
Male	151	56.6	56.6
Female	116	43.4	100
Total	267	100	
Marital status			
Single	83	31.1	31.1
Married	178	66.7	97.8
Divorced/separated	5	1.9	99.6
Widowed	1	0.4	100
Total	267	100	
Race			
Bumiputera	92	34.5	34.5

(continued)

Table 7.3 (continued)

Demographic characteristics	*N*	%	Cum. %
Chinese	125	46.8	81.3
Indians	44	16.5	97.8
Others	6	2.2	100
Total	267		
Highest education level			
Doctoral	2	0.7	0.7
Masters	31	11.6	12.4
Bachelor/advanced diploma	150	56.2	68.5
Diploma	69	25.8	94.4
Secondary school	14	5.2	99.6
Primary school	1	0.4	100
Total	267	100	
Educational background			
Engineering/production	84	31.5	31.5
Finance/accounting	46	17.2	48.7
Economics/business	41	15.4	64.0
Human resource management	13	4.9	68.9
Marketing/sales	14	5.2	74.2
Science/technology	35	13.1	87.3
Others	34	12.7	100
Total	267	100	
Years of working experience			
Less than 1 year	5	1.9	1.9
1–2 years	19	7.1	9.0
3–5 years	39	14.6	23.6
6–10 years	68	25.5	49.1
11–15 years	69	25.8	74.9
More than 15 years	67	25.1	100
Total	267	100	
Length of service			
Less than 1 year	23	8.6	8.6
1–2 years	48	18.0	26.6
3–5 years	71	26.6	53.2
6–10 years	58	21.7	74.9
11–15 years	51	19.1	94.0
More than 15 years	16	6.0	100
Total	267	100	
Position			
CEO/general manager	6	2.2	2.2
Manager	65	24.3	26.6
Assistant manager	26	9.7	36.3
Section head	33	12.4	48.7
Engineer/executive	137	51.3	100

(continued)

Table 7.3 (continued)

Demographic characteristics	*N*	%	Cum. %
Total	267	100	
Department in the organisation			
Marketing	33	12.4	12.4
Manufacturing/operations/engineering	121	45.3	57.7
Accounting/finance	50	18.7	76.4
Human resource management	14	5.2	81.6
IT/MIS	16	6.0	87.6
Research and development	15	5.6	93.3
Top management/corporate	15	5.6	98.9
Purchasing	1	0.4	99.3
Others	2	0.7	100
Total	267	100	

Screening the Data

Checking for Errors

To ensure that statistical analyses are valid, the data was checked for values that were not within the range of possible values for a variable. For categorical variables, frequencies and the minimum and maximum values for each variable were inspected. Values that were outside the possible range were rectified. Similarly, continuous variables were also checked for errors using descriptives. The mean, standard deviation and minimum and maximum values for each item were examined. Out-of-range values were detected using sort cases command or search command provided by SPSS. Errors that were identified were corrected to avoid distortion during statistical analyses.

Detection of Missing Data and Outliers

The collected data was screened for completeness to avoid biased statistical inferences. Some respondents may not have answered certain items in the questionnaire for various reasons – the respondent did not understand the question, did not know the answer, was unwilling to respond to the question or simply felt not obligated to complete the questionnaire. Nine of the questionnaires received were unusable due to excessive missing data.

As outliers distort statistics and lead to results that are not generalisable (Tabachnick and Fidell 2007), the data was examined for extreme values using scatter plots. Additionally, descriptives were used to check if the responses were within the range of possible values for a variable. If outliers were detected, the data has to be inspected to identify the cause – incorrect data entry or failure to specify missing value codes. The results indicated that there was no major problem of outliers in the data.

Refining of Measures

Reliability

Though well-established scales were adopted, the reliability and validity of the scales were checked to assess the degree of measurement error. Reliability is the degree to which the measures are error free; it reflects the stability and consistency between items used to measure a variable. The scales were checked for internal consistency using Cronbach's alpha. The internal consistency of measures provides evidence for homogeneity of multiple measurements of a variable (Sekaran 2003) and may ideally be highly intercorrelated.

Cronbach's Alpha

Cronbach's alpha provides an indication of the average correlation among all the items in the scale. Values range from 0 to 1, with higher values indicating greater reliability. Cronbach's alpha for all the variables in the study was above 0.7, the minimum level recommended by Nunnally (1978) and De Vellis (2003). Thus, respondents' answers to all the items in the scales were consistent. In short, respondents understood and interpreted each of the items in the same way. Cronbach's alpha for the study are show in Table 7.4.

Variance Extracted Measure

To complement construct reliability, variance extracted measure was employed to assess whether the sum of variance in the indicators was accounted for by the latent variable. The indicators are representative of the latent construct if variance extracted

Table 7.4 Cronbach's alpha

Variable	Number of items	Cronbach's alpha
Procedural justice	7	0.888
Informational justice	5	0.866
Distributive justice	4	0.914
Interpersonal justice	4	0.868
Job satisfaction	4	0.865
Leader–member exchange	5	0.852
Courtesy	5	0.872
Sportsmanship	5	0.871
Altruism	5	0.845
Civic virtue	4	0.789
Conscientiousness	4	0.767

values are high. Average variance extracted of 0.5 or higher indicates adequate convergence (Fornell and Larcker 1981; Hair et al. 2010). This value can be calculated using standardised loadings:

$$\text{AVE} = \frac{\sum_{i=1}^{n} L_i^2}{\sum_{i=1}^{n} L_i^2 + \sum_{i=1}^{n} e_i}$$

L_i represents the standardised factor loading and i is the number of items.

Construct Reliability

As structural equation modelling models are used in the analyses, construct reliability (CR) is computed to assess if internal consistency exists. High construct reliability indicates that the measures all consistently represent the same latent construct. Construct reliability estimates of 0.7 and above demonstrates good reliability. If other indicators of a model's construct validity are good, reliability between 0.6 and 0.7 may be acceptable (Hair et al. 2010). Construct reliability can be computed from the square sum of factor loadings (L_i) for each construct and the sum of the error variance terms for a construct (e_i). Thus:

$$\text{CR} = \frac{\left(\sum_{i=1}^{n} L_i^2\right)}{\left(\sum_{i=1}^{n} L_i^2\right) + \left(\sum_{i=1}^{n} e_i\right)}$$

Validity

To test the goodness of measures, various validity tests can be used. One can test for content validity, face validity, criterion-related validity, concurrent validity, predictive validity, construct validity, convergent validity and discriminant validity. For the purpose of this study, content validity, convergent validity and discriminant validity were conducted. Convergent validity and discriminant validity were checked to demonstrate construct validity. Construct validity is established when the instruments tap the concept as theorised. The validity of a scale refers to the extent to which it accurately measures what it is supposed to measure.

Content Validity

The main aim of content validity was to establish if the measures adequately measure the concept. Content validity is high if more of the scale items are representative of the domain of the concept being measured (Sekaran 2003). Garver and Mentzer (1999) affirm that for content validity, the researcher's judgement and insight have to be complemented by the opinions of subject matter experts. Accordingly, extensive literature review was needed to establish the psychometric properties of the scales. All the scales adopted have been well established, and studies conducted using these scales have attested to the reliability and validity of the scales. Additionally, two academic experts in the field and two industry captains have scrutinised the scales. The scales were deemed relevant and adequate to measure the concept, and, therefore, content validity, specifically, face validity, was assured.

Convergent Validity

Assessing convergent validity was one of the two measures taken to confirm construct validity. Convergent validity is established when two measures of the same concept is highly correlated (Hair et al. 2010; Sekaran 2003). High correlations indicate that the scale is measuring the intended concept. Checking for convergent validity was relevant as different items were used to measure a construct. Correlations of the summated scale would determine convergent validity. In the study, the factor loadings from confirmatory factor analysis results were used to verify convergent validity. Significant factor loadings indicated convergent validity, and, therefore, insignificant factor loadings were excluded from further analysis. Average variance extracted was also used to examine convergent validity of each construct, and the results accounted for more than 50 % of the corresponding items (Fornell and Larcker 1981; Hair et al. 2010). Additionally, leading researchers have argued that although these are separate constructs, in practice, correlation should be found between them due to convergent validity of the constructs (Folger 1987).

Discriminant Validity

Discriminant validity is the extent to which two conceptually similar concepts are distinct. Discriminant validity is established when the measure has a low correlation with a variable that is supposed to be unrelated to that variable. The empirical tests have to demonstrate that the summated scale is sufficiently different from scales of other latent variables (Hair et al. 2010). Discriminant validity is established if indicators from one scale do not load closely to other scales. Alternatively, examining the correlation of measures would also indicate discriminant validity. Results of the correlation analysis provided support for the discriminant validity of the study. Examining further, none of the correlation coefficient is above 0.90, indicating that all the variables are distinct (Amick and Walberg 1975). McFarlin and Sweeney (1992) attest that earlier research has verified that these scales predict different endogenous latent variables and advocate that they are distinct variables representing different constructs. Additionally, to measure discriminant validity, the Chi-square values of the freely estimated measurement model were compared with the theoretical model where the correlation parameter was constrained to 1. Comparatively, the Chi-square values for the unconstrained model are significantly lower indicating discriminant validity (Bagozzi and Phillips 1982). The results of the correlation analysis are shown in Table 7.8, while the results for the Chi-square difference test are presented in the measurement and structural model findings discussion (Table 7.12).

Exploratory and Confirmatory Factor Analysis

Exploratory factor analysis (EFA) using principal component analysis was used to condense the information contained in a number of original variables into a smaller number of variables with a minimum loss of information (Hair et al. 2010). The objective was to define sets of variables that were highly interrelated and to determine the minimum number of factors needed to account for the maximum variance in the original variables. As shown in Table 7.5, results of the EFA showed that the Kaiser–Meyer–Olkin (KMO) measure of sampling adequacy for all the variables was above 0.80, indicating the factorability of the matrix as a whole. Additionally, Bartlett test of sphericity for all the variables were significant. Thus, factor analysis was strongly justified. The communalities for all the items in organisational justice, job satisfaction, leader–member exchange and organisational citizenship behaviour were estimated to be >0.5. The factors, therefore, intercorrelate significantly to contribute to the variance in the variables.

Assessment of Conformity with SEM Assumptions

In SEM, it is imperative that the data satisfied the assumptions of sample size; normality, linearity and homoscedasticity; and multicollinearity. Therefore, before proceeding with the full-model SEM analysis, the data has to be examined to ensure that there is no violation of SEM assumptions. This is done after the validity and reliability of measures of each construct have been confirmed through EFA and CFA. The discussion that follows verified that the assumptions of sample size, normality and absence of multicollinearity problems have been fulfilled.

Table 7.5 Results of exploratory factor analysis

Variable	KMO	Bartlett's test		Communalities
		Aprox. χ^2	Sig.	
Organisational justice	0.910	3319.080	.000	20/20
Job satisfaction	0.819	496.635	.000	4/4
Leader–member exchange	0.849	529.709	.000	5/5
Organisational citizenship behaviour	0.864	3040.627	.000	23/23

Sample Size

Relatively, SEM requires a larger sample size compared to other multivariate approaches as some of the statistical algorithms used by SEM programmes are unreliable with small samples (Hair et al. 2010). Kline (2011) asserts that some kinds of statistical estimates in SEM may not be accurate with small samples and the likelihood of technical problems in the analysis is greater. The required sample size for SEM depends on the multivariate normality of the data, estimation technique, model complexity, amount of missing data and average error variance among the reflective indicators. In SEM, maximum likelihood estimation (MLE) is used, and, thus, multivariate normally distributed continuous outcome variables are necessary. As data deviate more from the assumption of multivariate normality, a generally accepted ratio to minimise sampling error's impact is 15 respondents for each estimated parameter (Hair et al. 2010). Bentler and Chou (1987) proposed the minimum of 5:1 between subject and parameter, while Kline (2011) suggested that the sample size should be at least 200.

Model complexity also affects sample size requirements. Models with more measured variables, more constructs and constructs having fewer than three measured variables all required larger samples. Depending on the missing data approach and the extent of missing data anticipated, larger sample size may be necessary to offset any problems of missing data. To enhance convergence and model stability, a larger sample size is preferable for models containing multiple constructs with communalities of <0.5. Though there is no single answer to what a large enough sample size is in SEM, determining an appropriate sample size is important. Too large or too small a sample size will affect the accuracy and stability of SEM results (Hair et al. 2010).

The proposed model in the study has four latent variables (organisational justice, job satisfaction, leader–member exchange and organisational citizenship behaviour) and 18 observed variables. There are four items each for organisational justice and job satisfaction and five items each for leader–member exchange and organisational citizenship behaviour. For models with five or fewer constructs, each with more than three items, and item communalities of 0.6 or higher, the minimum sample size required is 100. Additionally, models with seven or fewer constructs, and modest item communalities of 0.5, and no underidentified constructs, the minimum sample size required is 150 (Hair et al. 2010). The sample size for this study is 267, and communalities for all the items are above 0.5 with 44 of the 52 items having communalities above 0.6, thus fulfilling the sample size requirement.

For two of the latent variables, namely, organisational justice and organisational citizenship behaviour, item parcelling procedure was utilised to improve the variable to sample size ratio (Bagozzi and Edwards 1998; Bandalos and Finney 2001). Item parcelling procedure reduces the number of parameter estimations and helps stabilise parameter estimates (Bagozzi and Edwards 1998), makes data conform to normality assumptions and simplifies complex models without compromising the concept of multiple indicator measurement (Garver and Mentzer 1999). The process involves aggregating several items that are valid individual measures of the construct. However, the items that represent the parcel must fulfil the requirement of unidimensionality, and the level of specificity must be the same within and across parcels. Item parcelling procedure was used in this study to enhance parsimonious estimation. The items aggregated to form scale indicators are shown in Table 7.6.

For organisational justice, items representing each dimension of organisational justice were individually aggregated to represent the observed variables – procedural justice, informational justice, distributive justice and interpersonal justice. Similarly, the observed variables of organisational citizenship behaviour were formed by aggregating individually the items representing courtesy, sportsmanship, altruism, civic virtue and conscientiousness. The procedure reduced the number of variables, and, hence, the sample–parameter ratio. However, item parcelling was performed to fulfil the sample–parameter ratio requirement in SEM only after validity and reliability measures had been adhered to. Therefore, before performing item parcelling procedures, unidimensionality of items in each parcel was ascertained through EFA and CFA. Items with low loadings, high correlations or cross-loadings were omitted in the item parcelling procedure. This was necessary to avert misrepresentation of the factor structure of the data (West et al. 1995).

Table 7.6 Aggregated items to form scale indicators

Observed variable	Indicators	Items
Organisational justice	Procedural justice	PJ1, PJ2, PJ3, PJ4, PJ5, PJ6, PJ7
	Informational justice	IJ5, IJ6, IJ7, IJ8, IJ8
	Distributive justice	DJ1, DJ2, DJ3, DJ4
	Interpersonal justice	IJ1, IJ2, IJ3, IJ4
Organisational citizenship behaviour	Courtesy	Cou1, Cou2, Cou3, Cou4, Cou5
	Sportsmanship	Spo1, Spo2, Spo3, Spo4, Spo5
	Altruism	Al1, Al2, Al3, Al4, Al5
	Civic virtue	Cv1, Cv2, Cv3, Cv4
	Conscientiousness	Con2, Con3, Con4, Con5

Normality, Linearity and Homoscedasticity

Normality refers to the shape of the data distribution for an individual metric variable and its correspondence to the normal distribution (Hair et al. 2010). It is the most fundamental assumption in multivariate analysis – large variation from the normal distribution indicates invalid statistically tested results. Various statistical tests can be used to detect violation of multivariate normality including Mardia's (1985) test and the Cox–Small test (Cox and Small 1978), among others (Kline 2011). Graphical and statistical analyses were employed to check for conformity of the data to normality in this study. Normal probability plot was used to detect departures from normality due to skewness and kurtosis. Statistical tests of normality substantiated visual inspection – statistical values of skewness of <3 and kurtosis of <10 indicated normal distribution (Kline 2011). Results of the graphical and statistical analyses showed conformity of the data to normality. The statistical values for skewness were within the threshold of + 3 with the highest value at 0.843. Similarly, the kurtosis values for all the variables were less than the specified critical value with the highest value at 2.701. The means, standard deviations, skewness and kurtosis are shown in Table 7.7.

In addition to the above, residual scatter plots in multiple regression analysis were visually examined to confirm multivariate normality. A visual examination of the scatter plots revealed linear relations and homoscedasticity, thus, confirming the presence of multivariate normality. Straight line approximation and equal variance dispersion observed in the scatterplots indicated that the assumptions of linearity and homoscedasticity were not violated.

Multicollinearity

In multivariate analysis, the problem of multicollinearity has to be addressed. Multicollinearity occurs when any single independent variable is highly correlated with a set of other independent variables. In essence, two separate variables are measuring the same thing and, therefore, may be redundant in measuring a construct (Kline 2011). The simplest way to detect collinearity is to examine the correlation matrix for the independent variables – correlations of 0.90 and higher indicates substantial collinearity (Hair et al. 2010).

In addition to the correlation analysis, tolerance and its inverse, the variance inflation factor (VIF), are used to detect multivariate collinearity. Tolerance indicates the proportion of total standardised variance that is not explained by all the other variables. Tolerance values <0.10 may indicate extreme multivariate collinearity. Variance inflation factor (VIF) is the ratio of the total standardised variance over unique variance (tolerance). VIF more than 10.0 indicates redundancy of the variable in question (Kline 2011). Correlation analysis of the data showed that there were no correlations above 0.90, and, therefore, further analysis and interpretation of the data were possible. Examination of tolerance and VIF generated from multiple regression analysis showed that tolerance was more than 0.10 and VIF was <10 for

Table 7.7 Means, standard deviations, skewness and kurtosis

Observed variable	Mean	Standard deviation	Skewness	Kurtosis
Procedural justice	3.296	0.603	−0.524	−0.025
Informational justice	3.485	0.582	−0.431	0.220
Distributive justice	3.443	0.726	−0.510	−0.204
Interpersonal justice	3.690	0.585	−0.462	0.836
Job satisfaction	3.479	0.646	−0.427	0.623
Leader–member exchange	3.437	0.584	−0.792	1.726
Courtesy	3.888	0.499	−0.552	1.090
Sportsmanship	3.440	0.743	−0.105	−0.453
Altruism	3.666	0.566	−0.843	2.701
Civic virtue	3.593	0.552	−0.399	0.465
Conscientiousness	3.739	0.562	0.098	−0.007

all the variables. This indicated that multicollinearity assumption was not violated. Results of the correlation analysis are shown in Table 7.8, and collinearity statistics are summarised in Table 7.9.

Measurement Model

A measurement model was specified and validated with CFA once a measurement theory has been proposed. The measurement model specified the indicators for each construct and enabled an assessment of construct validity. Measurement models were assessed independently prior to the structural model (Anderson and Gerbing 1988) to fully focus on establishing construct validity for all constructs (Hair et al. 2010). Each construct was assessed independently for unidimensionality to achieve an acceptable measurement model for each construct. Unidimensionality was critically important when there was more than one construct in the measurement model. Then, the overall measurement model containing all the constructs was assessed. All variables for the structural model were analysed after specifying the measurement relationships between indicators and constructs, correlational relationships between constructs and error terms for the items. Every variable was assumed to be correlated with each other.

Results of the CFA confirmed that the theoretical measurement model was valid. The fit of the measurement models for each construct and the overall model substantiated the unidimensionality of each construct. The results of the goodness-of-fit indices indicated a well-fitting model with $\chi^2 = 269.960$, $p < .05$, GFI = 0.896, TLI = 0.917, CFI = 0.930 and RMSEA = 0.064. The standardised regression weights showed that except for sportsmanship, all the items were significantly loaded into the intended factor with standard loadings ranging from 0.597 to 0.838. There was no empirical or theoretical justification to modify or re-specify any of the existing relationships in the hypothesised model. The CFA results confirmed that the theoretical measurement model was valid. Figure 7.1 shows the theoretical measurement model of the study.

Table 7.8 Correlation results for observed variables

Variable	1	2	3	4	5	6	7	8	9	10	11
Procedural justice	1										
Informational justice	0.537***	1									
Distributive justice	0.533***	0.509***	1								
Interpersonal justice	0.406***	0.557***	0.414***	1							
Job satisfaction	0.480***	0.525***	0.472***	0.413***	1						
Leader–member exchange	0.459***	0.518***	0.494***	0.459***	0.556***	1					
Courtesy	0.093	0.270***	0.138*	0.301***	0.297***	0.216***	1				
Sportsmanship	–0.070	0.041	–0.068	0.088	0.118	0.010	0.232***	1			
Altruism	0.202***	0.239***	0.150*	0.277***	0.269***	0.289***	0.461***	0.041	1		
Civic virtue	0.300***	0.252***	0.297***	0.295***	0.354***	0.316***	0.430***	–0.012	0.419***	1	
Conscientiousness	0.064	0.164**	0.036	0.313***	0.222***	0.216***	0.577***	0.186**	0.369***	0.435***	1

* $p<0.05$ (2-tailed); ** $p<0.01$ (2-tailed); *** $p<0.001$ (2-tailed)

Table 7.9 Collinearity statistics

Observed variable	Tolerance	VIF
Procedural justice	.589	1.698
Informational justice	.503	1.988
Distributive justice	.593	1.686
Interpersonal justice	.636	1.572
Job satisfaction	.578	1.731
Leader–member exchange	.567	1.764

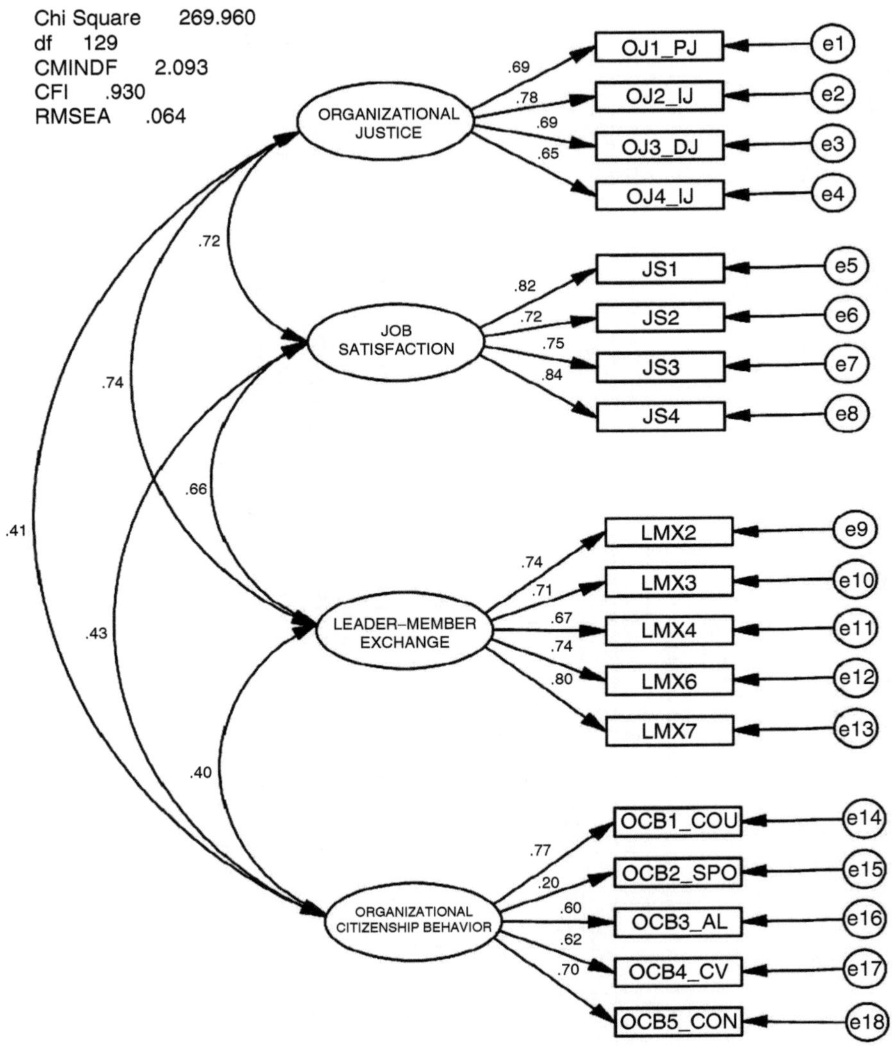

Fig. 7.1 Four-construct measurement model

Table 7.10 Testing for convergent validity

Factors/items	Std. loading	S.E.	C.R.	*P*
Procedural justice ← organisational justice	0.692			
Informational justice ← organisational justice	0.781	0.100	10.828	***
Distributive justice ← organisational justice	0.690	0.122	9.806	***
Interpersonal justice ← organisational justice	0.651	0.098	9.317	***
JS1 ← job satisfaction	0.824			
JS2 ← job satisfaction	0.724	0.066	12.644	***
JS3 ← job satisfaction	0.754	0.062	13.312	***
JS4 ← job satisfaction	0.838	0.066	15.179	***
LMX2 ← leader–member exchange	0.738			
LMX3 ← leader–member exchange	0.711	0.092	11.021	***
LMX4 ← leader–member exchange	0.671	0.084	10.404	***
LMX6 ← leader–member exchange	0.738	0.085	11.449	***
LMX7 ← leader–member exchange	0.797	0.084	12.335	***
Courtesy ← OCB	0.773			
Sportsmanship ← OCB	0.197	0.133	2.861	.004
Altruism ← OCB	0.597	0.104	8.462	***
Civic virtue ← OCB	0.618	0.101	8.726	***
Conscientiousness ← OCB	0.699	0.106	9.606	***

$^{***}p < 0.001$

Convergent Validity

Evidence for convergent validity was confirmed based on the factor loadings of all observed variables. As shown in Table 7.10, all standardised loading estimates were statistically significant and were 0.50 or higher except for sportsmanship, indicating that all the items converge on the intended construct that was measured.

To substantiate the size of factor loadings as an indicator of convergent validity, average variance extracted (AVE) and construct reliability (CR) were examined. The AVE and construct reliability of the indicators are shown in Table 7.11. An AVE of 0.50 or higher suggested adequate convergence, while a construct reliability of 0.7 or higher indicated good reliability (Hair et al. 2010). Reliability between 0.6 and 0.7 may be adequate if other indicators of a model's construct validity are good (Hair et al. 2010). As illustrated in Table 7.11, more of the variance in the measure was explained variance, that is, variance due to measurement error was smaller than variance explained by the construct. Except for sportsmanship, the AVE results ranged between 0.634 and 0.844 which exceeded the recommended threshold. Additionally, construct reliabilities provided further evidence that the measures were internally consistent, that is, the measures consistently measure the same latent construct. Therefore, the measures used in this study were valid.

Table 7.11 Average variance extracted and construct reliability of indicators

Constructs	Average variance extracted	Construct reliability
Procedural justice	0.717	0.717
Informational justice	0.822	0.822
Distributive justice	0.634	0.634
Interpersonal justice	0.684	0.684
Organisational justice	**0.715**	**0.889**
Job satisfaction	0.738	0.918
Leader–member exchange	0.681	0.914
Courtesy	0.844	0.844
Sportsmanship	0.069	0.069
Altruism	0.646	0.646
Civic virtue	0.690	0.690
Conscientiousness	0.745	0.745
Organisational citizenship behaviour	**0.6114**	**0.875**

Discriminant Validity

The extent to which a construct is truly distinct from other constructs was measured by discriminant validity. To measure discriminant validity, a Chi-square difference test was performed on the nested models. Four models that were specified provided evidence for discriminant validity. First, the four-construct model (Fig. 7.1) was specified where all constructs, namely, organisational justice, job satisfaction, leader–member exchange and organisational citizenship behaviour were treated as independent variables. Next, the model was changed to a three-construct model (Fig. 7.2) in which job satisfaction and leader–member exchange were loaded into one construct. Then, a two-construct model (Fig. 7.3) in which job satisfaction, leader–member exchange and organisational citizenship behaviour were loaded into one construct was specified. Finally, only one latent construct model (Fig. 7.4) was specified in which all 18 measured items were indicators. Each model was tested and its fit compared to the fit of the original four-construct model. As shown in Table 7.12, the model fits were significantly different, suggesting that the 18 items represented four separate constructs. Significant Chi-square differences ($\Delta\chi^2 > 3.84$ for df = 1) were observed in all cases, thus, providing evidence of discriminant validity. In essence, the model has fulfilled the criterion of distinctiveness. Having confirmed the adequacy of the measurement model, subsequent testing in the structural form was possible.

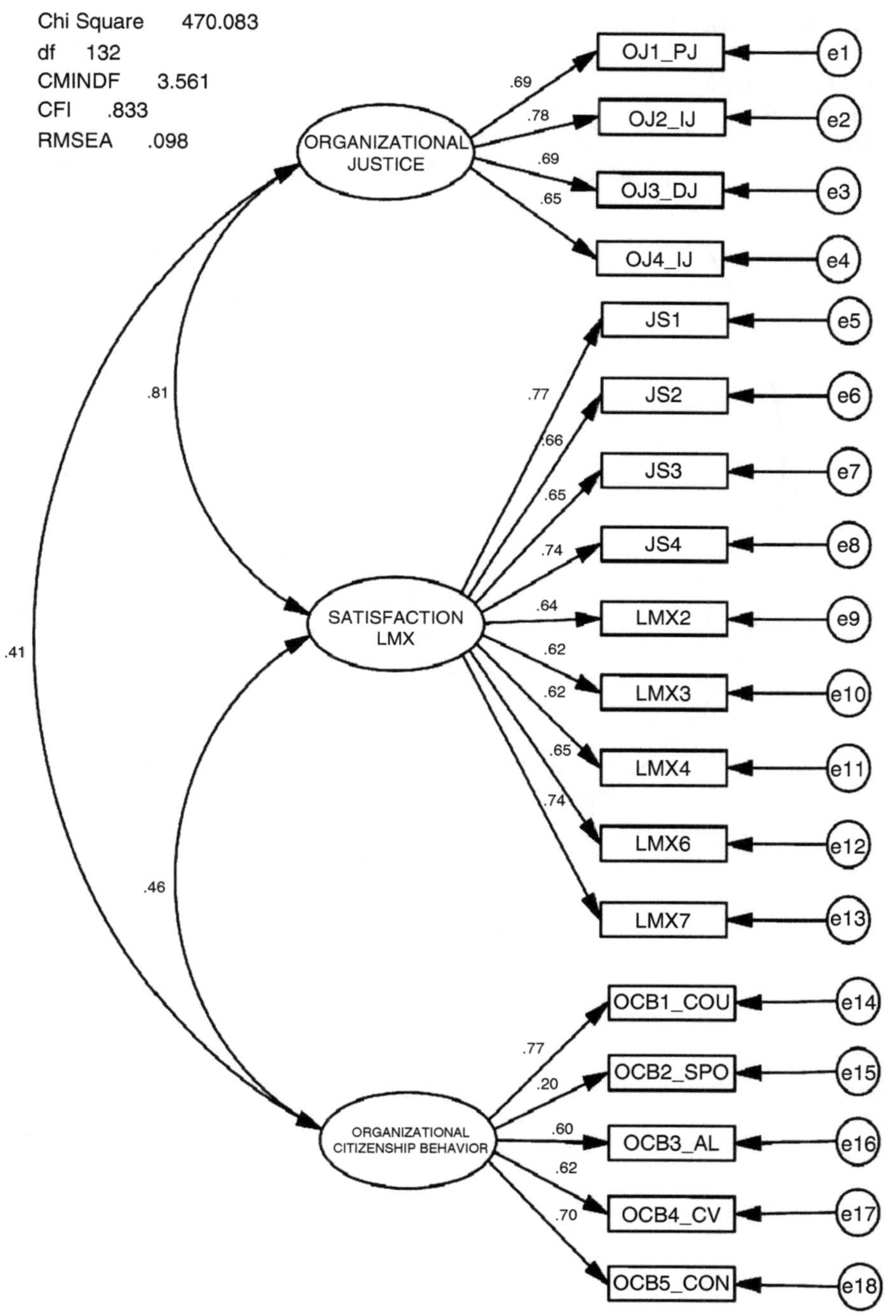

Fig. 7.2 Three-construct measurement model

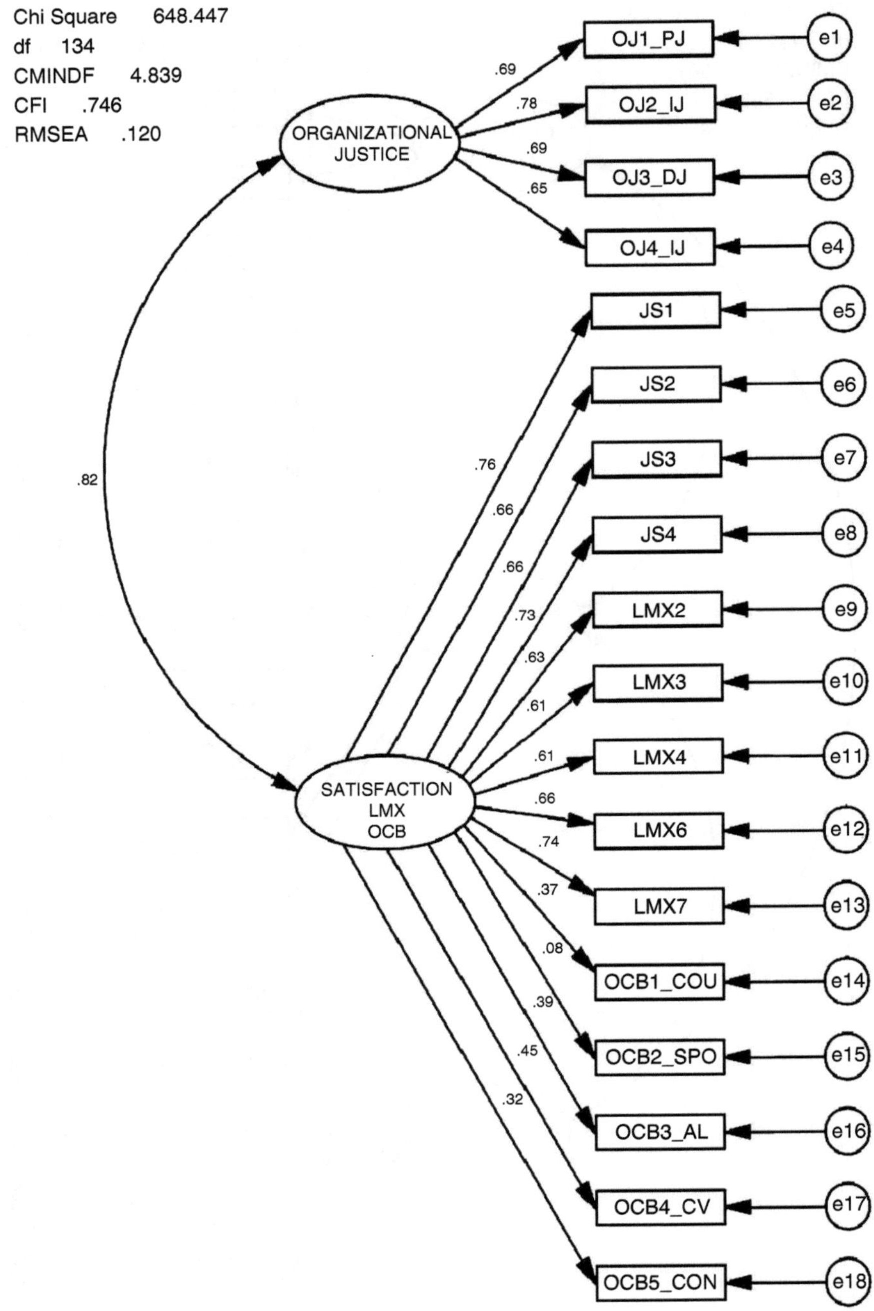

Fig. 7.3 Two-construct measurement model

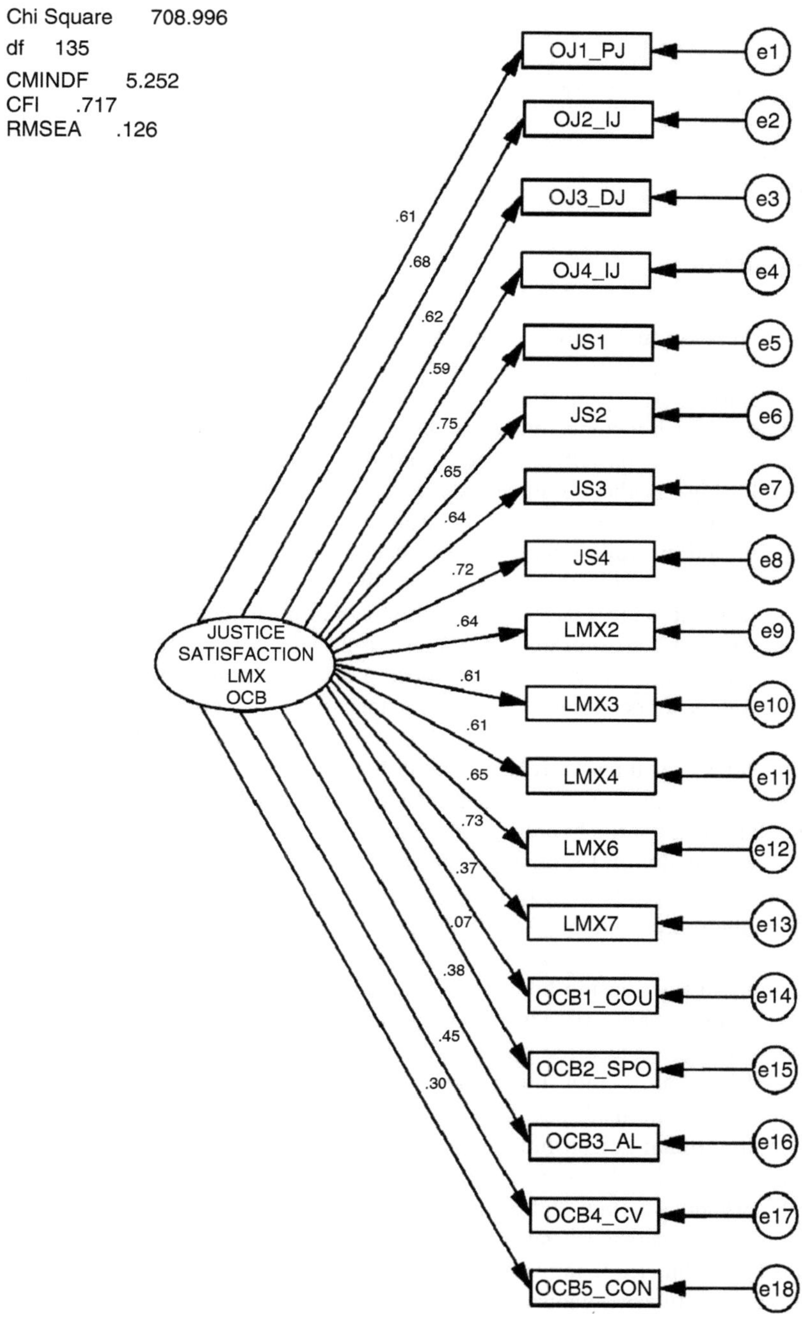

Fig. 7.4 One-construct measurement model

Table 7.12 CFA comparison of the measurement models

Model	χ^2	df	GFI	TLI	CFI	RMSEA
4-Factor model	269.960	129	0.896	0.917	0.930	0.064
3-Factor model	470.083	132	0.802	0.806	0.833	0.098
2-Factor model	648.447	134	0.745	0.710	0.746	0.120
1-Factor model	708.996	135	0.734	0.679	0.717	0.126

Conclusion

This chapter presented the preliminary results of the study. First, the sampling results were discussed in relation to data collection and entry, response rate and demography of the organisations and the respondents. This was followed by screening of data, which included detection of missing data and outliers. Then, refining of measures focusing on reliability and validity was elaborated. Scale reliability was assessed using Cronbach's alpha, average variance extracted and construct reliability. Factor loadings were used to determine convergent validity. The scales were then subjected to exploratory and confirmatory factor analysis. Based on statistical and theoretical considerations, items that did not fulfil convergent validity were deleted from the scale. In accordance with SEM requirements, adequacy of the data was determined. On confirmation of conformity with SEM assumptions, measurement and structural models were developed. Based on the statistical results, hypothesis testing was performed. The following four chapters provide a thorough discussion of the results of the hypothesis testing and the implications.

Chapter 8 expounds on relationship between perceptions of organisational justice and the dimensions of organisational citizenship behaviour. A summary of the research findings of the hypothesised relationships from the empirical analysis provides the groundwork for organisations to study the dynamics through which fairness perceptions render organisational citizenship behaviours appropriate. Chapter 9 outlines the research findings of the hypothesised relationships between organisational justice, job satisfaction and organisational citizenship behaviour. Findings on the empirical relationship between organisational justice and job satisfaction provide an insight of not only whether organisational justice is a primary antecedent of job satisfaction but also the importance of the job satisfaction–organisational citizenship behaviour relationship. Chapter 10 summarises the research findings of the hypothesised relationships between organisational justice, leader–member exchange and organisational citizenship behaviour. The findings give an indication of which type of organisational justice has a greater impact on leader–member exchange. The results further ascertain if leader–member exchange is indeed important in the organisational justice–organisational citizenship behaviour relationship. Finally, Chap. 11 establishes if job satisfaction and leader–member exchange mediate the relationship between organisational justice and organisational citizenship behaviour. An in-depth discussion on the outcomes of the findings provides indicators that practitioners could consider when implementing policies to enhance performance, in general, and organisational citizenship behaviours, in particular.

References

Amick, D. J., & Walberg, H. J. (1975). *Introductory multivariate analysis*. Berkeley: McCutchan Publishing Corporation.

Anderson, J. C., & Gerbing, D. W. (1988). Structural equation modeling in practice: A review and recommended two-step approach. *Psychology Bulletin, 103*(3), 411–423.

Bagozzi, R. P., & Edwards, J. R. (1998). A general approach to construct validation in organisational research: Application to the measurement of work values. *Organisational Research Methods, 1*(1), 45–87.

Bagozzi, R. P., & Phillips, L. W. (1982). Representing and testing organisational theories. A holistic construal. *Administrative Science Quarterly, 27*(3), 459–489.

Bandalos, D. L., & Finney, S. J. (2001). Item parceling issues in structural equation modeling. In G. A. Marcoulides & R. E. Schumacker (Eds.), *Advanced structural equation modeling: New developments and techniques*. Mahwah: Lawrence Erlbaum Associates.

Bentler, P. M., & Chou, C. P. (1987). Practical issues in structural modeling. *Sociological Methods & Research, 16*(1), 78–117.

Cooper, D. R., & Schindler, P. S. (2001). *Business research method*. New York: McGraw-Hill.

Cox, D. R., & Small, N. J. H. (1978). Testing multivariate normality. *Biometrika, 65*(2), 263–272.

De Vellis, R. F. (2003). *Scale development: Theory and applications* (2nd ed.). Thousand Oaks: Sage.

Folger, R. (1987). Distributive and procedural justice in the workplace. *Social Justice Research, 1*(2), 143–159.

Fornell, C., & Larcker, D. F. (1981). Evaluating structural equation models with unobservable variables and measurement error. *Journal of Marketing Research, 18*(1), 39–50.

Garver, M. S., & Mentzer, J. T. (1999). Logistics research methods: Employing structural equation modeling to test for construct validity. *Journal of Business Logistics, 20*(1), 33–57.

Hair, J. F., Black, W. C., Babin, B. J., & Anderson, R. E. (2010). *Multivariate data analysis* (7th ed.). Upper Saddle River: Pearson Prentice Hall.

Kline, R. B. (2011). *Principles and practice of structural equation modelling*. New York: The Guilford Press.

McFarlin, D. B., & Sweeney, P. D. (1992). Distributive and procedural justice as predictors of satisfaction with personal and organisational outcomes. *Academy of Management Journal, 35*(3), 626–637.

Nunnally, J. O. (1978). *Psychometric theory*. New York: McGraw-Hill.

Sekaran, U. (2003). *Research methods for business: A skill-building approach* (4th ed.). New York: Wiley.

Tabachnick, B. G., & Fidell, L. S. (2007). *Using multivariate statistics* (5th ed.). New York: Harper-Collins.

West, S. G., Finch, J. F., & Curran, P. J. (1995). Structural equation models with non-normal variables: Problems and remedies. In R. Hoyle (Ed.), *Structural equation modeling: Concepts, issues and applications* (pp. 56–75). Newbury Park: Sage.

Chapter 8
Organisational Justice–Organisational Citizenship Behaviour

Abstract This chapter delineates the research findings of the hypothesised relationship between organisational justice and organisational citizenship behaviour. A summary of the research findings of the hypothesised relationships from the empirical analysis provides the groundwork for organisations to study the dynamics through which fairness perceptions render organisational citizenship behaviours appropriate. Organisations in the manufacturing sector are able to see the effects of each type of organisational justice on each dimension of organisational citizenship behaviour. This helps organisations to decide which aspect of justice to work on to improve citizenship behaviour among their employees. Implications of the findings are discussed extensively to answer the research question identified for the hypothesised relationship.

Introduction

This chapter delineates the research findings on the assessment of reliability and validity of the hypothesised relationship between organisational justice and organisational citizenship behaviour and the outcome of the SEM analysis in confirming the hypothesised model. A summary of the research findings of the hypothesised relationships from the empirical analysis provides the underpinning for organisations to study the mechanisms through which justice perceptions are translated into behaviours (Colquitt and Greenberg 2003), specifically citizenship behaviours. It assists organisations in the manufacturing sector understand how each dimension of justice is translated into each kind of citizenship behaviour. This enhances managerial judgement of which aspect of justice to work on to improve citizenship behaviours among their employees. As organisational citizenship behaviour 'appears to be a reasonable and likely way in which an employee can exchange the social rewards brought on by perceptions of fairness' (Moorman 1991: 846), it is imperative that organisations foster justice investment. Justice investment drives employees to perform above and beyond formal job expectations to fulfil perceived 'unspecified obligations' (Blau 1964: 93). Implications of the findings are discussed extensively to answer the research question identified for the hypothesised relationship.

L.W. Hooi, *Organisational Justice and Citizenship Behaviour in Malaysia*, Governance and Citizenship in Asia, DOI 10.1007/978-981-10-0030-0_8

Organisational Justice

Organisational justice was conceptualised as three separate dimensions: distributive justice, procedural justice and interactional justice. The scale for the dimensions of organisational justice was adopted from a number of authors. Although well-established scales were adopted, EFA was carried out to uncover the underlying structure of a relatively large set of variables. The main aim is to examine the dimensionality of the scale (Kelloway 1995). From the EFA, four factors were extracted and classified as procedural justice, informational justice, distributive justice and interpersonal justice. This is shown in Table 8.1.

As shown in Table 8.1, procedural justice explained 42.4 % of the variance, informational justice 11 %, distributive justice 8.5 % and interpersonal justice 6.9 %. The KMO of 0.910 showed a high level of acceptance, and, therefore, all four dimensions were included to represent organisational justice. No items were dropped as factor loadings for all the items were above 0.50. Reliability for all the four factors was high with values of Cronbach's alpha above 0.80 – well above the level of 0.70 recommended by Nunnally (1978) and Robinson et al. (1991) and the range of between 0.56 and 0.82 suggested by Conant et al. (1990).

To assess the validity of the measure, all four factors were subjected to confirmatory factor analysis (CFA). First-order CFA was first carried out. This is shown in Fig. 8.1. The results shown in Table 8.2 indicated an acceptable fitting model with $\chi^2=382.388$; $p<0.001$; GFI = 0.877; TLI = 0.922; CFI = 0.932; and RMSEA = 0.071. None of the standardised factor loadings were less than 0.50, and no items were dropped. As for convergent validity, all items that represented organisational justice were significantly loaded into their intended factors with standardised loadings of more than 0.50. Cronbach's alpha for all four factors was above the recommended level of 0.7 indicating that the items were internally consistent in measuring organisational justice.

The organisational justice construct was then subjected to second-order CFA. As shown in Fig. 8.2 and Table 8.3, the results revealed an acceptable fitting model with $\chi^2=391.822$; $p<0.001$; GFI = 0.874; TLI = 0.920; CFI = 0.930; PNFI = 0.773; and RMSEA = 0.072. The standardised factor loadings for all the items were more than 0.50 and were significantly loaded into their intended factors, indicating convergent validity. The items were internally consistent in measuring organisational justice as Cronbach's alpha for all four factors was above the recommended level of 0.7 (Nunnally 1978).

Organisational Citizenship Behaviour

For organisational citizenship behaviour variable, the KMO index showed a high level of acceptance (0.864), and, therefore, all five factors, namely, courtesy, sportsmanship, altruism, civic virtue and conscientiousness, were included to represent

Table 8.1 Results of EFA on organisational justice

Items		**Value**	
Kaiser–Meyer–Olkin		0.910	
Bartlett's test of sphericity		3319.080 (sig. 0.000, df. 190)	
Factor	**Eigenvalue**	**Percentage of variance**	**Cumulative variance**
Procedural justice	8.479	42.397	42.397
Informational justice	2.210	11.048	53.445
Distributive justice	1.707	8.537	61.982
Interpersonal justice	1.378	6.891	68.873
Factors/items		**Factor loading**	
Factor 1: procedural justice			
PJ2	I have an influence over the (outcome) arrived at by the procedures used	0.773	
PJ3	The procedures used to arrive at the (outcome) have been applied consistently	0.765	
PJ6	I have been able to appeal the (outcome) arrived at by those procedures	0.739	
PJ7	The procedures used to arrive at the (outcome) have upheld ethical and moral standards	0.713	
PJ5	The procedures used to arrive at the (outcome) are based on accurate information	0.692	
PJ1	I have been able to express my views and feelings during the procedures used to arrive at the (outcome)	0.689	
PJ4	The procedures used to arrive at the (outcome) have been free of bias	0.670	
Internal consistency reliability (Cronbach's alpha)		0.888	
Factor 2: informational justice			
IJ6	(He/she) has explained the procedures thoroughly	0.801	
IJ7	(His/her) explanations regarding the procedures were reasonable	0.766	
IJ8	(He/she) has communicated details in a timely manner	0.749	
IJ5	(He/she) has been honest in (his/her) communication with me	0.663	
IJ9	(He/she) seemed to tailor (his/her) communications to individuals' specific needs	0.613	

(continued)

Table 8.1 (continued)

Internal consistency reliability (Cronbach's alpha)		0.866
Factor 3: distributive justice		
DJ2	The (outcome) I received is appropriate for the work I have completed	0.858
DJ1	The (outcome) I received reflects the effort I have put into my work	0.820
DJ3	The (outcome) I received reflects what I have contributed to the organisation	0.812
DJ4	The (outcome) I received is justified given my performance	0.797
Internal consistency reliability (Cronbach's alpha)		0.914
Factor 4: interpersonal justice		
IJ1	(He/she) has treated me in a polite manner	0.845
IJ3	(He/she) has treated me with respect	0.802
IJ2	(He/she) has treated me with dignity	0.792
IJ4	(He/she) has refrained from improper remarks or comments	0.721
Internal consistency reliability (Cronbach's alpha)		0.868

the construct. However, one item (Con1) was dropped due to low factor loading. This is further substantiated by a significant value for Bartlett's test of sphericity. Additionally, Cronbach's alpha for all the factors was above 0.70 indicating acceptable levels of reliability. As shown in Table 8.4, among the factors, courtesy explained more than 30 % of the variance. Except for Cv1, Con2 and Con5, factor loadings for all the other items representing the construct were above 0.70.

Results of the CFA shown in Fig. 8.3 and Table 8.5 signified an acceptable fitting model with $\chi^2=499.025$; $p<0.001$; GFI = 0.862; TLI = 0.889; CFI = 0.903; and RMSEA = 0.069. Standardised factor loadings for all items ranged from 0.599 to 0.836, and, therefore, no items were dropped. In terms of internal consistency reliability, Cronbach's alpha for all the five factors was above the recommended level of 0.7 (Nunnally 1978). As for convergent validity, all items that represented organisational citizenship behaviour were significantly loaded into their intended factors with standardised loadings of more than 0.50.

Second-order confirmatory factor analysis carried out implied an acceptable fitting model with $\chi^2=520.290$; $p<0.05$; GFI = 0.855; TLI = 0.885; CFI = 0.898; PNFI = 0.742; and RMSEA = 0.070. Except for sportsmanship, standardised factor loadings for all the other items were above 0.50, thus, confirming convergent validity. Most of the items that represented organisational citizenship behaviour were significantly loaded into their intended factors. As the Cronbach's alpha for all five factors was above the recommended level of 0.7 (Nunnally 1978), internal consistency reliability was maintained. The results are shown in Fig. 8.4 and Table 8.6.

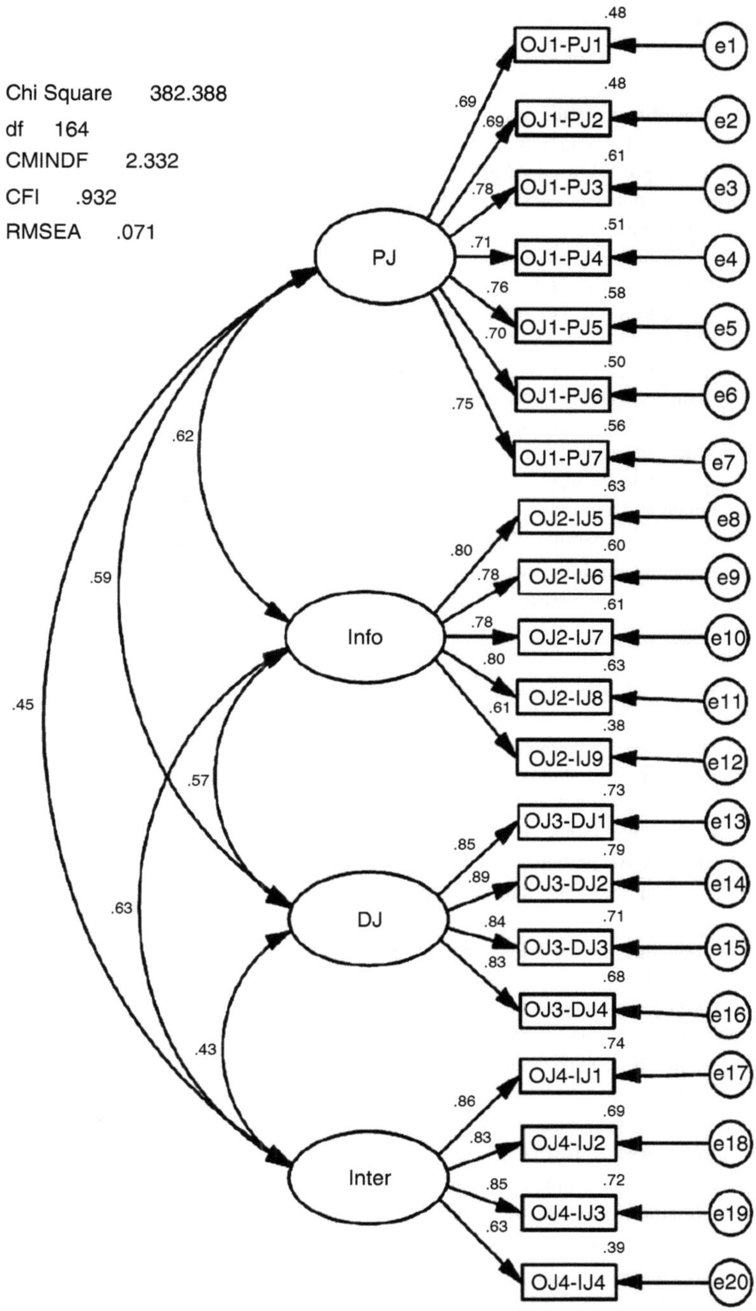

Fig. 8.1 First-order CFA model for organisational justice

Table 8.2 Results of first-order CFA on organisational justice

Factors/items		Std. loading	Std. error	C.R.
Factor 1: procedural justice				
PJ1	I have been able to express my views and feelings during the procedures used to arrive at the (outcome)	0.693		
PJ2	I have an influence over the (outcome) arrived at by the procedures used	0.691	0.098	10.473
PJ3	The procedures used to arrive at the (outcome) have been applied consistently	0.784	0.098	11.504
PJ4	The procedures used to arrive at the (outcome) have been free of bias	0.714	0.101	10.620
PJ5	The procedures used to arrive at the (outcome) are based on accurate information	0.763	0.098	11.121
PJ6	I have been able to appeal the (outcome) arrived at by those procedures	0.705	0.095	10.576
PJ7	The procedures used to arrive at the (outcome) have upheld ethical and moral standards	0.748	0.093	11.072
Internal consistency reliability (Cronbach's alpha)		0.888		
Factor 2: informational justice				
IJ5	(He/she) has been honest in (his/her) communication with me	0.796		
IJ6	(He/she) has explained the procedures thoroughly	0.776	0.078	13.155
IJ7	(His/her) explanations regarding the procedures were reasonable	0.779	0.073	13.565
IJ8	(He/she) has communicated details in a timely manner	0.795	0.077	13.508
IJ9	(He/she) seemed to tailor (his/her) communications to individuals' specific needs	0.614	0.076	10.012
Internal consistency reliability (Cronbach's alpha)		0.866		
Factor 3: distributive justice				
DJ1	The (outcome) I received reflects the effort I have put into my work	0.854		
DJ2	The (outcome) I received is appropriate for the work I have completed	0.889	0.056	18.828
DJ3	The (outcome) I received reflects what I have contributed to the organisation	0.843	0.059	17.296
DJ4	The (outcome) I received is justified given my performance	0.826	0.060	16.413
Internal consistency reliability (Cronbach's alpha)		0.914		
Factor 4: interpersonal justice				
IJ1	(He/she) has treated me in a polite manner	0.859		
IJ2	(He/she) has treated me with dignity	0.833	0.063	15.983
IJ3	(He/she) has treated me with respect	0.850	0.057	17.153
IJ4	(He/she) has refrained from improper remarks or comments	0.626	0.070	10.836
Internal consistency reliability (Cronbach's alpha)		0.868		

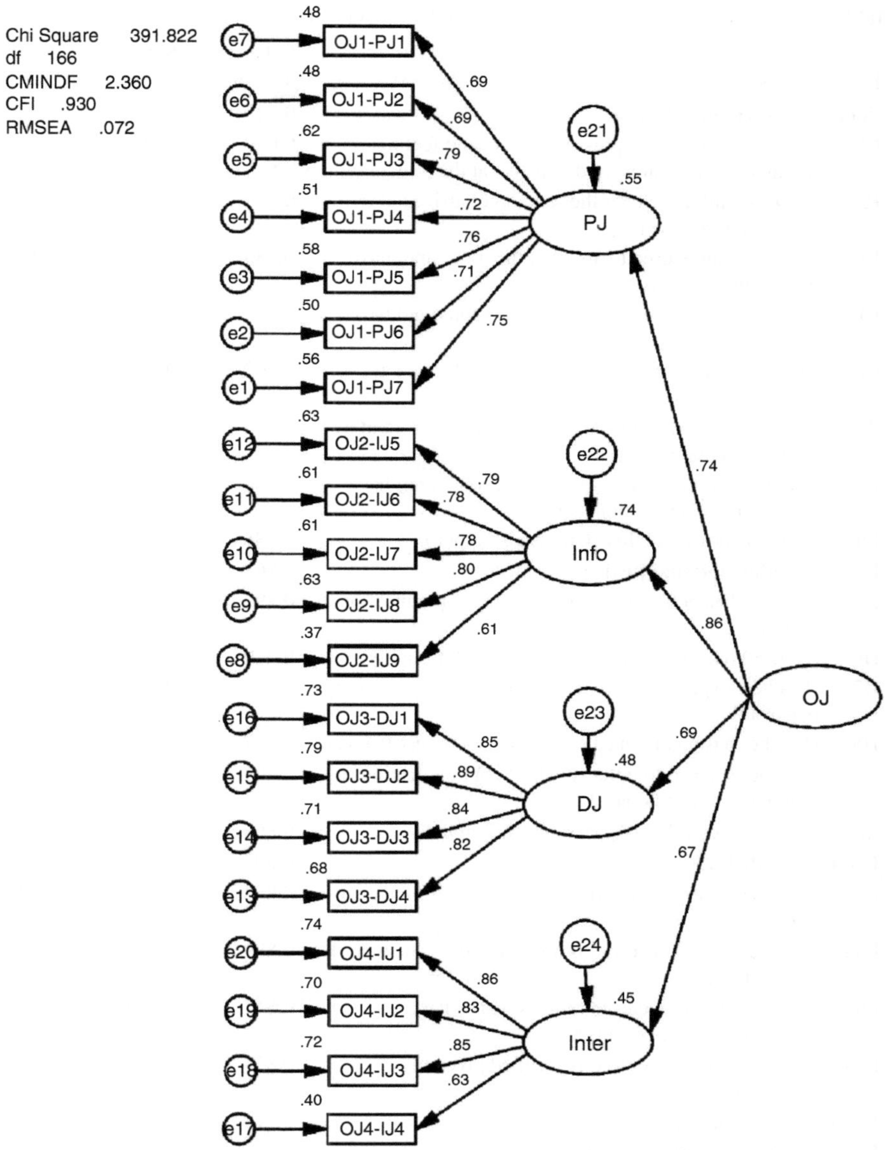

Fig. 8.2 Second-order CFA model for organisational justice

Table 8.3 Results of second-order CFA on organisational justice

Factors/items		Std. loading	Std. error	C.R.
Factor 1: procedural justice		0.741		
PJ1	I have been able to express my views and feelings during the procedures used to arrive at the (outcome)	0.690	0.087	11.084
PJ2	I have an influence over the (outcome) arrived at by the procedures used	0.690	0.090	11.075
PJ3	The procedures used to arrive at the (outcome) have been applied consistently	0.785	0.086	12.733
PJ4	The procedures used to arrive at the (outcome) have been free of bias	0.716	0.091	11.531
PJ5	The procedures used to arrive at the (outcome) are based on accurate information	0.762	0.086	12.328
PJ6	I have been able to appeal the (outcome) arrived at by those procedures	0.705	0.086	11.347
PJ7	The procedures used to arrive at the (outcome) have upheld ethical and moral standards	0.748		
Internal consistency reliability (Cronbach's alpha)		0.888		
Factor 2: informational justice		0.861	0.125	7.164
IJ5	(He/she) has been honest in (his/her) communication with me	0.793	0.131	10.025
IJ6	(He/she) has explained the procedures thoroughly	0.779	0.137	9.911
IJ7	(His/her) explanations regarding the procedures were reasonable	0.780	0.132	9.921
IJ8	(He/she) has communicated details in a timely manner	0.797	0.136	10.053
IJ9	(He/she) seemed to tailor (his/her) communications to individuals' specific needs	0.609		
Internal consistency reliability (Cronbach's alpha)		0.866		
Factor 3: distributive justice		0.693	0.145	7.747
DJ1	The (outcome) I received reflects the effort I have put into my work	0.854	0.062	16.588
DJ2	The (outcome) I received is appropriate for the work I have completed	0.889	0.062	17.552
DJ3	The (outcome) I received reflects what I have contributed to the organisation	0.844	0.065	16.309
DJ4	The (outcome) I received is justified given my performance	0.824		
Internal consistency reliability (Cronbach's alpha)		0.914		
Factor 4: interpersonal justice		0.674	0.109	6.757
IJ1	(He/she) has treated me in a polite manner	0.858	0.118	11.041
IJ2	(He/she) has treated me with dignity	0.834	0.120	10.846
IJ3	(He/she) has treated me with respect	0.848	0.115	10.963
IJ4	(He/she) has refrained from improper remarks or comments	0.630		
Internal consistency reliability (Cronbach's alpha)		0.868		

Table 8.4 Results of EFA on organisational citizenship behaviour

Items		Value	
Kaiser–Meyer–Olkin		0.864	
Bartlett's test of sphericity		3040.627 (sig. 0.000, df. 253)	
Factor	**Eigenvalue**	**Percentage of variance**	**Cumulative variance**
Courtesy	7.007	30.466	30.466
Sportsmanship	3.393	14.752	45.218
Altruism	1.819	7.910	53.127
Civic virtue	1.521	6.615	59.743
Conscientiousness	1.188	5.166	64.908
Factors/items		**Factor loading**	
Factor 1: courtesy			
Cou1	I always take steps to try to prevent problems with other workers	0.783	
Cou2	I am mindful of how my behaviour affects other people's jobs	0.745	
Cou4	I always try to avoid creating problems for coworkers	0.738	
Cou5	I always consider the impact of my actions on coworkers	0.718	
Cou3	I do not abuse the rights of others	0.714	
Internal consistency reliability (Cronbach's alpha)		0.872	
Factor 2: sportsmanship			
Spo2	I always focus on what is wrong rather than the positive side (R)	0.857	
Spo3	I tend to exaggerate (R)	0.849	
Spo4	I always find fault with what the organisation is doing (R)	0.843	
Spo1	I spend a lot of time complaining about trivial matters (R)	0.750	
Spo5	I always make sure that I am heard (R)	0.718	
Internal consistency reliability (Cronbach's alpha)		0.871	
Factor 3: altruism			
Al2	I always help others who have heavy work loads	0.814	
Al3	I always help orient new people even though it is not required	0.754	
Al4	I always willingly help others who have work-related problems	0.729	
Al5	I am always ready to lend a helping hand to those around me	0.724	
Al1	I always help others who have been absent	0.708	
Internal consistency reliability (Cronbach's alpha)		0.845	

(continued)

Table 8.4 (continued)

Factor 4: civic virtue		
Cv2	I make it a point to attend functions that are not required, but help the company image	0.775
Cv3	I always keep abreast of changes in the organisation	0.748
Cv4	I read and keep up with organisation announcements, memos and so on	0.724
Cv1	I make it a point to attend meetings that are not mandatory, but are considered important	0.690
Internal consistency reliability (Cronbach's alpha)		0.789
Factor 5: conscientiousness		
Con3	I obey company rules and regulations even when no one is watching	0.774
Con4	I am one of the most conscientious employees	0.734
Con2	I do not take extra breaks	0.658
Con5	I believe in giving an honest day's work for an honest day's pay	0.599
Internal consistency reliability (Cronbach's alpha)		0.767

Summary of Findings on Hypothesised Relationships

Hypothesis 1: Organisational Justice–Organisational Citizenship Behaviour

As summarised in Table 8.7, the main hypotheses relating employee perceptions of organisational justice to the dimensions of organisational citizenship behaviour were partially supported. Based on Table 8.7, distributive justice positively influenced civic virtue, while informational justice had a significant positive effect on courtesy. Procedural justice positively influenced civic virtue, but had a negative effect on courtesy and sportsmanship. Employee perceptions of interpersonal justice, however, positively influenced all dimensions of organisational citizenship behaviour. Comparatively, interpersonal justice had a more significant effect on conscientiousness than on courtesy, altruism, civic virtue or sportsmanship. The influence of interpersonal justice on civic virtue was stronger than the effect of procedural justice or distributive justice. Similarly, interpersonal justice was more significant on courtesy as compared to informational justice or procedural justice. Additionally, interpersonal justice had a stronger influence on sportsmanship than procedural justice. As shown in Table 8.8, Hypotheses 1, 1a, 1b and 1c were partially supported. The structural model for the organisational justice–organisational citizenship behaviour relationship is shown in Fig. 8.5

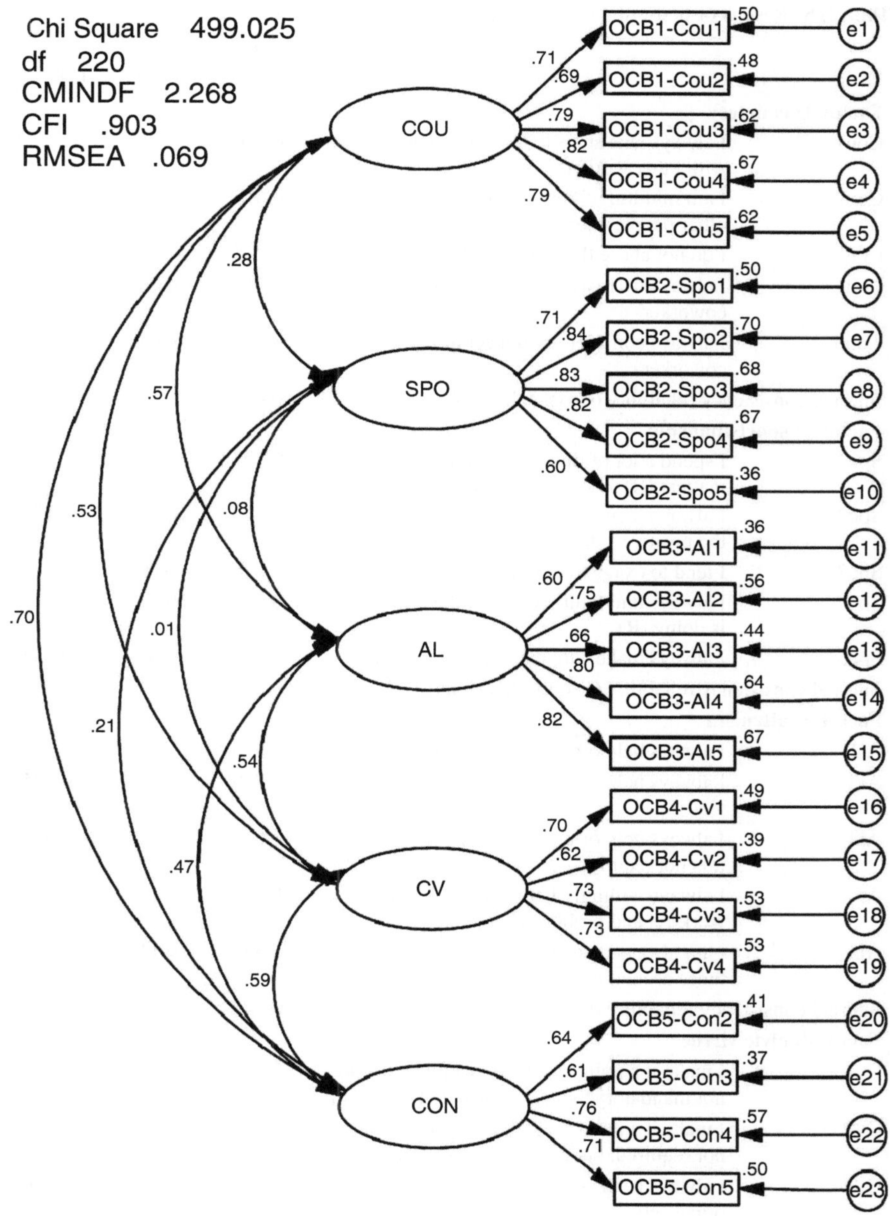

Fig. 8.3 First-order CFA model for organisational citizenship behaviour

Table 8.5 Results of first-order CFA on organisational citizenship behaviour

Factors/items		Std. loading	Std. error	C.R.
Factor 1: courtesy				
Cou1	I always take steps to try to prevent problems with other workers	0.710		
Cou2	I am mindful of how my behaviour affects other people's jobs	0.693	0.082	10.548
Cou3	I do not abuse the rights of others	0.788	0.091	11.926
Cou4	I always try to avoid creating problems for coworkers	0.819	0.095	12.361
Cou5	I always consider the impact of my actions on coworkers	0.787	0.089	11.908
Internal consistency reliability (Cronbach's alpha)		0.872		
Factor 2: sportsmanship				
Spo1	I spend a lot of time complaining about trivial matters (R)	0.707		
Spo2	I always focus on what is wrong rather than the positive side (R)	0.836	0.102	12.478
Spo3	I tend to exaggerate (R)	0.828	0.093	12.371
Spo4	I always find fault with what the organisation is doing (R)	0.817	0.098	12.236
Spo5	I always make sure that I am heard (R)	0.602	0.088	9.157
Internal consistency reliability (Cronbach's alpha)		0.871		
Factor 3: altruism				
Al1	I always help others who have been absent	0.599		
Al2	I always help others who have heavy work loads	0.749	0.131	9.345
Al3	I always help orient new people even though it is not required	0.661	0.123	8.583
Al4	I always willingly help others who have work-related problems	0.799	0.117	9.728
Al5	I am always ready to lend a helping hand to those around me	0.820	0.113	9.871
Internal consistency reliability (Cronbach's alpha)		0.845		
Factor 4: civic virtue				
Cv1	I make it a point to attend meetings that are not mandatory, but are considered important	0.701		
Cv2	I make it a point to attend functions that are not required, but help the company image	0.623	0.095	8.747
Cv3	I always keep abreast of changes in the organisation	0.731	0.089	9.960
Cv4	I read and keep up with organisation announcements, memos and so on	0.726	0.093	9.914
Internal consistency reliability (Cronbach's alpha)		0.789		

(continued)

Table 8.5 (continued)

Factors/items		Std. loading	Std. error	C.R.
Factor 5: conscientiousness				
Con2	I do not take extra breaks	0.640		
Con3	I obey company rules and regulations even when no one is watching	0.609	0.123	8.081
Con4	I am one of the most conscientious employees	0.757	0.110	9.418
Con5	I believe in giving an honest day's work for an honest day's pay	0.707	0.106	9.027
Internal consistency reliability (Cronbach's alpha)		0.767		

Discussion of the Findings

Organisational Justice–Organisational Citizenship Behaviour Relationship

The following discussion addresses the first research question of the study. Table 8.9 summarises the research question, hypotheses and the findings for the relationship between organisational justice and organisational citizenship behaviour. Table 8.10 shows the importance of each justice factor on each component of organisational citizenship behaviour.

The findings of the study affirm that there is indeed a positive relationship between organisational justice and organisational citizenship behaviour, albeit partially. This supports literature that research the relationship between organisational justice and organisational citizenship behaviour (e.g. Allen and Rush 1998; Ball et al. 1994; Cohen-Charash and Spector 2001; Colquitt et al. 2001; Erturk 2007; Eskew 1993; Greenberg 1993; Konovsky and Pugh 1994; Masterson et al. 2000; Moorman 1991; Moorman et al. 1993, 1998; Niehoff and Moorman 1993; Organ and Paine 1999; Podsakoff et al. 2000; Sheppard et al. 1992; Skarlicki and Latham 1996; Tansky 1993; Tschannen-Moran 2001; Williams et al. 2002; Yilmaz and Tasdan 2009). The findings establish the strong influence of interactional justice, in particular, interpersonal justice on organisational citizenship behaviour in the manufacturing sector in Malaysia. To a certain extent, the findings support the assertion that interactional justice is the sole dimension of fairness to relate significantly to organisational citizenship behaviour (Greenberg 1990a; Lazar et al. 2007; Moorman 1991; Williams et al. 2002). It is, therefore, crucial that organisations ensure politeness and treat employees with respect and dignity (Colquitt 2001; Greenberg 1993) as employees are more willing to accept unfavourable outcomes (Deutsch 2000). As the economy continues to expand and employment growth in the manufacturing sector experiences the highest growth, employees are likely to leave if organisational justice were not in place.

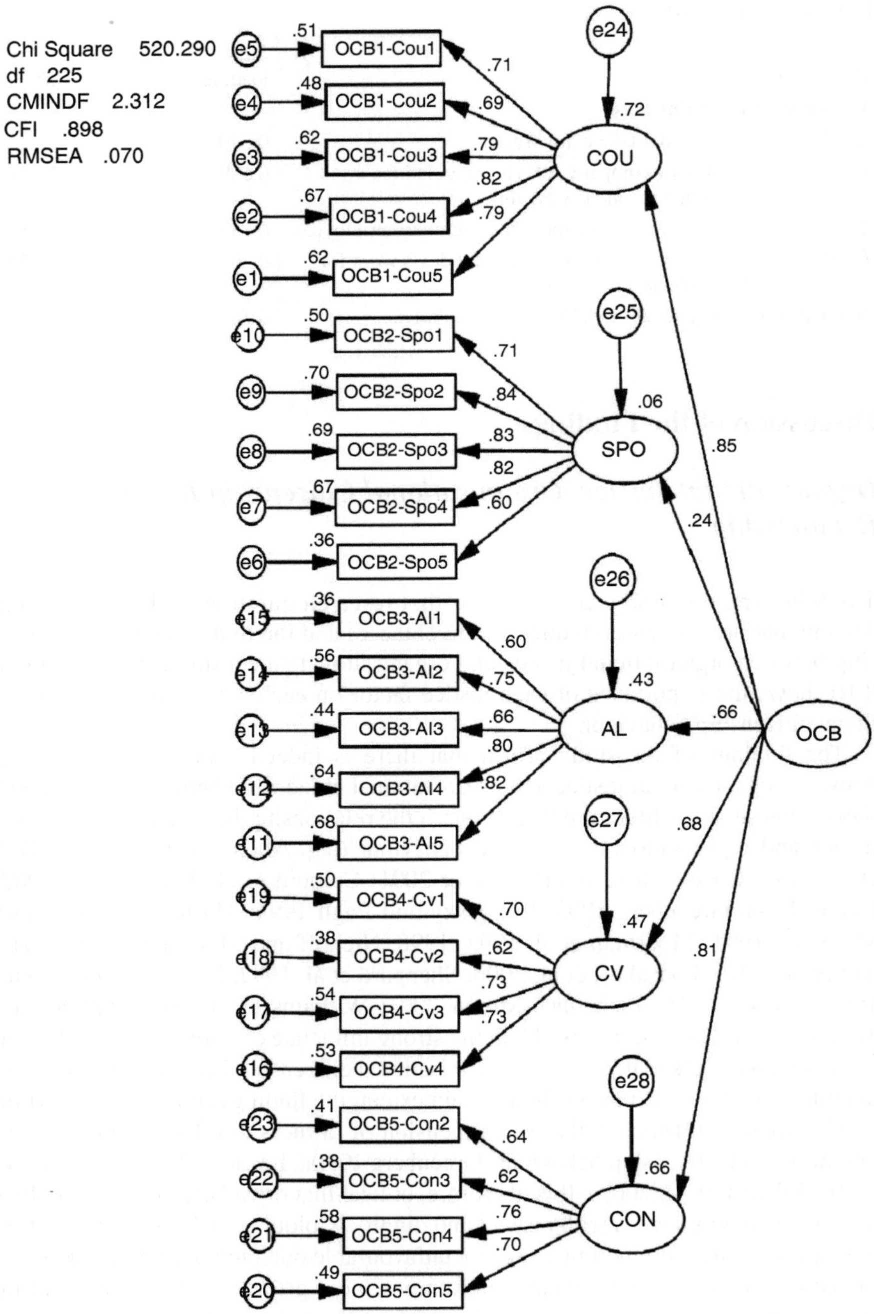

Fig. 8.4 Second-order CFA model for organisational citizenship behaviour

Table 8.6 Results of second-order CFA on organisational citizenship behaviour

Factors/items		Std. loading	Std. error	C.R.
Factor 1: courtesy		0.846		
Cou1	I always take steps to try to prevent problems with other workers	0.713	0.080	11.940
Cou2	I am mindful of how my behaviour affects other people's jobs	0.693	0.071	11.568
Cou3	I do not abuse the rights of others	0.785	0.077	13.378
Cou4	I always try to avoid creating problems for coworkers	0.820	0.079	14.061
Cou5	I always consider the impact of my actions on coworkers	0.787		
Internal consistency reliability (Cronbach's alpha)		0.872		
Factor 2: sportsmanship		0.236	0.098	3.099
Spo1	I spend a lot of time complaining about trivial matters (R)	0.707	0.136	9.131
Spo2	I always focus on what is wrong rather than the positive side (R)	0.836	0.155	10.171
Spo3	I tend to exaggerate (R)	0.829	0.141	10.120
Spo4	I always find fault with what the organisation is doing (R)	0.817	0.148	10.038
Spo5	I always make sure that I am heard (R)	0.601		
Internal consistency reliability (Cronbach's alpha)		0.871		
Factor 3: altruism		0.657	0.111	7.697
Al1	I always help others who have been absent	0.599	0.091	9.865
Al2	I always help others who have heavy work loads	0.747	0.085	12.826
Al3	I always help orient new people even though it is not required	0.664	0.085	11.127
Al4	I always willingly help others who have work-related problems	0.797	0.073	13.839
Al5	I am always ready to lend a helping hand to those around me	0.822		
Internal consistency reliability (Cronbach's alpha)		0.845		
Factor 4: civic virtue		0.684	0.115	7.294
Cv1	I make it a point to attend meetings that are not mandatory, but are considered important	0.705	0.111	9.875
Cv2	I make it a point attend functions that are not required, but help the company image	0.616	0.102	8.789
Cv3	I always keep abreast of changes in the organisation	0.734	0.095	10.177
Cv4	I read and keep up with organisation announcements, memos and so on	0.725		
Internal consistency reliability (Cronbach's alpha)		0.789		
Factor 5: conscientiousness		0.811	0.122	7.799
Con2	I do not take extra breaks	0.639	0.117	8.940
Con3	I obey company rules and regulations even when no one is watching	0.616	0.122	8.663
Con4	I am one of the most conscientious employees	0.758	0.107	10.217
Con5	I believe in giving an honest day's work for an honest day's pay	0.701		
Internal consistency reliability (Cronbach's alpha)		0.767		

Table 8.7 Organisational justice–organisational citizenship behaviour

Factors/items	Std. loading	S.E.	C.R.	*P*
Courtesy ← procedural justice	–.128	.051	–1.988	**.047**
Sportsmanship ← procedural justice	–.136	.076	–2.007	**.045**
Altruism ← procedural justice	.101	.054	1.497	.134
Civic virtue ← procedural justice	.170	.060	2.382	**.017**
Conscientiousness ← procedural justice	–.069	.058	–1.036	.300
Courtesy ← informational justice	.177	.071	2.656	**.008**
Sportsmanship ← informational justice	.082	.103	1.208	.227
Altruism ← informational justice	.072	.074	1.067	.286
Civic virtue ← informational justice	–.022	.080	–.311	.756
Conscientiousness ← informational justice	.045	.079	.675	.500
Courtesy ← distributive justice	–.029	.043	–.467	.640
Sportsmanship ← distributive justice	–.113	.064	–1.705	.088
Altruism ← distributive justice	–.046	.046	–.699	.485
Civic virtue ← distributive justice	.153	.051	2.207	**.027**
Conscientiousness ← distributive justice	–.109	.050	–1.647	.100
Courtesy ← interpersonal justice	.389	.077	5.206	***
Sportsmanship ← interpersonal justice	.191	.102	2.750	**.006**
Altruism ← interpersonal justice	.334	.082	4.324	***
Civic virtue ← interpersonal justice	.327	.087	4.183	***
Conscientiousness ← interpersonal justice	.480	.097	5.608	***

*** $p < 0.001$

Table 8.8 Hypotheses on organisational justice–organisational citizenship behaviour

	Hypotheses	Findings
1	Employee perceptions of organisational justice positively influence the dimensions of organisational citizenship behaviour	Partially supported
1a	Employee perceptions of distributive justice positively influence the dimensions of organisational citizenship behaviour	Partially supported
1b	Employee perceptions of procedural justice positively influence the dimensions of organisational citizenship behaviour	Partially supported
1c	Employee perceptions of interactional justice positively influence the dimensions of organisational citizenship behaviour	Partially supported

Besides, only interpersonal justice relates positively to sportsmanship. In short, employee perceptions of justice do not necessarily encourage avoidance of negative behaviours and complaints. Employees avoid negative behaviours only if superiors treat them with respect and dignity and would likely restrain positive behaviours if they were not given 'face'. Equity in the distribution of outcomes, objectivity in decision procedures as well as adequate and honest explanations do not deter pessimistic behaviours. To avoid negative behaviours from escalating, it is desirable that organisations provide adequate training to enhance interpersonal skills of superiors. Enhanced interpersonal skills improve social relations among employees and

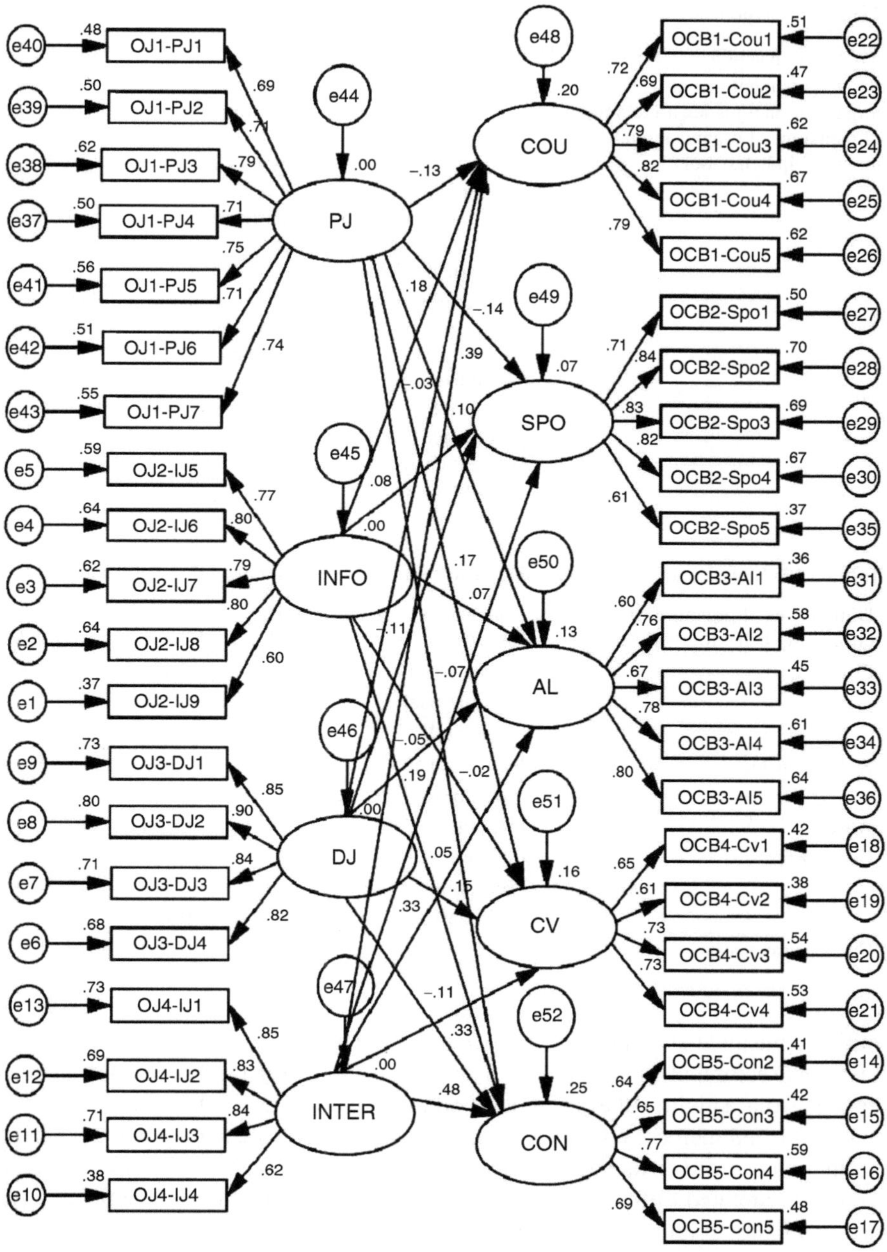

Fig. 8.5 Organisational justice–organisational citizenship behaviour

Table 8.9 Hypotheses and the findings for research question 1

Research question	Hypotheses		Findings
How do perceptions of organisational justice affect the dimensions of organisational citizenship behaviour?	1	Employee perceptions of organisational justice positively influence the dimensions of organisational citizenship behaviour	Partially supported
	1a	Employee perceptions of distributive justice positively influence the dimensions of organisational citizenship behaviour	Partially supported
	1b	Employee perceptions of procedural justice positively influence the dimensions of organisational citizenship behaviour	Partially supported
	1c	Employee perceptions of interactional justice positively influence the dimensions of organisational citizenship behaviour	Partially supported

Table 8.10 Significance of organisational justice on organisational citizenship behaviour

Dimensions of organisational citizenship behaviour	Dimensions of organisational Justice	Beta	Rank
Courtesy	Interpersonal	0.389	2
	Informational	0.177	6
	Procedural	–0.128	10
Sportsmanship	Interpersonal	0.191	5
	Procedural	–0.136	9
Altruism	Interpersonal	0.334	3
Civic virtue	Interpersonal	0.327	4
	Procedural	0.170	7
	Distributive	0.153	8
Conscientiousness	Interpersonal	0.480	1

mitigate misunderstanding and conflict at the workplace. Specifically, in the manufacturing sector that employs a significant number of foreign workers, organisations benefit from activities that promote workplace harmony, as such activities foster teamwork and increase employee morale. Besides, workforce in the manufacturing sector comes from different ethnic groups. Tensions are inevitable if different racial groups are treated differently. Additionally, well-established grievance procedures are also likely to improve sportsmanship at the workplace.

Furthermore, the results establish that interactional justice has a significant effect on courtesy, but only interpersonal justice significantly affects the other dimensions of organisational citizenship behaviour. The association between interpersonal justice and altruism supports the findings of Giap et al. (2005) which affirm that employees do extra-role work to help when their supervisors treat them respectfully, akin to Organ's (1997) contention that employees contain extra-role behaviour if employees perceive injustice. Similarly, Sweeney and McFarlin (1993) assert that employee perceptions of injustice restrict employee willingness to help other employees. Informational justice enhances employees' obligation of cooperation with others and has no significant effect on other dimensions of organisational citizenship behaviour. Employees that have limited access to information will perceive that they belong to the out-group and feel alienated. Hence, they may constrain cooperative behaviours, especially with the in-group, as they perceive that they will not benefit much even if they contribute to organisational effectiveness.

However, the current findings dispute prior studies that contend that procedural justice is an important determinant of organisational citizenship behaviour (e.g. Farh et al. 1990; Lind and Tyler 1988; Moorman 1991; Niehoff and Moorman 1993; Tansky 1993). Studies reveal a correlation between procedural justice and altruism (e.g. Farh et al. 1990; Konovsky and Folger 1991). Other studies substantiate a positive correlation between procedural justice and altruism, courtesy, sportsmanship and conscientiousness (Moorman 1991; Niehoff and Moorman 1993). The current findings are also incongruent with the findings of Nadiri and Tanova (2010) where distributive justice is a stronger predictor of organisational citizenship behaviour and that distributive justice is associated with altruism and conscientiousness (Organ and Konovsky 1989). It further differs from meta-analytic data that show positive correlations between both procedural and distributive justice and organisational citizenship behaviour (Cohen-Charash and Spector 2001; Colquitt et al. 2001; Farh et al. 1997; Folger 1987; Giap et al. 2005; Konovsky and Organ 1996; LePine et al. 2002; Moorman and Byrne 2005). The current study suggests that perceived fairness of interpersonal treatment by managers as well as adequate and sincere communication of procedures and outcomes rather than fairness of a firm's procedures would have a stronger impact on organisational citizenship behaviour. This is probably because Malaysians value trust, courtesy, mutual respect and face and believe in developing relationships. In high context cultures such as Malaysia, greater attention must be given to additional forms of communication such as voice tone, body language, eye contact and facial expressions to enhance interactional justice. Therefore, to promote organisational citizenship behaviour, managers may have to make a concerted effort to treat employees with greater respect and dignity.

In the current study, employee perceptions of procedural justice relate negatively to courtesy and sportsmanship. Hence, the results challenge prior research that contend the linear relationship between procedural justice and altruism (Farh et al. 1990) and altruism, courtesy, sportsmanship and conscientiousness (Moorman 1991; Niehoff and Moorman 1993). The inverse correlation indicates that employees have a tendency of containing cooperative behaviours and complain more if procedures in decision outcomes were perceived as fair. On the contrary, employees maintain courtesy despite low procedural justice. One possible explanation for this is that employees avoid displaying negative behaviour in public. Losing control of one's emotions openly is perceived as 'losing face'. In Malaysian culture, face is a vital element. Therefore, to mask one's true feelings, employees show courtesy and cooperate with others as well as make great efforts so as not to be seen as loud, noisy trouble makers. Besides, saving face is not only crucial to the employee but also other coworkers. Causing coworkers to lose face because of one's intolerance may influence team spirit and knowledge sharing. Thus, employees in Malaysia refrain from direct answers, particularly negative ones, to prevent disagreement and preserve harmony – two very important aspects of Malaysian culture.

In essence, perceptions of procedural justice reduce employees' efforts in avoiding negative behaviours and not complaining in case of problems. Concisely, employees are less tolerant and tend to behave negatively when equity in decision outcome procedures exists. As Malaysia scores highly on Hofstede dimensions of power distance and uncertainty avoidance, organisations tend to be highly rule-oriented with laws, rules, regulations and controls in order to reduce the amount of uncertainty. Given this, employees probably perceived that being discourteous, uncooperative or unsporting might have little effect on decision outcomes, as the system does not allow significant upward mobility. Moreover, as a collectivist and tolerant society, employees anticipate support from coworkers despite their shortcomings. Nonetheless, procedural justice hinders helpful behaviours, as well as discourages teamwork and collaboration among employees. Instead, the negative relationship may encourage employees to engage in behaviours that are damaging to fellow employees and the organisation itself. Such attitudes may be detrimental to organisations, as collaboration and consultation are sometimes instrumental in mitigating the severity of a foreseen problem.

The current study ascertains that distributive, procedural and interpersonal justices positively influence civic virtue in the manufacturing sector in Malaysia. This confirms the findings of Robinson and Morrison (1995) that employee perceptions of fairness enhance civic behaviour. This indicates that organisational justice is a key determinant of whether employees take an interest in company affairs and developments and make efforts that promote self as well as organisation interest. Succinctly, organisational justice is a strong determinant of whether employees respond appropriately and responsibly to the political life of the organisation. Fair procedures encourage employees to stay up-to-date with important issues of the organisation and support the needs of the group (Moorman and Blakely 1995). Awareness of happenings at the workplace not only helps employees respond quickly but also promotes citizenship behaviours in the long run. This is instrumental for organisational effectiveness in the current challenging global environment where external demand is increasingly uncertain.

The effect of employee behaviours on the bottom line (Alder and Tompkins 1997; Ball et al. 1994; Fernandes and Awamleh 2006; Gilliland 1994; Greenberg 1986; Welbourne et al. 1995) suggests that it may be beneficial for organisations to ensure justice at the workplace. Employee perceptions of organisational justice foster positive citizenship perceptions, which further enhance organisational justice perceptions (Yilmaz and Tasdan 2009). When employer initiates fair treatment of its employees, employees feel obligated to reciprocate (Blau 1964; Homans 1961) by exhibiting extra-role behaviours (Dittrich and Carrell 1979; Eskew 1993; Robinson and Morrison 1995; Scholl et al. 1987) such as organisational citizenship behaviours (Moorman and Blakely 1995; Organ 1988; Organ and Ryan 1995; Williams et al. 2002). A mutually beneficial social relationship is established as perceptions of equity motivate employees to support the organisation (Fuller and Hester 2007) in achieving its vision and mission. Nonetheless, employees may change their mindset with regard to their relationship with the organisation if they are treated unfairly (Erturk 2007). Given the increasing demand for skilled and talent workers, employee may be lured by competitors if organisational citizenship behaviour is not well established in the organisation.

Besides, perceptions of organisational justice affect employee health and well-being (Elovainio et al. 2002; Kausto et al. 2005; Kivimaki et al. 2003; Schmitt and Dorfel 1999; Tepper 2001). Negative feelings from perceptions of organisational injustice have an effect on stress (Judge and Colquitt 2004; Lind and Tyler 1988; Thibaut and Walker 1975; Tyler and Lind 1992), and the impact may be even more intense in the manufacturing sector due to the perilous nature of the workplace and the diverse workforce. This affects not only the productivity and performance of employees, but may also trigger employee intention to leave (e.g. Alexander and Ruderman 1987; Ansari et al. 2000; Bagdadli et al. 2006; Barling and Phillips 1992; Carson et al. 1994; Dailey and Kirk 1992; Harris et al. 2005; Lemons and Jones 2001; Masterson and Taylor 1996; Olson-Buchanan 1996; Porter and Steers 1973; Price 1977; Schaubroeck et al. 1994; Stroh et al. 1996; Vecchio and Gobdel 1984; Wayne et al. 1997), discrimination suits (Cole and Latham 1997; Peterson and Danehower 1994), theft behaviour (Greenberg 1994), increased sexual harassment proclivities (Krings and Facchin 2009), increased absenteeism and on-the-job accidents (Sashkin and Williams 1990). Thus, employee perceptions of organisational justice strongly affect attitudes and affective reactions towards the organisation (Cohen-Charash and Spector 2001). Accordingly, it is imperative for organisations to promote a positive image to mitigate negative behaviours that are costly to the organisation. Employee turnover, for example, increases recruitment and training costs and lost productivity (Sagie et al. 2002). Additionally, organisational commitment is essential to enhance sustainability as well as fulfil corporate social responsibility. With continuous financing and investment concentrated in the manufacturing sector, organisations should harness citizenship behaviours to gain competitive advantage. Assurance of organisational justice that augments organisational citizenship behaviour is vital to enhance commitment of employees in the manufacturing sector in Malaysia.

In summary, the findings of this study support prior research in asserting the significance of organisational justice in enhancing organisational citizenship behaviour (Dittrich and Carrell 1979; Farh et al. 1990; Konovsky and Folger 1991; Moorman 1991; Scholl et al. 1987). Specifically, particular attention should be paid to interpersonal justice, as it is significant on all dimensions of organisational citizenship behaviour. It is, therefore, imperative to provide industry captains or organisational leaders in the manufacturing sector with the interpersonal skills to communicate perceived fairness in decision-making. This involves giving employees due respect and increasing transparency in the decision-making processes. This concurs with DeConinck (2010) assertion that for interactional justice to improve, supervisors need to not only explain the procedures but also respond to queries regarding the process. With financial support from various sources and the enforcement of the Human Resource Development Act, training could be carried out to enhance the interpersonal skills of decision-makers. In essence, it may be necessary for HR practitioners and developmental specialists to prioritise leadership training for all employees involved in decision-making. Though autonomy in decision-making may be encouraged, perceived injustice will strain relationships and hamper citizenship behaviours.

Therefore, it is crucial that organisations promote a culture of fairness and influence employee perceptions of a quality relationship between organisational justice and organisational citizenship behaviour (Tansky 1993). Employees reciprocate with discretionary behaviours when they are treated fairly and vice versa (Organ 1997). Justice initiates neutrality and standing, which accordingly heightens reciprocation and communication (Allen and Meyer 1990; Brockner and Siegel 1996). As behaviour intent is the most important determinant of a person's behaviour (Ajzen and Fishbein 1980), employee perceptions of organisational justice will likely motivate employees to intentionally reciprocate positively. A mutually beneficial social relationship is established once the employer initiates fair treatment of its employees, as employees feel obligated to reciprocate (Blau 1964; Homans 1961). Employees reciprocate by exhibiting extra-role behaviours (Robinson and Morrison 1995) such as organisational citizenship behaviours (Organ 1988).

Studies show that employees exhibit feelings of anger, outrage and resentment (Bies 1987; Folger 1993; Folger and Cropanzano 1998; Greenberg 1989, 1990b; Sheppard et al. 1992) when treated unfairly. Ultimately, acts of retribution or retaliation (Greenberg and Scott 1996; Sheppard et al. 1992; Skarlicki and Folger 1997) may surface. Shaw et al. (2003) reiterate that informational justice decreases potential retaliatory behaviour of employees. Moreover, perceived fairness affects employees' decision to pursue activities that advance their own self-interest or pursue activities that promote group interests (Fuller and Hester 2007; Lind 2001). For organisational effectiveness, a potential win–win situation is to help further the self-interest of employees in achieving positive outcomes (Posthuma et al. 2007) and enhance employees' faith in organisational systems.

Conclusion

This chapter presented the results of the relationship between organisational justice and organisational citizenship behaviour. Factor loadings were used to determine convergent validity. The scales were then subjected to exploratory and confirmatory factor analysis. Based on statistical and theoretical considerations, items that did not fulfil convergent validity were deleted from the scale. In accordance with SEM requirements, adequacy of the data was determined. On confirmation of conformity with SEM assumptions, measurement and structural models were developed. Based on the statistical results, hypothesis testing was performed.

The findings showed that the relationship between perceptions of organisational justice and the dimensions of organisational citizenship behaviour was partially substantiated. Procedural justice and distributive justice perceptions of employees had a significant positive effect on civic virtue. However, there was a negative relationship between procedural justice and the organisational citizenship behaviour dimensions of courtesy and sportsmanship. Informational justice positively influenced courtesy. Among justice factors, employee perceptions of interpersonal justice were an important determinant of organisational citizenship behaviour. All dimensions of organisational citizenship behaviour were significantly related with interpersonal justice. Hence, the findings of the study affirmed a positive relationship between organisational justice and organisational citizenship behaviour, albeit partially. The chapter concluded with a comprehensive discussion of the implications of the findings for theory and practice. The next chapter focuses on the results and discussions on the relationship between organisational justice, job satisfaction and organisational citizenship behaviour.

References

Ajzen, I., & Fishbein, M. (1980). *Understanding attitudes and predicting social behavior*. Englewood Cliffs: Prentice Hall.

Alder, S. A., & Tompkins, P. K. (1997). Electronic performance monitoring: An organizational justice and concretive control perspective. *Management Communications Quarterly, 10*(3), 259–289.

Alexander, S., & Ruderman, M. (1987). The role of procedural and distributive justice in organisational behavior. *Social Justice Research, 1*(2), 177–198.

Allen, N. J., & Meyer, J. P. (1990). The measurement and antecedents of affective, continuance and normative commitment to the organization. *Journal of Occupational Psychology, 63*(1), 1–18.

Allen, T. D., & Rush, M. C. (1998). The effects of organizational citizenship behavior on performance judgements: A field study and a laboratory experiment. *Journal of Applied Psychology, 83*(2), 247–260.

Ansari, M. A., Kee, D. M. H., & Aafaqi, R. (2000). Fairness of human resource management practices, leader-member exchange, and intention to quit. *Journal of International Business and Entrepreneurship, 8*, 1–19.

Bagdadli, S., Roberson, Q., & Paoletti, F. (2006). The mediating role of procedural justice in responses to promotion decisions. *Journal of Business and Psychology, 21*(1), 83–102.

Ball, G. A., Trevino, L. K., & Sims, H. P., Jr. (1994). Just and unjust punishment: Influences on subordinate performance and citizenship. *Academy of Management Journal, 37*(2), 299–322.

Barling, J., & Phillips, M. (1992). Interactional, formal, and distributive justice in the workplace: An exploratory study. *The Journal of Psychology, 127*(6), 649–656.

Bies, R. J. (1987). Beyond "voice": The influence of decision-maker justification and sincerity on procedural fairness judgments. *Representative Research in Social Psychology, 17*(1), 3–14.

Blau, P. (1964). *Exchange and power in social life*. New York: Wiley.

Brockner, J., & Siegel, P. (1996). Understanding the interaction between procedural and distributive justice: The role of trust. In R. M. Kramer & T. R. Tyler (Eds.), *Trust in organizations – Frontiers of theory and research* (pp. 390–413). Thousand Oaks: Sage.

Carson, P. P., Carson, K. D., Griffeth, R. W., & Steel, R. P. (1994). Promotion and employee turnover. Critique, meta-analysis, and implications. *Journal of Business and Psychology, 8*(4), 455–466.

Cohen-Charash, Y., & Spector, P. E. (2001). The role of justice in organizations: A meta-analysis. *Organizational Behavior and Human Decision Processes, 86*(2), 278–321.
Cole, N. D., & Latham, G. P. (1997). Effects of training in procedural justice on perceptions of disciplinary fairness by unionised employees and disciplinary subject matter experts. *Journal of Applied Psychology, 82*(5), 699–705.
Colquitt, J. A. (2001). On the dimensionality of organizational justice: A construct validation of a measure. *Journal of Applied Psychology, 86*(3), 386–400.
Colquitt, J. A., & Greenberg, J. (2003). Organizational justice: A fair assessment of the state of the literature. In J. Greenberg (Ed.), *Organizational behavior: The state of the science* (pp. 165–210). Mahwah: Erlbaum.
Colquitt, J. A., Conlon, D. E., Wesson, M. J., Porter, C. O. L. H., & Ng, K. Y. (2001). Justice at the millennium: A meta-analytic review of 25 years of organizational justice research. *Journal of Applied Psychology, 86*(3), 425–445.
Conant, J. S., Mokwa, M. P., & Vadarajan, P. R. (1990). Strategic types, distinctive marketing competencies and organizational performance. *Strategic Management Journal, 11*, 365–383.
Dailey, R. C., & Kirk, D. J. (1992). Distributive and procedural justice as antecedents of job dissatisfaction and intent to turnover. *Human Relations, 45*(3), 305–317.
DeConinck, J. B. (2010). The effect of organizational justice, perceived organizational support, and perceived supervisor support on marketing employees' level of trust. *Journal of Business Research, 63*(12), 1349–1355.
Deutsch, M. (2000). Justice and conflict. In M. Deutsch & P. T. Coleman (Eds.), *The handbook of conflict resolution: Theory and practice* (pp. 41–64). San Francisco: Jossey Bass.
Dittrich, J. E., & Carrell, M. R. (1979). Organizational equity perceptions, employee job satisfaction and departmental absence and turnover rates. *Organizational Behavior and Human Performance, 24*(1), 29–40.
Elovainio, M., Kivimaki, M., & Vahtera, J. (2002). Organizational justice: Evidence of a new psychosocial predictor of health. *American Journal of Public Health, 92*(1), 105–108.
Erturk, A. (2007). Increasing organizational citizenship behaviors of Turkish academicians: Mediating role of trust in supervisor on the relationship between organizational justice and citizenship behaviours. *Journal of Managerial Psychology, 22*(3), 257–270.
Eskew, D. E. (1993). The role of organizational justice in organizational citizenship behavior. *Employee Responsibilities and Rights Journal, 6*(3), 185–194.
Farh, J., Podsakoff, P. M., & Organ, D. W. (1990). Accounting for organizational citizenship behavior: Leader fairness and task scope versus satisfaction. *Journal of Management, 16*(4), 705–721.
Farh, J. L., Earley, P. C., & Lin, S. C. (1997). Impetus for action: A cultural analysis of justice and organizational citizenship behavior in Chinese society. *Administrative Science Quarterly, 42*(3), 421–444.
Fernandes, C., & Awamleh, R. (2006). Impact of organisational justice in an expatriate work environment. *Management Research News, 29*(11), 701–712.
Folger, R. (1987). Distributive and procedural justice in the workplace. *Social Justice Research, 1*(2), 143–159.
Folger, R. (1993). Justice, motivation, and performance beyond role requirements. *Employee Responsibilities and Rights Journal, 6*(3), 239–248.
Folger, R., & Cropanzano, R. (1998). *Organisational justice and human resource management*. Beverly Hills: Sage Publications.
Fuller, J. B., & Hester, K. (2007). Procedural justice and the cooperative worker: An interactional model of union participation. *Journal of Labor Research, 28*(1), 189–202.
Giap, B. N., Hackermeier, I., Jiao, X., & Wagdarikar, S. P. (2005). Organizational citizenship behavior and perception of organizational justice in student jobs. In: *Research study, psychology of excellence instructional design, job analysis & job design* (pp. 1–14). Munich: Ludwig-Maximilians-University.
Gilliland, S. W. (1994). Effects of procedural and distributive justice on reactions to a selection system. *Journal of Applied Psychology, 79*(5), 691–701.

Greenberg, J. (1986). Determinants of perceived fairness of performance evaluations. *Journal of Applied Psychology, 71*(2), 340–342.
Greenberg, J. (1989). Cognitive reevaluation of outcomes in response to underpayment inequity. *Academy of Management Journal, 32*(1), 174–184.
Greenberg, J. (1990a). Looking fair vs. being fair: Managing impressions of organizational justice. In B. M. Shaw & L. L. Cummings (Eds.), *Research in organizational behavior* (pp. 111–157). Greenwich: JAI Press.
Greenberg, J. (1990b). Employee theft as a reaction to underpayment inequity: The hidden cost of pay cuts. *Journal of Applied Psychology, 75*(5), 561–568.
Greenberg, J. (1993). The social side of fairness: Interpersonal and informational classes of organizational justice. In R. Cropanzano (Ed.), *Justice in the workplace: Approaching fairness in human resource management* (pp. 79–103). Hillsdale: Lawrence Erlbaum.
Greenberg, J. (1994). Using socially fair procedures to promote acceptance of a work site smoking ban. *Journal of Applied Psychology, 79*(2), 288–297.
Greenberg, J., & Scott, K. S. (1996). Why do workers bite the hand that feeds them? Employee theft as a social exchange process. In B. M. Shaw & L. L. Cummings (Eds.), *Research in organizational behavior* (pp. 111–156). Greenwich: JAI Press.
Harris, K. J., Kacmar, K. M., & Witt, L. A. (2005). An examination of the curvilinear relationship between leader-member exchange and intent to turnover. *Journal of Organizational Behavior, 26*(4), 363–378.
Homans, G. C. (1961). *Social behaviour: Its elementary forms*. London: Routledge and Kegan Paul.
Judge, T. A., & Colquitt, J. A. (2004). Organizational justice and stress: The mediating role of work-family conflict. *Journal of Applied Psychology, 89*(3), 395–404.
Kausto, J., Elo, A. L., Lipponen, J., & Elovainio, M. (2005). Moderating effects of job insecurity in the relationships between procedural justice and employee well-being: Gender differences. *European Journal of Work and Organizational Behavior, 14*(4), 431–452.
Kelloway, E. K. (1995). Structural equation modelling in perspective. *Journal of Organizational Behavior, 16*(3), 215–224.
Kivimaki, M., Elovainio, M., Vahtera, J., & Ferrie, J. E. (2003). Organisational justice and health of employees: Prospective cohort study. *Occupational and Environmental Medicine, 60*(1), 27–34.
Konovsky, M. A., & Folger, R. (1991). The effects of procedures, social accounts, and benefits level on victims' layoff reactions. *Journal of Applied Social Psychology, 21*(8), 630–650.
Konovsky, M. A., & Organ, D. W. (1996). Dispositional and contextual determinants of organizational citizenship behavior. *Journal of Organizational Behavior, 17*(3), 253–266.
Konovsky, M. A., & Pugh, S. D. (1994). Citizenship behavior and social exchange. *Academy of Management Journal, 37*(3), 656–669.
Krings, F., & Facchin, S. (2009). Organizational justice and men's likelihood to sexually harass: The moderating role of sexism and personality. *Journal of Applied Psychology, 94*(2), 501–510.
Lazar, A., Zinger, A., & Lachterman, B. (2007). The influence of prefeedback selection justice on perceptions of overall procedural justice and organizational attractiveness in a real-life selection procedure. *European Journal of Work and Organizational Psychology, 16*(1), 94–109.
Lemons, M. A., & Jones, C. A. (2001). Procedural justice in promotion decisions: Using perceptions of fairness to build employee commitment. *Journal of Managerial Psychology, 16*(4), 268–280.
Lepine, J. A., Erez, A., & Johnson, D. E. (2002). The nature and dimensionality of organizational citizenship behavior: A critical review and meta-analysis. *Journal of Applied Psychology, 87*(1), 52–65.
Lind, E. A. (2001). Fairness heuristic theory: Justice judgments as pivotal cognitions in organizational relations. In J. Greenberg & R. Cropanzano (Eds.), *Advances in organizational justice* (pp. 56–88). Stanford: Stanford University Press.

Lind, E. A., & Tyler, T. R. (1988). *The social psychology of procedural justice*. New York: Plenum Press.

Masterson, S. S., & Taylor, M. S. (1996). *The broadening of procedural justice: Should interactional and procedural components be separate theories?* Paper presented at annual meeting of the Academy of Management, Cincinnati.

Masterson, S. S., Lewis, K., Goldman, B. M., & Taylor, M. S. (2000). Integrating justice and social exchange: The differing effects of fair procedures and treatment of work relationships. *Academy of Management Journal, 43*(4), 738–748.

Moorman, R. H. (1991). Relationship between organizational justice and organizational citizenship behavior: Do fairness perceptions influence employee citizenship? *Journal of Applied Psychology, 76*(6), 845–855.

Moorman, R. H., & Blakely, G. L. (1995). Individualism-collectivism as an individual difference predictor of organizational citizenship behavior. *Journal of Organizational Behavior, 16*(2), 127–142.

Moorman, R. H., & Byrne, Z. S. (2005). How does organizational justice affect organizational citizenship behavior? In J. Greenberg & J. A. Colquitt (Eds.), *Handbook of organizational justice* (pp. 355–380). Mahwah: Lawrence Erlbaum Associates.

Moorman, R. H., Niehoff, B. P., & Organ, D. W. (1993). Treating employees fairly and organizational citizenship behavior: Sorting the effects of job satisfaction, organizational commitment, and procedural justice. *Employee Responsibilities and Rights Journal, 6*(3), 209–225.

Moorman, R. H., Blakely, G. L., & Niehoff, B. P. (1998). Does perceived organizational support mediate the relationship between procedural justice and organizational citizenship behavior? *Academy of Management Journal, 41*(3), 351–357.

Nadiri, H., & Tanova, C. (2010). An investigation of the role of justice in turnover intentions, job satisfaction, and organizational citizenship behavior in hospitality industry. *International Journal of Hospitality Management, 29*(1), 33–41.

Niehoff, B. P., & Moorman, R. H. (1993). Justice as a mediator of the relationship between methods of monitoring and organizational citizenship behavior. *Academy of Management Journal, 36*(3), 527–556.

Nunnally, J. O. (1978). *Psychometric theory*. New York: McGraw-Hill.

Olson-Buchanan, J. B. (1996). Voicing discontent: What happens to the grievance filer after the grievance? *Journal of Applied Psychology, 81*(1), 52–63.

Organ, D. W. (1988). *Organizational citizenship behavior: The good solider syndrome*. Lexington: Lexington Books.

Organ, D. W. (1997). Organizational citizenship behavior: It's construct clean-up time". *Human Performance, 10*(2), 85–97.

Organ, D. W., & Konovsky, M. A. (1989). Cognitive versus affective determinants of organizational citizenship behavior. *Journal of Applied Psychology, 74*, 157–164.

Organ, D. W., & Paine, J. B. (1999). A new kind of performance for industrial and organizational psychology: Recent contributions to the study of organizational citizenship behavior. In C. L. Cooper & I. T. Robertson (Eds.), *International review of industrial and organizational psychology* (pp. 338–368). Chichester: Wiley.

Organ, D. W., & Ryan, K. (1995). A meta-analytic review of attitudinal and dispositional predictors of organizational citizenship behavior. *Personnel Psychology, 48*(4), 775–802.

Peterson, R. C., & Danehower, V. C. (1994). *Judicial decisions in promotion selection in employment: An empirical study of discrimination cases*. Paper presented at the Southwest Academy of Management meeting in Dallas.

Podsakoff, P. M., MacKenzie, S. B., Paine, J. B., & Bachrach, D. G. (2000). Organizational citizenship behaviors: A critical review of the theoretical and empirical literature and suggestions for future research. *Journal of Management, 26*(3), 513–563.

Porter, L. W., & Steers, R. M. (1973). Organisational, work, and personal factors in employee turnover and absenteeism. *Psychological Bulletin, 80*(2), 151–176.

Posthuma, R. A., Maertz, C. P., & Dworkin, J. B. (2007). Procedural justice's relationship with turnover: Explaining past inconsistent findings. *Journal of Organizational Behavior, 28*(4), 381–398.

Price, J. L. (1977). *The study of turnover*. Ames: Iowa State University Press.

Robinson, S. L., & Morrison, E. W. (1995). Psychological contracts and the OCB: The effect of unfulfilled obligations on civic virtue behavior. *Journal of Organizational Behavior, 16*(3), 289–298.

Robinson, J. P., Shaver, P. R., & Wrightsman, L. S. (1991). Criteria for scale selection and evaluation. In J. P. Robinson, P. R. Shaver, & L. S. Wrightsman (Eds.), *Measures of personality and social psychological attitudes*. San Diego: Academic.

Sagie, A., Birati, A., & Tziner, A. (2002). Assessing the costs of behavioral and psychological withdrawal: A new model and an empirical illustration. *Applied Psychology: An International Review, 51*(1), 67–89.

Sashkin, M., & Williams, R. L. (1990). Does fairness make a difference? *Organisational Dynamics, 19*(2), 56–71.

Schaubroeck, J., May, D. R., & Brown, F. W. (1994). Procedural justice explanations and reactions to economic hardship: A field experiment. *Journal of Applied Psychology, 79*(3), 455–460.

Schmitt, M. J., & Dorfel, M. (1999). Procedural injustice at work, justice sensitivity, job satisfaction and psychosomatic well-being. *European Journal of Social Psychology, 29*(4), 443–453.

Scholl, R. W., Cooper, E. A., & McKenna, J. F. (1987). Referent selection in determining equity perceptions: Differential effects on behavioral and attitudinal outcomes. *Personnel Psychology, 40*(1), 113–124.

Shaw, J. C., Wild, R. E., & Colquitt, J. A. (2003). To justify or excuse?: A meta-analytic review of the effects of explanations. *Journal of Applied Psychology, 88*(3), 444–458.

Sheppard, B. H., Lewicki, R. J., & Minton, J. W. (1992). *Organizational justice: The search for fairness in the workplace*. New York: Lexington Books.

Skarlicki, D. P., & Folger, R. (1997). Retaliation in the workplace: The roles of distributive, procedural, and interactional justice. *Journal of Applied Psychology, 82*(3), 434–443.

Skarlicki, D. P., & Latham, G. P. (1996). Increasing citizenship behaviour within a labor union: A test of organizational justice theory. *Journal of Applied Psychology, 81*(2), 161–169.

Stroh, L. K., Brett, J. M., & Really, A. H. (1996). Family structure, glass ceiling, and traditional explanations for the differential rate of turnover of female and male manager. *Journal of Vocational Behaviour, 49*(1), 99–118.

Sweeney, P. D., & McFarlin, D. B. (1993). Workers' evaluations of the 'ends' and the 'means': An examination of four models of distributive and procedural justice. *Organisational Behavior and Human Decision Processes, 55*(1), 23–40.

Tansky, J. W. (1993). Justice and organizational citizenship behavior: What is the relationship? *Employee Responsibilities and Rights Journal, 6*(3), 195–207.

Tepper, B. J. (2001). Health consequences of organizational injustice: Test of main and interactive effects. *Organizational Behavior and Human Decision Processes, 86*(2), 197–215.

Thibaut, J., & Walker, L. (1975). *Procedural justice: A psychological analysis*. Hillsdale: Erlbaum.

Tschannen-Moran, M. (2001). Collaboration and the need for trust. *Journal of Educational Administration, 39*(4), 308–331.

Tyler, T. R., & Lind, E. A. (1992). A relational model of authority in groups. In M. P. Zanna (Ed.), *Advances in experimental social psychology* (pp. 115–191). San Diego: Academic.

Vecchio, R. P., & Gobdel, B. C. (1984). The vertical dyad linkage model of leadership: Problems and perspectives. *Organizational Behavior and Human Performance, 34*(1), 5–20.

Wayne, S. J., Shore, L. M., & Liden, R. C. (1997). Perceived organizational support and leader-member exchange: A social exchange perspective. *Academy of Management Journal, 40*(1), 82–111.

Welbourne, T. M., Balkin, D. B., & Gomez-Mejia, L. R. (1995). Gainsharing and mutual monitoring: A combined agency-organizational justice interpretation. *Academy of Management Journal, 38*(3), 881–899.

Williams, S., Pitre, R., & Zainuba, M. (2002). Justice and organizational citizenship behavior intentions: Fair rewards versus fair treatment. *The Journal of Social Psychology, 142*(1), 33–44.

Yilmaz, K., & Tasdan, M. (2009). Organizational citizenship and organizational justice in Turkish primary schools. *Journal of Educational Administration, 47*(1), 108–126.

Chapter 9
Organisational Justice–Job Satisfaction–Organisational Citizenship Behaviour

Abstract This chapter outlines the research findings of the hypothesised relationships between organisational justice, job satisfaction and organisational citizenship behaviour. Findings on the empirical relationship between organisational justice and job satisfaction provide an insight of not only whether organisational justice is a primary antecedent of job satisfaction but also the importance of the job satisfaction–organisational citizenship behaviour relationship. The findings establish if job satisfaction affects the dimensions of organisational citizenship behaviour. An in-depth discussion on the outcomes of the findings provides indicators that practitioners could consider when implementing policies to enhance performance, in general, and organisational citizenship behaviours, in particular.

Introduction

This chapter investigates the extent to which organisational justice affects job satisfaction and the relationship between job satisfaction and organisational citizenship behaviour. The relationship between job satisfaction and organisational citizenship behaviour is well established in the literature. Podsakoff et al. (1993) conclude that job satisfaction is likely to be highest in organisations where organisational citizenship behaviour is prevalent. Despite the proliferation of research in job satisfaction and organisational citizenship behaviour, remarkably little research has examined the relationship between job satisfaction and organisational citizenship behaviour in the Malaysian manufacturing context. Moreover, due to the reciprocal relationship between job satisfaction and organisational citizenship behaviour, findings are still inconclusively pertaining to the direction of causality between job satisfaction and organisational citizenship behaviour. This chapter sets out to verify if the relationship between job satisfaction and organisational citizenship behaviour in the manufacturing sector in Malaysia concurs with prior studies. The findings would establish if manufacturing organisations ought to focus on job satisfaction to enhance organisational citizenship behaviour.

Additionally, should manufacturing organisations consider organisational justice as an antecedent of job satisfaction? A section of the current chapter outlines the effect of the four justice factors in explaining job satisfaction in the manufacturing sector in Malaysia. The findings provide valuable insights for manufacturing

L.W. Hooi, *Organisational Justice and Citizenship Behaviour in Malaysia*, Governance and Citizenship in Asia, DOI 10.1007/978-981-10-0030-0_9

organisations to focus on the specific type of justice to improve job satisfaction and ultimately organisational citizenship behaviour. Considering the hazardous nature of the manufacturing environment, job satisfaction level of the employees is more likely to be affected. Despite high power distance and the emphasis on collectivism in the Malaysian work culture, it is hypothesised that organisational justice affects employees' level of job satisfaction. Therefore, this study sets out to demonstrate if this is indeed important as job satisfaction may affect discretionary involvement in the workplace. It may be vital to the survival of the organisation. Satisfied employees can maximise efficiency and promote organisational effectiveness.

Job Satisfaction

The results of the exploratory factor analysis (EFA) on job satisfaction showed that only one factor was extracted, explaining 71.2 % of the variance. As shown in Table 9.1, the KMO index for job satisfaction was relatively high; a value of 0.819 indicated that intercorrelations in the data matrix were commendable. One item was dropped due to low factor loading (JS5). Cronbach's alpha was 0.865, and, therefore, reliability of the scale was high.

Table 9.1 Results of EFA on job satisfaction

Items		**Value**	
Kaiser–Meyer–Olkin		0.819	
Bartlett's test of sphericity		496.635	
		(sig. 0.000, df. 6)	
Factor	**Eigenvalue**	**Percentage of variance**	**Cumulative variance**
Job satisfaction	2.849	71.220	71.220
Factors/items		Factor loading	
Factor 1: job satisfaction			
JS4	I find real enjoyment in my job	0.876	
JS1	I am very satisfied with my job	0.857	
JS3	I like my job better than the average worker does	0.834	
JS2	Most days I am enthusiastic about my job	0.807	
Internal consistency reliability (Cronbach's alpha)		0.865	

Table 9.2 Results on organisational justice–job satisfaction relationship

Factors/items	Std. loading	S.E.	C.R.	*P*
Job satisfaction ← procedural justice	.229	.064	3.486	***
Job satisfaction ← informational justice	.347	.095	4.820	***
Job satisfaction ← distributive justice	.276	.055	4.267	***
Job satisfaction ← interpersonal justice	.161	.083	2.478	.013

***$p < 0.001$

Hypothesis 2: Organisational Justice–Job Satisfaction Relationship

As evidenced in Table 9.2 and Fig. 9.1, employee perceptions of organisational justice positively influenced job satisfaction. All dimensions of organisational justice were significantly related to job satisfaction. Among the justice factors, informational justice had a greater influence on job satisfaction than distributive justice, procedural justice or interpersonal justice. The findings as summarised in Table 9.3 showed that hypotheses 2, 2a, 2b and 2c were substantiated.

Hypothesis 4: Job Satisfaction–Organisational Citizenship Behaviour

As evidenced in Table 9.4, job satisfaction positively influenced all dimensions of organisational citizenship behaviour. Thus, as shown in Table 9.5, the hypothesis that job satisfaction positively influence organisational citizenship behaviour was substantiated. As shown in Fig. 9.2, the effect of job satisfaction on organisational citizenship behaviour was most significant on civic virtue, followed by courtesy, conscientiousness, altruism and sportsmanship.

Discussion of the Findings

Organisational Justice–Job Satisfaction Relationship

The second research question of the study emphasises the relationship between organisational justice and job satisfaction. Table 9.6 presents the research question, hypotheses and the findings for this relationship. The discussion that follows authenticates the significance of organisational justice on job satisfaction. These findings are important, as job satisfaction is likely to have an effect on organisational citizenship behaviour. If job satisfaction is indeed apparent in the organisational justice–organisational citizenship behaviour relationship, then organisations may target job satisfaction to increase organisational citizenship behaviours.

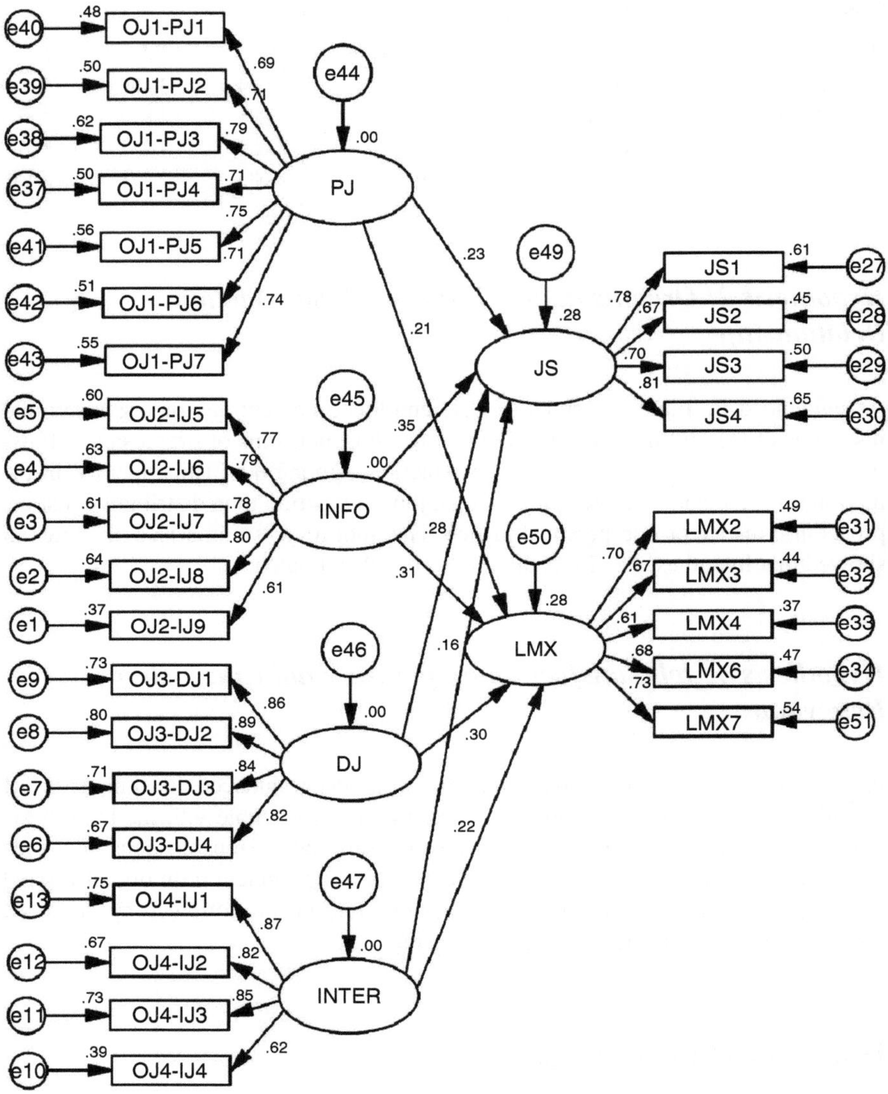

Fig. 9.1 Organisational justice–job satisfaction and organisational justice–leader–member exchange

The results of the study show that all dimensions of organisational justice positively influence job satisfaction. Informational justice has the most significant influence followed by distributive justice, procedural justice and interpersonal justice. This is consistent with prior research that affirms the relationship between fairness and job satisfaction (Alexander and Ruderman 1987; Ball et al. 1994;

Table 9.3 Hypotheses on organisational justice–job satisfaction

	Hypotheses	Findings
2	Employee perceptions of organisational justice positively influence job satisfaction	Supported
2a	Employee perceptions of distributive justice positively influence job satisfaction	Supported
2b	Employee perceptions of procedural justice positively influence job satisfaction	Supported
2c	Employee perceptions of interactional justice positively influence job satisfaction	Supported

Table 9.4 Job satisfaction–organisational citizenship behaviour

Factors/items	Std. loading	S.E.	C.R.	*P*
Courtesy ← job satisfaction	.345	.049	4.819	***
Sportsmanship ← job satisfaction	.189	.069	2.707	.007
Altruism ← job satisfaction	.234	.050	3.288	.001
Civic virtue ← job satisfaction	.369	.057	4.815	***
Conscientiousness ← job satisfaction	.286	.055	3.716	***

***$p < 0.001$

Table 9.5 Hypotheses on job satisfaction–organisational citizenship behaviour

	Hypotheses	Findings
4	Job satisfaction positively influences the dimensions of organisational citizenship behaviour	Supported

Brief 1998; Cohen-Charash and Spector 2001; Colquitt et al. 2001; Folger and Cropanzano 1998; Greenberg 1990; Hassan and Mohd Noor 2008; Hendrix et al. 1999; Latham and Pinder 2005; McFarlin and Sweeney 1992; Organ 1988, 1990; Organ and Konovsky 1989; Price and Mueller 1986). Specifically, distributive justice and procedural justice are related to job satisfaction (Colquitt et al. 2001; Greenberg 1990; Lee et al. 2000; Phillips 2002; Sweeney and McFarlin 1993), while interactional justice has a significant impact on both job satisfaction (Azman et al. 2011; Cohen-Charash and Spector 2001; Colquitt et al. 2001; Konovsky and Cropanzano 1991; McFarlin and Sweeney 1992) and performance (Fernandes and Awamleh 2006). Employees' perception of equity in distribution enhances employees' satisfaction with supervisors (Alexander and Ruderman 1987; Fields et al. 2000; Folger and Konovsky 1989; Konovsky and Cropanzano 1991; Schaubroeck et al. 1994; Sweeney and McFarlin 1993). Others concur that only procedural fairness enhances job satisfaction (Bartol 1979; Fields et al. 2000; Igbaria and Greenhouse 1992; Korsgaard et al. 1995; Quarles 1994). Nonetheless, the current study disagrees with other studies that indicate that procedural justice rather than distributive justice is more strongly related to job satisfaction (Schaubroeck et al. 1994).

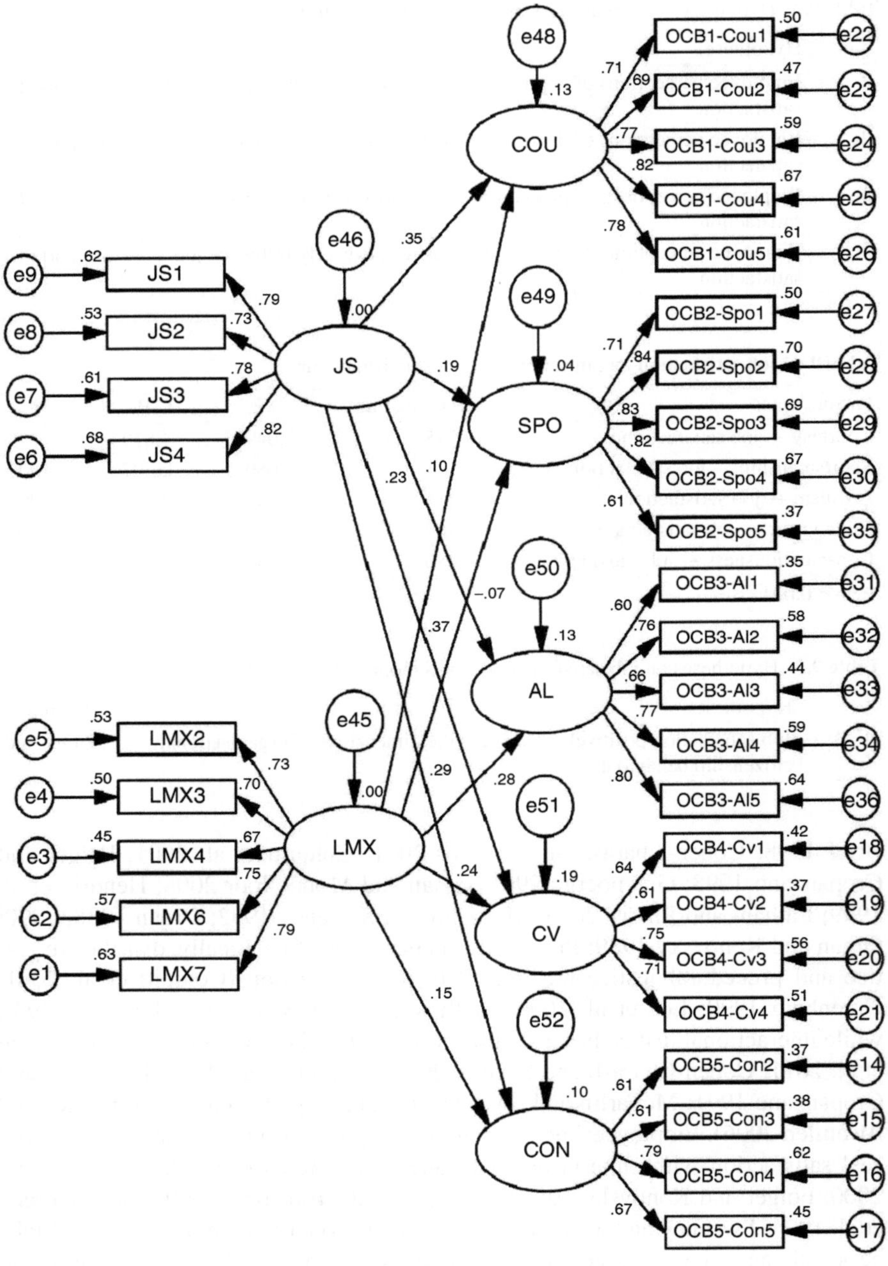

Fig. 9.2 Job satisfaction–organisational citizenship behaviour and leader–member exchange–organisational citizenship behaviour

Table 9.6 Hypotheses and the findings for research question 2

Research question	Hypotheses		Findings
How do employee perceptions of organisational justice affect job satisfaction?	2	Employee perceptions of organisational justice positively influence job satisfaction	Supported
	2a	Employee perceptions of distributive justice positively influence job satisfaction	Supported
	2b	Employee perceptions of procedural justice positively influence job satisfaction	Supported
	2c	Employee perceptions of interactional justice positively influence job satisfaction	Supported

In this study, distributive justice rather than procedural justice is a stronger predictor of job satisfaction in the manufacturing sector in Malaysia. At a score of 50 according to Hofstede's dimension, Malaysia can be considered a masculine society – highly success oriented and driven. People 'live in order to work', and being the best in the field rather than quality of life is the sign of success. Managers are expected to be decisive, and the emphasis is on equity, competition and performance. The manufacturing sector is no exception, as employees are driven by competition, achievement and success. Visibility is much emphasised, and at times, conflicts are resolved by fighting them out. In the current study, fairness of decision outcomes matters more, as the majority of the respondents (67.8 %) are young (25–40 years of age) and married (66.7 %). Family obligations and material needs probably top the list of priorities in this age group.

Furthermore, as competition intensifies, obtaining a higher education may be a solution for some employees who have been struggling to reach the upper echelons. Currently, pursuing a postgraduate degree, especially an MBA, is considered a norm for ambitious, young employees to remain competitive. In the current study, only 11.6 % of the respondents have a master's degree. As positions play a significant part in determining compensation and status in many Malaysian organisations, employees hope for justice in decision outcomes though most employees accept decisions unquestionably (Hooi et al. 2012). Given the strong labour market in the current economic growth, key employees may be enticed to join organisations that offer better prospects.

The importance of informational justice among justice factors in enhancing job satisfaction suggests that organisational decisions are not perceived as transparent and impartial. If honest and adequate explanations for decisions were given, employees are unlikely to perceive informational justice as the key determinant of job satisfaction. As job satisfaction affects other organisational phenomena that may have an impact on organisational performance, it is of paramount significance that organisations ensure transparency in decisions. Employees tend to lose confidence in ambiguous and partial decisions that affect their career and tenure with the organisation. Being in a high power distance environment, employees are unlikely to confront openly disputable decisions. Enduring in silence potentially aggravates employee feelings of discontentment and may result in unfavourable outcomes for the organisations. Therefore, organisations would probably benefit from investing in developing decision-makers to effectively articulate organisational decisions. Furthermore, with a diverse workforce, misunderstanding may arise if decision-makers lack the competence to communicate fair decisions effectively.

Alternatively, organisations can involve employees in decision-making, as participation in decision-making is likely to instill organisational citizenship behaviour. Opportunity to participate in decision-making enhances employee perceptions of procedural justice (Organ 1988; Thibaut and Walker 1975; Van Yperen et al. 1999) and promotes social exchange relationships between employees and their supervisors (Organ 1988). Based on the norm of reciprocity (Gouldner 1960), employees are likely to reciprocate by exhibiting organisational citizenship behaviour (Organ 1988; Van Yperen et al. 1999). Thus, regardless of nationality or race, every employee should be given a fair opportunity to participate in organisational affairs and decision-making.

As mentioned earlier, distributive justice rather than procedural justice has a more significant influence on job satisfaction in this study. This suggests that employees are concerned about fairness in decision outcomes. Organisations, therefore, have to reward accordingly (Homans 1961) and ensure that outcomes adhere to expectations (Blau 1964). Employees are less concern with the fairness in procedures in the decision-making process. As long as outcomes are consistent with implicit norms for allocation (Colquitt 2001), employees experience job satisfaction. The results imply that employees in general tend to be materialistic. Regardless of the procedures involved, equality of outcomes is of prime concern. This is probably attributed to the escalating cost of living in Malaysia. A lack of perceived fairness in procedures probably will not affect job satisfaction if employees perceive that rewards were contingent on the level of contribution (Yilmaz and Tasdan 2009). Hence, organisations may have to focus on improving distributive justice to enhance job satisfaction.

Interpersonal justice has the least effect on job satisfaction. Employees do not seem concerned with respectful treatment from their superiors. As long as explanations in decision procedures are honest and adequate, outcomes received meet expectations and procedures in decision outcomes are fair, employees experience job satisfaction. On the one hand, the indifferent attitude of employees towards the authorities implies that the superior–subordinate relationship in the organisations may not be strong. On the other hand, high interpersonal justice probably exists at the workplace, and, therefore, the impact on job satisfaction is not strong. In this case, organisations probably benefit more from improving other justice factors to enhance work performance. Organisations in the former situation may have to work on strengthening the bond between superior and subordinates and improving employee interest in the organisation to foster greater employee commitment. The mentor–mentee system, which has proven to be highly successful in Japanese manufacturing corporations, may be considered by manufacturing companies in

Malaysia to enhance employee engagement and loyalty. Furthermore, Malaysia is a collectivistic society. A collectivist culture fosters strong, close long-term relationships and commitment, where everyone takes responsibility for fellow members of their group. In most organisations, job satisfaction is likely to improve in extended relationships, and, hence, organisational citizenship behaviours.

Job Satisfaction–Organisational Citizenship Behaviour Relationship

The research question, hypotheses and the findings for the job satisfaction–organisational citizenship behaviour relationship are summarised in Table 9.7.

The fourth hypothesis that job satisfaction positively influences the dimensions of organisational citizenship behaviour is supported. In order of importance, job satisfaction has a significant effect on civic virtue, courtesy, conscientiousness, altruism and sportsmanship. The findings support empirical studies that show a significant association between job satisfaction and some dimensions of organisational citizenship behaviour (e.g. Bateman and Organ 1983; Foote and Tang 2008; Graham 1986; Murphy et al. 2006; Tansky 1993). Smith et al. (1983) affirm the influence of job satisfaction on altruism and conscientiousness, while Williams and Anderson (1991) emphasise the effect on conscientiousness. The current study, on the contrary, shows a stronger correlation between job satisfaction and civic virtue, as well as courtesy. In essence, job satisfaction increases employee interest to participate appropriately and responsibly in company matters to enhance corporate governance. Proactive, responsible participation in the political life of the organisation improves employee awareness of the affairs and developments at the workplace. Employees are likely to go for self-improvement to enhance competencies to stay up-to-date with important issues of the organisation. However, if employees are dissatisfied in their jobs, employees are generally not interested in developments at the workplace and limit participation in company affairs, as employees realise that they are not empowered to make a difference. It is unlikely things will change in their favour and the best solution for most employees is to look for better opportunities elsewhere.

Results of the study further emphasise the importance of job satisfaction on courtesy. As courtesy concerns undertaking and carrying out the obligation of cooperation with others, increased job satisfaction would probably enhance teamworking, create a more disciplined and committed workforce and improve

Table 9.7 Hypotheses and the findings for research question 4

Research question	Hypotheses		Findings
How does job satisfaction affect the dimensions of organisational citizenship behaviour?	4	Job satisfaction positively influences the dimensions of organisational citizenship behaviour	Supported

behaviours and attitude at the workplace. As these worker attitudes and behaviours enhance productivity, creativity, innovation, performance and openness to change (Clegg and Dunkerley 1980; Mathieu and Zajac 1990; Witt and Wilson 1991), it is crucial that organisations improve job satisfaction. Such supportive behaviours encourage communication and collaboration at the workplace to alleviate the intensity of job-related problems. Besides, it promotes social interaction, mutual understanding, tolerance, team spirit and harmony at the workplace. Problems of diversity at the workplace, which could escalate into intolerance, discrimination, harassment, hostility, conflicts and social alienation, could be better managed.

As job satisfaction has a significant effect on conscientiousness, organisations are likely to benefit from leveraging employee conscientiousness for achieving organisational goals. For organisational effectiveness, employees' sincere devotion to the organisation and respect for company policies beyond the organisation's requirements (Eskew 1993; Koopmann 2002; Tansky 1993) are fundamentals. Organisational effectiveness is essential for sustainability, and the importance of positive work behaviours is indisputable. However, as Malaysian workers maintain a more relaxed attitude and deviance from the norm is more easily tolerated, schedules are flexible. Precision and punctuality do not come naturally and hard work is undertaken when necessary. Furthermore, employees may find it unnecessary to adhere to rules that are ambiguous or do not work. Thus, the system can be abused if not managed properly.

Therefore, measures to improve job satisfaction to ensure that employees contribute beyond roles specified in the job description are crucial. Introducing incentive programmes to reward employees that adhere to organisational rules, procedures and regulations is a way to motivate employees to display characteristics of conscientiousness. Considering the damaging consequences of negative work behaviours, it may be worthwhile for organisations to invest in grooming conscientious workers. Conscientious workers naturally are role models to be exemplified and could be a source of motivation for other employees. A motivated and productive workforce translates to better quality of goods, which in turn enhances not only job satisfaction but also customer satisfaction and loyalty.

Since job satisfaction also influences altruism, improving job satisfaction becomes increasingly important. Organisations stand to gain if altruism is present at the workplace, as productivity and performance are likely to improve. In the manufacturing sector where interdependence is high, the voluntary behaviour of helping coworkers in the organisation in work-related matters not only promotes prosocial, helpful behaviours and neighbourliness among employees but also expedite completion of work-related tasks. Employees should be groomed, not only to step into each other's shoes but also each other's mind. Such discretionary behaviours have positive effects for the organisation and may even be instrumental for a company's survival. To avoid distracting and showing supervisors their lack of competence, employees may engage in knowledge sharing. Employees reap benefits from both knowledge donation and knowledge collection, which may in turn inspire them to further acquire new knowledge. A knowledgeable workforce in a learning organisation is valuable for gaining competitive advantage in an uncertain, challenging global environment.

Thus, it is advantageous for organisations to improve job satisfaction to garner the benefits of organisational citizenship behaviour though enhancing job satisfaction may entail increasing salaries and improving working conditions (Nadiri and Tanova 2010). Flexitime and working remotely may also enhance job satisfaction. Increased job satisfaction together with effective training has the potential to contribute significantly to the bottom line of any organisation. Furthermore, as job dissatisfaction causes anxiety (Spector et al. 1988), depression (Bluen et al. 1990), lower affective organisational commitment (Meyer et al. 2002), poorer in-role performance (Judge et al. 2001) and contextual performance (Podsakoff et al. 2000), ignoring job satisfaction may be detrimental to organisational effectiveness. Therefore, it is recommended that organisations implement policies and practices that augment job satisfaction. Job satisfaction is of utmost importance as it is significantly related to all dimensions of organisational citizenship behaviour. Organisations may have to focus on job satisfaction to enhance organisational citizenship behaviour.

Conclusion

This chapter focuses on the research findings of the hypothesised relationships between organisational justice, job satisfaction and organisational citizenship behaviour. Empirical results verify that employee perceptions of organisational justice positively influence job satisfaction. In order of importance, employee perceptions of informational justice, followed by distributive justice, procedural justice and then interpersonal justice, significantly influence job satisfaction. Manufacturing organisations in Malaysia may need to review the justice climate and pay more attention to informational justice if job satisfaction were low. The significant effect of informational justice on job satisfaction suggests that employees in the manufacturing sector are much concern about the quality of communication regarding decisions that directly affect them. Employees probably do not receive adequate explanation for the decisions made. Besides this, manufacturing organisations need to address the issue of perceived fairness of outcomes, the perceived fairness of the policies and procedures used to make decisions and the degree to which authorities treat employees with politeness, dignity and respect.

As for the job satisfaction–organisational citizenship behaviour relationship, job satisfaction has the strongest influence on civic virtue, followed by its effect on courtesy, conscientiousness, altruism and sportsmanship. These findings establish the importance of job satisfaction in enhancing organisational citizenship behaviour. The findings suggest that job satisfaction encourages employees to responsibly participate in the political life of the organisation, treat others with respect, carry out in-role behaviours well beyond the minimum required levels, help others and have positive attitudes. Therefore, it is imperative for organisations to understand the significance of job satisfaction. Understanding how job satisfaction improves organisational citizenship behaviour helps policy-making management executives and human resource specialists to design relevant initiatives to enhance the survival and profitability of business operations. In essence, it contributes to organisational efforts in adopting strategies to survive the challenges of the highly competitive and ever-changing global market of the twenty-first century. The following chapter analyses leader–member exchange in the organisational justice–organisational citizenship behaviour relationship.

References

Alexander, S., & Ruderman, M. (1987). The role of procedural and distributive justice in organisational behavior. *Social Justice Research, 1*(2), 177–198.

Azman, I., Mohamed, H. A., Hamid, N. S., Sulaiman, A. Z., Girardi, A., & Abdullah, M. M. (2011). Relationship between performance based pay, interactional justice and job satisfaction: A mediating model approach. *International Journal of Business and Management, 6*(11), 170–180.

Ball, G. A., Trevino, L. K., & Sims, H. P., Jr. (1994). Just and unjust punishment: Influences on subordinate performance and citizenship. *Academy of Management Journal, 37*(2), 299–322.

Bartol, K. (1979). Individual versus organizational predictors of job satisfactions and turnover among professionals. *Journal of Vocational Behavior, 15*(1), 55–67.

Bateman, T. S., & Organ, D. W. (1983). Job satisfaction and the good soldier: The relationship between affect and employee citizenship. *Academy of Management Journal, 26*(4), 587–595.

Blau, P. (1964). *Exchange and power in social life*. New York: Wiley.

Bluen, S. D., Barling, J., & Burns, W. (1990). Predicting sales performance, job satisfaction, and depression by using the achievement strivings and impatience-irritability dimensions of type A behavior. *Journal of Applied Psychology, 75*(2), 212–216.

Brief, A. P. (1998). *Attitudes in and around organizations*. Thousand Oaks: Sage.

Clegg, S., & Dunkerley, D. (1980). *Organization, class and control*. Boston: Routledge and Kegan Paul.

Cohen-Charash, Y., & Spector, P. E. (2001). The role of justice in organizations: A meta-analysis. *Organizational Behavior & Human Decision Processes, 86*(2), 278–321.

Colquitt, J. A. (2001). On the dimensionality of organizational justice: A construct validation of a measure. *Journal of Applied Psychology, 86*(3), 386–400.

Colquitt, J. A., Conlon, D. E., Wesson, M. J., Porter, C. O. L. H., & Ng, K. Y. (2001). Justice at the millennium: A meta-analytic review of 25 years of organizational justice research. *Journal of Applied Psychology, 86*(3), 425–445.

Eskew, D. E. (1993). The role of organizational justice in organizational citizenship behavior. *Employee Responsibilities and Rights Journal, 6*(3), 185–194.

Fernandes, C., & Awamleh, R. (2006). Impact of organisational justice in an expatriate work environment. *Management Research News, 29*(11), 701–712.

Fields, D., Pang, M., & Chiu, C. (2000). A comparative field study of the effects of distributive and procedural justice in Hong Kong. *Journal of Organizational Behaviour, 21*(5), 547–562.

Folger, R., & Cropanzano, R. (1998). *Organisational justice and human resource management*. Beverly Hills: Sage.

Folger, R., & Konovsky, M. A. (1989). Effects of procedural and distributive justice on reactions to pay raise decisions. *Academy of Management Journal, 32*(1), 115–130.

Foote, D. A., & Tang, T. L. (2008). Job satisfaction and organizational citizenship behavior (OCB): Does team commitment make a difference in self-directed teams? *Management Decision, 46*(6), 933–947.

Gouldner, A. (1960). The norm of reciprocity. *American Sociological Review, 25*(2), 165–167.

Graham, J. W. (1986). *Organizational citizenship informed by political theory*. Paper presented at the meeting of Academy of Management, Chicago.

Greenberg, J. (1990). Looking fair vs. being fair: Managing impressions of organizational justice. In B. M. Shaw & L. L. Cummings (Eds.), *Research in organizational behavior* (pp. 111–157). Greenwich: JAI Press.

Hassan, A., & Mohd Noor, K. (2008). Organizational justice and extra-role behavior: Examining the relationship in the Malaysian cultural context. *IIUM Journal of Economics and Management, 16*(2), 187–208.

Hendrix, W., Robbins, T., Miller, J., Summers, T. P. (1999). *Procedural and distributive justice effects on turnover.* Paper presented at the annual meeting of the Society for Industrial and Organizational Psychology, Atlanta, GA.

Homans, G. C. (1961). *Social behaviour: Its elementary forms.* London: Routledge and Kegan Paul.

Hooi, L. W., Sulaiman, M., & Omar, A. (2012). Procedural justice in promotion decisions of managerial staff in Malaysia. *Asia Pacific Business Review, 18*(1), 99–121.

Igbaria, M., & Greenhouse, J. H. (1992). The career advancement prospects of managers and professionals: Are MIS employees unique? *Decision Sciences, 23*, 478–499.

Judge, T. A., Thoresen, C. J., Bono, J. E., & Patton, G. K. (2001). The job satisfaction-job performance relationship: A qualitative and quantitative review. *Psychological Bulletin, 127*(3), 376–407.

Konovsky, M. A., & Cropanzano, R. (1991). Perceived fairness of employee drug testing as a predictor of employee attitudes and job performance. *Journal of Applied Psychology, 76*(5), 698–707.

Koopmann, R. (2002). The relation between perceived organization justice and organizational citizenship behaviors: A review of the literature. *Journal of Student Research.* Retrieved March 15, 2010, from www.uwstout.edu/rs/uwsjsr/table.htm

Korsgaard, M. A., Schweiger, D. M., & Sapienza, H. J. (1995). Building commitment, attachment, and trust in strategic decision-making teams: The role of procedural justice. *Academy of Management Journal, 38*(1), 60–84.

Latham, G., & Pinder, C. (2005). Work motivation theory and research at the dawn of the twenty-first century. *Annual Review of Psychology, 56*(1), 485–516.

Lee, C., Pillutla, M., & Law, K. S. (2000). Power distance, gender and organizational justice. *Journal of Management, 26*(4), 685–704.

Mathieu, J. E., & Zajac, D. M. (1990). A review and meta-analysis of the antecedents, correlates, and consequences of organizational commitment. *Psychological Bulletin, 108*(2), 171–194.

McFarlin, D. B., & Sweeney, P. D. (1992). Distributive and procedural justice as predictors of satisfaction with personal and organisational outcomes. *Academy of Management Journal, 35*(3), 626–637.

Meyer, J., Stanley, D., Herscovich, L., & Topolnytsky, L. (2002). Affective, continuance, and normative commitment to the organization: A meta-analysis of antecedents, correlates, and consequences. *Journal of Vocational Behavior, 61*(1), 20–52.

Murphy, C., Ramamoorthy, N., Flood, P. C., & MacCurtain, S. (2006). Organisational justice perceptions and employee attitudes among Irish blue collar employees: An empirical test of the main and moderating roles of individualism/collectivism. *Management Revue, 17*(3), 328–343.

Nadiri, H., & Tanova, C. (2010). An investigation of the role of justice in turnover intentions, job satisfaction, and organizational citizenship behavior in hospitality industry. *International Journal of Hospitality Management, 29*(1), 33–41.

Organ, D. W. (1988). *Organizational citizenship behavior: The good solider syndrome.* Lexington: Lexington Books.

Organ, D. W. (1990). The motivational basis of organizational citizenship behavior. *Research in Organizational Behavior, 12*(1), 43–72.

Organ, D. W., & Konovsky, M. A. (1989). Cognitive versus affective determinants of organizational citizenship behavior. *Journal of Applied Psychology, 74*, 157–164.

Phillips, J. M. (2002). Antecedent and consequences of procedural justice perceptions in hierarchical decision-making teams. *Small Group Research, 31*(1), 32–64.
Podsakoff, P. M., MacKenzie, S. B., & Fetter, R. (1993). Substitutes for leadership and the management of professionals. *Leadership Quarterly, 4*(1), 1–44.
Podsakoff, P. M., MacKenzie, S. B., Paine, J. B., & Bachrach, D. G. (2000). Organizational citizenship behaviors: A critical review of the theoretical and empirical literature and suggestions for future research. *Journal of Management, 26*(3), 513–563.
Price, J. L., & Mueller, C. W. (1986). *Handbook of organizational measurement.* Marshfield: Pittman.
Quarles, R. (1994). An examination of promotion opportunities and evaluation criteria as mechanism for affecting internal auditor commitment, job satisfaction and turnover intentions. *Journal of Managerial Issues, 6*(2), 176–194.
Schaubroeck, J., May, D. R., & Brown, F. W. (1994). Procedural justice explanations and reactions to economic hardship: A field experiment. *Journal of Applied Psychology, 79*(3), 455–460.
Smith, C. A., Organ, D. W., & Near, J. P. (1983). Organizational citizenship behavior: Its nature and antecedents. *Journal of Applied Psychology, 68*(4), 653–663.
Spector, P. E., Dwyer, D. J., & Jex, S. M. (1988). Relation of job stressors to affective, health, and performance outcomes: A comparison of multiple data sources. *Journal of Applied Psychology, 73*(1), 11–19.
Sweeney, P. D., & McFarlin, D. B. (1993). Workers' evaluations of the 'ends' and the 'means': An examination of four models of distributive and procedural justice. *Organisational Behavior and Human Decision Processes, 55*(1), 23–40.
Tansky, J. W. (1993). Justice and organizational citizenship behavior: What is the relationship? *Employee Responsibilities and Rights Journal, 6*(3), 195–207.
Thibaut, J., & Walker, L. (1975). *Procedural justice: A psychological analysis*. Hillsdale: Erlbaum.
Van Yperen, N. W., den Berg, A. E., & Willering, B. M. (1999). Towards a better understanding of the of the link between participation in decision-making and organizational citizenship behavior: A multilevel analysis. *Journal of Occupational and Organizational Psychology, 72*, 377–392.
Williams, L. J., & Anderson, S. E. (1991). Job satisfaction and organizational commitment as predictors of organizational citizenship and in-role behaviours. *Journal of Management, 17*(3), 601–617.
Witt, L. A., & Wilson, J. (1991). Moderating effect of job satisfaction on the relationship between equity and extra-role behaviors. *Journal of Social Psychology, 13*(2), 247–252.
Yilmaz, K., & Tasdan, M. (2009). Organizational citizenship and organizational justice in Turkish primary schools. *Journal of Educational Administration, 47*(1), 108–126.

Chapter 10
Organisational Justice–Leader–Member Exchange–Organisational Citizenship Behaviour

Abstract This chapter summarises the research findings of the hypothesised relationships between organisational justice, leader–member exchange and organisational citizenship behaviour. The findings give an indication of which type of organisational justice would have a greater impact on leader–member exchange. The results further ascertain if leader–member exchange is indeed important in the organisational justice–organisational citizenship behaviour relationship. Discussions on the theoretical and practical implications of the findings offer an insight of what is best for the organisations. This is particularly important in the manufacturing sector as prior studies show that superior–subordinate relationship is an important determinant of decision outcomes in the manufacturing sector.

Introduction

The previous two chapters discuss thoroughly the findings of the relationship between organisational justice, job satisfaction and organisational citizenship behaviour. Chapter 8 delineates the significant effect of organisational justice on organisational citizenship behaviour, while Chap. 9 integrates the effect of job satisfaction in this relationship. This chapter analyses the effect of leader–member exchange on justice–citizenship behaviour based on the research findings. As the effective functioning of an organisation is closely dependent on employees' discretionary behaviours, the role of leaders in championing employees' organisational citizenship behaviour becomes crucial. Indubitably, leaders engender organisational citizenship behaviour. Hence, the quality of leader–member exchange is vital for organisational effectiveness. Leader–member exchange shapes employees' discretionary behaviour as subordinates reciprocate in response to the benefits they received. In essence, employees restore equity by displaying citizenship behaviours if they perceive that they receive more than they give to the leaders. This chapter outlines if this is indeed true in the Malaysian manufacturing context. This enhances understanding of how contextual settings can strengthen the effect of leader–member exchange on organisational citizenship behaviour.

Although high-quality leader–member exchange stimulates organisational citizenship behaviour, it is also interesting to draw attention to how justice climate affects the quality of leader–member exchange. As organisations in Malaysia are

L.W. Hooi, *Organisational Justice and Citizenship Behaviour in Malaysia*, Governance and Citizenship in Asia, DOI 10.1007/978-981-10-0030-0_10

high on power distance and emphasise collectivism, subordinates tend to respect hierarchical relationships and submit to superior authority (Farh and Cheng 2000). However, it is argued that the quality of leader–member exchange should be better when subordinates perceive organisational justice. Tyler and Lind (1992) assert that procedural justice enhances employees' relationships with their employers. Similarly, Alexander and Ruderman (1987) and Manogran et al. (1994) affirm that leader–member exchange is positively related to procedural and interactional justice, while Erdogan and Liden (2002) establish the association between distributive justice and leader–member exchange. Additionally, several studies confirm the positive association between leader–member exchange and distributive and procedural justice (e.g. Lee 2001; Pillai et al. 1999). Furthermore, Cohen-Charash and Spector (2001) found relationships between leader–member exchange and distributive, procedural and interactional justice. Moreover, studies indicate that leader–member exchange is associated with perceptions of positive organisational climate (Dunegan et al. 1992; Kozolowski and Doherty 1989). The next section outlines the findings of the relationships between the three variables as well as discusses the theoretical and practical implications of the findings.

Leader–Member Exchange

For the leader–member exchange variable, only one factor was extracted with an eigenvalue of more than 1, explaining 62.9 % of the variance. Five items were used to represent the variable after two items were dropped due to low factor loadings (LMX1, LMX5). The EFA results as shown in Table 10.1 revealed that the KMO index for this construct was greater than 0.80 which was above the minimum value of 0.60 for a good factor analysis (Tabachnick and Fidell 2007), indicating the meritorious presence of intercorrelations in the data matrix. Bartlett's test of sphericity was significant at 10 degrees of freedom, and, therefore, the factor analysis was considered appropriate. Factor loadings for all items were more than 0.70, well-above the minimally acceptable level of 0.50.

Hypothesis 3: Organisational Justice–Leader–Member Exchange Relationship

Table 10.2 and Fig. 9.1 showed the results for the hypotheses related to the organisational justice–leader–member exchange relationship. As indicated in Table 10.3, all the hypotheses were supported. Employee perceptions of organisational justice positively influenced leader–member exchange. Informational justice had a more significant influence on leader–member exchange as compared to distributive justice, interpersonal justice or procedural justice.

Table 10.1 Results of EFA on leader–member exchange

Items		**Value**	
Kaiser–Meyer–Olkin		0.849	
Bartlett's test of sphericity		529.709	
		(sig. 0.000, df. 10)	
Factor	**Eigenvalue**	**Percentage of variance**	**Cumulative variance**
Leader–member exchange	3.144	62.875	62.875
Factors/items		**Factor loading**	
Factor 1: leader–member exchange			
LMX7	I would characterise my working relationship with my supervisor as extremely effective	0.823	
LMX2	My supervisor understands my job problems and needs very well	0.802	
LMX6	I have enough confidence in my supervisor that I would definitely defend and justify his/her decisions if he/she were not present to do so	0.799	
LMX3	My supervisor recognises my potential very well	0.789	
LMX4	Regardless of the amount of formal authority my supervisor has built into his/her position, the chances that he/she would use his/her power to help me solve problems in my work are very high	0.749	
Internal consistency reliability (Cronbach's alpha)		0.852	

Table 10.2 Organisational justice–leader–member exchange

Factors/items	Std. loading	S.E.	C.R.	P
Leader–member exchange ← procedural justice	.207	.056	3.101	.002
Leader–member exchange ← informational justice	.311	.082	4.290	***
Leader–member exchange ← distributive justice	.304	.049	4.508	***
Leader–member exchange ← interpersonal justice	.223	.074	3.277	.001

***$p < 0.001$

Table 10.3 Hypotheses on organisational justice–leader–member exchange

	Hypotheses	Findings
3	Employee perceptions of organisational justice positively influence leader–member exchange	Supported
3a	Employee perceptions of distributive justice positively influence leader–member exchange	Supported
3b	Employee perceptions of procedural justice positively influence leader–member exchange	Supported
3c	Employee perceptions of interactional justice positively influence leader–member exchange	Supported

Table 10.4 Leader–member exchange–organisational citizenship behaviour

Factors/items	Std. loading	S.E.	C.R.	P
Courtesy ← leader–member exchange	.105	.053	1.551	.121
Sportsmanship ← leader–member exchange	–.074	.078	–1.064	.287
Altruism ← leader–member exchange	.276	.059	3.761	***
Civic virtue ← leader–member exchange	.241	.063	3.288	.001
Conscientiousness ← leader–member exchange	.152	.060	2.062	.039

***$p < 0.001$

Table 10.5 Hypotheses on leader–member exchange–organisational citizenship behaviour

	Hypotheses	Findings
5	Leader–member exchange positively influences the dimensions of organisational citizenship behaviour	Partially supported

Hypothesis 5: Leader–Member Exchange–Organisational Citizenship Behaviour

As shown in Table 10.4 and Fig. 9.2, leader–member exchange positively influenced altruism, civic virtue and conscientiousness. Thus, as shown in Table 10.5, hypothesis 5 was partially supported.

Discussion of the Findings

Organisational Justice–Leader–Member Exchange Relationship

Table 10.6 summarises the hypotheses and findings of the third research question. The third research question that needs to be addressed focuses on whether employee perceptions of organisational justice positively influence leader–member exchange. Specifically, the objective is to discover if organisational justice is an antecedent of leader–member exchange. As the quality of leader–member exchange affects other organisational phenomena, a profound understanding of the relationship between organisational justice and leader–member exchange is fundamental for organisational success.

As shown in Table 10.6, the hypothesis that employee perceptions of organisational justice positively influence leader–member exchange is supported. While other studies show that procedural or interactional justice are more related to leader–member exchange (e.g. Alexander and Ruderman 1987; Brockner and Siegel 1996; Brockner et al. 1997; Folger and Konovsky 1989; Jablin 1979; Konovsky and Pugh 1994; Lind and Tyler 1988; Manogran et al. 1994; McFarlin and Sweeney 1992; Napier and Ferris 1993), the current study affirms that informational justice is the most important, followed by distributive justice, interpersonal justice and procedural justice. That informational justice is highly significant on leader–member exchange

Table 10.6 Hypotheses and the findings for research question 3

Research question	Hypotheses		Findings
How do employee perceptions of organisational justice affect leader–member exchange?	3	Employee perceptions of organisational justice positively influence leader–member exchange	Supported
	3a	Employee perceptions of distributive justice positively influence leader–member exchange	Supported
	3b	Employee perceptions of procedural justice positively influence leader–member exchange	Supported
	3c	Employee perceptions of interactional justice positively influence leader–member exchange	Supported

supports the notion that organisations may not be communicating enough to convince employees that equity is in place. It further indicates the lack of objectivity and transparency in decision outcomes. Being in a high power distance society, decision-makers probably assume that employees have respect for authority and will accept inequality irrefutably. Malays, in particular, prefer to be guided by subjective feelings along with the Islamic faith rather than rely on empirical evidence or hard facts. Therefore, decision-making is sometimes viewed in a more personal light, and information may be held back in order to prevent disagreement and preserve harmony.

The current findings suggest that the use of honest and adequate explanations for decisions is imperative for a higher degree of emotional support and exchange of valued resources between the leader and the subordinates. To enhance leader–member exchange, the supervisor has to explain explicitly the procedures involved in decision outcomes and to communicate with the employees to assure consistency and transparency of procedures and outcomes. The reason for this is explanations often provide the information needed to justify the procedures and decisions taken. The quality of leader–member exchange would be further strained if new leadership were to arise from the ultimate power, rather than from diplomatic or democratic change.

Comparatively, distributive justice is more important than interpersonal justice as a predictor of leader–member exchange. This shows that employees are more concerned about fairness in distribution of outcomes and care less of whether superiors treat them with respect and dignity. This disputes Aryee et al.'s (2007) contention that perceived interactional injustice creates resentment towards the supervisor. Procedural justice has the least effect on the quality of leader–member exchange. Whether equity exist in decision-making procedures is relatively insignificant in determining the quality of leader–member exchange. The quality of leader–member exchange is greatly influenced by how much employees perceived that explanations for decisions are given adequately and honestly. However, this challenges prior studies that maintain that leader–member exchange is positively related to procedural and interactional justice (Alexander and Ruderman 1987; Manogran et al. 1994).

Earlier studies focus mainly on trust in supervisors (Aquino et al. 1997; Folger and Konovsky 1989; Kim and Mauborgne 1998; Korsgaard et al. 1995; Lind and Tyler 1988; McFarlin and Sweeney 1992; Naumann and Bennett 2000) and maintain that procedural justice (Brockner and Siegel 1996; Folger and Konovsky 1989; Konovsky and Pugh 1994) and interactional justice (Ambrose and Schminke 2003; DeConnick 2010; Hopkins and Weathington 2006; Moorman et al. 1998; Roch and Shanock 2006; Stinglhamber et al. 2006) are important predictors of leader–member exchange. The current study demonstrates that though employee perceptions of organisational justice influence leader–member exchange, the effect is less likely attributed specifically to one dimension of organisational justice. It concurs with past research that indicates a significant relationship between each component of organisational justice and trust in the supervisor (Camerman et al. 2007; Konovsky and Pugh 1994; Stinglhamber et al. 2006). However, it differs from prior studies in terms of the significance of each component of organisational justice on the quality of leader–member exchange.

To enhance the quality of leader–member exchange, appropriate policies that address inequity at the workplace are essential. Specifically, measures taken to develop communication skills of managers in conveying decision outcomes may be instrumental in enhancing social exchange relations (Organ 1988) and harmony at the workplace. Additionally, organisations may groom leaders to be more decisive and consistent in decisions, and, hence, better decision-makers. Leadership training that emphasises on the importance of fairness, interpersonal skills, mentoring and joint development of goals may increase their knowledge, skills and self-confidence on the job. Leaders should be trained to make decisions based on merit or performance and not personal judgement. Emphasis should also be placed on the necessity to be explicit in whatever decisions made in order to mitigate perceptions of injustice.

Inadequate and dishonest explanations for decision outcomes or the availability of such information to certain groups of employees are likely to result in political factions among employees. This is especially so in the manufacturing sector, which employs a significant number of foreign workers. Indubitably, dissatisfaction sets in, as the quality of the leader–member exchange relationship is perceived to vary from one subordinate to another (Yukl et al. 2009). In-group subordinates usually have more autonomy, support and leader's consideration (Dansereau et al. 1975; Podsakoff et al. 1990). Such developments may jeopardise relationships at the workplace, especially in high power distance organisations where employees are expected to accept decision outcomes unquestionably. As perceived justice lowers job stress and enhances workplace safety (Erdogan and Liden 2002), assuring organisational justice is vital for organisational excellence, especially in a perilous manufacturing environment.

To further improve leader–member exchange at the workplace, authorities may consider promoting a culture of intelligibility. Fairness in explanations may enhance leader–member exchange, which in turn may create a sense of belonging to the organisation. Fostering commitment and loyalty among employees can be a competitive advantage in today's business world (Nadiri and Tanova 2010). As Malaysia is a collectivist society, organisations benefit from integrating employees into strong, cohesive in-groups and continue developing them in exchange for unquestioning loyalty. Opportunities to progress within the organisation promote a long-term pragmatic future-oriented perspective of employees' association with the organisation and reduce employee intention to leave. Strategic planning to enhance organisational effectiveness and continuous development of staffs would be more effective.

On the contrary, hoarding of information may hinder mutual trust and reciprocal influence, which further aggravates the leader–member exchange relationship. It may be necessary to increase employee involvement in decision-making process to improve the quality of leader–member exchange relationship as it enhances employee perceptions of procedural justice (Thibaut and Walker 1975; Van Yperen et al. 1999). As group interaction is essential for high-quality leader–member exchange relationship, occasional informal gatherings such as Family Day, team building workshops at resort locations, parties and sporting events are also likely to improve group morale and organisational effectiveness. Communication between the superiors and the subordinates tends to be less cautious, and the informality would probably lead to better understanding among staffs. Employees are likely to reciprocate with positive behaviours that reinforce leader–member exchange if they perceive that leaders are supportive of their endeavours.

Leader–Member Exchange–Organisational Citizenship Behaviour Relationship

The research question, hypotheses and the findings for the leader–member exchange–organisational citizenship behaviour relationship are summarised in Table 10.7. As shown in Table 10.7, the fifth hypothesis posits if leader–member exchange positively influences the dimensions of organisational citizenship behaviour.

The results of the current study partially support the hypothesis. In order of importance, leader–member exchange relates positively to altruism, civic virtue and conscientiousness (Table 10.4). To a certain extent, it concurs with the findings of Wayne and Green (1993) and Truckenbrodt (2000) that leader–member exchange specifically relates to altruism. However, it confirms the findings of other studies which indicate significant correlations between leader–member exchange and organisational citizenship behaviour (e.g. Dirks and Ferrin 2000; Konovsky and

Table 10.7 Hypotheses and the findings for research question 4

Research question	Hypotheses		Findings
How does leader–member exchange affect the dimensions of organisational citizenship behaviour?	5	Leader–member exchange positively influences the dimensions of organisational citizenship behaviour	Partially supported

Pugh 1994; Moorman 1991; Organ 1988; Podsakoff et al. 1990; Tansky 1993; Van Yperen et al. 1999). As employees characterise that their working relationship with supervisors is extremely effective (LMX7), the quality of leader–member exchange is probably high. Consequently, trust, liking and respect as well as expectations of mutual exchange (Yukl et al. 2009) are likely to be high. Besides a favourable working relationship with supervisors, employees opine that supervisors understand their job problems and needs very well (LMX2). Employees believe that supervisors recognise their potential (LMX3) and would use their authority to help employees solve work-related problems (LMX4). These are not possible without emotional support and exchange of valued resources between the leader and members (Kang and Stewart 2007). In exchange for desired outcomes provided by the supervisor, among others, subordinates reciprocate by defending and justifying supervisors' decisions in their absence (LMX6).

This can be seen in employees' willingness to voluntarily help coworkers in work-related matters, increased interest in company matters and personal development and sincere devotion and adherence to company endeavours. However, the results reveal that the quality of leader–member exchange does not influence courtesy and sportsmanship. High-quality leader–member exchange relationships do not enhance employees' obligation to cooperate with others. This is probably attributed to the importance of superior–subordinate relationship in decision outcomes (Hooi 2011) rather than courtesy or sportsmanship. Having a close bond with the superiors negates the necessity to adhere to certain obligations or to display sportsmanship, as employees experienced immunity to negative outcomes. Similarly, employees prefer to switch jobs rather than trying to improve a strained relationship. It would be much easier in the current labour market where demand for labour in the manufacturing sector is greater than supply. Thus, courtesy and sportsmanship are a matter of personal choice for most employees in this case.

Basically, employees are least concerned about actions that could affect their responsibilities. If left unchecked, such behaviours could possibly lead to disastrous consequences for the organisation. Organisations should, therefore, be aware and cautious that high-quality leader–member exchange relationships do not necessarily augment courteous behaviours from employees. Similarly, high-quality leader–member exchange relationships do not guarantee constructive behaviours that would contribute to organisational effectiveness. The quality of leader–member exchange does not deter employees from exhibiting disapproving behaviours. On the contrary, employees opt for other alternatives if they perceive lower than desirable quality in leader–member exchange relationships.

The significant correlation between leader–member exchange and altruism, civic virtue and conscientiousness demonstrates that high-quality leader–member exchange relationships are fundamental for positive employee attitudes. Thus, much empirical research link the quality of leader–member exchange with positive employee attitudes (e.g. Ang et al. 2005; Bhal and Ansari 2007; Gestner and Day 1997; Graen 2006; Graen et al. 1982; Harris et al. 2007; Hofmann et al. 2003;

Krishnan 2004; Lapierre et al. 2006; Lee 2005; Lee and Ansari 2005; Pellegrini and Scandura 2006; Schriesheim et al. 1999; Sparrowe et al. 2006). As employee behavioural intentions are determined by their attitudes, positive attitudes augment affirmative behaviours. Rational, volitional and systematic behaviour (Chang 1998; Fishbein and Ajzen 1975) in which the individual has control (Thompson et al. 1994) is essential for productive behaviours. Despite being highly motivated by own attitudes and subjective norms, the lack of volitional control will constrain employees from giving their best. As altruism, civic virtue and conscientiousness are employee behaviours that contribute significantly to organisational performance, it may be beneficial for organisations to invest in improving employee attitudes. The manufacturing sector in Malaysia specifically should capitalise on improved domestic demand driven by private and government initiatives such as the Bantuan Rakyat 1Malaysia (BR1M) in which RM350 is given to single individuals earning RM2,000 and below, RM950 to households earning RM3,000 and below, RM750 to households earning between RM3,001 and RM4,000 and the Family Bereavement Scheme which will entitle the next of kin of BR1M recipients to receive RM1,000 effective for a year. Moreover, every Malaysian student from Primary 1 to Form Five in both public and private schools (5.4 million students) is given a cash assistance of RM100 for the new school year, while a RM250 book voucher is given to each university or college student (1.3 million students). Furthermore, growth is expected to improve further in 2015 in tandem with stronger external demand for manufactured products, in particular electrical and electronic products, and steady demand for commodities (Economic Report 2014/2015).

Additionally, increasing the quality of leader–member exchange may probably enhance teamworking, create a more disciplined and committed workforce and improve behaviours and attitudes at the workplace. Employees are likely to exhibit extra-role behaviours – helping or cooperating with coworkers on organisation-related matters. Employees may be more accommodating to fresh recruits, relieve a sick coworker or volunteer to help others (Truckenbrodt 2000). Besides, employees are expected to go beyond what is minimally required relating to attendance and punctuality at work, coffee and lunch breaks, working hours, notice on absenteeism and general rule compliance. Positive work attitudes may result in a favourable organisational culture of growth and innovation. Human relations are likely to improve in an environment where high-quality leader–member exchange relationships can thrive. Improving the quality of leader–member exchange will enhance subordinates' sense of commitment and citizenship behaviour and aids in organisational growth and success (Truckenbrodt 2000). A strong dyadic relationship will be beneficial to all – the leaders, the subordinates and the organisation.

In essence, leader–member exchange motivates employees to perform beyond the formal requirements of their jobs and provide mutual support to achieve organisational goals. Employees are likely to go for self-improvement to enhance soft skills and competencies at the workplace. Additionally, it has a big impact on employees' interest in the affairs and developments of the organisation. Good leader–member exchange relationship augments a sense of commitment and identification with the organisation. Employees proactively improve self-awareness of happenings in the organisation and responsibly participate in company matters. Thus, practitioners may have to improve leader–member exchange if organisational citizenship behaviour were to increase. This may entail an open communication system, allocative procedures that are consistent across persons and over time (Leventhal 1976), greater employee involvement and increase transparency in procedures. Open communication is necessary to establish a sense of trust in the leader–member exchange relationship. Feedback sessions could be established to encourage constructive feedback from subordinates and superiors. A corporate culture that encourages open two-way communication is highly recommended.

Conclusion

This chapter analyses the role of leader–member exchange in justice–citizenship behaviours in the manufacturing companies in Malaysia. Although the current study concurs with extant literature on a positive relationship between organisational justice and leader–member exchange (e.g. Alexander and Ruderman 1987; Tansky 1993), the findings reveal that employee perceptions of informational justice has a more significant effect on leader–member exchange relative to distributive justice, interpersonal justice or procedural justice. This probably indicates that employees in the manufacturing organisations in Malaysia perceive that explanation for decisions is neither adequate nor credible. It reflects the importance of transparency in decisions as employees are likely to refrain from a quality relationship with superiors that are dishonest. It also suggests the powerful influence of people in authority in decision-making in the manufacturing environment. All these culminate in a lack of mutual trust and cooperation, a tense environment and organisational politics and conflict.

In the leader–member exchange–organisational citizenship behaviour relationship, leader–member exchange has a more significant influence on altruism in comparison to its effect on civic virtue or conscientiousness. This indicates that the relationship between the superior and subordinates determines the extent to which employees are willing to help their coworkers on the job. Employees probably perceive that the performance of the team as a whole will contribute to the performance of the superior. If the quality of leader–member exchange were low, employees would likely restrain their efforts in supporting their superiors. Thus, it is imperative that leaders foster good relations with their subordinates as the lack of cooperation among workers affects performance, which ultimately impacts the bottom line of the organisation. Besides, good quality leader–member exchange stimulates employee interest in the organisation and encourages employees to respond appropriately to how the organisation governs. Moreover, it enhances employees' dutiful respect to organisational rules that exceeds organisational expectations. Chapter 11 analyses if job satisfaction and leader–member exchange mediate the relationship between organisational justice and organisational citizenship behaviour.

References

Alexander, S., & Ruderman, M. (1987). The role of procedural and distributive justice in organisational behavior. *Social Justice Research, 1*(2), 177–198.

Ambrose, M. L., & Schminke, M. (2003). Organizations structure as a moderator of the perceived relationship between procedural justice, interactional justice, perceived organizational support, and supervisory trust. *Journal of Applied Psychology, 88*(2), 295–305.

Ang, C. H., Ansari, M. A., & Jantan, M. (2005, August). *Upward influence and work outcomes: The mediating role of LMX and organizational support*. Paper presented at the annual meeting of the Academy of Management, Honolulu.

Aquino, K., Griffeth, R. W., Allen, D. G., & Hom, P. W. (1997). Integrating justice constructs into the turnover process: A test of a referent cognitions model. *Academy of Management Journal, 40*(5), 1208–1227.

Aryee, S., Chen, Z. X., Sun, L. Y., & Debrah, Y. A. (2007). Antecedents and outcomes of abusive supervision: Test of a trickle-down model. *Journal of Applied Psychology, 92*(1), 191–201.

Bhal, K. T., & Ansari, M. A. (2007). Leader-member exchange-subordinates outcomes relationship: Role of voice and justice. *Leadership & Organization Development Journal, 28*(1), 20–35.

Brockner, J., & Siegel, P. (1996). Understanding the interaction between procedural and distributive justice: The role of trust. In R. M. Kramer & T. R. Tyler (Eds.), *Trust in organizations – Frontiers of theory and research* (pp. 390–413). Thousand Oaks: Sage.

Brockner, J., Siegel, P. A., Daly, J. P., Tyler, T., & Martin, C. (1997). When trust matters: The moderating effect of outcome favorability. *Administrative Science Quarterly, 42*(3), 558–583.

Camerman, J., Cropanzano, R., & Vandenberghe, C. (2007). The benefits of justice for temporary workers. *Group and Organizational Management, 32*(2), 176–207.

Chang, M. K. (1998). Predicting unethical behavior: A comparison of the theory of reasoned action and the theory of planned behavior. *Journal of Business Ethics, 17*(16), 1825–1834.

Cohen-Charash, Y., & Spector, P. E. (2001). The role of justice in organizations: A meta-analysis. *Organizational Behavior & Human Decision Processes, 86*(2), 278–321.

Dansereau, F. J., Graen, G., & Haga, W. J. (1975). A vertical dyad linkage approach to leadership within formal organizations – A longitudinal investigation of the role making process. *Organizational Behavior and Human Performance, 13*(1), 46–78.

DeConinck, J. B. (2010). The effect of organizational justice, perceived organizational support, and perceived supervisor support on marketing employees' level of trust. *Journal of Business Research, 63*(12), 1349–1355.

Dirks, K. T., & Ferrin, D. L. (2000). The effects of trust in leadership on employee performance, behavior, and attitudes: A meta-analysis. In S. J. Havlovic (Ed.), *Academy of Management Best Papers Proceedings*, OB: H1.

Dunegan, K. J., Duchon, D., & Uhl-Bien, M. (1992). Examining the link between leader-member exchange and subordinate performance: The role of task analyzability and variety as moderators. *Journal of Management, 18*(1), 59–76.

Erdogan, B., & Liden, R. C. (2002). Social exchanges in the workplace: A review of recent developments and future research directions in leader-member exchange theory. In L. L. Neider & C. A. Schriesheim (Eds.), *Leadership* (pp. 65–114). Greenwich: Information Age Publishing.

Farh, J. L., & Cheng, B. S. (2000). A cultural analysis of paternalistic leadership in Chinese organizations. In J. T. Li, A. S. Tsui, & S. E. Walton (Eds.), *Management and organizations in Chinese context* (pp. 95–197). London: Macmillan.

Fishbein, M., & Ajzen, I. (1975). *Belief, attitude, intention, and behavior*. Reading: Addison-Wesley.

Folger, R., & Konovsky, M. A. (1989). Effects of procedural and distributive justice on reactions to pay raise decisions. *Academy of Management Journal, 32*(1), 115–130.

Gerstner, C. R., & Day, D. V. (1997). Meta-analytic review of leader-member exchange theory: Correlates and construct issues. *Journal of Applied Psychology, 82*(6), 827–844.

Graen, G. B. (2006). In the eye of the beholder: Cross-cultural lesson in leadership from project GLOBE. *Academy of Management Perspectives, 20*(4), 95–101.

Graen, G. B., Novak, M. A., & Sommerkamp, P. (1982). The effect of leader-member exchange and job design on productivity and satisfaction: Testing a dual attachment model. *Organization Behavior and Human Performance, 30*(1), 109–131.

Harris, K. J., Harris, R. B., & Eplion, D. M. (2007). Personality, leader-member exchanges, and work outcomes. *Journal of Behavioral and Applied Management, 8*(2), 92–107.

Hofmann, D. A., Morgeson, F. P., & Gerras, S. J. (2003). Climate as a moderator of the relationship between leader-member exchange and content-specific citizenship: Safety climate as an exemplar. *Journal of Applied Psychology, 88*(1), 170–178.

Hooi, L. W. (2011). The role of leader-member exchange in organisational justice-organisational citizenship behavior relationship. *Research and Practice in Human Resource Management, 19*(2), 71–91.

Hopkins, S. M., & Weathington, B. L. (2006). The relationship between justice perceptions, trust, and employee attitudes in a downsized organization. *Journal of Psychology, 140*(5), 477–498.

Jablin, F. M. (1979). Superior-subordinate communication: The state of the art. *Psychological Bulletin, 86*(6), 1201–1222.

Kang, D. S., & Stewart, J. (2007). Leader-member exchange (LMX) theory of leadership and HRD: Development of units of theory and laws of interaction. *Leadership & Organization Development Journal, 28*(6), 531–551.

Kim, W. C., & Mauborgne, R. A. (1998). Procedural justice, strategic-decision making, and the knowledge economy. *Strategic Management Journal, 19*(4), 323–338.

Konovsky, M. A., & Pugh, S. D. (1994). Citizenship behavior and social exchange. *Academy of Management Journal, 37*(3), 656–669.

Korsgaard, M. A., Schweiger, D. M., & Sapienza, H. J. (1995). Building commitment, attachment, and trust in strategic decision-making teams: The role of procedural justice. *Academy of Management Journal, 38*(1), 60–84.

Kozlowski, S. W. J., & Doherty, M. L. (1989). Integration of climate and leadership: Examination of a neglected issue. *Journal of Applied Psychology, 74*(4), 546–553.

Krishnan, V. (2004). Impact of transformational leadership on followers' influence strategies. *Leadership and Organization Development Journal, 25*(1), 58–72.

Lapierre, L. M., Hackett, R. D., & Taggar, S. (2006). A test of the links between family interference with work, job enrichment and leader-member exchange. *Applied Psychology: An International Review, 55*(4), 489–511.

Lee, J. (2001). Leader-member exchange, perceived organizational justice, and cooperative communication. *Management Communication Quarterly, 14*, 574–589.

Lee, J. (2005). Effects of leadership and leader-member exchange on commitment. *Leadership and Organization Development Journal, 26*(8), 655–672.

Lee, F. H., & Ansari, M. A. (2005, April). *Affect and organizational citizenship behavior: The impact of leader-member exchange*. Paper presented at the 20th annual meeting of the Society for Industrial and Organizational Psychology, Los Angeles.

Leventhal, G. S. (1976). The distribution of rewards and resources in groups and organizations. In L. Berkowitz & W. Walster (Eds.), *Advances in experimental social psychology* (pp. 91–131). New York: Academic.

Lind, E. A., & Tyler, T. R. (1988). *The social psychology of procedural justice*. New York: Plenum Press.

Manogran, P., Stauffer, J., & Conlon, E. J. (1994). Leader-member exchange as a key mediating variable between employees' perceptions of fairness and organizational citizenship behavior. *National Academy of Management Meeting Proceedings*, Dallas.

McFarlin, D. B., & Sweeney, P. D. (1992). Distributive and procedural justice as predictors of satisfaction with personal and organisational outcomes. *Academy of Management Journal, 35*(3), 626–637.

Moorman, R. H. (1991). Relationship between organizational justice and organizational citizenship behavior: Do fairness perceptions influence employee citizenship? *Journal of Applied Psychology, 76*(6), 845–855.

Moorman, R. H., Blakely, G. L., & Niehoff, B. P. (1998). Does perceived organizational support mediate the relationship between procedural justice and organizational citizenship behavior? *Academy of Management Journal, 41*(3), 351–357.

Nadiri, H., & Tanova, C. (2010). An investigation of the role of justice in turnover intentions, job satisfaction, and organizational citizenship behavior in hospitality industry. *International Journal of Hospitality Management, 29*(1), 33–41.

Napier, B. J., & Ferris, G. R. (1993). Distance in organizations. *Human Resources Management Review, 3*(4), 321–357.

Naumann, S. E., & Bennett, N. (2000). A case for procedural justice climate: Development and test of a multilevel model. *Academy of Management Journal, 43*(5), 881–889.

Organ, D. W. (1988). *Organizational citizenship behavior: The good solider syndrome*. Lexington: Lexington Books.

Pellegrini, E., & Scandura, T. A. (2006). Leader-member exchange (LMX), paternalism, and delegation in the Turkish culture: An empirical investigation. *Journal of International Business Studies, 37*(2), 264–279.

Pillai, R., Schriesheim, C. A., & Williams, E. S. (1999). Fairness perceptions and trust as mediators for transformational and transactional leadership: A two-sample study. *Journal of Management, 25*(6), 897–933.

Podsakoff, P. M., MacKenzie, S. B., Moorman, R. H., & Fetter, R. (1990). Transformational leader behaviors and their effects on followers' trust in leader, satisfaction, and organizational citizenship behaviors. *The Leadership Quarterly, 1*(2), 107–142.

Roch, G., & Shanock, L. R. (2006). Organizational justice in an exchange framework: Clarifying organizational justice distinctions. *Journal of Management, 32*(2), 299–322.

Schriesheim, C. A., Castro, S. L., & Cogliser, C. C. (1999). Leader-member exchange (LMX): A comprehensive review of theory, measurement, and data-analytic practices. *Leadership Quarterly, 10*(1), 63–113.

Sparrowe, R. T., Soetjipto, B. W., & Kraimer, M. L. (2006). Do leaders' influence tactics relate to members' helping behavior? It depends on the quality of the relationship. *Academy of Management Journal, 49*(6), 1194–1208.

Stinglhamber, F., De Cremer, D., & Mercken, L. (2006). Perceived support as a mediator of the relationship between justice and trust. *Group and Organizational Management, 31*(4), 442–468.

Tabachnick, B. G., & Fidell, L. S. (2007). *Using multivariate statistics* (5th ed.). New York: Harper-Collins.

Tansky, J. W. (1993). Justice and organizational citizenship behavior: What is the relationship? *Employee Responsibilities and Rights Journal, 6*(3), 195–207.

Thibaut, J., & Walker, L. (1975). *Procedural justice: A psychological analysis*. Hillsdale: Erlbaum.

Thompson, K. E., Haziris, N., & Alekos, P. J. (1994). Attitudes and food choice behavior. *British Food Journal, 96*(11), 9–17.

Truckenbrodt, Y. B. (2000). The relation between leader-member exchange and commitment and organizational behavior. *Acquisition Review Quarterly, 7*(3), 233–244.

Tyler, T. R., & Lind, E. A. (1992). A relational model of authority in groups. In M. P. Zanna (Ed.), *Advances in experimental social psychology* (pp. 115–191). San Diego: Academic.

Van Yperen, N. W., den Berg, A. E., & Willering, B. M. (1999). Towards a better understanding of the of the link between participation in decision-making and organizational citizenship behavior: A multilevel analysis. *Journal of Occupational and Organizational Psychology, 72*, 377–392.

Wayne, S. J., & Green, S. A. (1993). The effects of leader-member exchange on employee citizenship and impression management behavior. *Human Relations, 46*(12), 1431–1440.

Yukl, G., O'Donnell, M., & Taber, T. (2009). Influence of leader behaviors on the leader-member exchange relationship. *Journal of Managerial Psychology, 24*(4), 289–299.

Chapter 11
The Mediating Role of Job Satisfaction and Leader–Member Exchange in Justice–Citizenship

Abstract This chapter analyses the mediating role of job satisfaction and leader–member exchange in the organisational justice–organisational citizenship behaviour relationship. For the purpose of this study, the fully mediated model, the partially mediated model and the non-mediated model are examined. Based on the above models, results of the analysis using SEM offer an insight of whether manufacturing organisations in Malaysia that contemplate enhancing organisational citizenship behaviour ought to capitalise on organisational justice, job satisfaction or leader–member exchange to maximise results. Merely attending to organisational justice issues may be ineffective to entice employees to engage willingly in proactive work behaviours that exceed those dictated by organisational policies and prescribed role requirements. Perhaps, it is crucial for organisations to enhance job satisfaction or/ and the quality of leader–member exchange while managing justice effectively. Discussions on the theoretical and practical implications of the findings give an indication of what is best for the organisations.

Introduction

A mediating effect is created when a third construct intervenes between two other related constructs. In evaluating mediation, there must be a significant correlation between the independent variable and the dependent variable, the independent variable and the mediator and the mediator and the dependent variable. Mediation is not supported if there is a significant correlation between the independent variable and the dependent variable when the mediator is included in the model as an additional predictor. If the correlation between the independent variable and the dependent variable is reduced, but remains significant when the mediator is included, partial mediation is supported. Full mediation is supported if there is no significant correlation between the independent variable and the dependent variable when the mediator is included. An examination of the absolute size of the coefficients is necessary due to the presence of multicollinearity between the independent variable and the mediator. The presence of multicollinearity may reduce the power in the coefficient estimates and result in ambiguous results.

L.W. Hooi, *Organisational Justice and Citizenship Behaviour in Malaysia*, Governance and Citizenship in Asia, DOI 10.1007/978-981-10-0030-0_11

For the purpose of this study, the fully mediated model, the partially mediated model and the non-mediated model are examined. Firstly, a fully mediated model is developed. In the fully mediated model, it is assumed that there is no correlation between the four dimensions of organisational justice and organisational citizenship behaviour when job satisfaction or leader–member exchange is included. In the partially mediated model, the correlation between the four dimensions of organisational justice and organisational citizenship behaviour though much reduced remains significant. In the non-mediated model, a significant correlation is expected between the four dimensions of organisational justice and organisational citizenship behaviour when job satisfaction or leader–member exchange is controlled. The models for mediation test comparison are shown in the Fig. 11.1.

Based on the above models, a sequence of test is performed using SEM. To confirm significance of the correlations, the coefficient estimates between the variables are examined. The value of χ^2 is estimated as a relative measure to indicate comparative fitness. As χ^2 is rather sensitive to sample size, this study uses multiple indices of model fit (GFI, RMSEA, CFI and TLI) to validate the inevitability and adequacy of mediated relationships. Typically, all estimated parameters must be significant in all situations.

Mediation Analysis

Having established the validity and reliability of the measurement model and before proceeding to the analysis of the structural model, a mediation test was performed to confirm the significant paths between variables that best explained the whole model. The procedure proposed by Hair et al. (2010) was adopted to show the mediating effect of job satisfaction and leader–member exchange in the structural model. The purpose is to explain why a relationship between organisational justice and organisational citizenship behaviour exists. The mediators – job satisfaction and leader–member exchange – explain why a relationship exists between the two original constructs. To understand how mediators affect the structural model, the direct and indirect effects of the model were estimated.

Direct effects link two constructs with a single arrow and represent the direct effect of one construct on another construct. The relationship between organisational justice and organisational citizenship behaviour in the study represents a direct effect. Indirect effects involve a sequence of relationships with at least one intervening construct between the original constructs (Hair et al. 2010) transmitting some of the causal effects of prior variables onto subsequent variables (Kline 2011). Represented visually by multiple arrows, an indirect effect is a sequence of two or more direct effects. The indirect effect in the study represents the mediating effect of the constructs job satisfaction and leader–member exchange on the relationship between organisational justice and organisational citizenship behaviour. Direct effect is estimated by controlling all prior and intervening variables in the model

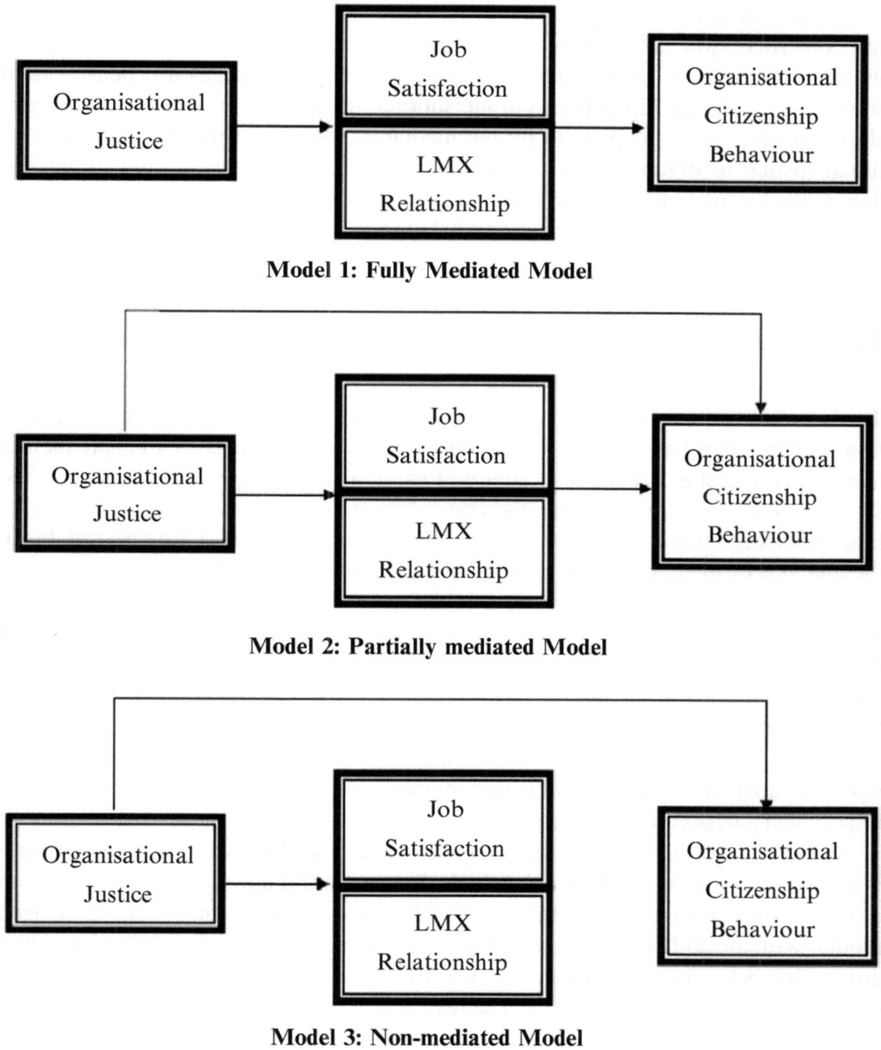

Fig. 11.1 Models of mediation test comparison

and measuring the partial coefficient between two variables. Indirect effect is measured statistically as the product of direct effects that link the two variables and interpreted as path coefficients (Kline 2011).

The mediation analysis involves job satisfaction and leader–member exchange as mediators between organisational justice and the dimensions of organisational citizenship behaviour. The mediation models are graphically represented in Fig. 11.1. For the full mediation model, the direct path from organisational justice to organisational citizenship behaviour is restricted to zero to show that the mediating constructs (job satisfaction and leader–member exchange) completely explain the relationship between the two original constructs. However, as it is possible that some of the relationship between organisational justice and organisational citizenship behaviour is not explained by the mediators, the direct paths from organisational justice to organisational citizenship behaviour is not restricted to zero to denote partial mediation. In the non-mediation model, the paths from the mediating constructs to organisational citizenship behaviour are set to zero.

Job Satisfaction and Leader–Member Exchange as Mediators

The possibility that the relationship between organisational justice and organisational citizenship behaviour is mediated by the two constructs of job satisfaction and leader–member exchange is analysed using a two-step process. At Step 1, the significant relationships between the constructs are established. For this, the correlations between constructs in the CFA model shown in Table 11.1 are referred. From the analysis of the correlations that are obtained after standardisation, the interconstruct correlations are significant for all the four constructs. As shown in Table 11.1, organisational justice is significantly related to organisational citizenship behaviour (0.410), ensuring that the direct, unmediated relationship is significant. Organisational justice is also significantly related to job satisfaction (0.722) and leader–member exchange (0.742), establishing relationship with both potential mediators. Finally, organisational citizenship behaviour is significantly related to both job satisfaction (0.426) and leader–member exchange (0.398), thus, supporting relationships between mediators and the outcome variable.

Step 2 is to estimate the mediated model and assess the level of mediation. First is to estimate the original model, which does not estimate the direct effect from organisational justice to organisational citizenship behaviour. Then, a revised model, with the added direct path between organisational justice and organisational citizenship behaviour, is estimated. This is to assess if adding the direct effect would substantially change the model fit. The results in Table 11.2 based on Figs. 11.2 and 11.3 show that the revised model with the direct relationship has a slight decrease in

Table 11.1 Construct correlation matrix (standardised)

	OJ	JS	LMX	OCB
OJ	1.000	0.521	0.551	0.168
JS	0.722***	1.000	0.432	0.181
LMX	0.742***	0.657***	1.000	0.158
OCB	0.410***	0.426***	0.398***	1.000

Values below the diagonal are correlation estimates among constructs, diagonal elements are construct variances, and values above the diagonal are squared correlations
Significance level: * = 0.05, ** = 0.01, *** = 0.001

Table 11.2 Testing for mediation in organisational justice–organisational citizenship behaviour

Model element	Original model	Revised model
Model fit		
Chi square (χ^2)	270.764	269.960
Degrees of freedom	130	129
Probability	0.000	0.000
CMINDF	2.083	2.093
RMSEA	0.064	0.064
CFI	0.930	0.930
Standardised parameter estimates		
OJ → JS	0.725***	0.722***
OJ → LMX	0.562***	0.558***
JS → OCB	0.290**	0.234*
JS → LMX	0.251**	0.255**
LMX → OCB	0.212*	0.144
OJ → OCB	0.000	0.134

Significance level: *=0.05, **=0.01, ***=0.001

Chi square ($\Delta\chi^2=0.804$, df=1, $p=0.000$) and an insignificant path estimate for the organisational justice–organisational citizenship behaviour relationship. These indicate that there is complete mediation, that is, the existence of a fully mediated model. Three paths reflect indirect causal mediated effects: OJ → JS → OCB, OJ → JS → LMX → OCB and OJ → LMX → OCB.

In the revised model, the path estimates between organisational justice (OJ) and the mediators (JS and LMX) are still significant. However, only job satisfaction has a significant relationship with organisational citizenship behaviour (JS → OCB is significant) at 0.05 significant level ($p=0.048$). The other relationship from leader–member exchange to organisational citizenship behaviour (LMX → OCB) is insignificant. In short, though leader–member exchange does not act as a mediator, job satisfaction still has a mediating effect. In the three indirect mediated effects, the insignificant relationship (LMX → OCB) is only a part of the second and third effects. The other indirect mediating effect still has statistically significant individual paths. As OJ → JS → OCB contains paths that are all significant, and the OJ → OCB path estimate is not significant, the model supports full mediation. In essence, there is only a significant indirect effect through job satisfaction in the organisational justice–organisational citizenship behaviour relationship.

The magnitude of the mediating effects is demonstrated by breaking down the total effects into direct and indirect effects. Direct effects represent the direct effect of one variable on another variable. Indirect effect or mediator effect involves one or more mediator variables that transmit some of the causal effects of prior variables onto subsequent variables (Kline 2011). A breakdown of the effects of OJ → OCB both in the original model (no direct effects from OJ → OCB) and the revised model (direct effect added for OJ → OCB) is shown in Table 11.3. In the original model, substantial indirect effects are present, thus, supporting the presence of mediating effects of job satisfaction and leader–member exchange. Although the indirect

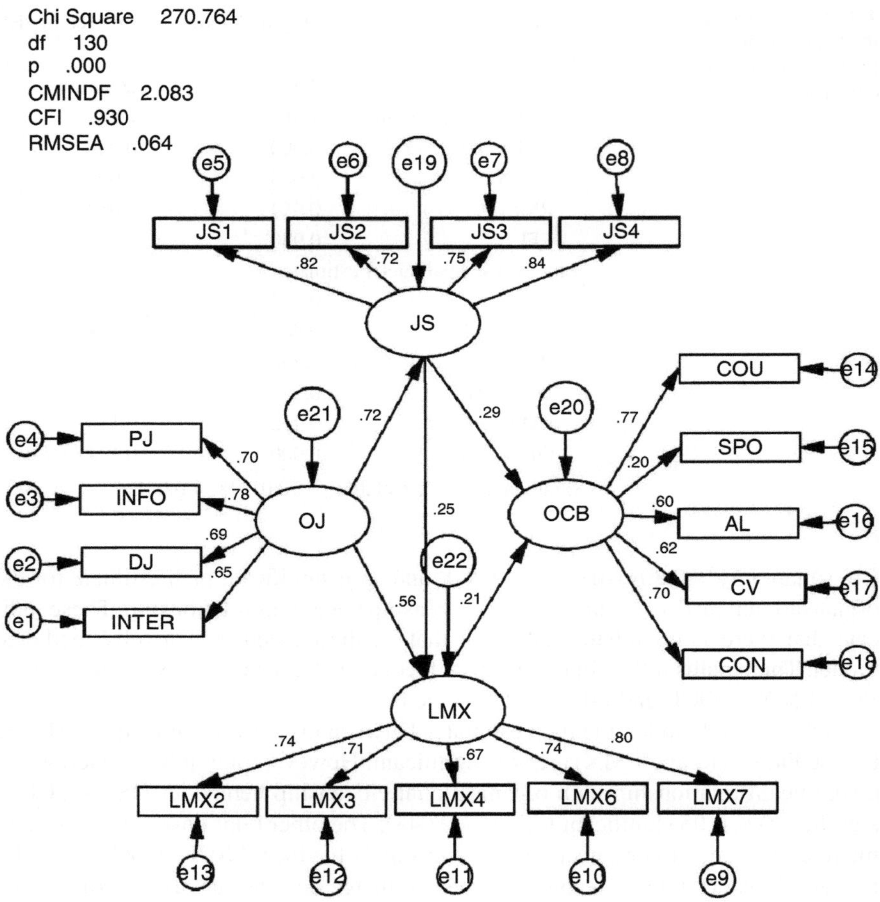

Fig. 11.2 Testing mediation in organisational justice–organisational citizenship behaviour

effects do decrease, the insignificant direct effect makes this a full mediation situation. As the LMX → OCB relationship is insignificant, all the mediating effects come from OJ → JS → OCB mediating relationship.

Hypothesis 6: Mediated Relationships

The results of the mediated relationships illustrated in Table 11.4 imply that only job satisfaction mediates the relationship between organisational justice and organisational citizenship behaviour. The findings shown in Table 11.4 indicate that job satisfaction fully mediates the relationship between organisational justice and organisational citizenship behaviour. In short, organisational justice has no direct

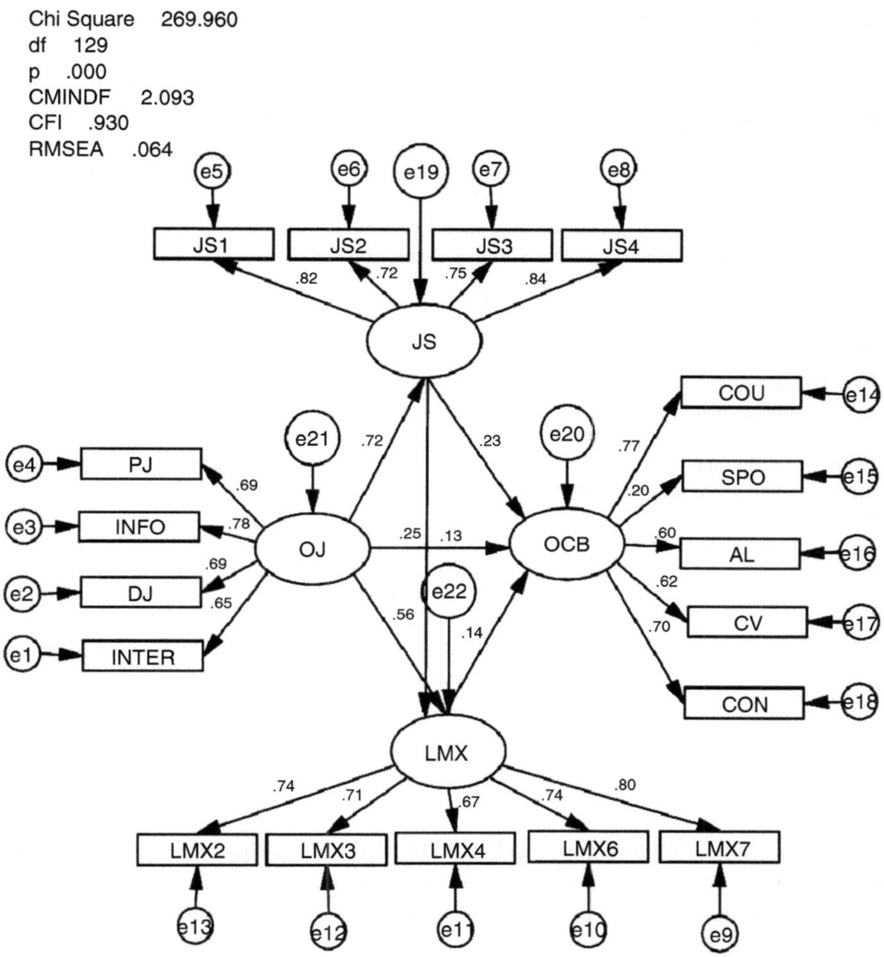

Fig. 11.3 Adding direct effects in testing mediation in the organisational justice–organisational citizenship behaviour model

Table 11.3 Assessing direct and indirect effects in a mediated model

Effects[a] of OJ → OCB	Original model (only indirect effects)	Revised model (indirect and direct effects)
Total effects	0.368	0.410
Direct effects	0.000	0.134
Indirect effects	0.368	0.276

[a]Values in the table represent standardised effects

Table 11.4 Hypotheses on the mediating factors in the organisational justice–organisational citizenship behaviour relationship

	Hypotheses	Findings
6	Job satisfaction and leader–member exchange mediate the relationship between organisational justice and organisational citizenship behaviour	Partially supported
6a	Job satisfaction mediates the relationship between organisational justice and organisational citizenship behaviour	Supported
6b	Leader–member exchange mediates the relationship between organisational justice and organisational citizenship behaviour	Not supported

Table 11.5 Hypotheses and the findings for research question 5

Research question	Hypotheses		Findings
Do job satisfaction and leader–member exchange act as mediators in the organisational justice–organisational citizenship behaviour relationship?	6	Job satisfaction and leader–member exchange mediate the relationship between organisational justice and organisational citizenship behaviour	Partially supported
	6a	Job satisfaction mediates the relationship between organisational justice and organisational citizenship behaviour	Supported
	6b	Leader–member exchange mediates the relationship between organisational justice and organisational citizenship behaviour	Not supported

effect on organisational citizenship behaviour, but is fully mediated by job satisfaction. Though organisational justice is significantly related to leader–member exchange, leader–member exchange does not have a significant relationship with organisational citizenship behaviour. Leader–member exchange does not act as a mediator, and, therefore, hypothesis 6b that leader–member exchange mediated the relationship between organisational justice and organisational citizenship behaviour is not supported. Nonetheless, job satisfaction still has a mediating effect.

The Mediating Role of Job Satisfaction and Leader–Member Exchange in the Organisational Justice–Organisational Citizenship Behaviour Relationship

Table 11.5 summarises the research question, hypotheses and the findings for the mediating roles of job satisfaction and leader–member exchange in the organisational justice–organisational citizenship behaviour relationship. The results of the study show that while job satisfaction fully mediates the relationship between organisational justice and organisational citizenship behaviour, leader–member exchange does not. In the current study, the relationship between organisational justice and the mediators remains significant with the addition of the direct path between organisational justice and organisational citizenship behaviour. However, only job satisfaction has a significant relationship with organisational citizenship behaviour. In essence, leader–member exchange has no mediation effect. As the direct path between organisational justice and organisational citizenship behaviour is insignificant, job satisfaction fully mediates the relationship. Additionally, the magnitude of the mediating effects shows that all the mediating effects come from job satisfaction. Therefore, job satisfaction is an important factor in enhancing organisational citizenship behaviours in the manufacturing sector in Malaysia. In the discussion that follows, the findings of job satisfaction as a mediator is first delineated and then, the role of leader–member exchange.

Discussion of the Findings

The following discussion addresses the fifth research question of the study. Table 11.5 summarises the research question, hypotheses and the findings for the mediating role of job satisfaction and leader–member exchange in the relationship between organisational justice and organisational citizenship behaviour.

It is hypothesised that job satisfaction and leader–member exchange mediate the relationship between organisational justice and organisational citizenship behaviour in the manufacturing sector in Malaysia. The findings reveal full mediation for job satisfaction, and, therefore, hypothesis 6a is substantiated. However, this contradicts extant literature that asserts that employee perceptions of fairness and not job satisfaction is the main determinant of organisational citizenship behaviour if job satisfaction and perceptions of fairness were both measured (Konovsky and Organ 1996; Lepine et al. 2002; Moorman 1991; Nadiri and Tanova 2010; Organ 1988, 1990). Organ (1990) further reiterates that the relationship between job satisfaction and organisational citizenship behaviour probably reflects employee perceptions of organisational justice. Nadiri and Tanova (2010) contend that though employees may be satisfied, employees will not demonstrate organisational citizenship behaviours if employees do not perceive organisational justice. Tension escalates in response to perceive injustice, and this translates into lower citizenship behaviours. Moreover, employees that favour social exchange are more likely to demonstrate organisational citizenship behaviours if equity exists. Despite the importance of organisational justice rather than job satisfaction in determining organisational citizenship behaviours, the current study shows that job satisfaction is a more significant predictor.

Full mediating effect of job satisfaction in the organisational justice–organisational citizenship behaviour relationship demonstrates that job satisfaction is indeed an important predictor. Thus, in contrast, organisational justice may not be as significant on organisational citizenship behaviour as expounded in prior studies.

This implies that practitioners should aim to improve organisational citizenship behaviour through improved job satisfaction. The effect on organisational citizenship behaviour would be minimal if practitioners were to focus on improving organisational justice. Increased job satisfaction potentially enhances morale, motivation and teamwork; creates a more disciplined and committed workforce; and improves behaviours and attitude at the workplace. Employees are more likely to engage in civic behaviour, hence, generating renewed interest in happenings in the organisation. Employees' concern and attention in organisational affairs augment organisational citizenship behaviour.

Leader–member exchange, however, does not act as a mediator in the organisational justice–organisational citizenship behaviour relationship. As empirical findings reveal the importance of trust in the leader–member exchange–organisational citizenship behaviour relationship (e.g. Dirks and Ferrin 2000; Erturk 2007; Giap et al. 2005; Konovsky and Pugh 1994; Mahfooz et al. 2007; Rhoades and Eisenberger 2002; Tan and Tan 2000), perhaps organisations should focus on improving trust to enhance organisational citizenship behaviours. Trust enhances employees' confidence in supervisors and may instigate organisational citizenship behaviours. This translates into positive work attitudes and volitional behaviours that may be valuable for organisational sustainability. In tandem with supervisor support, employee trust in supervisor probably works well in augmenting mutual reciprocation over time (Rhoades and Eisenberger 2002). Mahfooz et al. (2007) assert that mutual leader–member interpersonal trust and support are vital for maximum business results. Additionally, mutual reciprocation further promotes quality leader–member exchange and induces a continuous win–win relationship.

The results of the study suggest that organisations need to pay more attention to programmes and policies that encourage job satisfaction rather than leader–member exchange if organisational citizenship behaviour were the priority of management. In this case, organisations obviously benefit from exploring the so called 'happy-productive worker' hypothesis (Landy 1989; Weiss and Cropanzano 1996), as organisations tend to ignore the human factor to focus on maximising the productivity and financial performance of the organisation (Peccei 2004). Rather than focusing on more managerially oriented performance outcomes, it may be valuable for organisations to study the actual impact of human resource systems on employees' quality of working life, their experienced sense of satisfaction and well-being at work. As employee satisfaction and well-being play a central role in the relationship between human resource practices and organisational performance (e.g. Appelbaum et al. 2000; Becker and Huselid 1998; Guest 1997; Paauwe and Richardson 1997), progressive human resource policies and practices help to maximise employee positive affective reactions at work. This, in turn, enhances conscientiousness and altruism, thus, actively contributing to the overall productivity and effectiveness of the system. Along these lines, job satisfaction and organisational performance, far from being incompatible, go hand in hand and are inextricably positively linked.

Additionally, greater delegation of responsibility to workers (Peccei 2004), job enrichment (Guest 2002) and participative work practices (Appelbaum et al. 2000) may, for instance, help to increase intrinsic job satisfaction. However, it may also lead to an increase in job pressure, thereby cancelling out the positive psychological effects deriving from increased job autonomy, task variety and job involvement. Moreover, given the presence of expatriates in some manufacturing organisations, delegation of responsibility should be fair to mitigate negative behaviours. Therefore, the right balance is essential to augment job satisfaction. Generally, reasonable levels of control and variety at work, reasonable workloads, good wage-effort bargain, reasonable job security and treated with consideration and respect by management improve job satisfaction (Peccei 2004). In short, numerical flexibility (hours of work are kept within reasonable bounds), job design (multi-skilling and flexibility), pay and rewards (comparatively good pay and generous non-pay benefits), communications (systematic sharing and disclosure of both financial and nonfinancial information) and employee welfare (family friendly and work–life balance policies) help to sustain and underpin job satisfaction.

Nonetheless, organisations need to focus on overall justice to enhance job satisfaction and leader–member exchange, and, hence, organisational citizenship behaviour. As organisational justice has a significant influence on job satisfaction and the quality of leader–member exchange, it is crucial for organisations to manage fairness effectively to enhance organisational citizenship behaviour. The current study shows that the relationship between organisational justice and job satisfaction is more significant than the organisational justice–organisational citizenship behaviour relationship. Similarly, organisational justice has a stronger influence on leader–member exchange than the effect of leader–member exchange on organisational citizenship behaviour. Nevertheless, it may be beneficial for organisations to enhance leader–member exchange as there is a significant correlation between job satisfaction and leader–member exchange. To further justify the need to improve overall justice, the study concurs with the assertion that positive justice perceptions possibly reinforce affirmative citizenship perceptions, and, therefore, the more robust the organisational citizenship perceptions are, the more positive the organisational justice perceptions will be (Yilmaz and Tasdan 2009).

Conclusion

Precisely how justice perceptions are translated into citizenship behaviours is a challenging concern in the eyes of justice and citizenship scholars. Contemporary studies on justice–citizenship show that justice investment has resulted in exchanges based on mutual fulfilment of unspecified obligations (Blau 1964; Cropanzano and Mitchell 2005). Employees not only reciprocate by performing contractual tasks but also may perform above and beyond formal job expectations to fulfil perceived unspecified obligations. The theory of reasoned action (Blau 1964) provides a theoretical basis for this process as organisational citizenship behaviour (behavioural intention) is much dependent on attitudes and subjective norms. Perceptions of fairness will influence attitudes towards organisational citizenship behaviour, and important others' positive perceptions of organisational citizenship behaviour will motivate employees to display organisational citizenship behaviour. Furthermore, this study includes two sets of mediators: job satisfaction and leader–member exchange to enhance understanding of how each dimension of justice is translated into each kind of citizenship behaviour. Although contemporary justice–citizenship has been rich and diverse, prior research has not examined these separate constructs within a single study.

Based on the mediation analysis, the relationship between organisational justice and organisational citizenship behaviour is fully mediated by job satisfaction, while leader–member exchange does not have a mediating effect. Contradicting extant literature which shows that the effect of organisational justice is stronger than job satisfaction in determining organisational citizenship behaviour (e.g. Konovsky and Organ 1996; Lepine et al. 2002; Moorman 1991; Nadiri and Tanova 2010), employees will demonstrate citizenship behaviours if they experience job satisfaction despite organisational injustice. In essence, it may be imperative for manufacturing organisations in Malaysia to focus on improving organisational citizenship behaviour through improved job satisfaction to maximise results. Simply addressing organisational justice issues may be inadequate to generate employee work behaviours that exceed those dictated by organisational policy and one's job description. Thus, it is crucial for organisations to enhance job satisfaction while managing justice effectively. The next chapter recapitulates the entire study.

References

Appelbaum, E., Bailey, T., Berg, P., & Kalleberg, A. (2000). *Manufacturing advantage*. Itahaca: Cornell University Press.

Becker, B., & Huselid, M. A. (1998). High performance work systems and firm performance: A synthesis of research and managerial implications. *Research in Personnel and Human Resource Management, 16*(1), 53–101.

Blau, P. (1964). *Exchange and power in social life*. New York: Wiley.

Cropanzano, R., & Mitchell, M. (2005). Social exchange theory: An interdisciplinary review. *Journal of Management, 31*(6), 874–900.

Dirks, K. T., & Ferrin, D. L. (2000). The effects of trust in leadership on employee performance, behavior, and attitudes: A meta-analysis. In S. J. Havlovic (Ed.), *Academy of Management Best Papers Proceedings*, OB: H1.

Erturk, A. (2007). Increasing organizational citizenship behaviors of Turkish academicians: Mediating role of trust in supervisor on the relationship between organizational justice and citizenship behaviours. *Journal of Managerial Psychology, 22*(3), 257–270.

Giap, B. N., Hackermeier, I., Jiao, X., & Wagdarikar, S. P. (2005). Organizational citizenship behavior and perception of organizational justice in student jobs. In: *Research study, psychology of excellence instructional design, job analysis & job design* (pp. 1–14). Munich: Ludwig-Maximilians-University.

Guest, D. (1997). Human resource management and performance: A review and research agenda. *International Journal of Human Resource Management, 8*(3), 263–276.

Guest, D. E. (2002). Human resource management, corporate performance and employee wellbeing: Building the worker into HRM. *The Journal of Industrial Relations, 44*(3), 335–358.

Hair, J. F., Black, W. C., Babin, B. J., & Anderson, R. E. (2010). *Multivariate data analysis* (7th ed.). Upper Saddle River: Pearson Prentice Hall.

Kline, R. B. (2011). *Principles and practice of structural equation modelling*. New York: The Guilford Press.

Konovsky, M. A., & Organ, D. W. (1996). Dispositional and contextual determinants of organizational citizenship behavior. *Journal of Organizational Behavior, 17*(3), 253–266.

Konovsky, M. A., & Pugh, S. D. (1994). Citizenship behavior and social exchange. *Academy of Management Journal, 37*(3), 656–669.

Landy, F. J. (1989). *Psychology of work behaviour*. Pacific Grove: Brooks/Cole.

Lepine, J. A., Erez, A., & Johnson, D. E. (2002). The nature and dimensionality of organizational citizenship behavior: A critical review and meta-analysis. *Journal of Applied Psychology, 87*(1), 52–65.

Mahfooz, A. A., Kee, D. M. H., & Aafaqi, A. (2007). Leader-member exchange and attitudinal outcomes: Role of procedural justice climate. *Leadership & Organization Development Journal, 28*(8), 690–709.

Moorman, R. H. (1991). Relationship between organizational justice and organizational citizenship behavior: Do fairness perceptions influence employee citizenship? *Journal of Applied Psychology, 76*(6), 845–855.

Nadiri, H., & Tanova, C. (2010). An investigation of the role of justice in turnover intentions, job satisfaction, and organizational citizenship behavior in hospitality industry. *International Journal of Hospitality Management, 29*(1), 33–41.

Organ, D. W. (1988). A restatement of the satisfaction-performance hypothesis. *Journal of Management, 14*(4), 547–557.

Organ, D. W. (1990). The motivational basis of organizational citizenship behavior. *Research in Organizational Behavior, 12*(1), 43–72.

Paauwe, J., & Richardson, R. (1997). Introduction to special issue: Strategic human resource management and performance. *International Journal of Human Resource Management, 8*, 257–262.

Peccei, R. (2004). *Human resource management and the search for the happy workplace* (Inaugural address research in management series, pp. 1–19). Rotterdam: Erasmus Institute of Management.

Rhoades, L., & Eisenberger, R. (2002). Perceived organizational support: A review of the literature. *Journal of Applied Psychology, 87*(4), 698–714.

Tan, H. H., & Tan, C. S. (2000). Toward the differentiation of trust in supervisor and trust in organization. *Genetic, Social, and General Psychology Monographs, 126*(2), 241–260.

Weiss, H. M., & Cropanzano, R. (1996). Affective events theory: A theoretical discussion of the structure, causes and consequences of affective experiences at work. *Research in Organizational Behavior, 18*, 1–74.

Yilmaz, K., & Tasdan, M. (2009). Organizational citizenship and organizational justice in Turkish primary schools. *Journal of Educational Administration, 47*(1), 108–126.

Chapter 12
Conclusions and Recommendations

Abstract This chapter encapsulates the entire study. The chapter meticulously discusses if the findings are consistent with previous studies and identifies contributions to extant literature. Justification for insignificant correlations and supportive arguments for significant relationships are detailed. It establishes the linkage between the findings and the research gaps in the literature review. Implications for research and practice are also outlined. Finally, limitations of the study and directions for future research are highlighted. The conclusion of the chapter recapitulates the contributions of this study to the existing wealth of knowledge in the domain.

Introduction

This chapter encapsulates the entire study. It is divided into six sections and meticulously discusses the findings and identifies contributions to extant literature and practice. It establishes the linkage between the findings and the research gaps in the literature review. After a brief introduction, an overview of the study and a summary of the research findings from the empirical analysis are presented. Next, the theoretical and practical contributions as well as the managerial implications of the study are delineated. Then, limitations of the study and recommendations for future research are presented. The conclusion of the chapter recapitulates the contributions of this study to the flourishing literature in contemporary citizenship research.

In essence, this study contributes to contemporary research needs by integrating the literature of organisational justice and organisational citizenship behaviour through an application of the theory of reasoned action. The study explores the effects of each dimension of organisational justice perceptions on organisational citizenship behaviour. This enhances understanding of how each of the dimensions of justice is translated into each kind of citizenship behaviour. Furthermore, the model includes job satisfaction and leader–member exchange as mediators. Specifically, based on extant literature, organisational justice is instrumental in enhancing job satisfaction and leader–member exchange. Employees' positive perceptions of these in turn are expected to influence feelings of personal obligations and gratitude. In the current study, the findings reveal that while job satisfaction mediates justice–citizenship, leader–member exchange does not.

L.W. Hooi, *Organisational Justice and Citizenship Behaviour in Malaysia*,
Governance and Citizenship in Asia, DOI 10.1007/978-981-10-0030-0_12

An Overview of the Study

This research studied the link between organisational justice and organisational citizenship behaviour taking into consideration the effects of job satisfaction and leader–member exchange in the manufacturing sector in Malaysia. The study began with outlining the manufacturing sector in Malaysia and its contribution to the gross domestic product of the economy as well as the production performance, investment, exports, employment and financing of the sector. Justification for the importance of studying organisational justice–organisational citizenship behaviour relationship in the manufacturing sector was also discussed. Then, the discussion focused on a comprehensive review of related literature to elaborate on the issues related to the constructs of the study. After identifying the research gaps, the aims of the study were explicitly delineated. Accordingly, the research problem, research questions, research objectives and hypotheses specific to the study were outlined. Then, based on the research design, data was collected and analysed. The analysis of the collected data was done expansively to fully understand the relationship between the various constructs.

The discussion in the literature review established the importance of organisational justice in enhancing organisational citizenship behaviour. All justice factors had a significant impact on the dimensions of organisational citizenship behaviour. Though literature review indicated the correlation between organisational justice and organisational citizenship behaviour, the significance of each component of organisational justice on the dimensions of organisational citizenship behaviour varied. Prior studies reiterated the importance of procedural and distributive justice on organisational citizenship behaviour. Findings were, therefore, inconclusive as to specifically which justice factor was pertinent on organisational citizenship behaviour. For organisations to improve organisational citizenship behaviour, it would be imperative for organisations to understand precisely which justice factor influenced organisational citizenship behaviour. Hence, this study hoped to narrow the gap in existing literature and further advance knowledge in the organisational justice–organisational citizenship behaviour relationship by studying the relationship between each justice factor and each dimension of organisational citizenship behaviour, specifically in the manufacturing sector in Malaysia, as there is limited research in the sector.

The effect of each justice factor on job satisfaction and leader–member exchange as well as the effect of job satisfaction and leader–member exchange on each dimension of organisational citizenship behaviour was analysed. As past research emphasised that job satisfaction was not a significant predictor of organisational citizenship behaviour, but leader–member exchange was, this study included job satisfaction and leader–member exchange in the organisational justice–organisational citizenship behaviour relationship to confirm if these two variables were indeed mediators. This is particularly important in the manufacturing sector as prior studies showed that superior–subordinate relationship is an important determinant of decision outcomes in the manufacturing sector (Hooi 2002; Hooi et al. 2012). Furthermore, ensuring job satisfaction is more crucial in a high power distance and collectivistic society like Malaysia, as organisational justice is not expected. The working environment in the manufacturing sector, in particular, is comparatively not so conducive and may easily trigger undesirable employee behaviours such as office politics, absenteeism and job-hopping if employees were not satisfied. This is further complicated by the presence of a large number of foreign workers in the manufacturing sector in Malaysia.

The study, which focused specifically on the manufacturing sector in Malaysia, was divided into six parts – each part addressed the hypotheses of the study. The first part specifically focused on the organisational justice–organisational citizenship behaviour relationship. The purpose was to see the effect of each justice factor on each dimension of organisational citizenship behaviour. As job satisfaction and leader–member exchange were added as mediators in the study, the next part analysed the relationship between organisational justice and job satisfaction. The objective was to observe the effects of each justice factor on job satisfaction in order to understand which among the justice factors strongly influenced job satisfaction. Similarly, the effect of organisational justice on leader–member exchange was studied to determine how the justice factors influenced leader–member exchange. Then, the direct effects of the mediators on organisational citizenship behaviour were analysed to establish if job satisfaction and leader–member exchange significantly influenced the dimensions of organisational citizenship behaviour. Finally, the study looked at how job satisfaction and leader–member exchange mediated the relationship between organisational justice and organisational citizenship behaviour.

The study tested the hypotheses based on surveyed data collected from 267 employees of a sample of manufacturing companies listed in the Federation of Malaysian Manufacturers Directory (2010). The results of exploratory factor analysis showed that organisational justice was explained by procedural justice, informational justice, distributive justice and interpersonal justice. Similarly, organisational citizenship behaviour was accounted for by courtesy, sportsmanship, altruism, civic virtue and conscientiousness. Using structural equation modelling, the findings of the study established that the hypothesis that organisational justice positively influenced organisational citizenship behaviour was partially supported. On the contrary, the positive relationship between organisational justice and job satisfaction and organisational justice and leader–member exchange was supported. Though job satisfaction significantly influenced organisational citizenship behaviour, the hypothesis that leader–member exchange significantly influenced organisational citizenship behaviour was partially supported. As mediators, job satisfaction significantly predicted organisational citizenship behaviour, while leader–member exchange did not. In the study, job satisfaction fully mediated the organisational justice–organisational citizenship behaviour relationship.

Summary of the Research Findings

Using a cross-sectional survey design, this study examined the organisational justice–organisational citizenship behaviour relationship in the Malaysian manufacturing industry. The four variables involved in the study, namely, organisational justice, job satisfaction, leader–member exchange and organisational citizenship behaviour, were measured using scales adapted from previous studies. The research framework proposed a direct positive relationship between organisational justice and organisational citizenship behaviour, job satisfaction and leader–member exchange as well as a direct relationship between job satisfaction and leader–member exchange and organisational citizenship behaviour. The framework also proposed mediating hypotheses related to job satisfaction and leader–member exchange. Structural equation modelling was used to assess the framework. Table 12.1 summarised the research gaps, research objectives and findings of the study.

The research findings revealed mixed results. The analysis of the relationship between organisational justice and organisational citizenship behaviour showed that all the justice factors had a significant effect on only certain dimensions of organisational citizenship behaviour. Courtesy was negatively related to procedural justice, but positively related to interactional justice. Similarly, the correlation between sportsmanship and procedural justice was negative, but had a linear relationship with interpersonal justice. Civic virtue was significantly correlated with all dimensions of organisational justice except informational justice. Only interpersonal justice had a significant effect on altruism and conscientiousness. Therefore, the first hypothesis that employee perceptions of organisational justice positively influenced the dimensions of organisational citizenship behaviour was partially substantiated.

As for the relationship between organisational justice and job satisfaction, the results of the study confirmed that all dimensions of organisational justice had a significant effect on job satisfaction. Job satisfaction was more dependent on employee perceptions of informational justice than on distributive justice, procedural justice or interpersonal justice. Similarly, organisational justice had a significant impact on leader–member exchange. Among justice factors, informational justice had a stronger correlation with leader–member exchange than distributive justice, interpersonal justice or procedural justice. Thus, the findings supported both hypotheses 2 and 3 that employee perceptions of organisational justice positively influenced job satisfaction and leader–member exchange. Comparatively, informational justice and distributive justice are important predictors of job satisfaction and leader–member exchange.

Analysing the effect of job satisfaction and leader–member exchange on the dimensions of organisational citizenship behaviour, the results showed that job satisfaction had a significant effect while leader–member exchange correlated positively with altruism, civic virtue and conscientiousness. Job satisfaction has a significant effect on civic virtue, followed by courtesy, conscientiousness, altruism and sportsmanship. Thus, hypothesis 4 that job satisfaction positively influenced the dimensions of organisational citizenship behaviour was supported. However, hypothesis 5 that leader–member exchange positively influenced the dimensions of organisational citizenship behaviour was partially supported. Leader–member exchange had no significant effect on courtesy and sportsmanship.

The findings of the study established that the relationship between organisational justice and organisational citizenship behaviour was insignificant when job satisfaction and leader–member exchange were added as mediators. As the indirect mediation effect in the OJ→LMX→OCB was insignificant, leader–member exchange did not act as a mediator in the relationship. Though OJ→LMX was significant,

Table 12.1 Research gaps, research objectives and research findings

Research gaps	Research objectives	Research findings
Among many justice factors that have been studied to understand the organisational justice–organisational citizenship behaviour relationship, the findings of prior research are still inconclusive. Many studies linked organisational justice to specific organisational phenomena, but the effect of each justice factor on each component of organisational citizenship behaviour has not been extensively examined, especially in the manufacturing sector in Malaysia.	To examine the relationship between employee perceptions of organisational justice and the dimensions of organisational citizenship behaviour in the manufacturing sector in Malaysia	The findings partially supported the relationship between organisational justice and organisational citizenship behaviour. Distributive and procedural justice positively influenced civic virtue; procedural justice negatively influenced courtesy and sportsmanship; informational justice positively influenced courtesy; and interpersonal justice positively influenced all dimensions of organisational citizenship behaviour.
Though there are many studies on job satisfaction, there is limited literature on job satisfaction as an outcome. Most studies have included job satisfaction as a cause rather than an outcome (Organ 1988a, 1988b, 1990).	To verify if employee perceptions of organisational justice in the manufacturing sector in Malaysia influence job satisfaction	The direct relationship between organisational justice and job satisfaction was supported. Employee perceptions of organisational justice (informational, distributive, procedural, interpersonal) and job satisfaction were positively correlated.
Studies on organisational justice, as an antecedent of leader–member exchange, is not well established. More studies have been conducted on the influence of leader–member exchange on other organisational factors such as justice (Bhal and Ansari 2007) and human resource development (Kang and Stewart 2007) or the effect of organisational justice on other organisational outcomes such as employee work engagement (Hassan and Jubari 2010). No research has been recorded for organisational justice as an antecedent of leader–member exchange in the manufacturing sector in Malaysia.	To determine if employee perceptions of organisational justice in the manufacturing sector in Malaysia influence leader–member exchange	The direct relationship between each component of organisational justice and leader–member exchange was supported. Employee perceptions of organisational justice (informational justice, distributive justice, interpersonal justice and procedural justice) and leader–member exchange were positively correlated.

(continued)

Table 12.1 (continued)

Research gaps	Research objectives	Research findings
Though the relationship between job satisfaction and organisational citizenship behaviour has long been known, it is still ambiguous (Foote and Tang 2008). Empirical studies on leader–member exchange and organisational citizenship behaviour focus primarily on the role of trust (e.g. Dirks and Ferrin 2000; Erturk 2007; Konovsky and Pugh 1994; Mahfooz et al. 2007; Rhoades and Eisenberger 2002; Tan and Tan 2000). There is still limited knowledge on the direct relationship between leader–member exchange and organisational citizenship behaviour. In line with the conclusion of previous research on leader–member exchange, examining a broader range of outcome variables would enhance generalisability of leader–member exchange to other outcomes (Jawahar and Carr 2007). In Malaysia, the direct relationship between leader–member exchange and organisational citizenship behaviour has not been exploited in the manufacturing sector.	To establish if job satisfaction and leader–member exchange positively affect the dimensions of organisational citizenship behaviour in the manufacturing sector in Malaysia	The findings revealed that the job satisfaction–organisational citizenship behaviour relationship was supported, while the leader–member exchange–organisational citizenship behaviour relationship was partially supported. Job satisfaction had a significant effect on civic virtue, courtesy, conscientiousness, altruism, and sportsmanship while leader–member exchange had a positive correlation with altruism, civic virtue and conscientiousness.
Extant literature reveals limited studies on job satisfaction and leader–member exchange as a mediator in the organisational justice–organisational citizenship behaviour relationship, especially in the manufacturing sector in Malaysia. Furthermore, to enrich understanding of the dynamics of organisational behaviour, simply examining the direct relationships between organisational justice and organisational citizenship behaviour is insufficient to provide a universal view from a human capital management perspective.	To assess if job satisfaction and leader–member exchange mediate the relationship between organisational justice and organisational citizenship behaviour in the manufacturing sector in Malaysia	Only job satisfaction was a contingent factor in the organisational justice–organisational citizenship behaviour relationship. Job satisfaction fully mediated the relationship between organisational justice and organisational citizenship behaviour. On the contrary, leader–member exchange did not act as a mediator in the organisational justice–organisational citizenship behaviour relationship. However, there was a strong correlation between job satisfaction and leader–member exchange.

LMX→OCB was not. On the contrary, job satisfaction fully mediated the relationship between organisational justice and organisational citizenship behaviour. The indirect mediation effect in the OJ→JS→OCB was significant. As the OJ → OCB path estimate was insignificant, the model supported full mediation.

Theoretical Contributions

Drawing from the theory of reasoned action, the current study tested a theoretical model in which justice perceptions affect job satisfaction and leader–member exchange, which in turn influence organisational citizenship behaviour. Employee attitudes and subjective norms vis-à-vis organisational citizenship behaviour would indicate if organisational justice effects on job satisfaction and the quality of leader–member exchange relationship would result in organisational citizenship behaviour. Extant literature on organisational justice and organisational citizenship behaviour suggests that organisational justice is a strong determinant of organisational citizenship behaviour (Moorman 1991; Nadiri and Tanova 2010). The emphasis is on organisational justice rather than job satisfaction or leader–member exchange as a more significant predictor. The findings of the present study indicate that attention should be given to job satisfaction in particular and to a certain extent leader–member exchange. Results of this study contribute to advance knowledge in the organisational justice–organisational citizenship behaviour relationship in a number of ways.

Firstly, the study contributes to this field by providing insights on the justice factors that seem to affect organisational citizenship behaviour, job satisfaction and leader–member exchange in the manufacturing sector in Malaysia. Limited research has been carried out to study the direct and indirect effects of each justice factor, job satisfaction and leader–member exchange on each dimension of organisational citizenship behaviour in Malaysia. However, this study evidently shows the extent to which each justice factor, job satisfaction and leader–member exchange affects the dimensions of organisational citizenship behaviour, specifically in the manufacturing sector in Malaysia.

This is important as composite scores do not reflect the role that more specific subfactors play in the correlational relationship among variables (Tabachnick and Fidell 2007). An interesting finding of the current study is the inverse relationship between procedural justice and courtesy as well as sportsmanship. This implies that perceived fairness of decision-making procedures does not necessary make employees feel obligated to cooperate with others to check actions that could affect their responsibilities or motivate employees to refrain from negative behaviours. One possible explanation for this is, as employees perceived that decision-making procedures are fair, decision outcomes are not affected even if they were discourteous or seen as uncooperative. Therefore, there is no necessity to be courteous or cooperative, especially if the fair system meets or exceeds an employee's expectations and needs. On the contrary, employees may perceive that it would be better to pursue their own goals and limit teamwork and knowledge sharing to enhance their chances of progressing within the organisation. In essence, employees would rather focus on working towards what benefits them instead of being obligated to help achieve organisational goals. Additionally, there may be a tendency to assume that despite limited involvement or cooperation, job gets done if there were conscientious coworkers to complete the task. In another perspective, it may be because people are displaying courtesy and sportsmanship because society and their culture expect them to do, but deep underneath they may believe or think procedural justice is grossly lacking.

Similarly, if employees perceive justice in decision-making procedures, negative behaviours would have little effect on decision outcomes. Therefore, employees do not see the need to refrain from undesirable behaviours and are not afraid of displaying negative behaviours when their expectations are not met. Furthermore, a complaint may result in actions taken to rectify a problem that may be beneficial to the organisation. Instead of being punished, the complainant gets credit and perhaps rewarded for highlighting an issue. When procedural justice is high, employees that avoid negative behaviours do not benefit much comparatively. In short, outstanding sportsmanship has little effect on decision outcomes. The hazardous environment in the manufacturing sector sometimes justifies the negative behaviours of employees as stress levels increase. Furthermore, as decision-making procedures become fairer, expectations of employees may increase, and if these are not met, sportsmanship is affected.

The study further establishes the importance of interpersonal justice among justice factors in influencing organisational citizenship behaviour. Interpersonal justice positively influences all dimensions of organisational citizenship behaviour, in particular, conscientiousness followed by courtesy, altruism, civic virtue and sportsmanship. This partially supports Moorman's (1991) findings, which affirm the relationship between interactional justice and four dimensions of organisational citizenship behaviour, namely, courtesy, sportsmanship, conscientiousness and altruism. However, it differs in the significance of the effect on each dimension of organisational citizenship behaviour and does not influence civic virtue. It also supports the findings of Ishak and Alam (2009) that indicate a significant relationship between interactional justice and altruism. Additionally, distributive and procedural justice positively influences civic virtue while informational justice positively affects courtesy. This contradicts prior research that emphasises the insignificance of distributive and procedural justice in predicting organisational citizenship behaviour (Ishak and Alam 2009; Moorman 1991) and research that shows a strong relationship between procedural justice and altruism (Farh et al. 1990; Konovsky and Folger 1991). However, it is consistent with the findings of Abdullah and Mohd Nasurdin (2008) that assert the significance of distributive and procedural justice in influencing organisational citizenship behaviour.

Secondly, from the mediation perspective, this study includes job satisfaction and leader–member exchange as mediators in the relationship and establishes which of the two mediators has a more significant effect on organisational citizenship behaviour. This is perhaps among the first to test empirically the mediating effects of job satisfaction and leader–member exchange in the organisational justice–organisational citizenship behaviour relationship specifically in the manufacturing sector in Malaysia. This study advances existing literature in advocating that job satisfaction rather than organisational justice or leader–member exchange is a more significant predictor of organisational citizenship behaviour. Prior studies place great emphasis on organisational justice as an antecedent of organisational citizenship behaviour (e.g. Moorman 1991; Organ 1988b, 1990) and recommend on improving organisational justice to enhance organisational citizenship behaviour.

Additionally, though organisational justice significantly affects job satisfaction and leader–member exchange, only job satisfaction fully mediates the relationship between organisational justice and organisational citizenship behaviour. Leader–member exchange directly affects altruism, civic virtue and conscientiousness, but does not act as a mediator. This contradicts research that shows leader–member exchange fully mediating the relationship between interactional justice and organisational citizenship behaviour (Hassan and Jubari 2010). Though the findings support prior studies on the significance of organisational justice on job satisfaction and leader–member exchange, the current study shows that job satisfaction is of paramount importance if organisations in the manufacturing sector in Malaysia wish to enhance organisational citizenship behaviour.

Thirdly, the study reveals the interactive effect of job satisfaction and leader–member exchange in the organisational justice–organisational citizenship behaviour relationship. The findings show a significant positive correlation between job satisfaction and leader–member exchange, congruent with prior empirical findings (e.g. Hassan and Chandran 2005; Hsu 2011; Mardanov et al. 2008; McCalister 2003; Ng and Sorensen 2008). The higher the job satisfaction is, the higher the quality of leader–member exchange is expected to be, and the increased quality of leader–member exchange further increases job satisfaction. This is probably attributed to the fact that satisfied employees are more optimistic and happier at the workplace, and this increases employee interest in organisational matters. This translates into enhanced employee participation and engagement at the workplace. The quality of leader–member exchange is likely to improve as both employees and managers work to provide mutual support to meet the vision and missions of the organisation. This enhances perceptions of interactional justice and possibly, employees' intention to exhibit organisational citizenship behaviour. Dedicated workers are less likely to leave, and, therefore, the findings suggest that job satisfaction should be improved in tandem with the quality of leader–member exchange.

Managerial Implications and Contributions

From a practical perspective, this study has important implications for managers and organisations. Of utmost significance is the indication of the importance of each justice factors on job satisfaction, leader–member exchange and the dimensions of organisational citizenship behaviour. This is useful for managers to monitor a wide range of employee behaviours that may be detrimental to organisational effectiveness. The current findings reveal explicitly which justice factor to focus on to enhance job satisfaction, leader–member exchange and each dimension of organisational citizenship behaviour in the manufacturing sector in Malaysia. Previous studies have offered one-dimensional analysis of the effect of organisational justice on job satisfaction, leader–member exchange and organisational citizenship behaviour (e.g. Yilmaz and Tasdan 2009); job satisfaction on organisational citizenship behaviour (e.g. Murphy et al. 2006) and leader–member exchange on organisational citizenship behaviour (e.g. Truckenbrodt 2000). Other studies have researched perceived organisational justice and organisational citizenship behaviours separately (e.g. Allen and Rush 1998; Chen et al. 1998; Sheppard et al. 1992; Skarlicki and Folger 1997). However, knowing how each independent construct affects the dimensions of organisational citizenship behaviour helps diagnose opportunities for intervention and improvement to enhance organisational citizenship behaviour in the workplace. Given the strong demand for skilled workers, this is necessary for retaining key workers.

Though managers may have little direct control over some employee attitudes and behaviours, the findings suggest that managers can increase organisational citizenship behaviour, in particular courtesy, through demonstrating interactional justice. By treating employees with dignity and respect, organisational citizenship behaviour is expected to improve as this aspect of interactional justice affects all dimensions of organisational citizenship behaviour. As workplace success among other factors depends on respect for people, the findings support that interpersonal justice is indeed important. The way managers treat employees has a significant influence on their attitudes and commitment and, as a consequence, on their performance. Employees generally are more likely to respond affirmatively to meet the demands of increased workload if they perceive equity in interpersonal treatment. A corollary of this implication is that perceptions of fairness based on interpersonal justice may be the easiest perceptions to manage, as it is not constrained by forces outside the manager's control. It much depends on a manager's sensitivity and tact in dealing with the employee and convincing them that it is in the manager's interest to be fair.

Greenberg (1988) contends that actively communicating fairness through interaction rather than merely relying on actual fair behaviour has greater success of improving perceptions of fairness. The findings propose that if managers practise effective and fair communication, there is a probability that organisational citizenship behaviour will improve. Enhancing informational justice does not cost an organisation much, but the absence of it may be a costly affair. In high power distance organisations, it is unlikely that employees exhibit confrontational behaviours when faced with any kind of injustice, in particular informational injustice. Employees would rather leave, and in the manufacturing sector where competition is severe, it is imperative that organisations avoid losing key workers. The implementation of informational justice is feasible if organisations were to invest in enhancing communication skills of managers to improve perceive fairness in decision-making.

Besides, fair personal treatment in decision-making processes is likely to augment affirmative employee behaviours. Therefore, prompt and honest feedback is essential to maintain trust and confidence in managerial decisions. Bias managerial decisions would aggravate the tendency to job-hop, as employees usually gain more in terms of salary increase when they job-hop, particularly in the Malaysian manufacturing sector (Hooi 2002, 2008). As perception of justice is formed quickly, inadequate information in decision-making may influence the perception of subsequent actions (Klendauer and Deller 2009). Indubitably, it is of paramount importance that organisations convince employees about management sincerity in ensuring equity in information sharing. Strategic manipulation intentions may generate counterproductive effects (Klendauer and Deller 2009) that can spiral beyond managerial control. Hence, organisations should work to increase the fairness of their interactions with the employees.

Moreover, providing adequate explanations for decisions and events that affect them improve job satisfaction and the quality of leader–member exchange. As job satisfaction has a significant influence on all dimensions of organisational citizenship behaviour, improving job satisfaction is likely to enhance organisational citizenship behaviour. Similarly, improving the quality of leader–member exchange has positive effects on altruism, civic virtue and conscientiousness. As 'happy' employees are 'productive' employees (Gannon and Noon 1971; Katzell and Yankelovich 1975), organisations benefit from promoting organisational citizenship behaviour to influence employees to enhance commitment and performance. Intuitively, identification with the organisation would reduce employee alienation and enhance collaboration at the workplace. Employees are more likely to cooperate to help achieve organisational goals, devote sincerely to the organisation, avoid disapproving behaviours and increase interest in organisational affairs. These traits are instrumental for gaining competitive advantage in the face of current global challenges. As the manufacturing sector recover from the economic slump, workforce engagement and involvement is of paramount importance.

These findings suggest that organisational justice may have a greater impact on organisational citizenship behaviour via job satisfaction when compared to the direct effect of organisational justice on organisational citizenship behaviour. Organisational justice has long been thought to lead to improved organisational citizenship behaviour, but the results of this study indicate that organisational justice may not play a significant role in enhancing organisational citizenship behaviour. On the contrary, enhancing job satisfaction may produce better results. This is probably because employees in Malaysia do not expect justice at the workplace (Hooi et al. 2012). In the manufacturing sector where managerial positions are scarce and promotion is ad hoc (Hooi 2002, 2008), cronyism has its role in promotional decisions (Hooi et al. 2012). Therefore, if organisations were to increase organisational citizenship behaviour, the focus would be on improving job satisfaction rather than organisational justice.

To improve job satisfaction, managers would probably have to focus on providing adequate and honest explanations for decision outcomes. In a society where it is not a norm to question organisational decisions, transparency in decision outcomes would likely enhance perceptions of justice, and, hence, job satisfaction. As employees in the manufacturing sector in Malaysia are exposed to a hazardous working environment, it is imperative to enhance job satisfaction to mitigate disruption due to high turnover. Questionable decision outcomes may lead to dissatisfaction and trigger undesirable work behaviours. Furthermore, informational justice is believed to improve the quality of leader–member exchange. As the quality of leader–member exchange influences some dimensions of organisational citizenship behaviour, efforts to improve the quality of leader–member exchange through enhanced organisational justice is highly recommended. This is particularly so in the manufacturing sector in Malaysia where most managers act as mentors to their subordinates (Hooi 2010). Workflow would be affected if team spirit were affected due to poor quality leader–member exchange relationship. Organisational leaders may improve employee perceptions of justice by providing timely information, ensuring equity in distribution of outcomes, enacting fair procedures and treating subordinates with dignity and respect.

Another implication from the study is the significant relationship between job satisfaction and leader–member exchange. If employees are satisfied in their jobs, there is a higher probability that workplace relations may improve. Better quality of leader–member exchange may further increase job satisfaction, which in turn may enhance leader–member exchange. Managers are central in ensuring job satisfaction and good quality leader–member exchange and, therefore, play an important role in instilling organisational citizenship behaviour. This finding demonstrates that the intercorrelation between the various constructs makes it necessary for organisations to pay attention to justice factors as well as mediators in advancing organisational citizenship behaviour. This study has specified precisely how each construct affects the other. Depending on which dimension of organisational citizenship behaviour needs to be improved, managers have the option to select the most appropriate intervention to be taken. Managers may have to observe if procedural justice is negatively related to courtesy and sportsmanship as revealed in the findings. If this is indeed the case, then an explanation is necessary before measures can be taken to reverse the relationship. Rationally, it is unlikely that negative citizenship behaviours would arise from positive perceptions of justice.

Consequently, the need for organisations to train and educate their managers on the impact of the perceived lack of justice on job satisfaction, the quality of leader–member exchange and organisational citizenship behaviour is inevitable. In the current era of globalisation, increased diversity at the workplace provides more challenges for organisations. Some foreign multinational companies in the manufacturing sector in Malaysia are managed by expatriates whose management style may convey high awareness of justice. In essence, a diverse workforce may influence employee perceptions of justice and no longer accept what used to be the norm at the workplace. Moreover, technological advancement has enable employees to communicate globally, thus, enhancing awareness of global opportunities, which may entice employees to leave. Besides, sharing knowledge globally creates awareness on employee rights, and perceived injustice may lead to dissatisfaction, and, hence, lower organisational citizenship behaviour. In essence, appropriate training to enhance managerial competences in ensuring organisational justice is crucial for improving organisational citizenship behaviour. Moreover, fair management initiates job satisfaction and high-quality relationships with leaders as well as citizenship behaviours that benefit the organisation directly. When an organisation's culture is characterised by impartial management, high job satisfaction and good quality supervisor–employee relationships, the ramifications for overall productivity and performance are remarkable.

Limitations of the Study

Taking into consideration the mediating effects of job satisfaction and leader–member exchange, the study hopes to enhance understanding of the relationship between organisational justice and organisational citizenship behaviour. By empirically testing several hypotheses advanced in the literature, the findings reveal the principal role of job satisfaction in the organisational justice–organisational citizenship behaviour relationship. However, as organisational justice significantly influences job satisfaction and leader–member exchange, overall justice in organisations is essential to enhance organisational citizenship behaviour. As leader–member exchange does not significantly influence all dimensions of organisational citizenship behaviour, the findings indicate that it would be more beneficial to focus on improving job satisfaction to reinforce organisational citizenship behaviour. But, the significant relationship between job satisfaction and leader–member exchange suggests that the quality of leader–member exchange could not be totally ignored.

Although the findings provide constructive insights into the dynamics of the various constructs of the study, inherent limitations are evident. Some of the limitations of this study are as follows.

1. As the study is constrained to the manufacturing sector in Malaysia, it hinders generalisation of the findings to other sectors. The validity of the current findings is limited to the manufacturing companies in Malaysia even though the data is from a range of manufacturing industries in the country. The generalisability of the current findings to other countries is somewhat limited as the setting is different. Different settings would likely yield different results.
2. As this is a cross-sectional study, causality cannot be established despite some inferences on the causal relationships. In the absence of longitudinal analysis, the findings give a superficial view of the issues at a specific timeframe.
3. The present study relies on survey methodology for data collection. The tendency to provide a socially desirable response in survey studies may adversely affect the size of the effects or misrepresent the construct.
4. Though each participating company has been advised to randomly select ten respondents for the questionnaire, it is impossible to verify if the respondents were indeed randomly selected. Respondents are also limited to executives and managerial staffs only. Generalisability of findings to all employees is still a major concern.
5. The responses may be constrained by respondents limited comprehension of the concepts in the study. It is not sure how respondents interpreted the items. Respondents may have given an inaccurate response either intentionally or unintentionally.

6. The collection of data for both independent and dependent variables using the same questionnaire suggests that there may be potential bias or presence of common variance problems.

All data limitations aside, this study has made progress towards addressing important gaps in the literature. It advances knowledge in aligning each justice factors with the dimensions of organisational citizenship behaviour as well as integrates job satisfaction and leader–member exchange in the organisational justice–organisational citizenship behaviour relationship. Thus, it has not only filled the gaps in literature but also highlights the significant role of job satisfaction in explaining organisational citizenship behaviour.

Recommendations for Future Research

To advance knowledge on the issues in the current study, further research is necessary to provide a more profound understanding. More research is needed to assess the causal relationships among all constructs examined in this study. Hence, the following proposals are recommended:

1. Future research can replicate the study in other sectors or countries to verify if the scales are applicable to other contexts. Studies in a wider context would reveal the strength and applicability of the measurement and establish the importance of the various constructs in the study.
2. As stratified random sampling is based on geographic location, future studies may consider sampling by industries, equity ownership or company size in the manufacturing sector. Comparative studies would further advance understanding of the relationship of the various constructs in the study.
3. To enhance understanding of the justice–citizenship relationship, future research may consider a longitudinal approach. Longitudinal studies with repeated measures and qualitative data from both management and employees are needed to firmly establish the causal inferences. To understand the stage at which employees develop organisational citizenship behaviour, a longitudinal approach is more appropriate. Such studies would reveal more conclusive results over time as employee perceptions of organisational justice, job satisfaction, leader–member exchange and organisational citizenship behaviour are developmental in nature.
4. An empirical examination of the relationship between procedural justice and the dimensions of organisational citizenship behaviour would help clarify inconsistencies in extant literature. The inverse relationship between procedural justice and courtesy and sportsmanship in this study requires further investigation.
5. Further research on the role of job satisfaction in the organisational justice–organisational citizenship behaviour relationship may be necessary as the results are inconclusive. The current findings contradict prior studies that assert the

importance of organisational justice rather than job satisfaction in promoting organisational citizenship behaviour.

6. Only job satisfaction and leader–member exchange are mediators in the current study. Future research may consider other factors such as job involvement, job engagement, organisational commitment, motivation, career advancement, felt obligation and intent to quit.
7. To fully capture the quality of leader–member exchange, future research may include the supervisor version of the LMX scale. Development and validation of a leader's version of the LMX scale are needed to reflect a supervisor's perspective of the value of exchange delivered by the subordinate. Development of new measurement scales using a wider range of criteria is also needed.
8. Research is also needed on potential moderators of these relationships such as cultural values and demographic variables. Future research may consider the moderating influences of person, situation and organisational-based factors.
9. Given the multicultural background and multi-ethnic workforce, further research may incorporate the challenges of managing workforce diversity. Specifically, the study could focus on the variation in employee perceptions of the various constructs based on multicultural background and ethnicity of the workforce. The study could also integrate the struggle regarding the Malaysian manufacturing organisational culture versus a multicultural/multi-ethnic workforce.

Conclusion

This study presented an integrated analysis of the organisational justice–organisational citizenship behaviour relationship in the manufacturing sector in Malaysia by including job satisfaction and leader–member exchange as mediators to provide a wholesome perspective of the associations between organisational justice and organisational citizenship behaviour. Although the intention of the study is to enrich understanding of the mediating role of job satisfaction and leader–member exchange in the organisational justice–organisational citizenship behaviour relationship, it provides guidelines for managing organisational citizenship behaviour. The study has expounded on the importance of job satisfaction in the organisational justice–organisational citizenship behaviour relationship, and, therefore, the correlation between these constructs must not be overlooked. The proper alignment between organisational justice, job satisfaction and leader–member exchange apparently determines employees' intention to exhibit organisational citizenship behaviour. Accordingly, it is important to remember that organisational justice is a significant predictor of organisational citizenship behaviour. A positive perception of organisational justice enhances organisational citizenship behaviour, which in turn helps an organisation to sustain dynamism. On the contrary, perceived inequity can reduce organisational citizenship behaviour, which may affect the bottom line. It suggests that the survival of any organisation depends upon the development of organisational mechanisms to achieve organisational citizenship behaviours (Murphy et al. 2006) to ensure sustainability in today's turbulent environment.

Overall, the results of the study show support for many of the hypotheses in the model with justice perceptions differentially influencing job satisfaction, leader–member exchange and the dimensions of organisational citizenship behaviour in the manufacturing sector in Malaysia. Organisational justice perception of employees is very crucial in influencing organisational citizenship behaviour in that it significantly affects job satisfaction and leader–member exchange, which then influence the dimensions of organisational citizenship behaviour. As the findings reveal that job satisfaction is a more important predictor of organisational citizenship behaviour than organisational justice or leader–member exchange when these factors are taken together, practitioners may have to focus on job satisfaction to enhance organisational citizenship behaviour. Increased job satisfaction together with effective training to improve managerial competence in decision-making will lead to increased organisational citizenship behaviours, which ultimately results in better performance. On the contrary, if employees do not perceive organisational justice, job satisfaction level will decline and employees are unlikely to demonstrate organisational citizenship behaviours. Thus, even if management attempts to ensure fairness, organisational citizenship behaviour will not improve if employees are not satisfied. Therefore, organisations have to improve organisational justice in tandem with job satisfaction and leader–member exchange in order to enhance organisational citizenship behaviour. Among justice factors, interactional justice is important in influencing organisational citizenship behaviour, in particular interpersonal justice. In brief, the findings indicate that personal factors are imperative for advancing organisational citizenship behaviours in the manufacturing sector in Malaysia.

In conclusion, the findings of this study give credence to the importance of job satisfaction in the organisational justice–organisational citizenship behaviour relationship. A critical examination is necessary to advance knowledge on the influence of job satisfaction in the organisational justice–organisational citizenship behaviour relationship, as empirical evidence is still ambiguous. Additionally, management needs to focus on the quality of leader–member exchange, as today's employees reciprocate according to how they are treated. Positive perceptions of fairness are likely to improve the quality of leader–member exchange and elicit affirmative employee behaviours. In time, the quality of leader–member exchange may promote organisational justice climate that will strengthen employees' intention to demonstrate organisational citizenship behaviours. Concisely, positive perceptions of fairness must be sustained at reasonably high levels in the manufacturing sector in Malaysia in order to facilitate positive justice climate that would lead to increased job satisfaction and quality of leader–member exchange and finally, increased organisational citizenship behaviour.

References

Abdullah, M. H., & Mohd Nasurdin, A. (2008). Investigating the influence of organizational justice on hotel employees' organizational citizenship behavior intentions and turnover intentions. *Journal of Human Resources in Hospitality & Tourism, 7*(1), 1–23.

Allen, T. D., & Rush, M. C. (1998). The effects of organizational citizenship behavior on performance judgements: A field study and a laboratory experiment. *Journal of Applied Psychology, 83*(2), 247–260.

Bhal, K. T., & Ansari, M. A. (2007). Leader-member exchange-subordinates outcomes relationship: Role of voice and justice. *Leadership & Organization Development Journal, 28*(1), 20–35.

Chen, X., Hui, C., & Sego, D. J. (1998). The role of organizational citizenship behavior in turnover: Conceptualization and preliminary tests of key hypotheses. *Journal of Applied Psychology, 83*(6), 922–931.

Dirks, K. T., & Ferrin, D. L. (2000). The effects of trust in leadership on employee performance, behavior, and attitudes: A meta-analysis. In S. J. Havlovic (Ed.), *Academy of Management Best Papers Proceedings*. OB: H1.

Erturk, A. (2007). Increasing organizational citizenship behaviors of Turkish academicians: Mediating role of trust in supervisor on the relationship between organizational justice and citizenship behaviours. *Journal of Managerial Psychology, 22*(3), 257–270.

Farh, J., Podsakoff, P. M., & Organ, D. W. (1990). Accounting for organizational citizenship behavior: Leader fairness and task scope versus satisfaction. *Journal of Management, 16*(4), 705–721.

Foote, D. A., & Tang, T. L. (2008). Job satisfaction and organizational citizenship behavior (OCB): Does team commitment make a difference in self-directed teams? *Management Decision, 46*(6), 933–947.

Gannon, M. J., & Noon, J. P. (1971). Management's critical deficiency. *Business Horizons, 14*(1), 49–56.

Greenberg, J. (1988). Cultivating an image of justice: Looking fair on the job. *Academy of Management Executive, 2*(2), 155–157.

Hassan, A., & Al Jubari, I. H. A. (2010). Organizational justice and employee work engagement: LMX as mediator. *Journal of International Business and Entrepreneurship Development, 5*(2), 167–178.

Hassan, A., & Chandaran, S. (2005). Quality of supervisors-subordinate relationship and work outcome: Organizational justice as mediator. *IIUM Journal of Economic and Management, 13*(1), 33–52.

Hooi, L. W. (2002). The impact of Japanese promotion practices on Malaysian enterprises. *Asia Pacific Business Review, 9*(1), 21–38.

Hooi, L. W. (2008). Current remuneration practices in the multinational companies in Malaysia: A case study analysis. *Research and Practice in Human Resource Management, 16*(1), 78–103.

Hooi, L. W. (2010). Technical training in the MNCs in Malaysia: A case study analysis of the petrochemical industry. *Journal of European Industrial Training, 34*(4), 317–343.

Hooi, L. W., Sulaiman, M., & Omar, A. (2012). Procedural justice in promotion decisions of managerial staff in Malaysia. *Asia Pacific Business Review, 18*(1), 99–121.

Hsu, Y. R. (2011). Work-family conflict and job satisfaction in stressful working environments: The moderating roles of perceived supervisor support and internal locus of control. *International Journal of Manpower, 32*(2), 233–248.

Ishak, N. A., & Alam, S. S. (2009). The effects of leader-member exchange on organisational justice and organisational citizenship behavior: Empirical study. *European Journal of Social Sciences, 8*(2), 324–334.

Jawahar, I. M., & Carr, D. (2007). Conscientiousness and contextual performance: The compensatory effects of perceived organizational support and leader-member exchange. *Journal of Managerial Psychology, 22*(4), 330–349.

Kang, D. S., & Stewart, J. (2007). Leader-member exchange (LMX) theory of leadership and HRD: Development of units of theory and laws of interaction. *Leadership & Organization Development Journal, 28*(6), 531–551.

Katzell, R. A., & Yankelovich, D. (1975). *Work, productivity, and job satisfaction*. New York: Psychological Corporation.

Klendauer, R., & Deller, J. (2009). Organizational justice and managerial commitment in corporate mergers. *Journal of Managerial Psychology, 24*(1), 29–45.

Konovsky, M. A., & Folger, R. (1991). The effects of procedures, social accounts, and benefits level on victims' layoff reactions. *Journal of Applied Social Psychology, 21*(8), 630–650.
Konovsky, M. A., & Pugh, S. D. (1994). Citizenship behavior and social exchange. *Academy of Management Journal, 37*(3), 656–669.
Mahfooz, A. A., Kee, D. M. H., & Aafaqi, A. (2007). Leader-member exchange and attitudinal outcomes: Role of procedural justice climate. *Leadership & Organization Development Journal, 28*(8), 690–709.
Mardanov, I. T., Heischmidt, K., & Henson, A. (2008). Leader-member exchange and job satisfaction bond and predicted employee turnover. *Journal of Leadership & Organizational Studies, 15*(2), 159–175.
McCalister, K. S. (2003). *Hardiness and support at work as predictors of work stress and job satisfaction*. Austin: The University of Texas at Austin.
Moorman, R. H. (1991). Relationship between organizational justice and organizational citizenship behavior: Do fairness perceptions influence employee citizenship? *Journal of Applied Psychology, 76*(6), 845–855.
Murphy, C., Ramamoorthy, N., Flood, P. C., & MacCurtain, S. (2006). Organisational justice perceptions and employee attitudes among Irish blue collar employees: An empirical test of the main and moderating roles of individualism/collectivism. *Management Revue, 17*(3), 328–343.
Nadiri, H., & Tanova, C. (2010). An investigation of the role of justice in turnover intentions, job satisfaction, and organizational citizenship behavior in hospitality industry. *International Journal of Hospitality Management, 29*(1), 33–41.
Ng, T. W. H., & Sorensen, K. L. (2008). Toward a further understanding of the relationships between perceptions of support and work attitudes: A meta analysis. *Group and Organization Management, 33*(3), 243–268.
Organ, D. W. (1988a). *Organizational citizenship behavior: The good solider syndrome*. Lexington: Lexington Books.
Organ, D. W. (1988b). A restatement of the satisfaction-performance hypothesis. *Journal of Management, 14*(4), 547–557.
Organ, D. W. (1990). The motivational basis of organizational citizenship behavior. *Research in Organizational Behavior, 12*(1), 43–72.
Rhoades, L., & Eisenberger, R. (2002). Perceived organizational support: A review of the literature. *Journal of Applied Psychology, 87*(4), 698–714.
Sheppard, B. H., Lewicki, R. J., & Minton, J. W. (1992). *Organizational justice: The search for fairness in the workplace*. New York: Lexington Books.
Skarlicki, D. P., & Folger, R. (1997). Retaliation in the workplace: The roles of distributive, procedural, and interactional justice. *Journal of Applied Psychology, 82*(3), 434–443.
Tabachnick, B. G., & Fidell, L. S. (2007). *Using multivariate statistics* (5th ed.). New York: Harper-Collins College Publishers.
Tan, H. H., & Tan, C. S. (2000). Toward the differentiation of trust in supervisor and trust in organization. *Genetic, Social, and General Psychology Monographs, 126*(2), 241–260.
Truckenbrodt, Y. B. (2000). The relation between leader-member exchange and commitment and organizational behavior. *Acquisition Review Quarterly, 7*(3), 233–244.
Yilmaz, K., & Tasdan, M. (2009). Organizational citizenship and organizational justice in Turkish primary schools. *Journal of Educational Administration, 47*(1), 108–126.

Index

L.W. Hooi, *Organisational Justice and Citizenship Behaviour in Malaysia*,
Governance and Citizenship in Asia, DOI 10.1007/978-981-10-0030-0

MIX
Papier aus verantwortungsvollen Quellen
Paper from responsible sources
FSC® C105338

If you have any concerns about our products,
you can contact us on
ProductSafety@springernature.com

In case Publisher is established outside the EU,
the EU authorized representative is:
Springer Nature Customer Service Center GmbH
Europaplatz 3, 69115 Heidelberg, Germany

Printed by Libri Plureos GmbH
in Hamburg, Germany